Economic Geography

Economic Geography

Second Edition

(Revised and Updated)

H.M. SAXENA

RAWAT PUBLICATIONS

Jaipur | New Delhi | Bangalore | Guwahati | Kolkata

ISBN 978-81-316-0949-1 (HB)

Reprinted, 2024

Published by
Prem Rawat for **Rawat Publications**
Satyam Apts., Sector 3, Jawahar Nagar, Jaipur 302 004 (India)
Phones: 0141 265 1748 / 265 7006
E-mail: info@rawatbooks.com
Website: www.rawatbooks.com

New Delhi Office
4858/24, Ansari Road, Daryaganj, New Delhi 110 002
Phone: 011 2326 3290

Also at *Bangalore, Guwahati* and *Kolkata*

Printed at Nice Printing Press, New Delhi

Contents

Preface

Economic geography is the study of the spatial variations on the earth's surface of activities related to producing, exchanging and consuming goods and services. An economic geographer wishes to display the spatial distribution of these economic activities and understand why they are located as they are. During the last six decades, economic geography has undergone several changes and has also developed a strong theoretical base. Not only contents but methods and approaches have also been changed, which shows its importance in planning and development. The present volume is the *second revised edition* and an attempt to discuss recent trends, resources and their utilisation as well as theoretical development in the subject.

The book has been organised into three parts with 18 chapters in all, supported by maps, diagrams and tables.

Part I is an introduction, dealing with nature, recent trends, and approaches to the study of economic geography. The other aspects discussed in this part are economy and economic activities and concept, classification and conservation of resources.

Part II is a comprehensive analysis of the resources and their utilisation. This part contains ten chapters. Three chapters are devoted to the study of world agriculture, its nature, types, production and distribution of cereals and commercial agricultural products. Livestock and fisheries, mineral resources, power resources, important industries, industrial regions and transportation patterns have also been discussed in this part under separate chapters.

Part III entitled 'Theoretical Economic Geography' comprising five chapters deals with theories of agricultural and industrial location, spatial variations in production and transport costs, decision-making process, and economic regions and regionalisation. Thus, it provides a complete knowledge of the theoretical basis of economic geography.

This book is ideally suited to the postgraduate and undergraduate students as well as to those appearing in competitive examinations. It will provide them a comprehensive knowledge of the subject in a clear and lucid manner.

Many scholars and friends have had a role, either direct or indirect, in the making of this book. Acknowledgements have been made throughout the book as a mark of gratitude towards the scholars, whose works I have cited in the book. I am also thankful to the entire team of Rawat Publications for this nice publication.

My wife Nirmal has, as ever, been my greatest source of strength; without her active cooperation and moral support of other members of my family, this book would have been much harder to write. I am thankful to all.

H.M. Saxena

Part I

Introduction

1

Economic Geography

An Introduction

Geography has become an extremely varied and versatile subject and its area of study has grown a great deal since its inception. The concepts of place names, natural environment or influence of natural environment on man's activity have become old and unacceptable notions in the light of the new and expanded concepts of geography. The present-day geography is the study of spatial variations on the earth surface; thus, it deals with relationships among spatial variables and can be termed as spatial or areal science. Among main branches of geography, Economic Geography is the highly developed branch. Although it is a branch of Human Geography, but now has a distinct status in geographical studies and deals with areal variations on the earth's surface in man's economic activities. Among the various fields of geography, economic geography has experienced remarkable changes within past fifty years, resulting in diverse specialised branches, viz., geography of agriculture, industry, transportation, marketing, resources, etc.

Economic geography deals with the distribution of economic activities and with the factors and processes affecting their spatial occurrence. Over the last five decades, the character of economic geography has changed, initially shifting its emphasis from description – amassing facts about production in different parts of the world – to explanation, from environmental determinism to economic determinism. Both these changes can be related to the inclusion of Neo-classical Economics into economic geography, with its mechanical assumptions about Economic Man and Optimum Location and has led to important fields of study, such as Industrial Location Theory and Regional Science. More recently, however, a Behaviourial Approach has been developed with its focus on the decision-making.

During last three decades, the focus of economic geography has moved to:

- the nature and causes of development and underdevelopment, putting the mode of production at the centre, and stressing the interrelationships between the less and more developed worlds;
- the link between economic systems and geography, particularly in interpretations of the spatial impacts of capitalism and its role in the development of the world economy;
- the impact of technological changes and the construction of new industrial spaces;

- the use of discursive, qualitative, and realist explanations that recognise that each economic agglomeration and development is locally embedded in its peculiar socio-institutional context;
- the dimensions of class, race, and gender in economic systems, stressing, and sometimes challenging, the way economic systems depend on discrimination on the basis of these three categories;
- 'non-economic' forces – cultures, institutions, and social practices – that are central to economic process;
- new explanations have been given for the location of economic activity, based on the assumptions of economic man and optimisation;
- behaviourial approach has modified the ideas, with the introduction of the concept of the decision-maker and the satisfier; and
- the concept of sustainable development in resource use; etc.

All these areas of enquiry have contributed to a philosophy of economic geography and also helped in regional development and planning.

Definitions and Scope

What is economic geography? This basic question has been explained by several scholars in their own way and also has undergone changes with the change in nature of the study of economic geography. Until recently, it was concerned largely with spatial distribution of economic phenomena. In the early 1960s, for instance, the subject saw it as "an enquiry into the production, exchange, and consumption of goods by people in different areas of the world". Most of the geographers have defined the scope and method of economic geography in terms of three basic questions, as under:

(i) Where is the economic activity located?

(ii) What are the characteristics of the economic activity?

(iii) To what other phenomena is the economic activity related?

To these three later studies have added two more:

(iv) Why is the economic activity located where it is?

(v) Would it not be better located elsewhere, to better satisfy certain economic and social criteria?

And more recently an answer has been given that these are the result of economic behaviour. This changing nature and change in emphasis on content of study shows that economic geography has proved the importance in various periods of its growth. Therefore, it is necessary to discuss the nature and scope of economic geography both from traditional to modern point of view.

As early as in 1882, the German scholar, **Gotz** had defined economic geography as "a scientific investigation of the nature of world areas in their direct influence of goods". Although, Gotz initiated the concept of economic geography but his influence was limited to Germany only. The abstract principles of that time could not be related to economic geography because they were not in their developed form. Economic geography owes its growth as an academic discipline to the interest of the British people in commerce. It is interesting to note that George Chisholm, the father of modern economic geography, had wanted *an* *intellectual interest to the study of geographical facts relating to commerce.* He thought that the primary use of economic geography is "to form some reasonable estimate of the future course of commercial development so far as that is governed by geographical conditions". In his treatment of the subject, however, Chisholm emphasised commercial development, and considered the physical features and climate in relation to products mainly. This emphasis on physical features and climate in relation to products led others subsequently to think of economic geography in terms of productive occupations. Jones and Darkenwald (1950) state that, "Economic geography deals with productive occupations and attempts to explain why certain regions are outstanding in the production and exportation of various articles and why others are significant in the importation and utilisation of the things." On the other hand, Ellsworth Huntington (1940), however, considers that all sorts of materials, resources, activities, customs, capabilities and types of ability that play a part in the work getting a living are the subject matter of economic geography.

Bengston and Van-Royen (1957), in his book *Fundamentals of Economic Geography*, have stated that:

> Economic geography investigates the diversity in basic resources of the different parts of the world. It tries to evaluate the effects that differences of physical environment have upon the utilisation of these resources. It studies differences in economic development in different regions or countries of the world. It studies transportation, trade routes and trade resulting from this different development and as affected by the physical environment.

Some of the other definitions of economic geography are as follows:

> "Economic geography is the study of influence exerted on the economic activities of man by his physical environment and more specially by the form and structure of the surface of land, the climatic conditions which prevail upon it, and the place relations in which its different regions stand to one another."
>
> —J. McFarlane

> "Economic geography has to do with similarities and differences from place to place in the ways people make a living."
>
> —R.E. Murphy

> "Economic geography is that aspect of the subject which deals with the influence of the environment – inorganic and organic – on the activities of man."
>
> —R.N. Brown

> "Economic geography is concerned with problem of making a living, with world industries, with basic resources and industrial commodities."
>
> —E.B. Shaw

> "Economic geography is concerned with the distribution of man's productive activities over the surface of the earth."
>
> —N.J.G. Pounds

It thus becomes clear from above definitions that economic geography mainly deals with the man's productive activities and their relationship with environmental conditions. These activities are of three types: primary, secondary and tertiary. The primary activities are those which obtain simple commodities or raw materials from the soil, the sea and the rocks. They are agriculture, forestry, fishing and mining. These goods are then manufactured, processed or fabricated in factories and workshops. This constitutes the secondary group of activities. After manufacturing, transport services as well as services of insurance, brokers, dealers, etc. are required. These services constitute tertiary activities. All these human activities are in some way or other linked with environmental conditions.

Wheeler, Muller, Thrall and Fik, in their book *Economic Geography* (1998), explain economic geography by considering two continua: a human – physical continuum and a topical – regional continuum. Accordingly, economic geography, emphasising human production, distribution and consumption activities, naturally falls toward the human end of the scale. In which climate, terrain, soil, and hydrology will play a critical role at some level of analysis. The second continuum represents an approach to the analysis of spatial variation in human and physical elements, in other words study of the economic geography of a region, a second region, a third region and so on, until all the world is covered. It also deals with the principles involved in the distribution of various kinds of economic activities.

A major change has occurred in the nature of economic geography with the inclusion of the theme, 'spatial variation' or 'areal variation'. Alexander and Gibson (1979) and Hartshorn and Alexander (1988) in their book *Economic Geography* have stated that "economic geography is the study of areal variation on the earth's surface in man's activities related to producing, exchanging and consuming wealth".

In pursuit of that goal the economic geographer asks three basic questions:

(i) Where is the economic activity located?

(ii) What are the characteristics of the economic activity?

(iii) To what other phenomena is the economic activity related?

According to Loyod and Dicken (1972), "As a behavioural science with spatial dimension of economic system, economic geography is concerned with the construction of general principles and theories that explain the operation of the economic system."

A major change in the study of economic geography has been in the form of behavioural approach and systems analysis. Behaviour denotes the actions of individuals or groups, it follows that economic phenomena in some way reflects individual and group values, policies and decisions. While system is a set of identified elements so related together that they form a complex whole. Systems analysis means considerations of such a whole as a whole, rather than as something to be analysed into separate parts. Economic geographers utilise the system concept in order to better understand the component elements of some part of reality, and the relations between them. In fact, economic geography now has grown as a developed branch of geography with specialised branches having their own status and importance.

Economic Activities as Core of Economic Geography

Economic Geography focuses on the distribution of production, distribution and consumption activities. The economic geographer wishes to display the spatial distribution of these economic activities and to understand why they are located as they are. A significant part of this understanding lies in recognising how economic activities are interrelated in particular areas and how the activities are tied to other economic activities at other locations. Economic activities still form the core of economic geography, whatever may be the approach of study. Economic activities can be grouped into three categories, viz., production, exchange and consumption.

Production

- *Primary production* includes age-old activities of production which are directly and indirectly taken from the earth such as hunting animals and gathering wild products; extracting minerals from the earth's crust; fishing from rivers, lakes and oceans; and growing trees. In general, five primary activities recognised are: agriculture, cattle grazing, forest production, hunting and fishing, and mining and quarrying.
- *Secondary production* increases the value or usefulness of a previously existing item by changing its form. Such activities include manufacturing and commercial agriculture.
- *Tertiary production* involves the service sector rather than the tangible goods. In tertiary production no particular article is directly related, various kinds of aids are rather used for transport, distribution and primary and secondary production.
- Quaternary services represent special type of services such as financial, health, education, information, data processing, etc.
- *Quinary activities* include high-level managerial and executive administrative services both public and private. Research scientists, legal authorities, financial advisers and professional consultants are included in this category.

Exchange

Exchange services are essential for goods produced. It is through exchange that a product reaches to its consumer. The following services are included in exchange activities:

(i) Transportation and distribution services.
(ii) Exchanging services and ideas by telecommunication or face-to-face contact.
(iii) Satisfying the needs of people by changing their location (passenger transportation).
(iv) Warehousing and distribution.
(v) Wholesale trade marketing activities.
(vi) Retail trade marketing activities.

These exchanges increase the value of an item because of services provided and also play an important role in modern economies.

Consumption

A third aspect of all the economic activity involves the consumption of goods and services. The term 'consumption' refers to the final or direct use of goods and services to satisfy the wants and needs of human beings. This aspect, i.e. geography of consumption has largely been ignored by geography. But now, there is a growing interest among geographers to study spatial aspects of consumer behaviour.

The above mentioned activities are having functional interrelationship at various stages of economic production. This functional interrelationship is related to secondary and tertiary production through various services. The direct or indirect functional relation of all the resources of production depends upon location, relief, climate, soil and technical know-how of those areas. Just as the various aspects of primary production have established functional interrelationship with one another, in the same way, all the factors of secondary production have established functional relation with the factors of primary production. In the same way tertiary production has functional relation with the primary and secondary production. This functional interrelationship of production not only changes the form and utility of material but also effects a transformation in their ownership and value.

Approaches to Economic Geography

In geography, several approaches have been developed for systematic analysis of the subject. The same has also been adopted in economic geography. The approaches to study economic geography can be divided into three categories:

1. Traditional Approaches
2. Philosophic Approaches
3. Modern Approaches

Traditional Approaches

These are the approaches which are common in geography and frequently used in economic geography. These are: (i) Regional Approach, (ii) Commodity or Topical Approach, and (iii) Principles Approach.

(i) *Regional Approach:* The term 'region' is very popular in geographical literature and refers to a suitable areal unit, e.g. a climatic region, a natural region, an industrial region, an agricultural region, an administrative or political region and so on. A region is having common geo-economic characteristics, a resource base, economic development and to some extent similarities in culture and demographic structure. Therefore, several geographers have chosen this region approach in economic geography. An advantage of the regional approach is that it gives a better knowledge of different parts of a unit, their relationship to each other and to the unit as a whole.

(ii) *Commodity or Topical Approach:* This approach provides a systematic description and interpretation of the world distribution pattern of a commodity (wheat), or an industry (cotton textile industry), or a human occupation (fishing). It analyses the whole sequence of their development, and catches them on their march to progression or retrogression. This topical or commodity approach is very popular. The systematic economic geography, if we choose this appellation, is the legitimate child of this very conception.

(iii) *Principles Approach:* In every sphere of human activity certain fundamental truths or principles hold good: indeed, they provide the rock-foundations upon which the varied and varying superstructures rest. The concepts of Economic Geography are through and through permeated with the same spirit whether we talk of Regional Economic Geography or Systematic

Economic Geography. Economic regions are based on certain fundamental principles; and similar is the case with the extraction of minerals (coals, iron ore or diamond), or the localisation of industries (metal fabricating or textile industries), or the exchange of commodities. At least four principles, viz., the principle of geonomic relationship, the principle of optimum location, the principle of regional specialisation and the principle of geonomic succession appear to be valid generalisations under all conditions. That is why it seems to be a sound proposition if we enunciate certain fundamental principles in the discussion of geonomic problems. This approach has two distinct advantages: firstly, it provides an analytical method which promotes critical acumen; and secondly, it does away with parrot learning of factual material.

Philosophic Approaches

The 1990s research in economic geography may be characterised by three major philosophic approaches. These are: (i) Positivism, (ii) Structuralism, and (iii) Humanism.

(i) *Positivism:* It employs the scientific method to interpret and understand issues in economic geography. The scientific approach is based on empirically verifiable and commonly agreed upon evidence through replication of analytical results. It involves informed hypothesis testing leading to empirical generalisations and law-like statements. GIS (Group Information System) is central to analytical and positivist approaches to geography in general and with especially numerous application in economic geography.

(ii) *Structuralism:* In economic geography, structuralism, posits that what we see in the world does not reveal the causes of what we see. The structure of the economy cannot be directly observed, and we should therefore, develop ideas and theories that will help us understand what we see and experience. While there is no way to directly test such theories, we can debate about them to achieve better understanding.

(iii) *Humanism:* It is a part of critique of positivism. Humanistic economic geographers object to both positivism and structuralism on the basis that these approaches view people as responding mechanically to spatial and structural forces.

Modern Approaches

In economic geography, three approaches have been developed during last three decades that can be considered as modern approaches. These are: (i) system analysis, (ii) behavioural approach, and (iii) institutional approach.

(i) *System Analysis:* A system is a set of identified elements so related that together they form a complex whole. System analysis is an approach or methodology rather than a philosophy or scientific paradigm. Economic geographers utilise the system concept in order to better understand the component elements of some part of reality, and the relations between them. The use of such a conception stresses the study of the whole as well as of the parts. Thus, the world economy can be regarded as a set of interlocking parts and sub-systems.

(ii) *Behavioural Approach:* Incorporation of the behavioural science outlook in geography is known as behaviouralism. In economic geography behavioural approach now has become very common. Economic geographers study the overall results of economically-oriented behaviour as they appear in the landscape. In economic geography, the study of decision-making process is an important aspect. The type of decision-making, which is the concern of economic geography, can be classified as problem-solving or behavioural decision-making with such results as new locations for shops, farms or factories. Similarly, the study of consumer behaviour, movement or trip behaviour, etc. are considered to be important. The decision-making process and other aspects of behavioural analysis will be discussed in detail in other chapters of the book.

(iii) *Institutional Approach:* Ron Martin (2003) has emphasised the need of institutional approach in economic geography. He stated that the form and evolution of the economic landscape cannot be fully understood without giving due attention to the various social institutions on which economic activity depends and through which it is shaped. In other words, economic activity is socially and institutionally situated and it cannot be explained by reference to atomistic individual motives alone, but has to be understood as enmeshed in wider structures of social, economic and political rules, procedures and conventions. It is the role of these systems, both formal and informal, which is the focus of an institutional approach to economic geography.

Recent Trends in Economic Geography

During last four decades, economic geography has experienced tremendous changes in methodology, contents and approaches. These changes have occurred both in theoretical as well as in applied field. All these changes are the part of the development of the subject, but because of these changes economic geography has gained a special status among other branches of geography. Some of the recent trends in economic geography are as follows:

Increasing Use of Quantitative Methods and GIS

In comparison to other branches of geography, the use of quantitative techniques has increased in economic geography. This has become more popular with the use of computers.

Through the use of high-speed digital computers, massive amounts of information can now be processed both quickly and easily. Moreover, a computer can be programmed to handle virtually any kind of statistical technique. The computer revolution, as it is aptly called, has affected economic geography no less than other disciplines, and a number of texts now show geographers how to take advantage of it. However, the use of computers has as many pitfalls as advantages.

Recent technological developments in large-scale data storage, and display (mapping) have had a beneficial impact on research in economic geography. GIS allows the input, storage, analysis and output of spatial data, with either point or area coordinates. Large data sets comprising of numerous variables, when viewed in overlaid fashion, frequently lead to new hypothesis and provide insights into geographic relationships that have not previously been noted or understood.

Impact of the Mathematics: Concept of Probability and Random Processes

For sometime, social scientists have been questioning the total predictability of human action and behaviour. The original impulse for this came from the pure sciences, especially physics, which has elevated unpredictability to a formal principle – the so-called uncertainty principle. According to Werner Heisenberg, who formulated the principle in 1927, some natural phenomena can never be completely described. Before the work of Heisenberg and his colleagues physicists had taken a more deterministic approach; specific results were thought to be wholly predictable from specific conditions. In contrast, the principle of uncertainty, or indeterminacy, introduced a world in which physical laws no longer completely described or predicted anything, but instead yielded statistical approximations of very high probability. Thus, the entire nature of science was changed.

There is no need, of course, for geographers to jump to the conclusion that the earth's surface is governed by the mechanics of a roulette wheel, or to see economic development as a 'permanent floating crap game'. More important it is a proper appreciation of the different ways in which chance, or randomness, can enter into economic affairs. It can stem from the imperfection, of human decisions, since the limits on man's perceptual abilities at any one time are considerable. It can arise from the many apparently equal choices that can confront us on occasion – for example, there are more potential route ways than routes, and more town sites than towns. It can arise because, after all, the goals of individuals and groups do vary over time. Finally, it can arise because of what has been called 'background noise', that is, the infinite number of factors that, although present, could not be taken into account at the time of the actual decision or occurrence.

In geography, recognition that the traditional modes of explanation do not always apply stems to a great extent from the influence of other social sciences, which have brought dissatisfaction with available methods and concepts, and an increasing realisation of the unpredictability and uncertainty of human choice. This recognition, as we have seen, has been accompanied by the growth of sophisticated statistical techniques.

Reliance on Models

A model is an idealised representation of reality that is intended to demonstrate certain properties of the real world. By model building we abstract certain factors from reality, so that rather than having to consider simultaneously a whole host of them, we can deal with what we perceive as the essential few. By their very definition models cannot convey the whole truth, but only a comprehensible part of it.

Models have many uses. They can be a set of working hypotheses for the researcher; guides for the visualisation of complex interactions; organisational frameworks for the classification and manipulation of data; or simple and effective teaching aids. Thus, models can be concepts, notions, or just hunches. They are useful chiefly because they are economical. Not only do they transmit general information in a highly compressed form; they can also in certain circumstances express a theory as precisely as any verbal formulation. They can also draw our attention to the differences between abstraction and reality, and provide a simple picture for the student. In short, models are designed to make understanding easier. Some of the simplest models are almost everyday used. They include maps, aerial photographs, floor plans, and flow charts. Others are used on the pioneer fringes of research.

Economic Location Theory

Economic geography is an extremely broad field in the sense that it examines a wide range of activities. This breadth is shared, of course, by the discipline of economics, and the social sciences in general. Like economics, economic geography is unified as a body of knowledge that is not so much identified by the subject matter studied as by a set of interlocking principles or theories, which are constantly evolving. In case of economic geography, these principles and theories are those of the location of economic activities, known formally and collectively by the term 'location theory'. Location theory seeks to explain the basic universal factors that determine and influence the location of all kinds of economic activity. In economic geography, several location theories have been adopted to explain agricultural and industrial location. But now theories related to decision-making process have become important.

Behavioural Focus

A new trend in economic geography is the behavioural focus, i.e. more attention now has been given to behavioural pattern, in which the emphasis is placed on how locational decisions are actually made. It is one thing to describe a region as producing a particular crop or combination of crops; it is another to understand how the farmers in the region have come to decide what crops to raise. The behavioural pattern of market participants, i.e. consumer, trader-wholesaler, retailer and producer now has become an important aspect of study in economic geography. Similarly, the behavioural pattern movement of the people now determines the selection and location of transport routes. The spatial analysis of the behavioural pattern in all the economic activities now has become focus of the economic geography.

Policy Implications

Contemporary economic geographers are also now interested in the policy implication of economic activities. It is recognised that the role of government is fundamental in affecting the level and location of economic activities. This role is carried out not only by the federal governments, but also by state and local governments. Alternative public policies lead to different – sometimes quite different – locational patterns.

Applied Economic Geography

Apart from theoretical developments in economic geography, it has now more inclination towards the applied aspect. Another trend in modern economic geography is referred to under the general label of applied geography. Since, many professional geographers are now working in planning organisations, government agencies, business and industry, now using geographic concepts and techniques to a wide range of practical problems. Closely related to developments in applied geography is the contemporary concern with problem-solving approaches in economic geography. A background of mathematics, statistics, and computer programming and location analysis is useful. Practical skills such as cartography, remote sensing, GIS, are extremely helpful in the analysis of spatial problems.

Globalisation Trends

The concept of globalisation has spread throughout the social sciences, including economic geography. This new outlook on geography is challenging the traditional approaches to economic geography. Such phrases as 'the global shopping mall', 'the global workplace', or 'the global city' attempt to capture the essence of globalisation. This concept is based on the new communication technologies and their impact on the local and global economy, as well as on social, cultural and political life. The significance of globalisation may be understood in terms of following characteristics :

(i) Capital has become more globally mobile.
(ii) The market has become less regulated, breaking down governmental and political control.
(iii) Multinational firms have become principal agents of change.
(iv) The national political forces have been weakened, giving way to multinational corporations.
(v) Dual trends have been set in motion, the one trend toward more homogeneous global conditions as a result of widespread competition, and the other toward enhanced differences as localities strive to maintain their identities.

Globalisation represents a complex set of processes, which economic geographers have only just begun to understand.

More Emphasis on Spatial Pattern and Processes

The distribution of economic activities over the earth's surface or within a region may be viewed as forming a pattern or spatial distribution. This pattern may be a nodal or point pattern, a linear pattern. Combining the linear and nodal pattern, one may define a nodal region, which is useful in many kinds of analysis in economic geography. These spatial patterns are often depicted on the choropleth map. Another type of spatial pattern is the surface, which may be illustrated cartographically in a variety of ways. The most common method of surface mapping is by use of isolines, these lines connect points of equal magnitude. Spatial patterns often combine to form hierarchies, interlocking sequences of patterns ranging from small to large scale. Such spatial hierarchy reflects the extent and dimensions of an economic system.

Apart from spatial pattern, economic geographers also deal with spatial processes. The word 'process' implies something happening over time. A spatial process, then, involves change within some or all the elements of a system. Geographers are concerned with the interplay between pattern and process and these two concepts are avenues that geographers use to analyse spatial economic system. Economic patterns change because of human decisions, which may be based on different economic goals, different perceptions of economic alternatives, different preference and cultural systems. In contemporary economic geography, emphasis has been given on spatio-temporal analysis.

Systems Analysis

Like other social scientists, economic geographers are also using systems analysis as a method of analysing economic activities. The basic concept is simple enough. A system is a set of identified elements so related that together they form a complex whole. Systems analysis mean considerations of such a whole as a whole, rather than as something to be analysed into separate parts. A system as opposed to a mere assemblage (one might almost say 'heap') is not just a totality of parts, but rather a totality of relations among and including those parts. Systems analysis is an approach or methodology rather than a philosophy or a scientific paradigm. In other words, it is an analytical technique or tool that can aid in the understanding or elucidation of complex structures, not a generalised theory in itself – although some of its champions may see it as one.

Economic geographers utilised the system concept in order to better understand the component elements of some part of reality, and the relations between them. To continue with our example, if we look at the world economic scene as an entity, we can break it down into component sub-systems. Given better understanding of the structure, we could then perhaps try to rearrange the elements spatially in order to maximise some human welfare function. And in fact the acceptance by some economic geographers of this notion of the world economy is regarded by some as one of the major conceptual advances of recent years.

Specialisation and Development of Sub-Branches

In economic geography, several branches have been developed due to specialisation. Since economic activities are diversified, their study has also been specialised. This specialisation has given new status to economic geography. The main branches of economic geography are:

(i) Agriculture Geography
(ii) Industrial Geography
(iii) Transport Geography
(iv) Marketing Geography
(v) Geography of Resources
(vi) Geography of Planning and Development

All these branches now have become independent fields of study, but at the same time link with economic geography too. Contemporary economic geography is developing at a fast rate due to new researches in these sub-branches and also its applied value is increasing in comparison to other branches of geography.

Environmental Concern and Sustainable Development

Nowadays, environmental problems are of great concern in most of the subjects. Economic geographers are also now taking interest in problems associated with environment, both global as well as regional. This is more because of the fact that economic activities are also one of the main causes of environmental degradation. The economic activities like mining, industry, transportation are directly responsible for pollution, climatic change and global warming. Therefore, there is a need to manage the economic activities in a sustainable way. Similarly, resource utilisation, especially over-exploitation of natural and economic resources is increasing day by day and it is high time to take steps for their proper utilisation so that not only the present generation but our future generations will also be able to use them. The concept of sustainable development has now become an integral part of the study of economic geography. Economic geographers know the distribution, production and potentialities of world resources and they are in a position to suggest their conservation policy. The beginning in the field of sustainable development has already been done, but there is still a long way to go.

Other Trends

Apart from the above mentioned major trends in economic geography, the other trends are as follows:

(i) New concepts of development
  (a) Integrated development
  (b) Regional development
  (c) Sustainable development
  (d) Economic development and quality of life
(ii) Study of market-oriented economy
(iii) Environmental relation of the economy
(iv) Interdisciplinary nature
(v) Decision-making process
(vi) Use of gravity model
(vii) Production and transport cost analysis
(viii) Concept of isotropic and anisotropic space
(ix) Concept of time and space in economic development
(x) New development in locational theories related to economic development
(xi) Use of remote sensing and GIS in studying resource distribution and utilisation
(xii) Economic geographical forecasting
(xiii) Planning for regional economic development
(xiv) Emphasis on the societal impact of economic activities
(xv) Feminism and economic geography, i.e. gendering work and working gender
(xvi) The economic geography of global trade
(xvii) Telecommunications and economic space

In brief, economic geography is a highly developed branch of human geography. To the centuries-old methods of description and synthesis, modern research in economic geography has been added by developments in the social and behavioural sciences, in computer science, in statistics, in mathematics, and in GIS. The use of the scientific method to study economic spatial systems has permitted new ways of understanding old questions. The principles of economic location theory have formed a core around which economic geography is focused.

2

Economy and Economic Activities

Geographical Perspective

ECONOMY

Generally, economy refers to the whole structure and function of a country, region or society, particularly the exploitation of resources and the production, distribution and consumption of goods and services. It has a potential saving or cost advantage. The cost advantages are obtained from concentrating production into large-scale processing units. There is a distinction between internal and external economies of scale. The former occur as a result of expansion of the individual firm. Whereas the external economies of scale occur where a firm takes advantage of developments within the industry as a whole and which result in a lowering of its own cost. In fact, economy is a complex system and related with the development of human civilisation. It is a reflection of human progress or in other words, human use of the earth's resources. It is also an indicator of man-environment relationship in changing techno-economic world. The growth, development, present pattern and potentialities of an economy are directly related with the geographical environment and have spatio-temporal variations based on physical, economic and technological status.

McCarty and Lindberg (1966), in their book *A Preface to Economic Geography* have stated, "An economy may be defined simply as a system of production, whose central purpose is to create a type of product, but whose operations also include all the related activities present in the area of production and necessary to the creation of that product." Thus, the primary element of economy is production, but production is done for the fulfilment of needs of the people. Both the needs and production varies from region to region, so does economy. The production involves distribution, i.e. the produce should reach the consumer, through various channels of distribution and agencies or organisations. Therefore, a network of transport and communication is required and also a place where these activities are performed, e.g. market place. This whole system is controlled by a framework of policies, rules and regulations, both national and international. All these aspects as well as those which direct and determine this system are the integral part of economy.

Michael Eliot Hurst (1972), in his book *A Geography of Economic Behavior,* has explained about economy in terms of utility, that is, what is added to resources so that they are converted into something useful to man.

- Through manufacture, man adds *form utility*.

- Through transportation, man adds *place utility*.
- Through storage, man adds *time utility*.

Taken together, these attempts to make the natural environment more amenable to exploitation creates an *economy*. According to Hurst, the economy has two basic functions:

1. To produce goods and services.
2. To distribute these goods and services among users.

The above functions are performed by two institutions known as the *firm* and its clients as the *consumers*. In between these two, the process of exchange is also involved. Basically a firm involved in four distinct but interrelated activities is labeled as primary, secondary, tertiary and quaternary. While a process of exchange is performed by transportation, which is also a tertiary production activity. The consumer is at the end of the line of the economic activity system.

According to Hodder and Lee (2008), "Economy refers to a network of economic decision makers." The interpretation derives from neo-classical economics as the source of theory in economic geography. The economics, as defined by Hodder and Lee, can exist at any scale. They range from simple subsistence village economics to those operating at the national or international scale. But even at its simplest, the economy is a complex phenomenon. The concept of economy can be understood by a simple model of the economy.

A Simple Model of the Economy

The economy in its simplest form can be explained by a simple model of the economy as given by Hodder and Lee in their book *Economic Geography*. The model has been depicted in Figure 2.1.

The economy, as revealed in Figure 2.1, may be said to consist of:

1. A set of decision-making elements identified as consumers (E_1); firms (E_2), often grouped into particular industries or sectors; resource owners (E_3); and government (E_4).

Figure 2.1

The simple model of economy

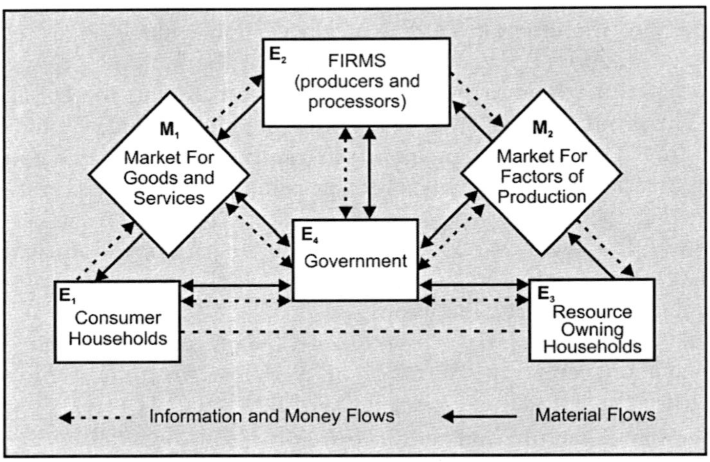

2. A set of relationships between the elements shown in Figure 2.1 by the dashed and continuous arrows connecting them, facilitated by the market for goods and services (M_1) and the market for factors of production (M_2).
3. A set of relationships between these components and the total environment, which may be simply defined as a higher order system within which the economy, or economic system, is but a part.

In this sense economic activity can be said to consist of the actions and interactions of four sets of elements. For a variety of reasons, the most basic of which is self-preservation, *consumers* (usually measured as consumer-households) generate wants and needs or demands for goods and services. *Firms*, or the technical and organisational units for production and processing, may respond to this demand by deciding to produce the goods demanded. To do this they need to acquire the resources of land, labour and capital from *resource owners* (resource-owning households). In other words, firms may generate a demand for resources and may try to attract them by the offer of some form of payment to the owners of the resources. If this offer is satisfactory the resource owners may decide to release at least some of their resources. Firms can then generate productive services (or factors of production) from the input of resources which are used in combination to make goods by the process known as production. The goods, or output produced by firms, can then be offered to the consumers. If the latter are satisfied with the goods and decide to accept them, then the firms receive a return, or payment, in exchange for the utility of the goods. In reality, all economically active households in the economy are both consumers and resources owners; the payment, or income, received from firms by resource owners may in turn be used to purchase goods from firms by the same individuals in their role as consumers. Transfer payments are made via government to those households which are unable, for reasons of old age, ill health or unemployment, to be economically active; such payments are supposed to enable these households to behave as consumers.

Firms are linked to consumers and resource owners along a network of communications via the *market for goods and services* and *the market for factors of production*. A market is a process of communication that enables buyers and sellers to exchange information about actual or latent demands and available or potential supplies, and helps them to organise the sale and purchase of goods and services. This type of activity may take place within well-defined market places which act as commercial foci for buyers and sellers and so are referred to as central places. But not all commodities and information are exchanged at a central place. The market for iron ore, for example, has no places of exchange at which buyers are able to meet and draw upon supplies from a particular market-supply area. Furthermore, the reduction in ore transportation costs is causing formerly discrete supply areas to coalesce, so that any one supplier of iron ore may well serve buyers in spatially separate locations (Manners 1971a). Sometimes the term market is used in a less specific context to include all the intermediate and final destinations of goods or resources being exchanged between buyers and sellers, but our present interest in markets is as the means by which information and goods are exchanged within economies.

This description of economic activity assumes that it is set in motion and controlled by decentralised decision makers whose activities are stimulated by the likelihood of private gain and co-ordinated through the markets. Although there are good theoretical reasons for such an arrangement the theory is not easily transferred to the real world. Furthermore, when the essential economic issues of social justice and ecological balance are considered, an economy based upon private decision-making is sadly lacking. Alternatively, economic activity can be generated and controlled by a single central decision-making body – the government. All decisions about demands, supplies, the use of resources and the behaviour of the individual elements may be contained in a centrally controlled economic plan and the government, whose interests in economic activity are less private than those of the individual elements of an economy, may take decisions on an entirely different basis. More common than either of these two extremes is a mixture of decentralised and centralised (private and public) decision making in which the government can influence individual actions; act as a consumer, producer or resource owner; and can outline and implement a co-ordinated economic plan.

The Operational Milieu

Culture, social institutions, the political and technological systems – all are powerful factors influencing the economy. The interrelationships between these factors are complex, but feedback occurs between the economy and the other components as shown in Figure 2.2.

Figure 2.2
The interrelatedness of the operational milieu

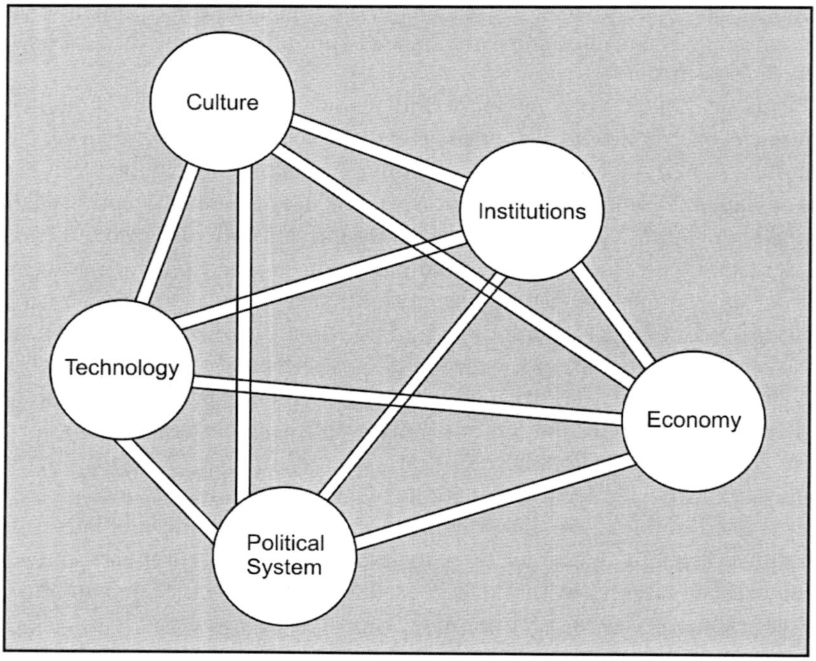

The economy, is seen at simplistic level as influenced by and influencing other operational components.

There are two views, according to Marxists, economy is the key institution, and it determines the form taken by all other institutions. Another is the Hegelian viewpoint which states that the economy is seen as only one element in an interrelated system. The brief characteristics of the different components of economy are discussed below:

Culture

Certain aspects of the cultural system influence economic activities. Man is surrounded by culture all his life. It shapes his thinking, his behaviour, his participation in ways of life; culture changes man from an organism into a human being. Culture is an historically transmitted pattern of meanings embodied in symbols. The cultural elements include – age grading, calendars, systems of counting, cosmologies, division of labour, food taboos, gift giving, laws, religious systems, tool making, etc. It operates by groups, classes and culture regions. The economic subsystem is linked to the whole societal milieu in three ways:

(a) Normative integration (economic values, part of general values of a society);

(b) Functional interdependence (joint roles played in society, some economic, some social); and

(c) Casual interaction (facilities shared by economic and social systems).

Political System

It is a system of sharing rights of territory and mutual services, like protection. The elements of a political system are: the nation state in international relations, the state within territorial framework and political relations among groups, i.e. firm, consumer, stockholders, labour unions, etc. It operates by dominance, coercion, use of power and authority, induction, laissez faire, etc. through government, legislation, political authority, judiciary, etc. The political system by its policies determines the economic system of a state. It also supports resource utilisation and also develops a system of internal and external marketing. The legislative, executive and judicial levels of it constitute a part of the operational milieu and affect economic activities.

Technological System

The economic system and technological system are closely linked with each other. Technology is a system of ideas, principles, techniques, and tools with which man attempts to control or modify his natural or phenomenal environment. Technology includes tools (like knifes, hammers, missiles, facilities, energy convertors, instruments, mechanical and non-mechanical devices). It operates by conceptions and applications concerning direct and indirect energy transmissions, etc. The computers, cybernetic techniques and information technology are important recent developments. All these make possible a great degree of control over power machines and other economic activities. It is now technologically feasible to place all spatial aspects of the economy under continuous electronic surveillance. Now, the interaction of technology and economic activity is entering a new stage.

Institutions

The concept of institution is closely connected not only with the economy but with the other three sectors of the operational milieu. Institutions are structures or normative patterns which represent and sanction standardised modes of behaviour. The standardised norms and modes of behaviour become institutionalised in a group of people when a large number of people accept the norms and take them seriously. The norms are also sanctioned. The institutions operate by conceptions and applications concerning direct and indirect energy transmissions, bodily motions, etc. The relations between institutions and the economy are complex, but have a profound effect on economic activity. Institutions provide the applications of labour and capital as well as design regulatory devices that limit and define economic action.

Economic System or the Economy

It is a system of allocation of scarce goods, the goods having alternative uses and varying satisfaction. The elements of economy or economic system are – firms, consumer, contract, property, division of labour, means of production, consumption and exchange market, quasi-market, trade, etc. This system operates by addition to form, place, and time utility, value, exploitation of resources and compensation for their uneven distribution in space and time. All these are a part of the organisational system.

In brief, culture, religion and education legitimate and motivate the economy, especially through legitimation of economic roles. Political system supply to the legal order in which economic decisions are made and the legal institutions that make credit and investment possible. But it is not a one way affair, there are feedbacks from the economy to the rest of the society – the economy returns wages and income, goods and services. A study of the economic system by a geographer would obviously be incomplete without reference to this milieu.

Types of Economic Organisations/Economies

An aspect in which economic geographers are interested is the distribution of different types of economies or economic organisations. Each type of economy exhibits distinct characteristics and forms and these are distributed in its various parts. The economies can be classified in a number of ways:

1. On the basis of production techniques economies can be classified as plant gathering, hunting and fishing, hoe and plough cultivation, pastoralism and manufacturing.
2. Similarly, on the basis of economic evolution, their categories are hunting and gathering, agricultural, industrial and scientific.
3. They can be classified into subsistence and profit economies or in modified terms as subsistence and exchange economy.

The subsistence economy, usually depends upon family, whether nuclear or extended and performs all the functions of production, exchange and consumption. Whatever is produced in subsistence economy is consumed by family or group of families. Some scholars have also termed it as 'primitive'. But it is still prevalent in some tribes of the world.

While in exchange economy, goods and services are distributed by formal and sophisticated methods over a wide area of a state or beyond state to several nations. An exchange economy can be *reciprocal, redistributive, peasant* and *market-oriented*. Thus, five types of economic organisations can be identified; these are:

1. Subsistence.
2. Reciprocal exchange with subsistence.
3. Peasant with primary reliance on self-produced food, but containing some exchange elements.
   (a) Market peasant.
   (b) Redistributive peasant.
4. Market-commercial.
5. Redistributive, or state socialist.

The characteristics of all the above mentioned economic organisations have been given in Table 2.1.

Table 2.1

Characteristics of economic organisations

<table>
<tr><th>Subsistence</th><th>Reciprocal</th><th>Peasant</th><th>Redistributive</th><th>Market commercial</th></tr>
<tr><td colspan="3">Absence of machine technology</td><td colspan="2">Complex technology</td></tr>
<tr><td>Limited exchange</td><td>Reciprocal exchange</td><td>Peripheral market</td><td>'State' market</td><td>Market</td></tr>
<tr><td colspan="2">Market less</td><td></td><td></td><td></td></tr>
<tr><td></td><td>Value of 'gifts'</td><td>Money variable</td><td colspan="2">All-purpose money</td></tr>
<tr><td colspan="3">Production unit: family, kinship</td><td>Production state-managed</td><td>Production by institutional units</td></tr>
<tr><td colspan="3">Distribution relatively complex</td><td>Distribution state organised</td><td>Distribution by market</td></tr>
<tr><td colspan="3">Production and distribution units: multipurpose social units</td><td colspan="2">Production and distribution units economically oriented</td></tr>
<tr><td colspan="3">Primary activities dominant</td><td colspan="2">Secondary and tertiary activities dominant</td></tr>
<tr><td>Craft specialised</td><td></td><td>Cottage industries</td><td colspan="2">Large industrial units</td></tr>
</table>

Another classification is based on theoretical and historical identification of different modes of production or forms of economic organisation, that are commonly recognised: 1. subsistence, 2. slavery, 3. feudalism, 4. capitalism, and 5. socialism. These are all broad categories, however, each can be broken down into more specific forms of economic organisation, for example, to differentiate between merchant capitalism, competitive capitalism (early phase of industrial capitalism), organised capitalism (later phase of industrial capitalism) and later advanced capitalism (globalised).

The contemporary world economy can be divided into three types based on their levels of economy. These types of economy are: *developed, developing* and *underdeveloped* (now referred to as developing). The economic organisations are also classified as *regional, metropolitan, world regional* and *global*.

In fact, economic organisations are closely linked with spatial change influenced by demographic change, political change, cultural change, social change and technological change as shown in Figure 2.3.

Figure 2.3

Interrelationships surrounding economic organisation and spatial change

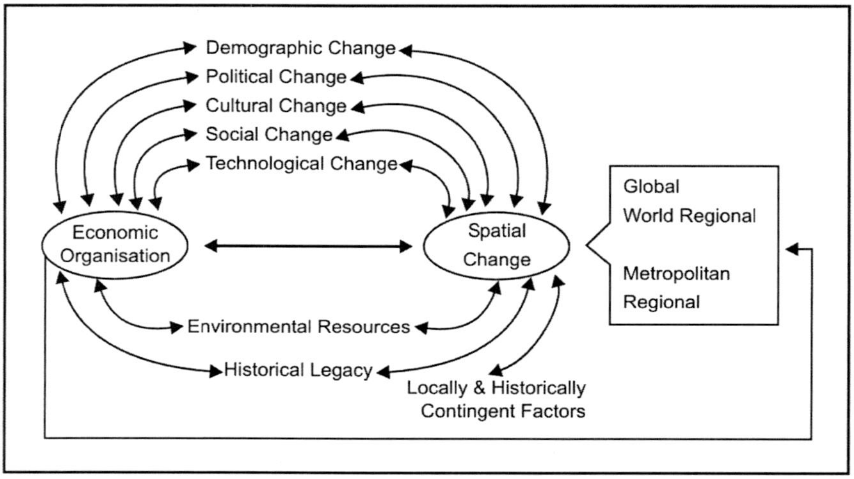

Figure 2.3 shows that economic organisation, with critical to spatial change, is itself implicated with demographic, political, cultural, social and technological change, as both cause and effect. The figure also shows that there are many interactions, for example, between political change and cultural change and between locally contingent factors and spatial change.

Social, Environmental and Spatial Relations of Economy

Economy cannot exist in isolation, but it is a part of the total wider environment. Thus, economy always has interrelations with social and physical environment and is also a part of spatial system. Therefore, it is necessary to discuss the relation of economy in social, ecological and spatial context.

Social Relations

Economic activities are closely associated with society because social needs or demands are used to direct and determine the nature and structure of the economy. One of the major problems facing societies, at all levels, is the social implication of the concentration of economic power. This may be defined as the power of economies or their individual elements to influence, by unilateral action, the course of economic events in a lasting or substantive fashion. The international inequalities in economic development are very well-known, one implication being that less than 25 per cent of the world's population generates over 60 per cent of its output. The remaining 75 per cent of the population is, in consequence, placed at a considerable bargaining disadvantage in attempting to obtain a share of the world economy's productive capacity and output commensurate with its needs. But some would go further than this and argue that the very process of development in one part of the world has the effect of impoverishing other parts because developed areas operate at higher levels of economic efficiency and so undercut less efficient producers. Furthermore, by offering higher remuneration, developed economies suck in resources from less-developed economies and so increase their own productive potential while decreasing the potential of the source areas. Without an efficient mechanism for redistributing such spatially concentrated wealth, major and increasing inequalities in social well-being develop. On the other hand, in the implementation (or perhaps more correctly imposition) of development programmes it is important not to transfer value systems from one situation to another. It is all too easy, for instance, to assume that the dream of each less-developed country is to become developed. Such a view can easily disregard highly developed local cultures. Self-respect is at least as important a measure of social and economic progress as are increases in urbanisation, specialisation, long-distance trading connections and material wealth (Adams, 1970).

A non-spatial and more frequently publicised example of inequality in economic power is symbolised by the struggle for shares in the wealth created by capitalist production between, on the one hand, the owners and controllers of capital and firms and, on the other, the owners of labour resources. The inequalities in the economic power of these elements are related to the private ownership of capital and the ability of capitalist institutions to make resource allocation decisions. Thus, the distribution of income amongst resource owners, which is determined by the type, amount and firms' evaluation of their resources and by the organised strength of their bargaining position, is an obvious symptom of their economic power and determinant of their social status and political influence. The work situation is a fundamental social variable of much wider significance than in the mere production of goods.

Ecological or Environmental Relation of Economy

Economy of any region depends upon the environmental factors. In spite of technological development, there are regions in the world which are still economically not at all developed because of either extreme cold or extreme hot and/or humid conditions. The Tundra region, equatorial regions, high mountainous regions and hot deserts are the best examples of economic backwardness due to physical conditions. On the other hand, wherever economic development has occurred, it also has close relations with ecological conditions. The links between economy and ecological environment are shown schematically in Figure 2.4.

A circular, physical flow of materials can be traced out of the ecosystem through the economy and back into the ecosystem. This flow suggests that a crude policy of economic growth attacks the ecosystem in two ways: (i) by increasing flows of EF it depletes the natural resource base and feeds the flows of FE and HE which (ii) pollute the ecosystem with their waste and often toxic substances. It is now widely felt that the ability of the ecosystem to withstand this two-pronged attack is limited and that the effect of damaging withdrawals and additions are often intensified as they make themselves felt throughout the system as a whole.

The demands made upon the ecosystem by the economy are increasing for two main reasons. First, the continued and increasing expansion of world population creates new demands upon the productive capabilities of economies and is partly responsible for the ever more widespread use of ecologically dangerous technology, especially chemical technology, in the short-term interest of increasing the output of goods. Secondly, the increasing standard of living of the members of advanced industrial economies results in an expanding range of sophisticated consumer tastes, especially for personal mobility which is threatening remote, ecologically fragile stretches of wilderness, congesting and polluting urban areas, and consuming vast quantities of non-renewable petroleum reserves. Increases in the flows within an economy automatically lead to increased demands upon the ecosystem, the cost of which can only be measured by the extension of conventional accounting systems adept at recording flows of HF and FH to include EF, FE, EH and HE (Figure 2.4).

The interaction of the economy with its higher order society and ecosystem illustrates the general problem posed by the boundaries and environment of a system under analysis: which elements are within the boundaries of the system, and which are in the environment and judged not to have any relevance for the analysis? While our emphasis in these pages is very much upon the economy per se, it is important to bear in mind the crucial links which exist between the economy, society and the ecosystem.

Figure 2.4
The economy and the ecosystem

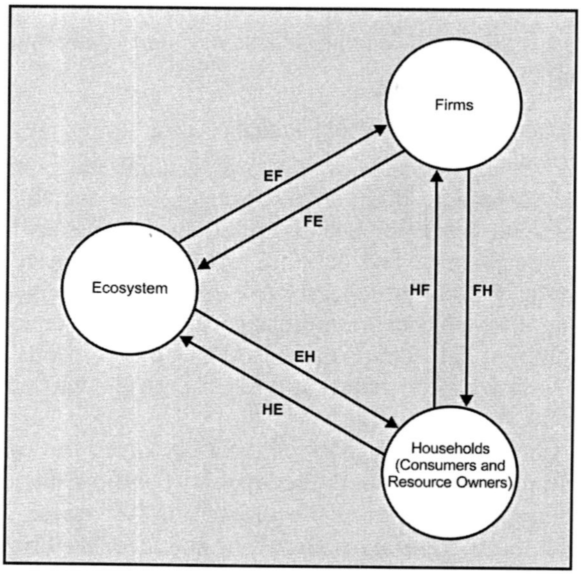

Spatial Structure of the Economy

Geographers are interested in the spatial aspect of the economy. Since economic activities are performed over a space, the problem of delimitation comes in the way of the economy. Firms, for example, may sell goods to local, regional, national or internal groups of consumers and may acquire resources, especially of capital equipments, from an equally wide distribution of resource owners. The world economy may be considered closed, but any attempt to delimit a sub-world economy in either spatial or sectoral terms must accept that the economy, so defined, is more or less open to interaction with other spatial units or sectors.

The spatial structure of an economy consists of the two-dimensional spread – spatial and functional. Such a spatial arrangement may be considered at several levels or scales of analysis. First, the individual elements within a particular sector of the economy may be regarded as nodes of activity dependent upon, and interacting with, the other elements along a network of communication. Much theorising about the location of firms has taken place at this scale, the problem being to minimise the cost of production and resource acquisition whilst at the same time trying to locate it in such a way relative to consumers that profits are maximised. Secondly, the individual elements may be coalesced into the space economies of cities and, at a larger scale, of world core areas forming zones of intense economic activity set in less intensively developed hinterlands. Although self-sufficient (or closed) in many respects, these concentrations need to draw upon the less densely distributed economic elements in their hinterlands for food and space-extensive resources and they interact with each other in the exchange of specialist products and information. The attempt to build a theory of the size, spacing and interaction of such economies, involving as it does the interdependence of a multitude of economic and social processes, is one of the most difficult problems in spatial economic analysis.

Both these levels of analysis are essentially functional in concept because they rely for their spatial definition upon the degree of closure of the economies. But closure is not necessarily determined by the existence of national, political or regional-administrative boundaries. However, nation states and some supra-national groups of states are important units in economic activity, if only because most government intervention takes place at this scale. Thus, a third level of analysis is defined by grouping the population of consumers, firms, resource owners and governments into politically delimited national or supra-national economies which may, however, develop strong international links.

A simple illustration of spatial economic organisation is given in Figure 2.5. The concept of spatially closed economies is indicated in Figure 2.5(a), which shows four completely isolated city-regions, each providing entirely for its own needs. The economy of each city-region is divided into four major sectors, A, B, C, D, located mainly within the major urban centre. Each of these sectors acquires resources and produces and markets goods and services entirely within the spatial confines of the city-region. There may well be a substantial amount of inter-sectoral exchange of goods and services – an agricultural sector, for example, may use some of the outputs of an engineering or chemical sector to aid production. But there is no interaction between the four city-regions, with the result that each is obliged to produce a minimum quantity of goods from all sectors but cannot produce too great a surplus without incurring considerable

Figure 2.5 (a, b, c)

Economic integration and locational specialisation

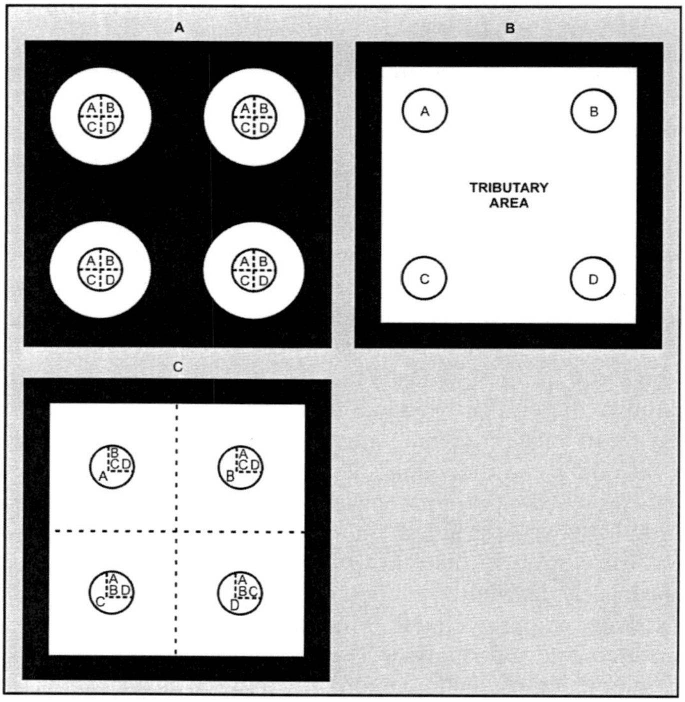

storage costs. By contrast, Figure 2.5 (b) shows four completely open economies operating effectively as one highly integrated economy. Here each centre specialises in one economic sector which can draw its resources from within the city in which it is located, from all parts of the tributary area and from the other three cities. Furthermore, exchange of goods and services can take place between all the cities so that the demands in each city can be fully met despite complete locational specialisation of supply.

Three major changes account for the differences between Figure 2.5 (a) and (b). First, the economic decision makers in each economy have perceived that there is advantage in local economic specialisation and exchange; secondly, the friction of space has been reduced so that economic interaction over long distances is possible; and thirdly, organisations enabling the large-scale exchange of resources and goods and services over long distances have grown. Figure 2.5 (c) shows an intermediate and more realistic situation. Specialisation has occurred but is not complete, and whilst each economy can draw upon the whole of the tributary rural area, it is more probable that intra-sectoral interaction will take place between elements close to rather than further from the town. But a precautionary note should be added here. Non-spatial factors may be more important than spatial factors in determining the nature of a space economy, for example, population growth may induce closure and economic diversity in the four economies by increasing economies of scale and by encouraging the production of an ever-increasing range of goods.

ECONOMIC ACTIVITIES

Economic activities are the integral part of economy. In fact, organisation of these activities determines the nature of economy. Economic activities are also considered as human occupation. Because human occupations are in a way an activity for the fulfilment of demands, i.e. gathering, hunting, fishing, livestock raising, mining, agriculture, manufacturing, etc. are human occupations and also economic activities. The economy of a region is the reflection of economic activities and these activities have changed with the development of civilisation. Geographers are interested in spatio-temporal analysis of these activities.

Man has steadily expanded his *ecumene*, as we shall call the region for his habitation, by following economic pursuits, and has thus, altered the face of the earth and organised the different parts of the ecumene gradually into a complex structure of world-wide economic relationships. In doing so, man is guided by his own will as well as by the possibilities bestowed by nature. In early phase of development the emphasis was on primary occupations or economic activities but afterwards secondary activities gained importance along with tertiary activities. Now tertiary activities are in prominence, although, primary and secondary activities are also equally important.

Figure 2.6
Major categories of economic activities

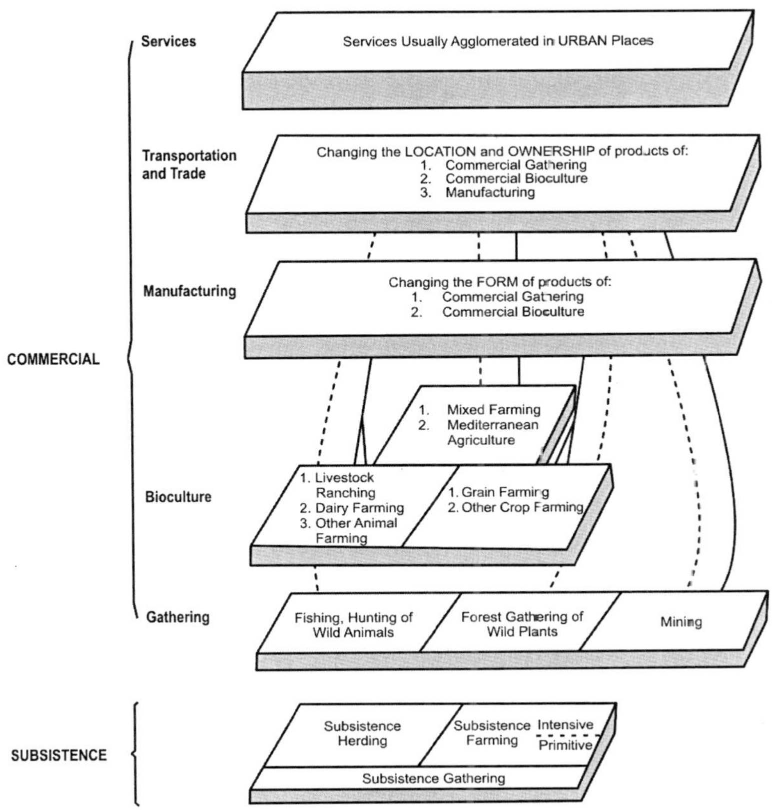

Alexander and Gibson (1979: 51) have classified economic activities in two broad categories, i.e. subsistence and commercial. The commercial activities have been further classified as – gathering, bioculture, manufacturing, transportation and trade, and services. Figure 2.6 shows the major categories of economic activities.

In a subsistence economy, where each family performs the roles of farmer, fisherman, hunter, miner and manufacturer, there is likely to be no surplus – or a very small one. But when a family concentrates on one of these roles and becomes a full-time farmer or fisherman or miner, the usual result is an immediate surplus – more of some commodity than a family can consume.

As the economy of a region tends more and more towards commercialism, producers intensify their specialisation and produce larger quantities of fewer items. Thus, there is specialisation in *agriculture, fishing, forestry* and *mining*. Specialisation appears also in secondary production, or *manufacturing*. With the increase in production, exchange is started. This exchange requires and gives rise to *transportation and trade*. With further intensification of commercialism, a new type of production arises – *commercial services*. Physicians, teachers, entertainers, government officials, computer experts, lawyers, repairmen, household helpers and other service types have been developed as an economic activity. All these developments have occurred along with the growth of economy.

Michael Eliot Hurst (1972) has given a *classification of economic activities* as under:

1. **Production:** Transformation of resources and producer goods, adding value and/or form.
   (a) *Primary:* Direct acquisition from the natural environment or systematised production from land or sea (agriculture, grazing, forest products, fishing and hunting, mining and quarrying).
   (b) *Secondary:* Transformation of primary products and producer goods (Manufacturing-handicraft to factory production).
   (c) *Tertiary:* Services, wholesaling and consumer goods (retailing, banking, trading, entertainment, office services, etc.)
   (d) *Quaternary:* Service for which advance training and education is required.
2. **Exchange:** The addition of time and place utility; the sale of goods in the market place.
   (a) *Trade* (wholesaling and retailing).
   (b) *Transportation* (passenger and freight).
3. **Consumption:** The using up of goods and services to satisfy human wants and needs.
   (a) *Consumer Goods:* Food, shelter, clothing, etc. used in direct satisfaction of human wants.
   (b) *Producer Goods:* Used for indirect satisfaction; consumed in the act of further production of goods.

The variations in economic activities depend upon the stage through which region's economy progresses. The following generalisations (hypotheses) seem to be correct:

1. The lower the level of commercial development in a region, the higher the proportion of its people who are engaged in *agriculture, fishing* and *forestry*.
2. As the degree of commercialism in a region begins to increase, the proportion of people engaged in those three activities tends to shrink, but the proportion engaged in *trade* and *transportation* rises.
3. As a region continues to advance up the ladder of commercialism, it reaches a third stage, at which *manufacturing* is the most rapidly expanding endeavour.
4. With further commercial development, the most rapid growth is seen in *services*, which ultimately take over as the leading endeavour in the region's economy.

3

Resources

Concept, Classification and Conservation

The modern economy is a resource-based economy and all the development of a country or a region is based on resources, especially on natural resources. Nature has given us abundant resources in the form of water, air, heat, natural vegetation, soil, wild animals, metals, fossil fuels, etc. and man by his technical skill and knowledge is using all these resources in some way or the other right from the dawn of civilisation.

Etymologically, 'resource' refers to two separate words – 're' and 'source' meaning any thing or substance that may occur unhindered many times. Although, resources have been utilised by man right from the beginning of human civilisation, but 'resource' as a concept had no special significance till the early part of the 20th century. Only in 1933, when eminent economist Erich W. Zimmermann promulgated his famous concept of 'resource', the idea became so popular that not only economists but geographers and other academicians also started to study this concept. This was also due to overexploitation of resources mostly by colonial powers and it was felt that these resources were not unlimited. Therefore, nations of the world have started to frame policies for their utilisation because development of a nation is always not only directed but also determined by its resources.

Definitions

'Resource' is a wider term and its dictionary definitions are:

- that upon which one relies for aid, support, or supply;
- means to attain given ends; and
- the capacity to take advantage of opportunities or to extricate oneself from difficulties.

According to Zimmermann, "the word 'resource' does not refer to a thing or a substance but to a function which a thing or a substance may perform or to an operation in which it may take part, namely, the function or operation of attaining a given end such as satisfying a want. In other words, the word resource is an abstraction reflecting human appraisal and relating to a function or operation." Thus, a resource satisfies individual human wants or attains social objectives. It also refers to the positive interaction between man and nature. Man is, of course, the most important and integral part of resource creation, as he is at the top of the hierarchy in resource consumption. Only the satisfaction of human beings converts any thing or a substance into a resource.

Small and Witherick (1997) have defined resource as "a feature of the environment (e.g. minerals, soils, climate) used in order to meet particular human needs (e.g. energy, housing, food, etc.). It is the act of exploitation which converts a feature or commodity into a resource." Further, they elaborated the statement that "often the term resource is taken to be synonymous with natural resource, but it can be extended to embrace human resources, such as manual skills, the innovative ability or entrepreneurial talents of a population."

Similarly, Susan Mayhew (2006) has defined resource as "some component which fulfils people's needs. Resources may be man-made – labour, skills, finance, capital and technology – or natural – ores, water, soil, natural vegetation or even climate." The perception of resource may vary over time; coal was of little significance to Neolithic man, while flint was of great importance. Such resources depend on relevant technology. Other resources, like landscapes and ecosystems, may be permanently valued whatever the technology be.

Resources are significant because:

(i) they satisfy human wants both individual and social,

(ii) they are a source or possibility of assistance,

(iii) they are a means of development and support,

(iv) they are an expedient,

(v) they have capacity to take advantage of opportunities, and

(vi) one relies on them for aid, support and supply.

In fact, "resources are those aspects of man's environment which facilitates the satisfaction of human wants and the attainment of social objectives" (*Encyclopedia of Social Sciences*). A thing is a resource so far as it affects man as a means of satisfying his wants. In other words, a thing becomes resource by its function in relation to man, therefore, it is said that resources do not exist, they become. For example, a lump of coal is a resource not because of its shape, colour or composition nor for its scarcity but because it functions for satisfying some human wants. Thus, resource is something functional but at the same time it must be beneficial to man.

Resources are always having two properties: first – function ability and second – utility. Both these qualities make anything or substance as a resource. Sometimes the word 'wealth' is also used for same purpose and meaning as the resource. But, both are not similar and have a difference. Wealth, as stated by noted economist J.M. Keynes, "consists of all potentially exchangeable means of satisfying human wants". So, wealth must possess: utility, functionability, scarcity and transferability. Similarly, wealth is measurable in terms of units. On the contrary, resource may be tangible as well as intangible substances. Resource covers a wider field than wealth, therefore, all material and non-material means of satisfying human and social needs are resources. Land, building, machinery, shares and stocks are resources. At the same time, air, water, sunshine, rivers, education, social institutions, a good government, health, knowledge, culture, etc. are all resources, because all these have both the attributes of the resources. So, all wealth are resources but all resources are not wealth. Resource incorporates much more than wealth in a sense that culture, technology, skill, knowledge and many other aspects are included in the realm of resource.

Conceptualisation

Resources are the gift of nature and also developed by man through his skill, knowledge and technology. Earlier man was not particular about resources, because his wants were limited and he used to fulfil them easily. But, with the industrialisation, technological development and growth of population, the use of resources has also increased. In this process of the utilisation of resources man often misuses their availability, thus affect the natural ecosystem as well as faces their scarcity. With the overexploitation of resources it was soon realised that resources are not unlimited and unless properly used the day is not far off when he will not only be deprived of them but he will also have to face ecological consequences. This apprehension has given a way to scientists and others to think about various aspects related to resources. Therefore, certain ideas/concepts have been developed. These are discussed as under:

Principle of Resource Adequacy and Scarcity

The concept of resource adequacy and scarcity has been developed in two different types of economy. The first is the capitalistic ideology/economy and the second is the socialistic economy. According to capitalistic thought, resources are adequate and their maximum use is possible. This is necessary for development and trade or for the capital gain. Capitalists believe that resources are the gift of nature, therefore, they can be used without any restriction. This concept has increased the overexploitation of resources for the benefit of certain states or group of people.

On the contrary, socialists believe that resources are limited, means there is scarcity of resources. Therefore, there use should be done in such a way that their utilisation is possible for a long time. If resources are utilised without planning, a stage will come when they will be finished. At the same time, overexploitation of resources will also create several ecological problems.

Resources: Static or Dynamic

In relation to resource, a static and dynamic concept has also been developed. Some scholars consider resources as 'static' and state that they are fixed asset and their quantity cannot be increased, whether it is minerals, water, soil or natural vegetation. This was an earlier concept, when widespread belief was that "resource cannot be created". It is a free gift of nature. This was because of the fact that only natural things or substances were considered as a resource and creation, modification or extension of resources was practically unknown.

By now resources are considered as 'dynamic' because with scientific knowledge and technological development several new resources have been developed and modification in several resources has also been done. The present concept is that "resources are not, they become". The role of man in overall resource creation process has now been understood. As Zimmermann remarks, "man's own wisdom is his premier resource – the key resource that unlock the universe". He further elaborated his statement that resource is as dynamic as the civilisation itself.

Functional Theory of Resources

"Resources were defined as means of attaining given ends, i.e. individual wants and social objectives. Means take their meaning from the ends which they serve. As ends change, means must change also." This statement of Zimmermann clearly states that resource is a function of space and time. It means that only those things or substances are considered as resources which are functional means useful for man. But, the situation changes with time and development of science and technology. The modern school of thought believes in resource use for human welfare and also in functional theory of resource, which entails that:

(a) Resource is functional and operational,

(b) It is made or created by efforts of man, and

(c) It is dynamic and not static.

The term 'functional' denotes functionable character, i.e. the capacity of satisfying human wants. As natural phenomena which can satisfy human wants, is functional and so a resource. The sunshine which helps our organic growth, the air which we breath, the earth on which we live, are automatically resources. They are functional in their original state and form. But, many natural things, e.g. minerals, soils, rivers, waterfalls, forests, etc. did not possess their functional capacity in their original state. It acquired its functional capacity when man by his efforts discovered it and learnt the art of putting it into various uses, then it became a resource. The tropical Africa is well-endowed with water resources. But, due to backward economy and technological drawbacks, inhabitants of that region could not convert it into energy. On the contrary, Japanese were able to produce huge energy from their limited water resources. Therefore, it is clear that resources although exist but their functional character makes them a resource, otherwise they are neutral stuffs. Without functional capacity coal was a neutral stuff, with functional capacity coal is a resource. So, with the efforts of man, through the functional or operational process, resource is dynamically created. The resource creation process is highly dynamic in nature.

Resource, Resistance and Neutral Stuff

Resource and resistance are closely linked with each other, where there is resource there is also resistance. Nature has given many things which can function as a resource, e.g. productive land, coal for energy, rain for agriculture and so on. But at the same time, nature also presents us with some harmful things, i.e. resistance such as barren and unproductive soil, floods, typhoon, hurricane, earthquakes, poisons, etc. which are harmful or restrict man and are called resistance. In social context education, training, improved health, social morality are resources, but illiteracy, ignorance, greed, over population, racial conflict, war, etc. are resistance. Similarly, in the field of culture, scientific development, tools, machines or technology, good government, finance, etc. are resources but obsolete equipments, conservative attitude, business depression, abortive policies, etc. are resistances.

Another aspect of resources is the neutral stuff. Any thing or any process that restricts subsistence becoming resource is called neutral stuff. Similarly, anything or substance which does not contain functionability or utility value, it is termed as neutral stuff. A neutral stuff should not be necessarily neutral forever. What is considered neutral stuff today may transform into resource tomorrow. Man by his knowledge, wisdom and technological innovation may transform neutral stuff into resource. For example, till 1859, petroleum was not considered a resource, because its use as a source of power was not known. But, with the development of science and technology, it has become now an important energy resource. Similar is the case with other minerals and several other resources. In fact, the process of economic development is directly proportional with the rate of conversion of neutral stuff into resource.

Concept of Phantom Pile

The concept of phantom pile has been applied to explain the nature and changing role of technology in resource development. The name 'phantom pile' suggests that it is technological knowledge that can derive extra resources hidden within the substance.

For example, formerly, for the production of 1 ton pig iron, 5 tons of coal were required. But in the contemporary world, 2 tons of coal is enough to produce 1 ton pig iron. In other words, 5 tons of coal can produce 2.5 tons of pig iron. So, functionability of coal has increased 2.5 times. It means same substance is yielding 2.5 times more energy resource. That excess hidden resource, which was unknown or invisible before is called phantom pile (Figure 3.1).

Figure 3.1
Phantom pile

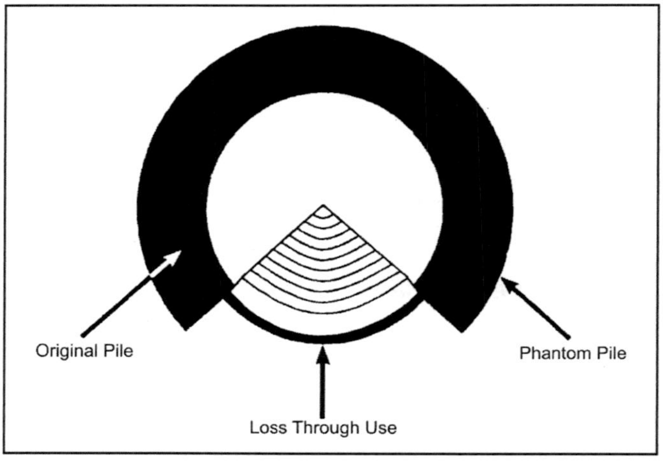

The concept of phantom pile was given by Zimmermann, which in later years, helped to develop the concept of resource conservation. There has been remarkable improvement in the utilisation of many minerals and natural substances. Due to improvement in the technique and skill, they are now more efficiently and economically used. For each of such instances, the phantom pile principle is applicable.

Resource Creating Factors

The three important resource creating factors are: (i) nature, (ii) man, and (iii) culture.

Nature

Nature is the biggest creator of resources. It is often said 'bountiful nature', but this should be kept in mind that to what extent is she bountiful? Air, water, light, space, etc. are free gifts of nature, which man enjoys without any effort. On the other hand, most of the nature's gift are really man-made. These resources such as minerals, land, water and so on are created by nature but these substances have become useful only after strenuous efforts of man.

Nature is both a friend and foe to man. She is a friend when she provides air, water, sunshine, fertile soil and other useful resources. But, nature becomes a foe when she brings floods, earthquakes and other natural calamities. Natural resources always have natural resistance. The distribution of natural resources is not uniform over the earth. Minerals and other natural endowments are unevenly distributed. The various regions of the world differ in respect of physiography, water bodies, climate, soil, natural vegetation. There are endless diversities in the distribution of natural resources and natural resistances. There are ubiquitous resources, which occur everywhere, on the other hand, localised resources occur only at few places. Similarly, in nature, there are flow resources which are perennial such as air, water and also fund resources which exhaust through use, all minerals are the fund resources.

Man

Man is a creator of resources. In fact, man acts both as *producer* and *consumer* of resources. As a producer of resource, man contributes his labour, mental and physical capabilities. He creates methods and technology to make labour more productive and to lessen the impact of resistances. He discovers new ways and invents new arts. Added by nature on the one hand and culture on the other, he builds up resources. Man's role as a consumer is equally important in the field of resources. In fact, human wants and needs initiate the process of resource building because resources are meant for satisfying human wants. Man is essentially an element of nature, but he is different from the other elements of nature because he has the capacity to think and act accordingly. Thus, he is not only a producer and consumer but also a planner and aspirer and his decision-making ability makes him a creator of resources in respect of their usefulness.

Human wants are of two types: basic and cultural. Basic wants include food, clothing and shelter. But, his demand is not limited to mere fulfilment of these wants at the minimum level, rather he demands more and more improvement in basic wants. In other words, he is always busy in improving the quality of life. This has resulted into resource development through technological and scientific development. The development of human resources now has become a key to progress.

Culture

According to Zimmermann, "Culture means education, learning, experience, religion, civilised behaviour, suppression of vicious animal instincts, cooperation, replacing conflict, the law of jungle." In other words, culture is the sum total of all the devices produced by man, with the aid, advice and consent of nature, to assist him in the attainment of his objectives. Culture has the duel function of enlarging resources and reducing the resistances. In fact, resource evolves out of the dynamic interaction of nature, man and culture.

Man and nature are original resource factors, while culture is a derived factor. Culture includes material things like machines, tools, transportational arrangements, warehouses, social institutions, management, etc. apart from those mentioned in the above paragraph. Culture not only reduces the influence of natural resistances but also removes the human constraints like illiteracy, poor health, conservative attitudes, etc. The utilisation of resources is always related with the cultural development, so is the 'conservation of resources'.

Classification of Resources

For resource classification, several scholars have adopted different criteria and explained their characteristics. Resources can be classified on the basis of their nature, durabilities, ownership, and distribution pattern. A general classification has also been done based on their general characteristics. The following chart depicts the classification of resources:

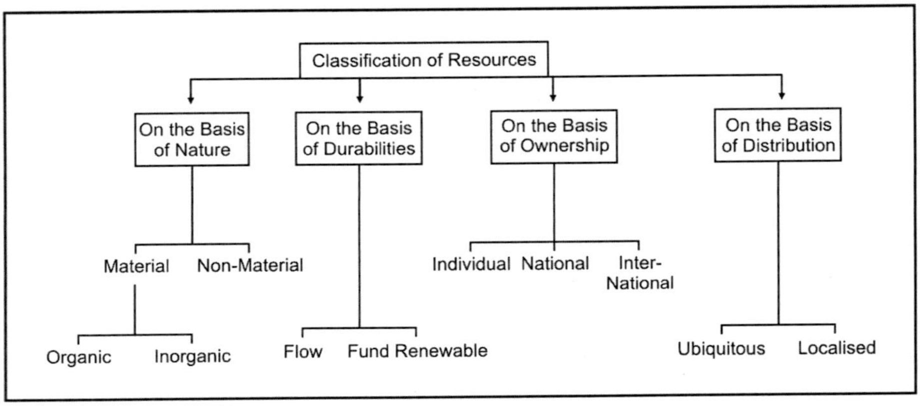

On the Basis of Nature of Resources

There are two types of resources:

(i) material resources, and

(ii) non-material resources.

Material resources are tangible substances, such as iron ore, copper, coal, petroleum and other minerals. Material resources may be further sub-divided into two groups:

(i) Organic resources: like forest, fish, livestock, etc.

(ii) Inorganic resources: all types of minerals.

Non-material resources are intangible substances like health condition, culture, freedom, environmental harmony, etc.

On the Basis of Durability of Resources

There are two types of resources based on durability. These are:

1. Fund or exhaustible resources: These resources are not everlasting and get finished after a particular time. These resources cannot be created or generated by man but are the result of long geological processes. All the minerals come in this category. Coal, petroleum, iron ore, uranium, copper, mica, etc. all are exhaustible resources.

2. Flow or inexhaustible resources: These resources can be used continuously because they have a tendency of renewal. Their supply remains unchanged even after renewed use. Such resources are river water, sunshine, wind, sea waves, etc. The forest if properly managed can also be used for a long time.

On the Basis of Ownership of Resources

Three categories of the resources have been identified on the basis of their ownership: (i) individual resources, (ii) national resources, and (iii) international resources.

(i) Individual resources are those which belong to the individuals. These are both tangible resources, i.e. property, money, wealth and intangible resources, i.e. knowledge, wisdom, health, etc.

(ii) National resources are those which belong to the nation. These resources include both natural and economic resources. Water, air, forest minerals, sea resources are mostly national resources. For the utilisation of these resources every nation has their own policies.

(iii) International resources are also known as world resources. These resources are owned by global population or by international organisations. The sum total of all material and non-material resources comes under this category.

On the Basis of Distribution or Availability of Resources

Resources can be classified into two groups on the basis of their distribution or availability. These are:

(i) Ubiquitous resources

(ii) Localised resources

Ubiquitous resources are found everywhere, e.g. sunshine, air, water, etc. while localised resources are found at some particular place(s) such as petroleum, uranium, iron ore and all other mineral resources, etc.

General Classification of Resources

The classification described above is based on some particular criterion. But, for the sake of their proper study, a general classification has been evolved by the scholars, which helps in proper understanding of resources. This is not a new classification but a combination of already described resource types, accordingly resources can be classified into three groups: (i) natural resources, (ii) economic resources, and (iii) human resources.

Natural Resources

Any element of our natural environment such as soil, water, forest, wildlife, minerals, etc. that man can utilise to promote his welfare may be identified as a natural resource. Natural resources vary greatly in quantity, mutability and reusability, therefore, can be classified into following categories:

Inexhaustible

(a) *Immutable:* Seemingly incapable of much adverse change through man's activities, such as:

(i) wind power
(ii) precipitation
(iii) tidal power
(iv) atomic energy

(b) *Misusable:* Little danger of complete exhaustion, but when improperly used their resource quality may be impaired, such as:
(i) solar power
(ii) atmosphere
(iii) ocean
(iv) flowing streams

Exhaustible

1. *Maintainable:* Those resources in which permanency is dependent upon method of use by man.
2. *Renewable:* The living or dynamic resources whose perpetual harvest is dependent upon proper planning and management by man. These are:
   (i) water in place
   (ii) soil fertility
   (iii) products of the land – agricultural products, forests, forage land, wild animals
   (iv) products of lakes, streams and impoundments – freshwater fish, black bass, lake trout, catfish
   (v) products of oceans – marine fish, marine mammals
   (vi) human resources
3. *Non-renewable:* Once gone there is no hope of replacement:
   (i) mineral resources
   (ii) fossil fuels
   (iii) species of wildlife

Economic Resources

In this category, those resources are included which are useful to man from economic point of view. Although, all the resources are in one way or the other useful to man, but resources like minerals, power resources, marine resources, agricultural resources, forest resources, animal resources are economically useful, therefore, called economic resources.

Human Resources

Human resources refer not to human beings as such, but to the qualities they possess and which can be used by the community for some useful purpose. Human resource does not originate spontaneously. It is cultivated through education and proper training. In fact, human resources are the energies, skills, talent and knowledge of people which potentially can and should be applied to the production of goods and services. Mere production of goods and services are not enough, unless and until it is consumed properly. Man is situated at the centre stage. On the one side he produces, on the other he consumes. Therefore, man plays a dual role in the development of resources.

Conservation of Resources

The word 'conservation' is derived from two Latin words, 'con' meaning 'together' and 'servare' meaning to 'keep' or 'guard'. Literally, therefore, conservation means "to keep together". The word was coined by Gifford Pinchot shortly after the White House Conference of 1908. Some of the definitions of resource conservation are:

According to P. Haggett, resource conservation is the scheduling of resource use so as to provide the greatest yield for the greatest number over the longest time period.

According to Ely, conservation means a sacrifice of the present generation to future generations, whenever it is carried for, this conflict beginning far before the ideal is reached which conservationists are inclined to advocate.

According to Harold M. Rose, the optimum allocation of natural, human and cultural resources in the scheme of national development, whereby maximum economic and social security will be assured.

John F. Kennedy, in a special message to the Congress in 1962, interpreted conservation as "the wise use of our natural environment, the prevention of waste and despoilment while preserving, improving and renewing the quality and usefulness of all our resources".

The conservation of natural resources is a concept that deals with the rational use of resources so that harmony between man's resource requirements and its availability can be established. While renewable resources need a proper resource management system (a part of conservation), the non-renewable resources require a long-term strategy for their proper use. This is not only necessary to assure long-term resource use but also to protect the ecosystem. Nowadays, every country is very particular regarding its natural resources and tries to genuinely adopt conservation policies. During the colonial period of 18th century to mid-20th century most of the countries of Asia, Africa and Latin America have suffered a lot due to their resource exploitation by colonial powers. Gradually, all these countries got their freedom but either for economic needs or for political adjustment their natural resources have been exploited unwisely, resulting in not only the loss of several resources but also was responsible for many problems of environmental degradation.

The conservation movement, in its present form, was first started in the USA under the guidance of Gifford Pinchot, Head of the US Forest Service from 1898 to 1910, with active support from Franklin D. Roosevelt. The first wave of conservation actually started when Roosevelt called the White House Conference on Natural Resources in 1908, followed by a number of important events in several subsequent decades, the enactment of several laws which regulated the manner in which the natural resources of the country can be protected. As a result of the conference, a fifty-men National Conservation Commission was formed which composed of scientists, statesmen and businessmen. After 1930, in USA, several agencies have been established and several acts have been passed to protect forests, soils, wildlife and other natural resources. This tradition was followed by other US presidents like John F. Kennedy, Lyndon B. Johnson, Richard M. Nixon and is still in force to this day. In 1970, Nixon set up the 'National Environmental Protection Agency'.

The conservation wave was not limited to the US only but started in European countries as well as in Russia and soon all the countries of the world realised the need to conserve natural resources. Therefore, apart from national efforts by each country, efforts on global level have also been started under United Nations. Different agencies of the UN are now playing a key role in setting the world on the long road towards conservation of natural resources and protection of the environment. The increase in public support for conservation measures both at international and local levels has given this movement a new life, but still there is a long way to go in this direction.

The conservation of important natural resources is discussed as under:

Forest Conservation

Where geographical conditions permit vegetation to take the form of trees, the forest is one of the major forms of the natural landscape. The forest resources are valuable as an integral part of the ecosystem, from the commercial point of view, and as providers of shelter to wildlife. Today forests provide the raw materials for over 5,000 products worth about 23 million dollars. They support industry which employs 1.3 million people. In fact, forests are still the natural habitats of several species of plants and animals, as well as of several tribal groups of the world. But, the most unfortunate setback came in the form of commercial exploitation, which resulted in mass destruction of forest cover year after year. Originally, over two-fifth of the land area of the earth, exclusive of the polar regions, or about 1,200 million hectares was covered with natural forests. But, now more than one-third of this area has been robbed by man of its natural protective cover and has been turned into barren land.

The history of the exploitation of forests is as old as man himself, but during earlier times it was balanced through a natural growth process because at that time forest cutting was done for personal or community use only. But with the expansion of agriculture, forest lands have been cleared. More destruction has been done after industrial revolution and urbanisation. During the colonial period commercial exploitation began and this was the main cause of the depletion of forests. The commercial use of forests nowadays has reached such an extent that it has become a threat to the environment in the form of:

(i) Increase in temperature,
(ii) Lesser precipitation,
(iii) Increased rate of soil erosion,
(iv) Increase in frequency and volume of floods,
(v) Loss of soil productivity,
(vi) Extinction of several species,
(vii) Non-availability of several essential forest products, and
(viii) Imbalance in ecosystem.

The harmful effects of deforestation are so much that all over the world people and authorities have realised that forest resources must be conserved properly in order to protect the ecosystem.

The forest is a national resource and a social asset. It yields a great social profit which lies wholly outside the realm of business. But, at present, most of the forests of the world are so over-used that experts predict dire calamities in the not-too-distant future and irreparable damage on a catastrophic scale. If properly used and put on a sustained yield basis, it will be one of man's greatest resources and for this, conservation of forest is the only alternative.

Methods of Forest Conservation

The following steps should be taken for the conservation of forests:

Regulated and Planned Cutting of Trees

One of the main reasons of deforestation is commercial felling of trees. According to an estimate, about 1,600 million cubic metres of wood have been used for various purposes in the world. Although trees are considered as perennial resource, when exploited on a very large scale, their revival cannot be possible. Therefore, cutting should be regulated by adopting methods like:

(i) clear cutting,

(ii) selective cutting, and

(iii) shelter wood cutting.

The clear cutting method is useful for those areas where the same type of trees are available over a large area. In that case, trees of same age group can be cut down in a selected area and then marked for replantation. In selective cutting only mature trees are selected for cutting. This process is to be followed in rotation. Shelter wood cutting is where first of all useless trees have been cut down followed by medium and best quality timber trees. The time gap between these cuttings is helpful in regrowth of trees. In regulated cutting only one-tenth of the forest area is selected for use and rotational system is always followed for their protection. The forest can be managed in such a way that a timber crop may be harvested indefinitely year after year without being depleted. This technique is called the 'sustained yield' method adopted by many countries of the world.

Control over Forest Fire

Destruction or loss of forest by fire is fairly common, because trees are highly exposed to fire and once started it becomes difficult to control. Sometimes, the fire starts by natural process, i.e. by lightning or by friction between trees during speedy winds, while in most cases it is started by man either intentionally or unintentionally. According to an estimate, during the period from 1940 to 1950, in the US alone, fires consumed an average of 21.5 million acres of timber yearly and as many as 1,175,664 cases of forest fires occurred during 1955 to 1964 period. Throughout the world, forest fire is common and in most cases they were begun by man. As John D. Guthrie, former fire inspector of US Forest Service, has written: "To stage a Forest Fire you need only few things – a forest, the right atmospheric conditions, and a spark either from a lightning bolt or a match in the hands of a fool or a knave. The formula is simple – the larger the forest, the drier the air, the bigger the fool, the bigger the fire you will have".

In order to save forests from fire it is necessary to adopt latest techniques of firefighting. Some of the fire suppression techniques are to develop three metre wide fire lanes around the periphery of the fire, back fires, arrangement of water spray, fire retardant chemicals should be sprayed from back tank and if possible by helicopters. There must be a trained staff of firefighters to control the fire.

Reforestation and Afforestation

The sustained yield concept dictates that whenever timber is removed, either by block cutting or by selective cutting, the denuded area must be reforested. This may be done by natural or artificial methods. Similarly, any forested land which has been destroyed by fire or mining activities should be reforested. In rugged terrain aerial seeding is the method of choice.

Besides all this, fresh afforestation programmes should be started. New plantations will not only increase the forest cover but also help in making up the eco-balance. For afforestation, selection of trees should be done according to local geographical conditions and care must be taken during initial growth of the trees.

Check over Forest Clearance for Agricultural and Habitation Purposes

Most of the present-day agricultural land was once forested and then cleared for the use of agriculture. But now it has reached the stage where further clearance will be dangerous for the entire ecosystem. There are tribals in some parts of Asia, Africa and South America, where shifting cultivation is still a part of their system of land procurement. According to an estimate, about 40 million sq km of land is used for this purpose by 200 million tribals of the world. For the conservation of forest, this should be checked and an alternative system should be suggested to them. Similarly, for the development of villages, towns and cities, forest lands have been cleared and this process continues to this day causing loss of forest cover. This also should be checked and green belts around cities should be developed.

Protection of Forest

The existing forests should be protected. Apart from commercial cutting, unorganised grazing is also one of the reasons. There are several forest diseases resulting from parasitic fungi, rusts, mistletoes, viruses and nematodes which cause the destruction of trees. The forests should be protected either by use of chemical spray, antibiotics or by development of disease resistant strains of trees.

Proper Utilisation of Forest Products and Forests

Generally, forests have been cut for logs and rest of the tree – stump, limbs, branches and foliage, etc. are left out in the forest as worthless debris. Further waste occurs at the sawmill. There is a need to use all this waste material. Now several uses have been developed and products like waterproof glues, board, etc. can be obtained.

Similarly, forests can easily be used or developed as tourist centres. By using them as tourist centres the country can earn substantial foreign exchange. This practice has been adopted by many countries, both developed and developing. The concepts of 'national park' and 'game sanctuary' have now become popular and every country has developed its unique forest area as a 'national park'. In India alone, there are as many as 21 national parks. This scheme is a good method of forest conservation.

Role of Government in Forest Conservation

Although the government of every country is very particular about conservation of its forest resources and have several rules and laws for the protection of forest, but their effective implementation is necessary. Both national and provincial governments can take some steps in this direction, such as:

(i) Pass acts for the conservation of forests,
(ii) Survey of the forest resources,
(iii) Categorisation of forest resources,
(iv) Categorisation of forest areas and proper delimitation of reserved forest areas,
(v) Find out the areas where reforestation can be done,
(vi) Regulate the commercial use of forest products,
(vii) Protect forest from fire, mining and other natural calamities,
(viii) Develop national parks,
(ix) Encourage forests developmental activities like social forestry, agro-forestry, etc. and
(x) Prepare master plans, both for long-term and short-term period, etc.

Forest Management

Management of forest resources is the key to all conservation efforts. In forest management, the following aspects should be taken into consideration:

(i) Survey of forest,
(ii) Categorisation of forest,
(iii) Economic use of forest,
(iv) Administrative setting for forest management,
(v) Training programmes for persons engaged in forest conservation activities,
(vi) Use of forest land as tourist centres,
(vii) Social and agro-forestry,
(viii) Development of new techniques for the conservation of forest,
(ix) Research for efficient use and conservation of forest, and
(x) Policy-decisions and their proper implementation.

In brief, conservation of forest resources can be done by cooperative efforts of the government, non-government organisations and the public through a proper management system.

Soil Conservation

Soil is the uppermost layer of earth's surface which supports all forms of life. It is in the soil that all plants have their roots and from which they absorb life-sustaining moisture and nutrients. Man, in turn, feeds directly upon these plants or upon plant eating animals. Thus, virtually all terrestrial life ultimately derives from the soil. If a nation's soil resources are fertile and abundant, in like measure will that state have vigour and stability. When this resource is exhausted because of mounting demands of a swelling population or long mismanagement, the nation's survival is in jeopardy. Some authorities believe that one of the causes of the decline of the Roman Empire was deterioration of soils. The loss of soil, either by natural process or by mismanagement, is harmful not only for agricultural development but to the whole ecosystem, therefore, its conservation has now become a matter of grave concern.

The main reason for the loss of soil is soil erosion which is of four types as under:

(i) normal soil erosion,
(ii) soil erosion by water,
(iii) wind soil erosion, and
(iv) accelerated soil erosion.

Normal soil erosion is a natural and a very slow process, therefore, not harmful, rather it helps in soil formation. Soil erosion by water is quite widespread and a main reason of soil loss and loss of fertility. Water soil erosion is of four types, viz. sheet erosion, rill erosion, gully erosion and riparian erosion. The third agent of soil erosion is wind. Winds are more effective in arid and semi-arid regions. While the accelerated soil erosion is done by human activities, which accelerate the process of soil erosion by deforestation, grazing, mining, defective agricultural practices, etc. landslide and leaching is also a reason of soil loss. The problem for soil loss now has become a worldwide problem and its conservation is necessary.

Techniques of Soil Conservation

Soil erosion can be controlled by adopting land management practices and also by changing the pattern of some human activities which accelerate soil erosion. The following techniques can help in controlling soil erosion:

(i) *Contour Farming:* Contour farming may be defined as ploughing, seeding, cultivating and harvesting across the slope, rather than with it. Thomas Jefferson, who wrote in 1813: "we now plough horizontally, following the curvature of the hills … . Every furrow thus acts as a reservoir to … retain waters … scarcely an ounce of soil is now carried off."

(ii) *Strip Cropping:* On land with a decided slope, planting crops on contour strips will be an effective erosion deterrent. For effective control the width of the contour strip should vary inversely with the length of the slope. Strip cropping should be combined with crop rotation, so that a strip planted to a soil depleting, erosion-facilitating corn crop one year will be sown to a soil enriching and protecting strip of legumes the next.

(iii) *Terracing:* The practice of terracing has been common in ancient China. The flat, step-like bench terraces are now not useful. The modern terrace is an embankment of earth constructed across a slope in such a way as to control water run-off and minimise erosion. To be effective, terrace must check water flow before it attains sufficient velocity to loosen and transport soil.

(iv) *Gully Reclamation:* Gullies are danger signals that indicate land is eroding rapidly and may become a wasteland as in the case of vast areas along the rivers Chambal and Yamuna. If a gully is small it may be ploughed in and then seeded to quick-growing crops like barley, maize, jowar, wheat in order to check erosion. In case of severe gullying, small check dams of manure and straw constructed at 5 metre intervals may be effective, because silt will collect behind the dams and gradually fill in the channel. Earthen, stone and even concrete dams may be built at intervals along the gully. Once dams have been constructed and water run-off has been restrained, soil may be stabilised.

(v) *Shelter Belts:* These are the 'green belts' of trees which help to break the force of strong winds and thus, prevent or cut to a minimum the blowing away of the loose top-soil. In areas where wind erosion is more, rows of trees may be helpful to check the flow of winds. Apart from this, these trees will also add colour to the landscape and help to control the desert spread. Soil blowing away can also be controlled if local shrubs and small trees are planted in a systematic way. Even useful trees can be planted and harvested after a regular interval of two to three years.

Other measures of soil conservation are:

(i) Expansion of vegetative cover and protective afforestation,
(ii) Controlled grazing,
(iii) Flood control,
(iv) Prohibition of shifting cultivation,
(v) Proper land utilisation,
(vi) Maintenance of soil fertility,
(vii) Land reforms, reclamation of wasteland,
(viii) Establishment of soil research institute and training of soil scientists, and
(ix) Effective agencies for soil management.

Conservation of Water

Water is an indispensable component of our ecosystem and the essence of our life. On an average, each individual uses 50 litres of water per day in rural areas and 150 litres in urban areas. Apart from drinking purposes, water is used for irrigation as well as in industries. Wherever available about 12,000 m^3 to 14,000 m^3 water is used annually to irrigate 1 hectare of land. The main source of water is rainfall occurring through 'hydrological cycle', while other sources include underground water and water from the melting of snow. The oceans are full of water but because of salinity this water is not usable, so is the case with several inland seas. In fact, usable water is very limited and there are areas in the world where water is a scare commodity. The unfortunate situation is that wherever water is available, users never think about its proper use and they not only misuse it but waste a large quantity of it too. Therefore, conservation of water is a necessity for all the countries of the world so that minimum water requirement can be fulfiled. A few steps in this direction are:

Proper Distribution System of Water

The water distribution system should be such that loss of water should be minimum and it should remain free from pollution. According to local/regional conditions the distribution system should be developed. A few general steps for distribution of water are:

(i) As far as possible water distribution should be done through pipes so that loss will be minimum and water will remain free from pollutants.

(ii) If water storage place is small it should be cemented and if its size is big, the selection of site should be done where non-porous rocks exist.

(iii) The channels and distributors of canals should be cemented, and in fields also either pipes should be used or cemented channels (*nala*) be constructed.

(iv) For irrigation, sprinkle and drip system should be used.
(v) If possible, water tanks should be covered to avoid evaporation and also for cleanliness.

Rational Use of Underground Water

Underground water is also a main source of water specially in arid and semi-arid regions. The overexploitation of underground water often results in the lowering of water table, intrusion of saline water, subsidence of land, etc. The prime need is the proper and limited use of water and also geológical and hydrological survey of the region for assessment of water availability.

Purification of Waste Water

The system of the recycling of water should be used so that waste water can be used for irrigation purposes. There are several mechanical devices for the waste water treatment, some methods are expensive also. But the government agencies and industrial establishments should establish treatment plants. This will also help in control of water pollution.

Control over Deforestation

The loss of vegetation is also a cause of drought and reduction of rainfall and indirectly a cause of lowering of the water table. In order to maintain humidity in the atmosphere which helps in rainfall and to minimise evaporation rate forest cover should be maintained.

Protection of Water from Pollution

Apart from availability of water, quality of water is also important, in other words water should be free from pollution. Nowadays, several techniques such as physico-chemical purification methods – hydrolysis, electrolysis, ion-exchange, absorption, coagulation, chlorination, ozonisation, etc. are in use. Similarly, biological purification method is also in use.

The conservation of water can be done only by water management system. Apart from above mentioned measures, water can be obtained from desalination of sea water and even by artificial rain-making. Apart from conservation of water, mutual cooperation in use of water resources is necessary.

Wildlife Conservation

Like forests, wildlife is also a national resource which not only helps in maintaining the ecological balance but is also beneficial from economic, recreational and aesthetic points of view. There was a time when human interference was minimum, the number of wild animals were quite high and there was no problem of their protection or conservation. But, with the expansion of agriculture, settlement, industrial and other developmental activities and mainly due to greed of man the number of wild animals gradually became lesser and lesser. As a result that several species of animals have been pronounced extinct and several others are at the verge of it. Deforestation is also one of the main reasons for the loss of wildlife. Mass scale killings of wild animals for their meat, bones, fur, teeth, hair, skin, etc. are going on throughout the world. Therefore, the need for wildlife conservation has now become a necessity.

Population growth, the expansion of agriculture and livestock raising, the building of cities and roads, and pollution are among the many pressures on the natural habitat of wildlife. Along with illegal hunting, habitat reduction and its degradation has threatened the biodiversity of the regions where these are rampant. Preservation of wildlife does not mean a blanket protection to all faunal and floral species; rather it implies a proper, judicious control over the multiplication of plants and animals which interact together to provide a proper environment to man whose very existence is in peril today. Due to the irrational use of natural and biotic resources of the earth in the past, most of the wildlife has been destroyed beyond retrieval. It is our urgent duty to protect the natural splendour of ecosystems and to evolve a system of co-existence with every living creature upon the earth.

Although countries of the world are very particular regarding conservation of wildlife, the number of wild animals is reducing day by day. World Wild Life Fund is the international agency doing commendable work in promoting the protection of wildlife. There are national agencies also engaged in conservation of wildlife. Some steps in the direction of wildlife conservation that can be taken are as follows:

(i) To survey and collect all the information about wildlife, especially, their number and growth.
(ii) To protect habitat by protecting forests.
(iii) To delimit the areas of their natural habitat.
(iv) To protect wildlife from pollution and from natural hazards.
(v) To impose complete restriction on hunting and capturing of wildlife.
(vi) To impose restrictions on export and import of wildlife products and severe punishment to be given to those who indulge in this activity.
(vii) To develop game sanctuaries for specific wild animals or for general wildlife.
(viii) To make special arrangements to protect those species whose number is very limited.
(ix) To develop general awareness at national and international level regarding protection of wildlife.
(x) A system of wildlife management be adopted through trained personnel.

India is a good example where several steps have been taken for wildlife conservation. It is a country of varied wildlife, where more than 500 types of wild animals, 2,100 types of birds and about 20,000 types of reptiles and fishes have been found. According to an estimate, in India about 200 species of wild animals and birds have become extinct and another 2,500 are on the verge of extinction. Some of them are black buck, chinkara, wolf, swamp deer, nilgai, Indian gazelle, antelope, tiger, rhinoceros, gir lion, crocodile, flamingo, pelican, bustard, white crane, grey heron, mountain quail, etc. In India, the government and NGOs are taking keen interest in protection of wildlife. The Wild Life Protection Act, 1972, has several provisions for the conservation of wildlife. As many as 165 game sanctuaries and 21 national parks have been developed to protect the natural habitat and wild animals. Apart from this, a Wild Life Conservation Week is also celebrated from 1st to 7th October every year. But still there is a long way to go in this direction.

Conservation of Energy Resources

Almost 90 per cent of the world's current energy supply is based on fossil or mineral sources, oil, coal, gas and uranium. Only 10 per cent comes from renewable sources, especially hydro-power and biomass, while the share of solar and wind energy is below 1 per cent. The following table indicates the pattern of primary consumption in the world:

Table 3.1

Primary energy consumption in the world

Energy source	*World-wide consumption*	*Percentage*
Oil	21678.10^6 barrels	34.2
Coal	4765.10^6 tons	30.2
Gas	1923.10^9 chm	19.1
Nuclear	1670 TWH	5.0
Hydro-power	2050 TWH	6.1
Wood/biomass	1219.10^6 tons	5.3
Wind	3 TWH	1.10^{-2}
Solar	0.1 TWH	1.10^{-3}
Geo-thermal energy	76 TWH	0.1

It is undisputed that this structure of supply involves three problems: if consumption rates do not change, reserves of non-renewable energy will largely run out in one or two generations; the waste products caused by consumption in the water, the earth and in the atmosphere threaten mankind and the environment; and finally the cost of this shortage and the effects on consumption will be too much. The use of energy is increasing day by day and according to an estimate oil and gas will be in shortage after 2050 AD and coal reserves will also fall short after 2200 AD. Even today, there are problems in coal mining. The world supply of natural gas is also limited.

Nuclear power, which amounted to over 5 per cent of global energy production accounts for very limited use and after the Chernobyl accident more technological precautions are needed. At present, there is a need for adopting methods for conservation of energy resources and also to develop and use more and more renewable energy sources.

The conservation methods should be applied for coal, petroleum and natural gas in order to preserve these resources, so that their use may be possible for a longer period and their environmental effects can be minimised. The coal mines have become deeper in most of the countries, therefore, new techniques should be applied. The new methods like gasification may help in deeper mining operations. The coal should be classified and cleared at production centres itself. The use of secondary coal products like coal tar, ammonium sulphate, gas, light oil, benzol, sulphur, etc. should be made. A better transportation and marketing system as well as research in use and mining of coal should be applied.

The conservation of petroleum or mineral oil is the need of the time because the availability of petro-reserves is limited and the use of oil is increasing day by day especially in the field of transportation. The following steps may help in conservation of petroleum:

(i) reduction of the consumption of petroleum,

(ii) development of such engines which consume lesser petroleum,

(iii) intensive survey for new resources,

(iv) exploitation of oil resources from ocean floors,

(v) correct estimation of available resources,

(vi) new techniques for oil drilling and refining should be developed,

(vii) to reduce petroleum consumption in certain areas such as for military purposes,

(viii) to develop alternative source of energy for automobiles, etc.

(ix) international cooperation in reduction of the consumption of petro-products, and

(x) research institutes working in this field should intensify their work.

The energy crisis can be solved to some extent by proper use of renewable sources of energy. The renewable energy sources include solar energy, wind energy, tidal energy, hydro-power, ocean energy and geo-thermal energy. Renewable energies are also called the energies of the future, because in principle they are inexhaustible and neutral in terms of CO_2. The renewable energy sources utilised by man come from three primary sources:

- isotopic disintegration in the earth's interior,
- thermo-nuclear conversion (fusion) in the sun, and
- the movement of planets, combined with mass attraction.

The greatest of the renewable energy sources is the solar energy or solar radiation reaching the earth's atmosphere year after year. Every 29 seconds the solar energy that falls on our planet is equivalent to human energy needs for one day at the 1980 consumption level. In case of solar-thermal utilisation, the solar energy is converted to heat through absorption. This can occur through passive systems, i.e. through constructional measures for collecting, storing and distributing solar energy which renounce thermal installations to a considerable degree or through active system, i.e. collectors or absorbers. The advantages of using solar energy are – limitless supply, no air pollution, no water pollution, no harmful wastes, no possibility of a large-scale explosion or disaster. There is a need to evolve cheaper technology to harvest solar energy. At least for tropical regions it is the greatest source of energy.

There is no need to stress the importance of water energy or hydro-power. Water energy is already in use in developed countries, but in developing countries vast energy potentials exist.

There is enough wind energy available to supply the world's energy needs, and it is technically feasible to build windmills capable of producing electricity. These can be built either as small home-sized units or as large central generators. Besides the conversion of rotation energy into electrical energy, the conversion of rotation energy into mechanical energy also finds application in pumping of water, etc.

Ocean energy refers to a number of different renewable energy sources – tidal energy, wave energy, ocean currents and ocean heat.

Today, the significant attempts at harnessing the energy of the ocean have been related to tidal power. In many coastal regions, the flow of the tide naturally funnels through narrow entrances into bays and estuaries, and strong currents can be used to generate power.

Energy derived from the heat of the earth's crust is called geo-thermal energy. In various places on the globe, hot springs, geysers and underground steam are available, which can be used for power generation.

Bio-energy can be produced by organic compounds through chemical and biological processes. The combustion, gasification and liquification helps in production of gas which can be used as a source of energy. The bio-gas plant has now become a common feature in rural India.

Viewed in the long-term perspective utilisation of renewable energy sources is of major significance, in terms of both the conservation of the reserves of fossil fuels and the reduction of pollutant emissions caused by the conversion of energy from coal, oil and gas. The renewable energy sources have good chances for the future energy supply. How large their contribution will be, depends upon the question of how safe, economical and environmentally friendly each particular 'new' energy is.

Part II

Resources and Their Utilisation

4

Agriculture

Nature and Types

Agriculture is the primary form of economic activity, including within its denotation a wide range, from simple to highly complex, of systems of utilising the soils for the production of foodstuffs or raw materials for human use. Agriculture not only includes cultivation but also stock ranching, dairy, forestry, lumbering and host of other economic activities. Etymologically, the word 'agriculture' is derived from two words, 'ager' means field or soil, and 'culture' means care of or the tilling of. But agriculture is now more than tilling of the field and now it has become a whole science and practice of farming. It implies a conscious and determined effort on the part of man to utilise the soil for his benefit. Agriculture is an example of man's modification of his environment. Agriculture is still the chief occupation of man, in which more than 50 per cent of the labour force is engaged.

Despite of the development of several other economic activities, agriculture still holds the key of economic life in most of the developing countries of the world. Even in developed countries the importance of agriculture cannot be underestimated, because it not only provides food and raw material for many industries but also plays an important role in internal trade. Agricultural sector contributed only 5 per cent of the global Gross Domestic Product (GDP). But its contribution is 14 per cent in developing countries. There are countries in which agricultural sector's contribution to GDP is much higher, for example, it is 67 per cent in Georgia, 58 per cent in Tanzania, 29 per cent in India and 21 per cent in China, etc.

It is still not known when agriculture actually originated. Primitive men must have begun as food gatherers, eating whatever fruits and roots they could obtain. Nature must have been bountiful in those days when human number was so small and wild plants grew everywhere. As time passed and human number grew, fishing and hunting became increasingly important in supplementing what was lacking in the field and an endless search for food.

It was soon realised that some form of food production was necessary if men were to live long and feel secure. Animals were tamed, seeds were sown in ploughed fields. Men were then able to live in settled communities. Without a settled agriculture, a measurable degree of civilisation is not possible. Naturally, as civilisation becomes more and more advanced, the demands upon the productivity of the environment becomes more exacting. In an ever-expanding community, ways and means have to be found to increase agricultural productivity of the land.

Canals were dug to bring more water; better seeds and improved methods of tillage helped to increase the annual harvests. With the spread of agriculture as a global activity, tremendous progress was made in every aspect of crop production. The use of mechanical power in agriculture was a great step towards commercial production of agro-products. Mechanisation created large crop surpluses so that international trade in agricultural crops became possible. Mechanisation process covered various aspects of farming system like irrigation, ploughing, harvesting, use of fertilisers, pesticides, insecticides, conservation and storage of crops, marketing and export of the product. The objectives of the farm mechanisation are:

(i) Less dependence on labour,
(ii) Prompt, speedy and trouble-free operation,
(iii) Enhanced efficiency,
(iv) Enhanced productivity, and
(v) Cost reduction.

With the adoption of modern scientific and technological methods as well as following crop-combination and crop-rotation techniques, now the world agriculture has become a commercial activity in many countries of the world.

Geographical Factors Influencing Agriculture

Growth and development of agriculture is always directed and determined by physical, economic, social and political factors. In fact, geographical factors play a vital role in agricultural development, in spite of the technological and scientific development. The important factors influencing agriculture are as follows:

Natural Factors

The natural factors that affect agriculture most are: (a) climate – mainly temperature and precipitation, (b) soil, and (c) topography. Most of these factors can be modified to some extent by man's effort. For example, man carries water to land where there is little rain, or supplies fertilisers to soil that are deficient in plant food. If necessary, he will adapt his agriculture to conditions that he cannot overcome.

Climate

All forms of agriculture are controlled largely by temperature. Areas deficient in heat are deficient in agriculture. For that is one element of climate that man has not been able to create at economic costs on a large scale. Temperature determines the growth of vegetation through determining the length of the vegetative period. Successful agriculture, therefore, requires a fairly long summer. In higher latitudes, however, the shortness of summer is compensated by the longer duration of the day. The total amount of heat received is enough for ripening of crops. In lower latitudes where the winters are never too cold to arrest the growth of vegetation, practically the whole year is the growing period, and the agricultural operations are timed according to the supply of rainfall.

The moisture requirements of the plant vary according to the heat received. In the higher latitudes, where the summers are not very hot or where the winds are not dry, the amount of moisture given out by plant transpiration is less than in the lower latitudes where the heat received is great and the capacity of the winds to suck up moisture considerable. The plants, therefore, require less moisture in the temperate regions than in the tropical regions. Thus, a certain amount of precipitation may be sufficient for flourishing agriculture in the temperate regions, while the same may not suffice for meager agriculture in the tropical regions.

Soil

A rich soil in plant food is the chief requirement of successful agriculture. It is essential as a support for plants, and as the main medium whereby water and all plant foods, except carbon dioxide, are brought to the roots of the plants where they are absorbed. Soils that are poor, either chemically or in texture, have low productivity, both in amount and variety.

Topography

Topography affects agriculture as it relates to soil erosion, difficulty of tillage and poor transportation facilities. Mechanisation of agriculture depends entirely on the topography of land. On rough, hilly lands, the use of agricultural machinery is impossible. In areas where the pressure on soil is great, even the slopes of mountains are terraced into small farms to provide agricultural land. In China, farm terraces may be seen clinging to hillsides to a height of several thousand feet. It is known that in extreme cases agriculture may succeed in conquering slopes of as much as 45 degrees.

Economic Factors

Market

Relation to market generally determines the character of farming, for the cost of transport to the market will generally affect the competitive power of the agricultural output. Places away from the market will generally grow such things which can afford the cost of transport to the market. Places near large centres of population generally develop market gardening and produce easily perishable goods which can be transported to the market for short distances without much damage.

Transportation Facilities

In commercial type of farming transportation facilities play a significant role. Indeed they determine its genus. In regions far flung from markets and ill-equipped with transportation facilities commercial farming is a remote possibility. The term 'truck farming' bears the unmistakable influence of transportation facilities on agriculture. The economic history of the world records the changes in agriculture patterns as induced by transportation facilities. Improvements in the realm of transportation and communication have rendered possible regional specialisation and thus made feasible fuller utilisation of the peculiar features of the specific soils and climates.

Labour

Labour supply determines the character of agriculture. Intensive agriculture is essentially labour-intensive and exemplifies the human pressure on land.

Agriculture requires skilled labour who can appreciate the subtle relations of seasons and soils with crops and adopt the requisite cultural practices. Again, it is the supply of agricultural labour that determines the timely sowing, harvesting and other cultural practices and ensures good returns.

Capital

The modern mechanised farming has become capital-intensive to a large extent. The occidental farmer has to invest large amount of capital in agriculture because he has to buy agricultural machinery and chemical fertilisers.

Social Factors

Social factors affect farming in a number of ways. The type of farming practised, be it shifting cultivation, subsistence farming, extensive cereal cultivation or mixed farming, etc. is always related to regional social structure. Social factors can also affect the type of crops that are grown. These factors are more effective in tribal cultures. Another way in which social factors can affect agriculture is in the ownership and inheritance of land. In many parts of the world the land of a father is divided between his children. This leads to the breaking up of already small farms into smaller units which are often uneconomic to farm, as in case of India.

Political Factors

Political factors also play a vital role in agricultural development. The political system, i.e. capitalistic, communist or socialistic system determine the pattern of agriculture. For example in China, agriculture is fully controlled by government, similar was the case of former USSR. On the other hand, in USA, Canada and in most of the other countries of the world, agriculture is a private concern. The government policies regarding land, irrigation, marketing and trade, etc. have a direct impact on agriculture. Similarly, subsidies, loan policy, purchase policies, agricultural marketing and international trade and tax policy of the government also have a direct impact on agricultural production and its development.

Types of Agriculture

The classification of the agricultural types of the world is very difficult because of the complexity of farming activities due to varied geographical and economic conditions. Economic geographers have classified the types of agriculture depending on their expansion, availability of water, cropping pattern, volume of production, season variations, regional concentrations, social system, ownership of land, etc. On the basis of these factors following types of world agriculture have been mentioned:

1. *On the basis of the expansion of land*
   (a) Intensive agriculture
   (b) Extensive agriculture
2. *On the basis of availability of water*
   (a) Humid farming
   (b) Irrigated farming
   (c) Dry farming
3. *On the basis of cropping pattern*
   (a) Monoculture: single crop agriculture

   (b) Duoculture: double crop agriculture
   (c) Oligoculture: multiple crop agriculture
4. *On the basis of seasonal variations*
   (a) Winter crop agriculture
   (b) Summer crop agriculture
   (c) Autumn crop agriculture
   or as in India – (a) kharif crops, (b) rabi crops
5. *On the basis of volume of production and their nature*
   (a) Simple subsistance agriculture
   (b) Intensive subsistance agriculture
   (c) Commercial grain farming
   (d) Plantation agriculture
6. *On the basis of social system*
   (a) Capitalistic
   (b) Socialistic
   (c) Feudalistic
7. *On the basis of ownership of land*
   (a) Collective state farming
   (b) Cooperative farming
   (c) Individual farming
8. *On the basis of regional characteristics*
   (a) Monsoon type of agriculture
   (b) Mediterranean agriculture
   (c) Mixed farming of North-West Europe
   (d) Tropical and sub-tropical plantation agriculture

In above mentioned agricultural types, a great deal of overlapping is there. Therefore, it creates complexities in classification. To avoid all such complications, it is better to group the world's agricultural types according to the characteristic features both of organisation and crops, which give each type a uniqueness. The main agricultural types of the world have been depicted in Figure 4.1.

Subsistence Farming

There are two types of subsistence farming:

(a) primitive or simple subsistence farming, and
(b) intensive subsistence farming.

Primitive or Simple Subsistence Farming

Primitive farming is the oldest form of agriculture and still prevalent in some areas of the world. From primitive gathering, some people have taken a step 'upward' on the economic ladder by learning the art of domesticating plants and their economy has moved into primitive cultivation. This type of farming is done on self-sufficient basis and farmers grow food only for themselves and their families. Some small surpluses may be either exchanged by barter or sold for cash. The resultant economy is thus static with little chance for improvement, but there is a high degree of rural independence because farmers are not tied to landlords or to trading centres.

Figure 4.1
Agricultural types of the world

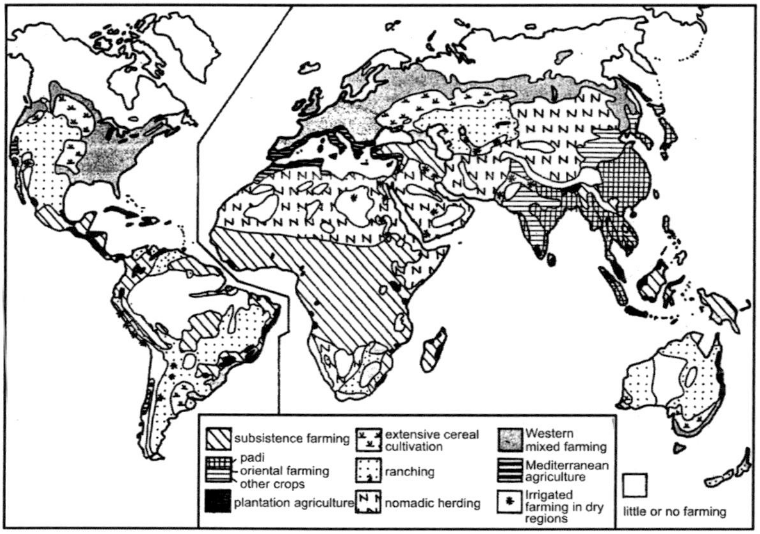

Location

This form of agriculture is widely practised by many tribes of the tropics, especially in Africa, in tropical South and Central America, and in South-East Asia. It is better known as shifting cultivation (Figure 4.2). Shifting cultivation is practised in the tropics by many different peoples and thus has many different names, e.g. *milpa* in Central America and parts of Africa, *conuco* in Venezuela, *roca* in Brazil, *masole* in Zaiire, *ladang* in Malaysia, *humah* in Indonesia, *caingin* in the Phillippines, *taungya* in Burma, *tamrai* in Thailand, *bewar* or *poda* in India and *chena* in Sri Lanka.

Figure 4.2
Areas of primitive subsistence farming

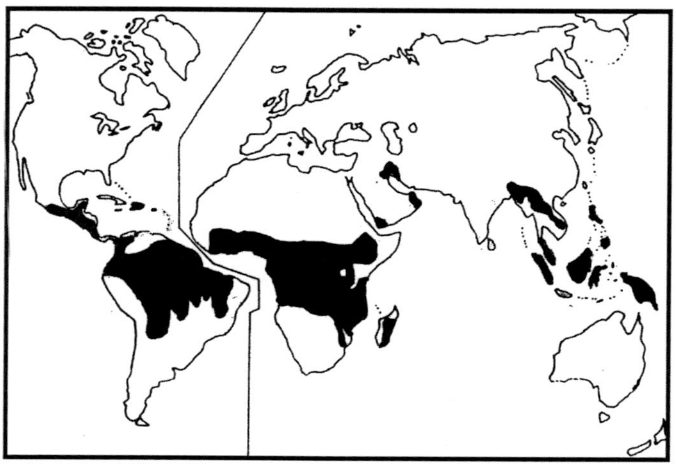

Characteristics

The primitive subsistence agriculture or shifting cultivation is characterised by the following features:

(i) Sites for the ladang are usually selected in the virgin forest by the experienced elders. Hill slopes are preferred because of better drainage. Many ladangs are located in the remote interiors, far from the main population centres. This is partly for historical reasons as most shifting cultivators have been forced into less favourable areas by the expansion of more advanced farmers into the lower and better lands. Their isolation hinders their progress and makes the spread of new ideas more difficult.

(ii) The forests are usually cleared by fire and the ashes add to the fertility of the soil. Trees that are not burnt are hacked out by the men or left to decay naturally. Shifting cultivation is thus also called 'slash-and-burn agriculture'.

(iii) The cultivated patches are usually very small, about 0.5–1 hectare (1–3 acres) scattered in their distribution and separated from one another by dense forests or bush.

(iv) Cultivation is done with very primitive tools such as sticks and hoes, without the aid of machines or even drought animals. Much manual labour is needed in land clearance to produce food for a few people. Thus, despite the fact that little attention is given to the crops when they are once planted, no other form of farming is so wasteful of human energy and so unrewarding as shifting cultivation.

(v) Few crops are raised in the ladangs. The main crops are starchy foods, e.g. tapioca, cassava or manioc, yams, maize or corn, millet, upland rice, beans and bananas. Crops are sown at calculated intervals, often between the other plants, so that the harvest can be staggered to provide food all the year round. Much the same types of crops are grown in all the farms.

(vi) Short periods of crop occupance alternate with long periods of fallowing. When the yields can no longer support the community because of soil exhaustion or the invasion of weeds and shrubs, the fields are abandoned and fresh areas cleared. 'Field rotation' rather than 'crop rotation' is practised.

(vii) This form of 'migratory agriculture' still supports many of the aboriginal tribes of the tropical rain forest, despite the efforts made by the local governments to resettle them. The exhaustion of soil nutrients, deterioration of the lightly constructed bamboo houses, attack by insect-pests, diseases or wild animals are some of the major reasons that make migration a necessity.

A more advanced form of subsistence farming is 'sedentary subsistence agriculture' in tropical lowlands, where the fallowed fields are frequently reused and the community stays permanently in one spot. Crop rotation is also practised in some places and greater attention is given to the land and the crops sown. Methods of tillage are more intensive, though crude hand implements are often still used and there is a greater employment of manpower in the fields. This type of economy is capable of sustaining a relatively larger population on a permanent basis. Many more animals are kept, including buffaloes, swine and horses, and animals are used for drought purposes on the farm as well as to supply milk or meat. Crops are sown in the cool season and grown throughout the rainy period to be harvested in the dry season. Many sedentary farmers in Central America and South-East Asia also find jobs on plantations and return to their homes periodically with their earnings. In South-East Asia and West Africa subsistence farming may be combined with the cultivation of cash crops or with the collection and sale of forest products.

Intensive Subsistence Farming

The term, 'intensive subsistence agriculture' is used to describe a type of agriculture characterised by high output per unit of land and relatively low output per worker. Although the nature of this agriculture has changed and in many areas now it is no more subsistence. But despite changes the term 'intensive subsistence' is still used today to describe those agricultural systems which are clearly more sophisticated than the primitive agriculture. Sometimes it is also known as 'monsoon type of agriculture'.

Location

This form of agriculture is best developed and practically confined to the monsoon lands of Asia. It is found in China, Japan, Korea, India, Pakistan, Sri Lanka, the greater part of continental South-East Asia and parts of insular South-East Asia (Java, Luzon, Visayan Inlands, coastal Sumatra and Malaysia) (Figure 4.3). Farming in both the wet lowlands and the terraced uplands has to be very intensive to support a dense population. Population densities in some agricultural areas in Asia are higher than those of industrial areas in the West. Many of the regions of intensive subsistence farming have a highly developed form of society and government and some such as China and India have a continuous history of civilisation going back more than 4,000 years. The

Figure 4.3
Areas of intensive subsistence farming

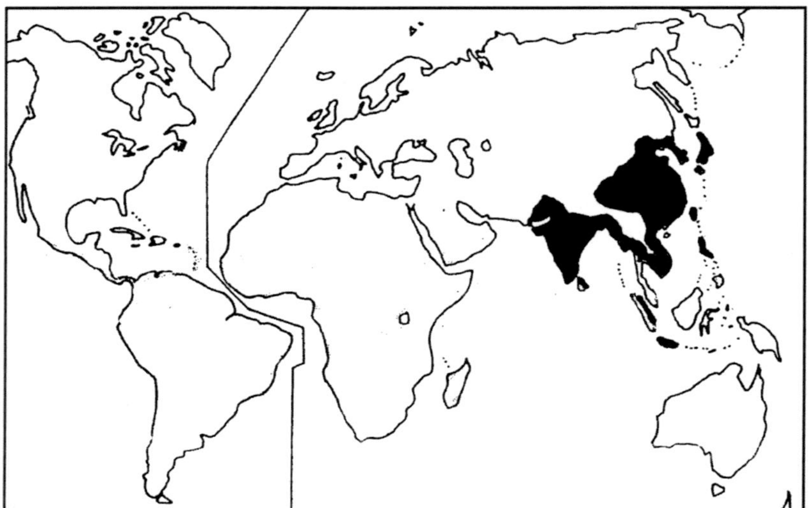

fast-growing population, almost unchecked for centuries, necessitates an ever greater intensity in the tillage of the lands. A small plot of land has to support 5 or 10 times the number of people that a similar plot on an extensive corn farm in the USA could feed.

Characteristics

The main characteristics of the intensive subsistence agriculture are as follows:

(i) *Very small holdings:* Farms have been subdivided through many generations so they have become extremely small and often uneconomic to run. An average farm in Japan is approximately 0.6 hectare (about 1.5 acres) but in India and elsewhere in Asia farms may be even smaller. Individual peasants grow crops mainly to support their own families, though there is some surplus for sale in some areas. In China, however, rapid agricultural changes took place after the agrarian revolution of 1949 when the tiny farms were consolidated, under communist rule, into large collectives.

(ii) *Farming is very intensive:* In Monsoon Asia, the peasants are so 'land hungry' that every bit of tillable land is utilised for agriculture. The fields are separated only by narrow, handmade ridges and footpaths by which the farmers move around their farms. These are kept very narrow to save space. Additional land is made available for cultivation by draining swampy areas, irrigating drier areas and terracing hill slopes to produce flat areas that are suitable for padi cultivation. Only the steepest hills and the most infertile areas, irrigating drier areas and terracing hill slopes to produce flat areas that are suitable for paddy cultivation. Only the steepest hills and the most infertile areas are left uncultivated. Farming is so intensive that double- or treble- cropping is practised, that is, several crops are grown on the same land during the course of a year. Where only one crop of padi can be raised, the fields are normally used in the dry season to raise other food or cash crops such as sugar, tobacco or oil-seeds.

(iii) *Much hand labour is entailed:* Traditionally, much hand labour is required in wet padi cultivation. Ploughing is done with the aid of buffaloes, the fields are raked by hand, the padi is planted painstakingly in precise rows by the women, harvesting is done with sickles and threshing is done by hand. Farm implements are often still very simple. The basic tools are simple ploughs, the *cangkul*, a kind of spade, and hoes. Nowadays machinery has been developed which is capable of working in the flooded fields and separate machines can plough, plant and harvest the padi. Such machines are not yet widely used because most farmers cannot afford to buy them, but they are extensively used in more affluent Japan and are gradually spreading throughout Monsoon Asia. They may be owned by firms or co-operatives and hired by individual farmers. Machinery has also been widely used in the state farms of China.

(iv) *Use of animal and plant manures:* To ensure high yields and continued fertility farmers make use of every available type of manure including farm wastes, rotten vegetables, clippings, fish wastes, guano, animal dung (especially those from the pigsties and poultry yards) and human excreta.

Increasing amounts of artificial fertilisers are now being used in Japan, India and China, usually with government advice or assistance. The basic fertilisers applied include phosphates, nitrates and potash, which help to replenish vital plant nutrients in the soil.

(v) *Dominance of padi and other food crops:* Padi is the most dominating crop produced in intensive subsistence agriculture. But due to differences in relief, climate, soil and other geographical factors, it is not practicable to grow padi in many parts of Monsoon Asia. Though methods are equally intensive and farming is done on a subsistence basis, a very wide range of other crops are raised. In most parts of North China, Manchuria, North Korea, northern Japan and Punjab, wheat, soya beans, barley or kaoliang (a type of millet) are extensively grown as major food crops. In the India Deccan and parts of the Indus basin sorghum or millet is the dominant crop due to the scarcity of rain and the poorer soils. In many parts of continental South-East Asia such as the Dry Zone of Myanmar, the Korat Plateau of Thailand and the interior regions of Indo-China, the annual precipitation is too low for wet padi cultivation, and the substitute crops are millet, maize and groundnuts grown together with cotton, sugarcane and oil-seeds.

During recent decades, this type of agriculture has registered a significant improvement in the form of mechanisation, use of improved seeds and fertilisers and other modern systems of agro-science. The countries like China, India, Japan, Malaysia, Korea, Taiwan, Philippines, etc. have adopted improved system of agriculture.

Plantation Agriculture

The tropical plantation is one of the world's oldest system of commercial agriculture. Since 1500 AD, the products from over a dozen tropical crops have been in constant demand by people in the temperate regions. The specialised commercial cultivation of cash crops on estates or plantations is a very distinctive type of tropical agriculture and is found in many parts of Asia, Africa and tropical and sub-tropical America. Its initiation by the Europeans during the colonial period has made possible the manufacture of a wide range of modern materials. Some of the main plantation crops are rubber, oil palm, cotton and copra, beverages like coffee, tea and cocoa, fruits like pineapples and bananas, as well as sugarcane, hemp and jute.

Plantation agriculture is the product of colonialism. Plantations have been developed in response to a demand in Europe for foods, spices, fibers, and beverages, which because of climatic constraints, could be produced only in the tropics or sub-tropics. Over the centuries the demand for most of these items has increased with the growth of world population and with the insatiable needs of modern western society. Plantation agriculture is an export-oriented specialised farming method where emphasis is given to raise a single crop – specially meant for export to the overseas countries. It is a large enterprise with sound infrastructure, where profit is the sole objective. It involves not only cultivation of crop but also processing, packaging, transporting and exporting of the product.

Location

Plantation agriculture is confined within tropical areas, i.e. both sides of the equator. Plantations exist on every continent possessing a tropical climate. The plantation system, however is considerably older in tropical America than in Asia and Africa. The tropical areas of Latin America, Asia and Africa are the areas where plantation agriculture has been developed. Some of the important plantation farming are coffee plantation in Brazil, Paraguay and Bolivia, Tanzania, Kenya; sugarcane plantation in Cuba, Brazil, Peru, Puerto Rico and Philippines; tea plantation in India, Sri Lanka, Indonesia; cocoa farming in West Indies, Ecuador, Brazil, Nigeria, Ghana; rubber plantation in Malaysia, Indonesia, Thailand, Sri Lanka, Cambodia, Myanmar, India; banana plantation in Mexico, Jamaica, Columbia, Brazil, Panama and Costa Rico (Figure 4.4).

Characteristics

Plantation agriculture is different than other forms of agriculture. The characteristic features of plantation agriculture are as follows:

(i) Plantation agriculture is highly sophisticated and scientific methods are used for large-scale production.

(ii) There is specialisation of single crop in plantation agriculture, e.g. coffee in Brazil, tea in India, rubber in Malaysia, etc.

(iii) *Estate farming:* Plantation crops are usually raised on large estates, of more than 40 hectares (100 acres) each, though the success of such crops has often encouraged other farmers to grow them so that small holdings exist side by side with the large estates. In some parts of West Africa small holdings are, however, more important than estates and small holding rubber production in Malaysia now exceeds that from estates. Seedlings are first

Figure 4.4

Major plantation areas of the world

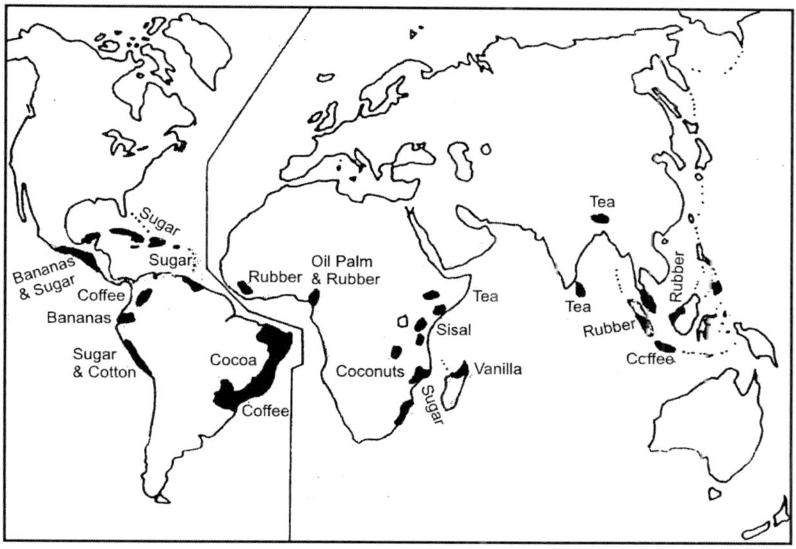

grown in nursery seed-beds and then transplanted in neat rows, well-spaced and regularly weeded, on the estates.

(iv) *Foreign ownership and local labour:* Most of the largest estates are owned by Europeans. For example, most Malaysian rubber estates were originally in the hands of British companies with their head offices in London, and were managed and supervised by Englishmen. Since independence, however, there has been an increase in local ownership. The tapping and processing of the rubber is done entirely by local people or by immigrant labourers from southern India. The British also established large tea gardens in India and Sri Lanka and banana and sugar plantations in the West Indies. The French have established cocoa and coffee plantations in West Africa, e.g. in Cameroun and Ivory Coast, but Ghana and Nigeria have fewer estates. The Dutch once monopolised the sugarcane plantations in Indonesia, especially in Java. Spanish and American capitalists invested heavily in coconut, abaca and sugar plantations in the Philippines. Some coffee fazendas in Brazil are still in the hands of the Portuguese, though most of them belong to wealthy Brazilians, and there is also some Spanish, American and Canadian interest in plantation agriculture in tropical America. Sugar plantations in Queensland, Australia, are unusual as they employ white labour.

(v) *Farming in estates is scientifically managed:* Work in estates is executed with specialised skill, and wherever possible with the application of machinery and fertilisers. It aims at high yields, high quality production and a large output, most of which is exported. The final products, whether sheet rubber, palm oil or tea, have to be carefully processed and standardised to meet world demand and specification.

(vi) *Heavy capital outlay:* To initiate and to maintain a tropical plantation, large sums of money are required. As many plantations are located in previously undeveloped or sparsely populated areas, far from urban centres, a minimum network of communication by road or rail has to be developed first, either with or without government assistance. This is a very expensive undertaking especially under tropical conditions where maintenance costs are also high. Plantations are manned more and more by local staff, however, less administrative expenses are incurred, but the overall production cost is still high, especially where labour is highly unionised as in Indian and Sri Lankan tea estates.

(vii) Plantation agriculture is an export-oriented agriculture. Nearly the entire product of plantation agriculture is generally exported to the international market. Therefore, it requires a better communication network, packaging and processing facilities.

(viii) Unlike other forms of agriculture, plantations are well-planned not only in terms of field structure but also having facilities like residence, transport, hospitals, retail markets, etc. for workers and associated people and their families.

(ix) Plantation agriculture often encourages migration from other countries. In colonial period thousands of people migrated from one place to another for work. In this way, cultural exchange occurs.

(x) Most of the crops grown in plantation agriculture have a life cycle of more than two years. Natural rubber, coconuts, oil palm, tea, cocoa, and coffee are all tree crops and take years to mature, but afterwards they are productive for long periods.

Although plantation agriculture is advantageous and profitable to owners. But there are several problems of plantation agriculture. The major problems or difficulties are as follows:

(i) *Climatic hazards:* The climatic requirements of crops like rubber, cocoa and oil palm, which need constantly high temperatures, high relative humidity and very heavy rainfall, are unfortunately, those least suited to human activities. The heat and high humidity sap human energy and reduce the amount of work people can do. Local winds like the harmattan, hurricanes and typhoons can cause great damage to plantation crops, and in sub-tropical areas excessive rainfall or an extended drought can also reduce output or damage trees. In marginal sub-tropical areas frost is a major hazard. Coffee production in Brazil has frequently suffered from the effects of unexpected frosts.

(ii) *Prevalence of diseases and insect pests:* The tropics with their hot, humid conditions, encourage the growth of insects and bacteria and also the spread of diseases. Consequently plantations may suffer from uncontrollable outbreaks of plant diseases, e.g. coffee blights, or the depredations by insect pests such as the boll-weevil of the cotton plantations. At the same time the labour force is also prone to virus diseases such as fevers which reduce productivity. In some areas malaria has not yet been completely eradicated.

(iii) *Difficulties of clearing and maintenance:* The hot, wet, tropical climates encourage the growth of a wide variety of vegetation. In rain forests, for instance, there is a multiplicity of species; tall trees, palms, undergrowth ferns and various kinds of herbaceous, epiphytic and parasitic plants. A dense vegetative cover is difficult to clear to make way for plantations and a sound communication network. It is even more expensive to prevent forest shrubs and trees encroaching on such clearings. Large sums of money are needed annually for the repair of estate roads and railways.

(iv) *Rapid deterioration of tropical soil:* Under tropical conditions of heavy rainfall, mineral nutrients in the soil are carried downwards with the rain water as it sinks into the ground. This leaching process proceeds very rapidly and magnesium, potassium and calcium are removed. The red lateritic soils that are so familiar in tropical lands are thus, rather infertile. Overexploitation and absence of crop rotation depletes soil fertility and increases soil erosion.

Mediterranean Agriculture

The term 'Mediterranean agriculture' applies to the agriculture done in those regions which are having Mediterranean type of climate. Mediterranean agriculture is unique because it is a mixture of diverse biocultural activities (both animal husbandry and crop farming) that has developed in five major world regions. This type of agriculture is determined by climatic conditions, which exert such an influence that both traditional and commercial agriculture flourish with a dominance of the agriculture of citrus fruits along with horticulture and floriculture.

Location

There are five major regions in the world having Mediterranean type of agriculture. The largest of these nearly encircles the Mediterranean Sea – and it is from there that the type derives its name. The regions having Mediterranean type of agriculture in the world are as follows:

(i) The Mediterranean Basin: France, Spain, Italy, Algeria, Morocco, Turkey, Tunisia, Israel, Northern Nile valley, i.e. all the regions around Mediterranean Sea

(ii) California in USA

(iii) Central Chile

(iv) Southern part of South Africa

(v) Lower Murray – Darling basin of South Australia

Characteristics

(i) The natural setting that lends itself to Mediterranean agriculture is distinguished by erratic rainfall, mild temperatures, irregular topography, and nearness to large water bodies.

(ii) In this type, farming is intensive, highly specialised and varied in the kinds of crops raised. Subsistence agriculture occurs side by side with commercial farming. Many crops such as wheat, barley and vegetables are raised for domestic consumption, while others like citrus fruits, olives, and grapes are mainly for export. The Mediterranean lands are also known as 'orchard lands of the world'.

Figure 4.5

Areas of Mediterranean agriculture in the world

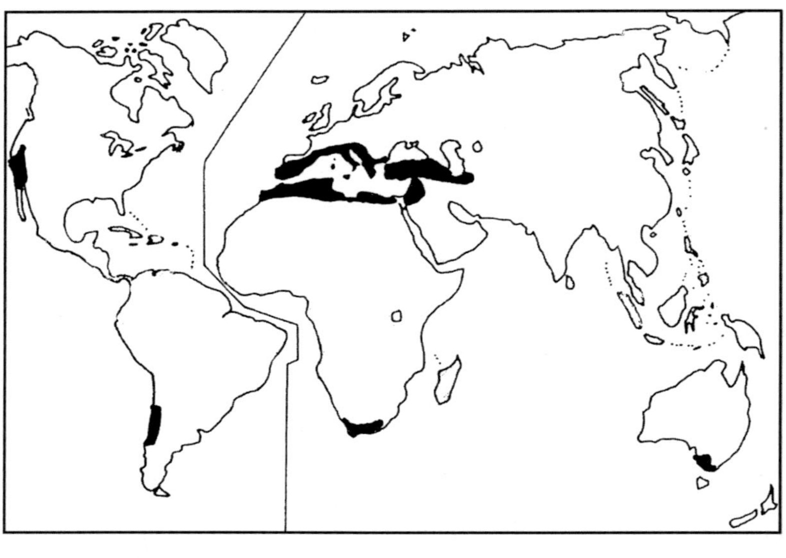

(iii) The land use in these areas is dependent on such factors as the total annual amount of rainfall, length of summer drought, availability of melting snow, local soil conditions, and price fluctuations in local and world market.

(iv) The four main aspects of Mediterranean agriculture are: (a) orchard farming, (b) viticulture, (c) cereal and vegetable cultivation, and (d) limited animal husbandry.

(a) *Orchard farming:* It represents a highly specialised commercial agriculture here. The world supply of citrus fruits, olives and figs comes almost exclusively from Mediterranean lands. Fruit culture has long been a traditional Mediterranean occupation because of the very special climatic features in Mediterranean areas. Citrus fruits (oranges, lemons, grapefruits), olives and figs, which have long, wide-spreading roots, scant foliage and fruits with thick skins are best adapted to the Mediterranean type of climate where annual precipitation can be as low as 380–635 mm (15–25 inches) and where summer droughts may last for more than six months. Fruits are sometimes raised on unirrigated ground and draw their moisture supply from deep in the soil. Irrigation is, however, practised in many areas, especially in California, Israel and parts of France, Spain and Italy. Olives and figs are indigenous to the Mediterranean region and can survive even on thin, calcareous soil with very little precipitation.

(b) *Viticulture:* Viticulture or grape cultivation is a speciality of the Mediterranean region. It represents a very intensive form of farming requiring not only good conditions of moisture, temperature and soil but also much personal care, if the grapes are to be of high quality. Grapes raised in different parts of the Mediterranean lands have distinctive flavours and wines made in the various areas maintain their exclusive names, e.g. sherry from the Andalusia district of southern Spain, port wine from the Doura basin of western Portugal, marsala from the Isle of Sicily, anti from the Chianti Hills of Tuscany, asti from the Piedmont district of northern Italy. In France, where wine-making is a national industry though much of the country does not have a Mediterranean climate, the specialisation is even more distinct. The great variation in relief, climate, soil and methods of preparation has produced many famous wines. The sparkling Champagne comes from the Paris basin; Burgundy from the limestone scarplands of the Côte d'Or; Claret, Brandy (Cognac), Barsac and Bordeaux from different parts of western France, especially the basin of Aquitaine. Wines are also produced in the Mediterranean lands of Australia, South Africa and South America, though these are not as famous.

(c) *Cereal and vegetable cultivation:* In acreage, cereal crops are the most important in Mediterranean agriculture. Wheat, especially hard winter wheat, is the principal food grain, and barley is grown in the poorer areas. In most Mediterranean countries cereals often occupy about half the total cultivated acreage and provide enough grain for home consumption. The warm and sunny Mediterranean climate also allows a wide range of other food crops and green vegetables to be harvested. Beans, lentils, onions, tomatoes, carrots, sugar beet and all the leafy vegetables of the warm temperate latitudes are grown. The seeds are sown in autumn when the showers come and cultivation continues into the following year, maintaining a constant supply to the urban markets.

(d) *Limited animal husbandry:* Mediterranean agriculture is also characterised by limited animal husbandry, which survives on grasslands available here. In areas like Lombardy plain, Ebro basin, San Joaquin valley of California, dairy farming is important. In mountain areas the practice of 'transhumance', moving the cattle up to mountain pastures in the summer and returning them to the valleys in winter, is very common.

Mixed Farming

In mixed farming, a farmer combines the cultivation of crops and the domestication of animals and gets income from both. Mixed farming can, therefore, serve as a transition between the animal-raising economics and the crop-raising ones. This type of mixed farming provides greater security than the growing of a single crop as in the extensive prairie wheat farms may suffer from market fluctuations and crop failures. Mixed farms are moderate in size and usually grow arable crops such as wheat, barley, oats or rye. Many practise crop rotation, growing root crops, like turnips or potatoes, and legumes, like peas, beans or clover, as an alternative to cereals in some years. This maintains the fertility of the soil. Many mixed farms also grow some industrial crops such as sugar beet, hops, tobacco or flax. In addition to the arable crops a herd of cattle or sheep is usually kept. These may be fed on the stubble of cereal crops, helping, with their dung, to enrich the soil or may be fed on fodder crops such as roots or legumes grown in the crop rotation system. Some part of the farm may be kept for beef or milk and sheep for meat. Pigs are also often kept, especially where dairying is practised as they can be fed on skim milk and other leftovers from the farm.

Location

The two most extensive regions of mixed farming are in Eurasia and the United States (Figure 4.6). This activity takes up more land than any other type of bioculture in Europe and is prevalent eastward in an ever narrowing belt that stretches from the Atlantic to the Pacific, with only one interruption in Eastern Siberia. This belt is the thickest between Ukraine and central Finland.

In United States mixed farming is the second most extensive type of agriculture, and covers a large part of eastern half of the country. It extends through Ohio, Indiana, Illinois, Iowa and Nebraska on the north, and Virginia, Tennessee, Georgia, Oklahoma and much of Texas on the south. A small area in Pacific North-West also has mixed farming.

Other regions of mixed farming are: Mexico, South America and Southern Africa.

Characteristics

(i) The mixed farming is done for
   (a) Sustenance of animals,
   (b) For own consumption, and
   (c) For commercial sale.

Figure 4.6
Mixed farming regions of the world

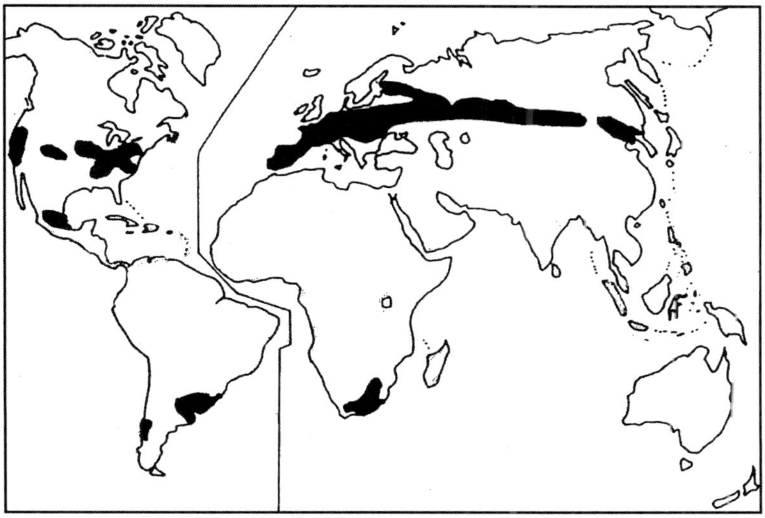

(ii) In mixed farming about 90 per cent land is devoted to agriculture.

(iii) In mixed farming crop rotation is followed in order to maintain soil fertility.

(iv) The sequence of cultivation in mixed farming is cereal and vegetable production for own consumption, followed by hay, alfalfa, clover, etc. for livestock consumption, and finally, some amount of cereal production, wheat, maize, etc. for commercial sale.

(v) This farming is more mechanised. The use of heavy machines like tractors, harrowers, thrashers, etc. is very common.

(vi) There is a large-scale use of both organic and inorganic fertilisers.

(vii) The degree of commercialism varies considerably. In west-central Europe, the northern United States, and Argentina, mixed farming is highly commercialised, while in other areas the commercialisation is limited.

Commercial Grain Farming

Commercial grain farming is an extensive and mechanised form of agriculture. This is a development in the continental lands of the mid-latitudes, which were once roamed by nomadic herdsmen. The continental position, well away from maritime influence, and the low precipitation (between 305 and 660 mm/12 and 26 inches) make crop cultivation a calculated risk. It was the invention of farm machinery which enabled farmers to cultivate grain on a large scale, and there is a marked specialisation in wheat monoculture in many areas. Communication with the outside world is mainly by railways and the bulk of the grain harvest is exported.

Location

The major world regions of commercial grain farming are shown in Figure 4.7. The largest one, in Eurasia, stretches from Kiew in southern Russia to Omsk in western Siberia in a width of about 1,000 km from Caucasus to Saratov on the Volga river.

In north America, there are several areas of commercial grain farming. The largest area runs from Alberta, through Saskatchewan and Manitoba to Dakotas. Another centre is in Kansas and spills over into neighbouring states. Smaller regions appear in eastern Washington and Oregon, eastern Illinois and northern Iowa.

In south America, Argentina has a large region of commercial grain farming. Australia has two areas, one in the south-west and another in the south-east. In fact, commercial grain farming is a mid-latitude activity and mostly done in between 30° to 55° N and S latitudes.

Characteristics

(i) *Specialisation in single crop:* Commercial grain farming is highly specialised and generally one single crop is grown. In most commercial grain regions that crop is wheat. Both winter wheat and spring wheat is grown in these areas.

(ii) *Farms are very large:* The wheat farms in mid-latitudes are very large, ranging from 240 to 16,000 hectares. Though average size of the farm in the USA is about 400 hectares. In these areas land is cheap that makes it possible for a farmer to own very large holdings.

(iii) *Highly mechanised:* The commercial grain farming is highly mechanised. Cultivation from ploughing to harvesting is often entirely mechanised. The use of tractors, ploughs, drills and combine harvests which reap, thresh, winnow and sack the grain all in one operation is common.

(iv) *Low yield per acre but high yield per man:* In this farming wheat grown gives comparatively low yields. The average yield is seldom more than 1,700 kg per hectare, whereas under intensive cultivation the yield is more in many countries. But because of mechanisation, less labour force is required, therefore, yield per man is high.

Figure 4.7
Areas of commercial grain farming

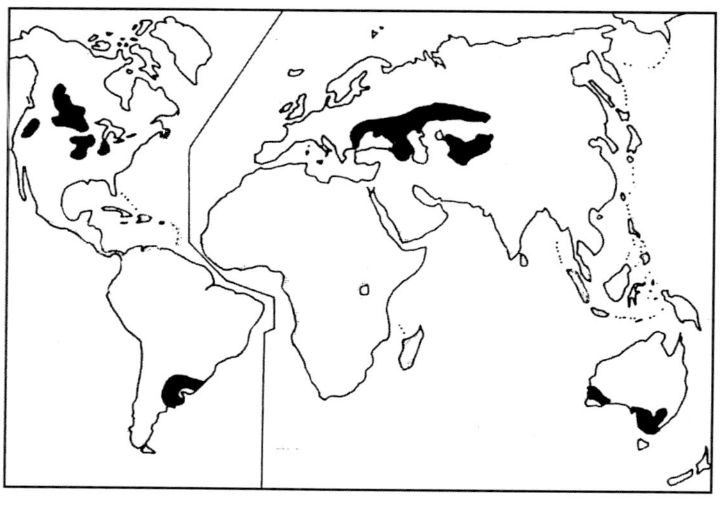

Other features of the commercial grain farming are:

(a) Lack of irrigation
(b) Farm ownership
(c) Prone to climatic hazards
(d) Dependance on market fluctuations, etc.

Irrigation Farming

Irrigation farming is prevalent in areas where rainfall is seasonal and confined to a particular season. In all parts of the world there is a long dry season, when irrigation is practised.

It is, however, the most important in monsoon and the sub-tropical regions. Here rainfall is precarious, or is confined to one season only, and the temperatures are suitable for crop cultivation throughout the year. Also large populations exist here whose mainstay is mostly agriculture, which may produce nothing in drought years.

One of the main advantages of farming under irrigation is that the water supply needed for the growth of crops, which is so uncertain in humid farming, is very largely under the control of the farmer. Growing a crop under irrigation requires more labour and cost than under humid farming. The higher yield of the crops, however, repays this extra labour and cost. In the United States the value of crops on irrigated land is 25 to 65 per cent greater per acre than in the country as a whole.

The sources of irrigation water are: (i) from the rivers which may be snow-fed and yield a continuous supply as in India, (ii) tanks or reservoirs which may be filled during rain, (iii) the underground supply tapped through the artesian wells in especially suited regions as in Australia or South Africa, or through the ordinary dug out wells as in India, and (iv) canal irrigation now has become very popular. This requires construction of dams on rivers. In many countries of the world, dams have been constructed to provide irrigation. Large dams have been built across the mighty rivers like Ganga, Indus, Irrawaddy, Menam, Mekolong, Nile, San-Joaquin, etc., which provide ample water in drier parts of the year for irrigation.

In fact, irrigation farming is not a special farming but it is simply a farming through irrigation facilities. Although, construction of dams and canals is a costly affair but the same has been compensated by high production of cereals and other cash crops. This has been done in India and China. Irrigation enables cultivation throughout the year and the farming system is practised intensively.

Dry Farming

The term 'dry farming' was first used in America to designate farming without irrigation in a section where irrigation was generally practised. The use of the term has been extended and it has come to mean specifically the production of crops without irrigation in regions of deficient rainfall. The factor that distinguishes dry farming from humid farming is the limited water supply. Water being the vital thing for agriculture, its conservation and economic utilisation becomes of primary importance in dry farming agricultural practice.

The essential part of dry farming is deep ploughing (20 to 30 cm), to enable greater and deeper sinking of water. This is done immediately after the harvest, so that any succeeding rain will soak in. The ploughed land also checks the drifting of snow that may fall in winter. The conservation of moisture is attained by the maintenance of a layer of dust or dust-mulch over the surface of the field. This 'mulch' prevents water from getting evaporated. Leaving the land fallow in occasional years and not allowing any weeds to grow is also sometimes necessary. While the land is lying fallow, it is carefully and repeatedly tilled to prevent the growth of weeds which would use up soil moisture. The ratio of fallow years to crop years varies with the amount and distribution of rainfall. Sometimes a crop may be grown only once in three years.

Wheat is perhaps the widest and most generally grown dry farming crop. It is fairly drought-resistant and economic in its use of water; and its early maturity enables it to make the best use of water stored in the soil, before it is seeded. As wheat has both winter and spring varieties, it is well-adapted to a wide range of climatic conditions that may occur in the dry farming lands. The wheat grown under dry farming is of the highest baking quality.

Oats, barley, rye, sorghum and beans are other important crops grown chiefly as fodder crops.

The most important dry farming area of the world is in the United States, where the largest area is located in the Great basin, Columbia river basin and the Snake river basin. Other regions where dry farming is practised to some extent or the other are in Australia, Canada, Western Asia and South Africa.

5

Agricultural Products

Cereals

There are three well-defined agricultural products, these are:

1. *Cereals* include rice, wheat, maize, rye, oats, barley, sorghum, etc.
2. *Beverages* include tea, coffee, cocoa, tobacco, etc.
3. *Fibre crops* include cotton, jute, hemp, sisal, etc.

Apart from these, there are certain *commercial crops*, such as sugarcane, sugar beet, rubber, fruits and vegetables, etc. The present chapter deals with cereals only.

Cereals is a collective term for all kinds of grass-like plants which have starchy edible seeds. The most common cereals include *rice, wheat, maize, barley, rye, oats, millet* and *sorghum*. Since the dawn of history, cereals have formed the basic diet of mankind. Cereals are contributing major energy to human beings from the early days, even from pre-historic period. The world's earliest civilisations such as China, India and Egypt were all founded on fertile alluvial basins where cereals could be easily grown. In the early part of human history food grains, as cereals, supplied food for men and fodder for livestock. In the past, when the pressure of population was not so great, every country had to be self-sufficient in their production of cereals. But afterwards the situation changed and now some countries produce large surpluses of cereals, while others have its deficit. This situation has given rise to the international trade in cereals. The production of cereals like any other crop is determined by geographical factors, therefore, it is essential to discuss these factors along with their spatial distribution and production.

RICE

Rice (*Oriza sativa*) has been cultivated since time immemorial. The origin of rice is not traceable, but it is believed that rice must have originated somewhere in China or India. Chinese literary works mentioned rice as long ago as 3000 BC. It has been the staple food of China for a long time and is consumed in many ways. Ancient Hindu scriptures also mentioned rice in connection with religious offerings as well as the peasants daily food. From China and India, rice cultivation spread to neighbouring Asian countries. Now rice is a special crop of the monsoon region, where alone it finds almost ideal conditions for growth.

Geographical Conditions for Cultivation

Temperature

Rice is a tropical crop and grown where the average temperature during the growing season is between 20°C and 27°C. Abundant sunshine is essential during its four months of growth. The minimum temperature should not go below 15°C as germination cannot take place below that temperature.

Rainfall

Paddy requires more water than any other crop. As a result, paddy cultivation is done only in those areas where minimum rainfall is 115 cm. Although the regions having average annual rainfall between 175–300 cm are the most suitable. Paddy also needs flooded conditions with the depth of water varying over 25 mm at the time of transplanting to as much as 150 mm for 10 weeks of the growing period.

Soils

Paddy is grown in wide range of soil, from the podzolic alluvium of China to the impermeable heavy clay of central Thailand. Fertile riverine alluvial soil is best for rice cultivation. Clayey loam soil in monsoon land is considered to be the best for rice cultivation as water retention capacity of this soil is very high. Rice is also grown in saline areas of deltic region. Rice cultivation needs high fertiliser application.

Surface

Unlike other crops, paddy needs a level surface to enable the fields to be flooded at least during the growing period. Its ideal habitat is therefore in the great alluvial deltas and river basins of the world: the Ganges, Siking, Yangtzekiang, Irrawaddy, Menam Chao Phraya and Mekong, where there is practically no gradient.

Fertilisers

Paddy requires three essential plant nutrients: nitrogen, phosphorus and potassium. Most paddy lands have a moderate quantity of such nutrients, but if they are deficient, organic manure or artificial fertilisers have to be used.

Labour

Paddy cultivation is extremely labour-intensive, therefore, requires more labour in comparison to other cereal crops. Labour is necessary for: preparing the field, weeding, sowing, transplanting, manuring, harvesting, threshing, winnowing and milling. For rice cultivation large number of cheap labour is required.

Methods of Cultivation and Varieties of Rice

Paddy is a growing plant or the yellowish unhusked grain from which rice (whitish husked grain) is obtained. Different varieties are grown in different parts of the world, and the methods of cultivation also vary. Farming methods also differ between the different oriental countries. But, in general, paddy cultivation is quite distinctive and observes following steps:

Preparation of Field

Paddy farmers used to get their fields ready before the rainy season. The weeds are cleared and the field is ploughed by buffaloes or tractors to a depth of few inches. Manures and fertilisers are added to the soil. The whole surface then remained covered with water of about 2.5 cm. The field is then ready for receiving seedlings from the nursery.

Transplantation

Generally paddy seedlings are first prepared in nursery and then transplanting is done in the field after about 40 days. Although in some areas of India and Sri Lanka seeds have been sown directly in the field and the seedlings sprout when the rain comes. But yield of paddy from transplanting is greater than the direct sowing. The transplanted paddy also grows faster because of regular spacing and matures within a shorter period.

Field Maintenance

Paddy fields also require regular maintenance, such as occasional weeding and thinning out the more crowded patches, level of water is to be maintained according to the growth and the fields are drained dry before the crop is harvested.

Harvesting

The traditional harvesting system is either through a curved knife or a sharp-edged knife. It is very labour-intensive. Harvesting is done in the dry season, when the weather is sunny. Mechanical combines which cut and thresh are used in Japan.

Threshing, Winnowing and Milling

After the paddy stalks have been gathered and dried for a brief spell, their threshing is usually done. By beating the sheaves against the bars, the grains are separated from the stalks. Now threshing machines have also been developed.

Winnowing is a process of removing the unwanted particles from the paddy grains. The simplest way is by pouring the paddy down from a height on a windy day to a large square mat on open ground. The grains fall to the mat while lighter chaff blows out. Sometimes hand-winnowing machines are also used.

Milling means removal of the yellowish husks from paddy so that white or polished rice is obtained. In a rice mill the paddy is made to pass between varying sets of huller or rollers till it is milled or polished.

Although, there are several varieties of rice, but on the basis of their location two varieties have been identified. These are: (i) *upland rice,* which is grown on upland areas; and (ii) *lowland rice*, which grows in low lying and marshy areas. Another classification is based on origin and geographical concentration, and accordingly, there are two types:

(i) *Japonica:* found in temperate climate and requires more fertiliser. Mostly found in Japan, Korea, Philippines, etc.

(ii) *Indian:* grown in warmer regions like India, Bangladesh, Indonesia, Thailand, etc.

World Distribution of Rice-Producing Areas

The tropical region of Asia or Monsoon Asia is the largest rice-producing area. The countries of this region together produce 90 per cent of the global output of rice. Major rice-producing countries are China, India, Indonesia, Thailand, Bangladesh, Myanmar, Vietnam, Laos, Cambodia, Korea, Japan and Philippines. Besides these South-East Asian countries, rice is also produced in Brazil, USA, France, Venezuela, Columbia, Egypt, Spain, etc. The world distribution of rice-producing areas has been depicted in Figure 5.1.

China

The greatest rice-producing country in the world is China. The average annual production of rice in China is 130 million metric tons, which is about 36 per cent of the world production. In 2015-16 the China's rice production was 145.77 million metric tons, while in 2016-17 it was little less i.e. 144.88 million metric tons. In China rice culture has been developed in early phase of civilisation, therefore, it is a traditional rice-producing country. With the introduction of several HYV rice seeds, China now has increased its production several times and is in a position to provide food to its large population. The major rice-producing regions of China are as follows:

(i) *Szechuan Region:* It is the largest rice-producing region in China. Favourable geographical conditions, cheap labour, fertile riverine alluvial soil and traditional skills enable this region to produce huge amount of high quality of rice.

(ii) Lower Yaugtze Basin

(iii) South-West Region of China

(iv) Kwantung Region

(v) Szechun-Hunan Region

Figure 5.1

Rice-producing areas of the world

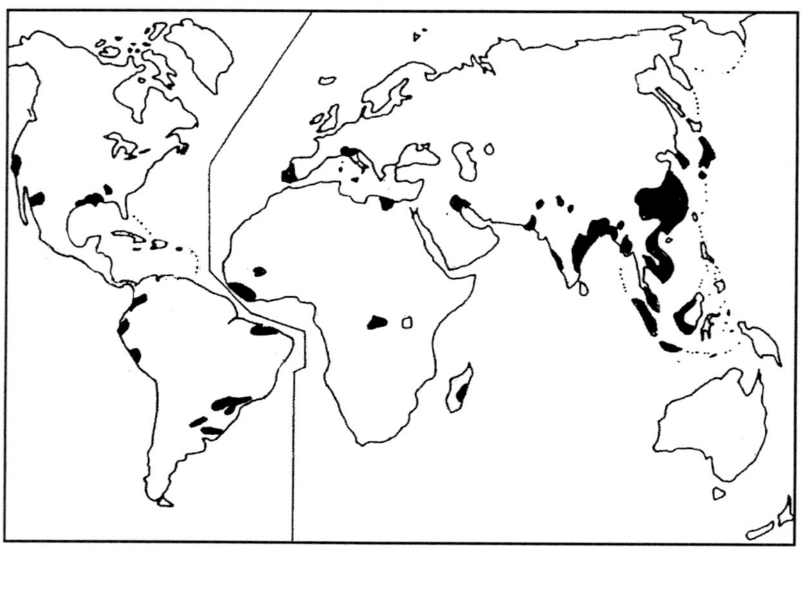

India

India is the second largest rice-producing country in the world. Its average annual production is 95 million metric tons, which is about 20 per cent of the world total. Although, in 2016-17 the production of rice in India was 108.06 million metric tons. Rice is the staple food and cultivated in most of the states of India. Among the regions Ganga-Brahmaputra valley contributes the largest amount of rice followed by coastal regions. The major rice-producing states in India are West Bengal, Bihar, Tamil Nadu, Andhra Pradesh, Uttar Pradesh, Madhya Pradesh, Karnataka, Assam and Odisha. With the help of irrigation, improved seeds, use of fertilisers, multiple cropping, the production of rice is increasing but its average yield is still low in comparison to other important rice-producing countries.

Indonesia

It is the third largest rice-producing country in the world. The average annual rice production of Indonesia is 37 million metric tons. In Indonesia rice is produced in many islands but the main rice-producing areas lie in Java, Sumatra and Borneo.

Bangladesh

The total rice average of nearly 10 million hectares and the annual cutput of nearly 30 million metric tons makes Bangladesh a major world rice producer. The bulk of the rice fields are unirrigated in the Ganges delta region, where annual rainfall is more than 250 cm and soil is heavy and wet all the time.

Japan

Japan is the country which has not only developed rice cultivation under adverse topographical conditions but is also a leading producer of rice. It ranks 10th in world rice production. In Japan rice dominates the low alluvial filled valleys and coastal plains. Kwanto plain is the main rice-producing region of Japan. The Japanese have introduced high-yielding 'Japonica' paddy hybrids which increase output tremendously. The average yield of rice in Japan is as high as 6,166 kg/hectare. Some of the fast maturing species that the Japanese agronomists have devised can be harvested within 95 days. Double cropping of rice is also practised in the southern regions of Japan.

Apart from above mentioned countries, South-East Asian countries are also leading producers of rice. In fact, all the countries of South-East Asia produce rice. But, the main countries are Vietnam, Thailand, Myanmar and Philippines. These countries rank 5th, 6th, 7th and 8th in world rice production. Thailand and Myanmar, are considered the 'rice bowl of Asia'. Other countries of South-East Asia which produce rice are Cambodia, Laos and Malaysia.

Pakistan also produces rice and ranks 12th in world's rice-producing countries. Rice is also produced in South Korea. In Taiwan, paddy is grown on the wetter west coast.

Outside Monsoon Asia, relatively little rice is grown. In *Egypt*, rice is grown both in the Nile delta and valley. It was originally cultivated by the basin irrigation system, in which annual flood water of the Nile river is used. Today, apart from basin irrigation, rice is grown in canal irrigated region of the Aswan dam.

Brazil is the important rice-growing country in the southern continents. Paddy is grown mainly in South-East Brazil where the heavy precipitation, the swampy coastal lowlands and the abundant sunlight all make the area ideal for wet paddy cultivation.

In *USA* also rice is produced, mainly in regions from the coast lands of the Gulf of Mexico. The leading rice state is Louisiana, followed by California, Texas and South Carolina.

In *Europe*, paddy farming is done in the North Italian plain, the Ebro basin of Spain, the Rhone delta of France and scattered areas of the Balkans.

Production

Two aspects of production are important, first – per hectare production, i.e. yield per hectare, and second – total production of the country or world as a whole.

The average yield per hectare in the world in 2016-17 is 4.51 metric tons but it varies from country to country. The highest yield of 8.18 metric tons has been registered in Egypt, followed by 8.11 metric tons in USA, 6.81 metric tons in Japan and 6.86 metric tons in China. In India, production of rice per hectare is 3.77 metric tons only. It is lowest in Burma and Nigeria with 2.77 and 1.71 metric tons per hectare respectively. This variation is mainly due to use of improved seeds, fertilisers as well as due to geo-economic conditions.

The country-wise production of rice is given in Table 5.1.

Table 5.1

Annual production of rice

Country	*Production (in million metric tons)*	
	2015–16	*2016–17*
China	145.77	144.85
India	104.41	108.06
Indonesia	36.21	37.15
Bangladesh	34.50	34.58
Vietnam	27.58	27.86
Thailand	15.80	18.60
Myanmar	12.16	12.40
Philippines	11.00	11.50
Brazil	7.21	8.16
Japan	7.67	7.78
USA	6.13	7.12
Pakistan	6.80	6.80
Korea Republic	4.33	4.20
Egypt	4.00	4.80
Cambodia	4.85	4.95

Cont'd...

...Cont'd

Nigeria	2.71	2.70
Madagascan	2.38	2.44
Iran	1.78	1.73
Peru	2.17	2.20
Laos	1.93	1.95
Korea Democratic	1.30	1.60
Malaysia	1.80	1.82
European Union	2.05	2.07
Others	21.18	22.22
World Total	471.87	483.10

Source: US Department of Agriculture, Foreign Agricultural Service, World Agricultural Production, June 2017.

It becomes clear from the above table that the total production of rice in the world during 2015–16 was 471.87 million metric tons and in 2016–17 it was 483.10 million metric tons. China is the largest producer of rice in the world with production 144.85 million metric tons in 2016–17, followed by India with 108.06 million metric tons. Bangladesh, Vietnam, Thailand, Myanmar and Philippines are the countries which produce more than 10 million metric tons of rice annually.

WHEAT

Wheat is the most important food crop. Its precise origin is lost in antiquity, and traces of its ancient cultivation have been found in many parts of the world. It is probably originated in Asia Minor and the Middle East, gradually spreading across the Mediterranean to the European countries. It is essentially a crop of temperate lands, but it is also grown in many other climatic regions, such as the warm temperate, western margin Mediterranean regions, the sub-tropical eastern margin regions, the tropical monsoon areas, the savanna lands, etc. Renner and others (1957: 231–32) have rightly remarked, "The culture of wheat, however, is so widespread in the world that it is easier to state where it is not grown rather than where it is grown. Its range of growth is so wide that somewhere in the world wheat is being seeded every month in the year, and likewise it is being harvested somewhere every month in the year."

Geographical Conditions for Cultivation

Temperature

The temperature required for wheat during growing season is around 15.5°C. The weather should be warm and moist during the early stage of growth and sunny and dry in the later stages. The average temperature of the hottest month should not exceed 20°C. A frost-free period of 100 days is usually required but some fast-ripening varieties may mature only in 90 days.

Rainfall

The amount of rainfall required for wheat cultivation varies between 30 cm and 100 cm. The major wheat lands of the temperate regions have an annual rainfall of 38 cm to 80 cm. The spring wheat region of Canadian Prairies only receives around 46 cm of rainfall, but it comes in the early summers when the wheat is growing. Wheat is also grown in areas having lesser amount of rainfall, i.e. 25 cm. This has been done by adopting dry farming method. Also where irrigation facilities are available, wheat is cultivated in dry lands also.

Soils

The soil suitable for wheat is either light clay or heavy loam. The world's best wheat comes from the *chernozem* soils in the 'Black Earth' region of the Ukrainian Steppes, the dark brown soil of North America and also the grey brown podzolic soils of the deciduous forest region.

Topography

Wheat is grown in plain as well as in rolling topography, which provides adequate drainage and at the same time facilities of the use of machinery. The world's largest commercial wheat lands are the undulating temperate grasslands of Steppes, Prairies, Pampas and the Australian Downs.

Economic Factors

The economic factors that favours wheat cultivation are:

(i) *Technology:* In wheat cultivation maximum use of technology is possible. The commercial wheat farming is technology-intensive cultivation which requires tractors, harvesters, threshers, elevators, etc.

(ii) *Transport:* Wheat farming is also linked up with export. Therefore, a good transport network is essential for its successful cultivation.

(iii) *Capital:* It is a capital-intensive farming, therefore, sufficient capital is required.

(iv) *Market:* Both internal and external markets are essential for the profitable wheat cultivation.

Types of Wheat

On the basis of the *season of sowing* wheat is of two types: *winter wheat* and *spring wheat*.

Winter wheat is usually grown in regions of the middle latitudes where winters are mild and cool but without severe frost. About 80 per cent of the world's wheat is winter wheat.

Spring wheat is grown in the colder north of the Canadian Prairies, where winter temperature may drop to 16°C to below freezing point and seeds can only be sown after the severe winter is over.

Commercially, wheat is divided into *hard* and *soft*. Both winter and spring wheat may be either hard or soft. The hard wheat has a low moisture content and best suited for bread making. While soft wheat, with its higher moisture content is more suited for making cakes, biscuits and pastries.

Wheat varieties may be grouped into five broad categories, according to hardness, softness and time of sowing. These are:

(i) Hard Red Spring Wheat

(ii) Hard Red Winter Wheat

(iii) Soft Red Winter Wheat

(iv) Soft White Wheat

(v) Durum Wheat

Production and Distribution

The following table indicates production of wheat in various countries:

Table 5.2

Production of wheat (in million metric tons)

Country	*Production year*	
	2015–16	*2016–17*
China	130.19	128.85
India	86.53	87.00
USA	56.12	62.86
Russia	61.04	72.53
Pakistan	25.10	25.60
Canada	27.59	31.70
Argentina	11.30	17.00
Kazakhstan	13.75	14.99
Turkey	19.50	17.25
Iran	15.00	15.50
Ukraine	27.27	26.80
Australia	24.17	35.00
Egypt	8.10	8.10
Uzbekistan	7.20	7.20
Brazil	5.54	6.73
Iraq	4.41	4.23
Syria	3.50	2.40
Ethopia	3.50	3.90
Afghanistan	5.00	5.10
Belarus	2.90	2.60
Uruguay	1.19	0.78
Morocco	8.06	2.73
Algeria	2.70	2.00
Nepal	1.74	1.72
European Union	160.48	145.47
Others	21.35	22.19
World	736.98	754.10

Source: US Department of Agriculture, Foreign Agricultural Service, World Agricultural Production, June 2017.

It becomes clear from the above table that the total wheat production in the world in 2016–17 was 754.10 million metric tons. China produces highest quantity of wheat in the world, i.e. 128.85 million metric tons, followed by India with 87 million metric tons. USA and Russia are at third and fourth position in wheat production in the world. The other leading countries in wheat production are France, Pakistan, Germany, Canada, Argentina, Kazakhstan, Turkey, Iran, Ukraine, Australia and Britain. All these countries used to produce more than 10 million metric tons of wheat annually.

The average yield of wheat in the world is 3.39 tons per hectare. Egypt has recorded highest yield i.e. 6.43 tons per hectare. While wheat yield in Mexico is

Figure 5.2
Wheat-producing areas of the world

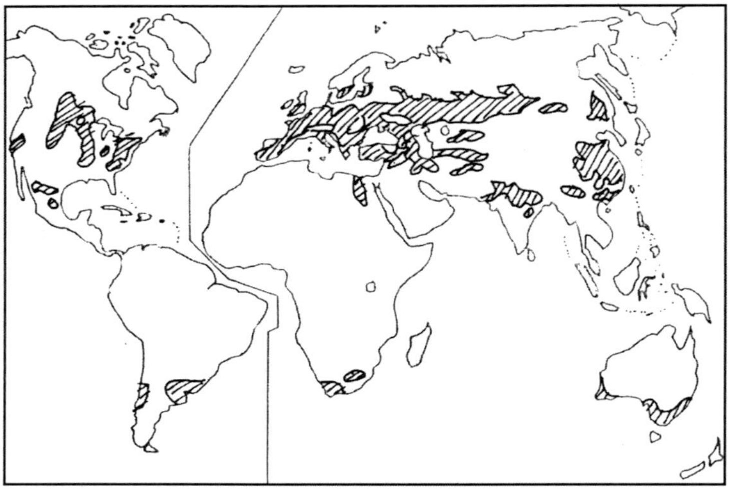

5.39 tons, European Union–5.35, Uzbekistan–5.14, Ukraine–4.16, USA–3.54, India–2.88 tons per hectare etc.

Wheat-producing areas of the world are distributed in all the continents, as shown in Figure 5.2.

China

China is the largest producer of wheat in the world and its average annual production is 110 million metric tons. Production of wheat in China has registered a spectacular increase in recent years. The productivity of wheat is 4.69 metric tons per hectare. In China intensive-mechanised wheat farming is done. Wheat is produced chiefly in the north of the country in the Huang He (Hwang Ho) basin and in Manchuria. But now wheat is also grown in other areas. The major wheat-producing areas of China are:

(a) *North-East China* includes Beijing and Manchurian plain.

(b) *South-East China* includes Human and Yangtze fertile plain. In this region spring wheat cultivation is done.

(c) *North China Plain and Kaoliang Region* are famous for winter wheat. The Hwang Ho valley is considered as the best wheat-producing region.

India

India is the second largest producer of wheat in the world. In 2016–17, it produced 87 million metric tons of wheat. India has registered a massive increase in wheat production after ‘Green Revolution’. Once an importer of wheat, now it not only fulfils the needs of its own large population but also has a surplus stock. The climate of northern plain of India with its mild, rainy winter and hot, dry summer is highly favourable for wheat production. The major wheat-producing states are: Punjab, Uttar Pradesh, Haryana, Madhya Pradesh, Bihar, Rajasthan, Maharashtra and Gujarat.

In India both spring and winter wheat is grown. Winter wheat is more popular in northern India, while spring wheat is cultivated in western India. Now wheat cultivation has become more mechanised and also commercial in nature. The yield of wheat in India is 2.79 tons per hectare, which is lower in comparison to other leading wheat-producing countries.

USA

In the world, USA is the third largest producer of wheat and produces 62.86 million metric tons of wheat in 2016–17. About 25 million hectare of land in USA is devoted to wheat cultivation. The cultivation of wheat in USA is highly mechanised, capital-intensive and commercial. The leading wheat-producing states are Kansas, North Dakota, Nebraska and Montana, although in many other states wheat is grown. The four major wheat-growing regions of USA are as follows:

The Hard Red Spring Wheat Region

This is a continuation of the Canadian Prairies and is leading commercial wheat region of America. It includes the states of North and South Dakota, Montana and Minnesota. In this region wheat is sown in early spring rain and grows through the warm summer and is harvested by autumn.

The Hard Red Winter Wheat Region

South of Minnesota and South Dakota is another great wheat region that grows hard red winter wheat. The states included in this region are Nebraska, Kansas, Missouri, Oklahoma, and Northern Texas. The wheat is sown in winter and harvested in early summer.

The Soft Red Winter Wheat Region

It includes such states as Illinois, Indiana, Ohio, Pennsylvania and most of the mid-Atlantic states. Increased moisture and higher relative humidity gives the winter-sown wheat a softer texture.

The Soft White Wheat Region

The soft white wheat is grown in two areas of USA, first, around lakes Michigan and Huron and second, the west coast including California and the Columbia plateau region. This wheat is sown in spring or winter depending on the local climate and relief.

Russia/Ukraine/Kazakhstan

Russia alone ranks fourth in world wheat production, which produces more than 50 million metric tons of wheat. Ukraine once the part of USSR is now an independent state and ranks 13th in wheat production. The black soil region of Russia and Ukraine is best for wheat cultivation. Both spring and winter wheat are grown. Since the Communist Revolution (1917) planned efforts were made to achieve self-sufficiency in wheat production. Large-scale mechanisation, extension of agriculture in the virgin land, state-sponsored community farming enabled the country to spectacularly increase wheat production. Large areas of the Steppes stretching from the Dnieper into Asiatic Russia have been brought under wheat cultivation. Besides Russia and Ukraine, Kazakhstan region (now independent) is another major wheat-producing country.

European Union

Almost all the countries of European Union grow wheat, but France, Germany and UK are the three leading countries. Other wheat-producing countries of Europe are Poland, Italy, Spain, Denmark and Hungary. Europe fulfils all requirements of wheat cultivation: a temperate maritime or continental climate with an annual precipitation of between 40 to 75 cm. Europe contributes nearly one-fourth of wheat production of the world. The productivity of wheat is also higher, for example, in UK, Germany and Denmark the per hectare yield of wheat is more than 7 metric tons which is highest in the world. Despite high productivity, due to high density of population, local consumption is also high, therefore, wheat surplus is not available, even some countries import wheat. The combined production of wheat in European Union in 2016–17 was 145.47 million metric tons.

Canada

Canada is not only a leading wheat producer of the world but also a leading exporter. The average annual production of wheat in Canada is 25 million metric tons and ranks 8th in world producers. Since Canada is having small population, most of the wheat is exported to other countries specially to Britain and other West European countries. In Canada 95 per cent wheat is grown in Saskatchewan, Alberta and Manitoba province. Other wheat-producing provinces are Ontario and British Columbia. The Canadian Prairies is one of the leading granaries of the world. This is because of the following factors: (i) extensive cheap land was available, (ii) good network of railways, (iii) fertile prairie soils, (iv) undulating topography, (v) suitable climate, and (vi) access to world market.

Argentina

In South America, the leading wheat producer is Argentina, which ranks 9th in the world wheat producer countries. Its average annual production of wheat is 10 million metric tons. In 2016–17 Argentina produced 17 million metric tons of wheat. Its greatest concentration is in the '*wheat crescent*' of the Pampas from Rosario to Bahia Blanca, where the cool temperate oceanic climate with mild winter and warm summer is almost ideal for wheat-growing. The rolling treeless Pampas facilitates the extensive use of machines. The dense network of railways allows the harvested grain to reach the coastal ports of Buenos Aires and Bahia Blanca for export.

Australia

Australia is the 14th wheat-producing country of the world. In 2016–17 Australia produced 35 million metric tons. Murray-Darling basin and South-Western Australia Region are the main wheat-producing regions, because these areas are having suitable climatic conditions for wheat production.

Pakistan

Pakistan is also a leading wheat-producing country in the world and ranks 6th in wheat production. Its wheat production in 2016–17 was 25.60 million metric tons. The Indus Plain is the main wheat-producing region of Pakistan. The geographical conditions of the Indus Plain are suitable for wheat production.

Apart from above mentioned important countries, wheat is also produced in many other countries of the world. The other important wheat-producing countries are Iran, Turkey, Egypt, Uzbekistan, Syria, Afghanistan, Romania, Morocco, Bulgaria, New Zealand, South Africa, Uruguay, Central Chile and Southern Brazil.

MAIZE

Maize is the third important cereal crop of the world after rice and wheat. Maize is often known as Indian corn or simply corn and is a widely cultivated cereal. It originated in America and has long been cultivated by the American Indians. It was grown by the people of ancient civilisations of the Incas and Aztecs and is still the staple food of many Latin American people. Afterwards it was introduced in Europe, Africa and Asia and is now grown in wide range of climatic conditions in many countries.

Types and Uses

There are seven types of maize, each one has distinctive characteristics and uses. These are:

1. *Dent corn:* This is a soft maize, widely cultivated and has great commercial value.
2. *Flint corn:* This is a hard corn that ripens rapidly.
3. *Sweet corn:* This corn contains both starch and sugar and thus tastes sweet.
4. *Pop corn:* The grain of this corn is very hard and small in size. This is a popular type of corn for human consumption.
5. *Flour corn:* Its starch is soft and shrinks when the corn ripens.
6. *Waxy corn:* This corn comprises of a soft, wax-like substance resembling tapioca starch.
7. *Pod corn:* This type of corn is not grown on a commercial basis. Unlike other maize, each grain of the pod corn is enclosed in a separate pod or husk.

Maize has a wide variety of uses. Its three main uses are: (i) animal feed, (ii) human food, and (iii) industrial products. The main use of corn is the animal feed and nearly 75 to 90 per cent corn is used for feeding animals. In USA 40 per cent corn is used to feed hogs or pigs, 25 per cent to feed cattle, 15 per cent for poultry and 10 per cent for horses and sheep. Another use of corn is as human food. In many parts of the world especially in Latin America, Africa, Southern Europe and some Asian countries, maize is consumed as food grain. The third use of maize is in making industrial products. Maize is used for making industrial alcohol. Maize is also used for making vegetable oil and starch is also obtained from it. On the other hand maize stalks are used in making rayon, plastics, paper and wall-boards.

Geographical Requirements for Cultivation

Maize is grown under divergent physical conditions. Maize is one of the most widely cultivated crop and grown in both tropical and warm temperate latitudes. The general requirement for maize cultivation are as follows:

1. *Temperature:* Maize is grown in temperatures between 18°C and 27°C during the day and around 14°C during the night. But the most important factor is the 140 frost-free days. The crop is very susceptible to frost, therefore, its cultivation in temperate latitudes is limited.
2. *Rainfall:* Maize is grown mostly in regions having annual rainfall between 60 cm to 110 cm. But it is also grown in areas having rainfall of about 40 cm.
3. *Soils:* Maize grows in a wide range of soils, ranging from temperate podzols to the leached red soils of the tropics. But, the best suitable soil for maize is deep, rich soils of the sub-tropics, where there is abundant nitrogen.
4. *Topography:* The plain regions are most suitable for maize cultivation, because this helps in use of machines. Although, maize is also cultivated on undulating lands as well as on lower slopes of the hills. Maize is also grown as a major crop of shifting cultivation.
5. *Economic Conditions:* Unlike other crops maize can be cultivated with small capital. Use of machines have reduced the labour requirements. Most of the maize grown is utilised within the country, although its limited international trade is also there.

Production and Distribution

The total production of maize in the world is as follows:

Year	*Maize production (in million metric tons)*
2007–08	791.63
2008–09	787.83
2009–10	785.14
2015–16	968.29
2016–17	1,067.21

The major maize producers in the world with their production data are shown in Table 5.3.

Table 5.3

Major maize-producing countries of the world

Country	*Year/Production (in million metric tons)*	
	2015–16	*2016–17*
USA	345.51	384.78
China	224.63	219.55
Brazil	67.00	97.00
Mexico	25.97	27.00
Argentina	29.00	40.00
India	22.33	26.00
Ukraine	23.33	28.00
South Africa	8.21	16.40
Canada	13.56	13.20
Russia	13.17	15.31
Indonesia	10.50	10.90
European Union	58.73	60.71

Figure 5.3
Maize-producing areas of the world

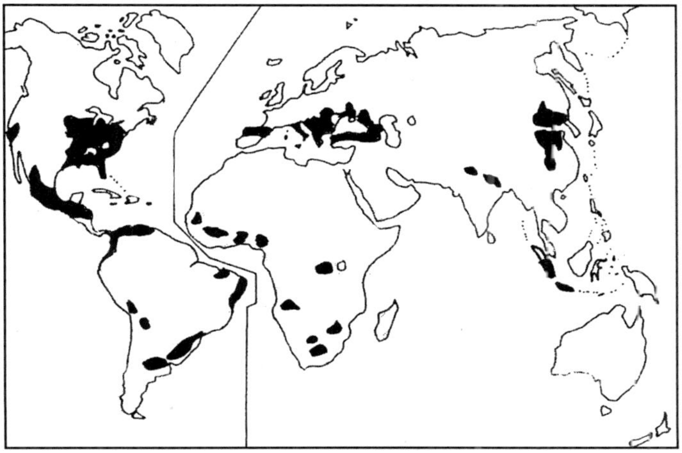

Apart from above mentioned major maize-producing countries, the other important countries are: Ukraine, Philippines, Nigeria, Egypt, Vietnam, Serbia, Hungary, Russia, Romania, Thailand, Ethiopia, Turkey, Poland, Zimbabwe, etc. USA, China and Brazil are the leading maize-producing countries in the world.

USA

USA is the largest producer of maize in the world. Its average annual maize production is 310 million metric tons. USA produces about 43 per cent of the global total maize production. Nearly 30 million hectare of land is devoted in USA to corn production. The Corn Belt of USA is a distinctive agricultural region, where the dominant crop is corn. The Corn Belt includes the states of Ohio, Indiana, Illinois, Iowa and Minnesota. The climatic conditions in this area are ideal for maize-growing. The higher summer temperatures of over 23°C and the rainy summer are ideal. The rolling topography and rich prairie soil are also the advantages. USA is also the largest exporter of corn.

China

China is the second largest maize-producing country. In 2016–17, it produced 219.55 million metric tons of maize, which is about 20 per cent of the world production. Corn is produced almost in all parts of China. The major producing areas are Hopei, Yuman and Kirin.

Brazil

Brazil is the third largest corn-producing country in the world. Its average annual production of maize is 55 million metric tons.

Argentina

Argentina is one of the important corn-producing countries of South America and ranks 5th in the world. Its average annual production of maize is 20 million metric tons. Most of the corn is grown in the Pampa region.

India

India ranks 6th in the global maize production. Its average annual production is 18 million metric tons. In 2016–17, the production of maize in India was 26 millon metrictons. Maize is widely grown in UP, Bihar, Chhattisgarh, Madhya Pradesh, Rajasthan, Gujarat, Maharashtra, Andhra Pradesh, etc.

The other leading countries in maize production are Mexico, France, South Africa, Canada, Italy, Indonesia, Ukraine, Philippines, Nigeria, Egypt, Vietnam, Serbia, Hungary, Russia, Turkey, etc. The distribution of maize in the world is shown in Figure 5.3.

BARLEY

Barley is the cereal that is believed to be one of the most ancient. It was cultivated by the Chinese, the Egyptians and Mediterranean peoples in early times. Barley is now very extensively cultivated. Barley is unique among the food crops for its short growing season. It has been estimated that, barley matures in about 90 to 100 days and, thus, is very popular as a food crop in the regions where physical constraints, either in the form of low temperature or short supply of moisture, restricts the cultivation of other crops.

The geographical conditions for barley cultivation are almost the same as for wheat, but barley is more tolerant of dry conditions and will ripen at lower temperatures. It is thus grown in a wide range of climatic, topographical and soil conditions, where wheat or other cereals fail to survive. The cultivation of barley is done in the following areas:

1. *Sub-Arctic Regions:* Barley can be grown in high latitudes, even beyond the Arctic circle. It is grown in Finland up to 70° North latitude where growing season is very short.
2. *Semi-Arid Regions:* Barley is grown in desert areas having semi-arid climatic conditions. Barley crop is having tolerance for arid conditions.
3. *High Altitudes:* Barley can be grown in upland regions also because it can ripen in cool temperatures.
4. *Steep Hill Slopes:* In mountainous areas of Japan, Norway and Switzerland barley is grown on steep hill slopes.
5. *Light, Limey Soils:* The most suitable soil for barley cultivation is the light, sandy or dry soil. But it is also grown on dry chalk and limestone regions in Europe.

Barley is used as human food, to feed animals and also used in malting. Barley is still used for bread-making, specially in those poor areas where wheat cannot be grown. Large quantities of barley is used nowadays to feed livestock. It is often cut green and is fed to cattle, pigs and poultry. The most important use of barley is for making beer and whisky.

Production and Distribution

In year 2016–17, the total world production of Barley was 147 million metric tons. The major producers of barley and their production figures have been given in Table 5.4.

Table 5.4

Major barley-producing countries and their production

Country	*Year/Production (in million metric tons)*	
	2015–16	*2016–17*
European Union	62.10	60.00
Russia	17.08	17.55
Spain	11.60	11.60
Canada	8.23	8.80
Germany	10.39	11.97
France	9.47	12.24
Australia	8.59	13.00
Turkey	7.40	4.75
Ukraine	8.75	9.90
Britain	5.08	5.14
USA	4.75	4.34
Argentina	4.04	3.30
Denmark	3.13	3.36

It becomes clear from the table that Russia is the largest producer of barley in the world and accounts for nearly 32 per cent of the world barley output.

Spain is the second largest barley producer in the world. Its production in 2016–17 was 11.60 million metric tons. Canada produces 8.80 million metric tons. The combined production of European Union in 2016–17 was 60 millon metric tons. The leading barley producing countries of EU are Germany, Spain, France, Great Britain, Poland and Denmark. Turkey, Ukraine, Australia, Britain and USA are also important producers of barley in the world.

The world distribution of barley is shown in Figure 5.4.

Figure 5.4

Barley-producing areas of the world

Barley is produced almost in all the continents. Apart from the countries mentioned above, the other barley-producing countries are Iran, China, Kazakhstan, Finland, Czech Republic, Belarus, Argentina, Sweden, Ethiopia, India, Italy, Iraq, Hungary, Mexico, Algeria, Austria, Morocco, etc. On the continental basis Europe is the greatest producer accounting for about half of the world's barley production.

6

Commercial Agricultural Products

The production of agricultural products for trade and commerce has started with the new innovations in the field of agriculture as well as under the colonial patronage. The commercial agriculture has been developed during last century. In first phase those tropical crops have been developed which were not grown in temperate regions and its objective was to fulfil the needs of colonial people. But, this trend has been changed with the decolonisation and independence of countries. Many developed and developing countries have realised that agriculture can provide a boost to the economy through export of agricultural products. Therefore, commercial agriculture has been started with the prime objective of export and production of cash crops. Plantation agriculture was first to develop. It is an export-oriented specialised farming, where emphasis is given to raise a single crop, specially meant for export to the overseas countries. Afterwards other crops have also been produced for commercial purpose. The agricultural products include *beverage* like tea, coffee, cocoa, tobacco; *fibre crops* such as cotton, jute, hemp, sisal, etc. and other *industrial crops* like rubber, sugarcane, sugar beet, fruits, etc. Cereals like wheat, maize, barley and oilseeds are also grown for commercial purpose.

In this chapter, a detailed analysis of the following important commercial agricultural products has been done: *tea, coffee, cocoa, rubber, cotton, jute, sugarcane, sugar beet* and *tobacco.*

TEA

Tea is the most important of the beverage crops of the world. A much larger proportion of the world population drinks tea than coffee or cocoa. Tea is grown exclusively in the tropical and sub-tropical regions, but consumed in all parts of the world. Tea is made from the leaves of a tropical shrub, of the *camellia* family. Tea cultivation is believed to have originated in Yangtze valley of China as early as the 6th century AD. It has always been valued for its flavour and stimulant qualities and was even used for medical purposes. Tea was introduced in Britain and rest of Europe in mid-17th century. Because of its popularity as a common drink large-scale commercial cultivation in plantation has started in India, Bangladesh, Sri Lanka and the former British colonies of East Africa.

Cultivation

Tea is a tropical shrub and is cultivated mostly as a plantation crop. In its natural state, the tree may grow to a height of 9 to 12 metres, but it is regularly pruned to form a bush of 1.2 to 1.5 metres high. Tea is cultivated in a wide range of physical and climatic conditions. Tea cultivation is different from other crops. The land, preferably on hill slopes, is first cleared. Tea seedlings or cuttings are raised in a nursery and when the plants reach a height of 20 cm, they are transplanted into the field. They are usually planted in straight rows 1.5 metres apart. Weeding, manuring and pruning are done at regular intervals. The first picking is done at the end of the second year.

Tea picking and *tea processing* require special skill. Tea picking is a very skilful job and is usually done by women. Two tender leaves and a bud are usually plucked from each stem and in a year generally three pickings are done. After picking, tea processing is also important, because it determined the quality of the finished tea. The three types of tea are the result mainly based on its processing. These are: (a) black tea, (b) green tea, and (c) brick tea.

Black tea is prepared in India, Bangladesh, Sri Lanka and Indonesia. The leaves after plucking are dried, crushed and fermented for sometime so as to reduce tannin content of tea by 50 per cent. Then, the fermented tea is fried and sieved into various grades.

Green tea is prepared in China, Japan and Taiwan. The green tea is not allowed to ferment. The leaves are dried, crushed and then rolled.

Brick tea is prepared from inferior leaves, broken twigs and dust tea. All these are mixed up and rolled into humps after mixing with rice paste.

Conditions of Growth

Climate

Climatically, tea belongs to the monsoon lands where high temperatures, long growing season and heavy rainfall help the growth of tea plants. A temperature of 21°C during the growing season of not less than eight months is ideal. Warm summers and frequent rains promote rapid leaf reproduction and increase the number of annual pickings. During the cool season, e.g. in China and Japan, the tea bushes lie dormant and there is no picking but where growth is not restricted by a distinct season, as in Sri Lanka, picking can be carried out all the year round. In India and Bangladesh, the highest yields are obtained from June to September when the weather is hot and rainy, but the best quality tea is derived from the earlier and later pickings when the climate is cooler and drier.

Relief

Almost all the commercially-managed tea plantations are located in the highlands and on hill slopes where the natural drainage is good. Tea cannot tolerate stagnant water and waterlogged lowlands are thus least suited to tea cultivation. Almost all the black tea that enters international trade comes from highland districts. Different grades of tea are obtained at varying altitudes, e.g. the low grade 'Low Crown Tea' from tea grown below 610 metres; the intermediate grade 'Medium Crown Tea' from altitudes of 610–1,200 metres, while the best quality 'High Crown Tea' comes from estates located at 1,220 metres and above. Mountain slopes have been adopted for tea gardens all over the tea regions of the monsoon lands. Undulating and well-watered tracts, where the water escapes freely without serious soil erosion, offer best conditions for tea cultivation.

Soils

Tea is grown in variety of soils. The best, however, is a light, friable loam with porous sub-soil which permits a free percolation of water, for tea is highly intolerant to stagnant water. In general the most suitable soils are slightly acidic and without calcium. The presence of iron in sub-soil is desirable. On the sloping land which is most suitable for tea, soil erosion is often a problem. This is combated by planting tea bushes in lines along the contours.

Shade

Tea shrubs grow better when shielded from strong sunlight or violent winds. It is therefore usual in plantations to plant some large trees in between the shrubs to give shade not only to tea plants but also to the pickers.

Labour

Tea cultivation and processing are labour-intensive tasks. The work of field preparation, weeding, manuring, pruning and picking goes on all the year round on tea estates. Female labour is preferred for tea picking because it is a tedious job, requiring both skill and patience. Picking is done entirely by hand, and pickers are paid by piece rate, i.e. by the amount of tea picked during the day. Workers are also required in the tea processing plants where the leaves are dried, rolled, fermented, sifted, graded and packed.

Capital

Tea cultivation is a capital-intensive farming. Tea cultivation requires large finances for the development of plantations, payment to labourers, for processing, etc. In early phase of development of tea gardens, foreign capital has been used. In other words all the tea gardens in Monsoon Asia were owned by colonial financers. But now these gardens are either owned by multinational companies, individuals or by semi-government organisations.

Production and Distribution

The world production of tea in 2013 was 5,063.9 thousand metric tons, which was raised to 4,364.7 thousand metric tons in 2010. The information about the leading producers of tea and their production quantity is given in Table 6.1.

Table 6.1

Major tea producting countries

Country	*Tea production (in thousand metric tons)*	
	2010	*2013*
China	1475.1	1924.5
India	970.3	1200.4

Cont'd...

...Cont'd

Kenya	403.3	436.3
Sri Lanka	331.4	363.1
Turkey	235.0	227.0
Vietnam	192.0	185.0
Indonesia	156.6	152.7
Japan	83.0	84.7
Bangladesh	60.0	66.2
Argentina	90.7	78.9
Malawi	51.6	46.5
Uganda	31.6	58.3

Source: FAOIGG Secretraiat.

The world distribution of tea-growing areas is shown in Figure 6.1.

Figure 6.1

Tea-growing areas of the world

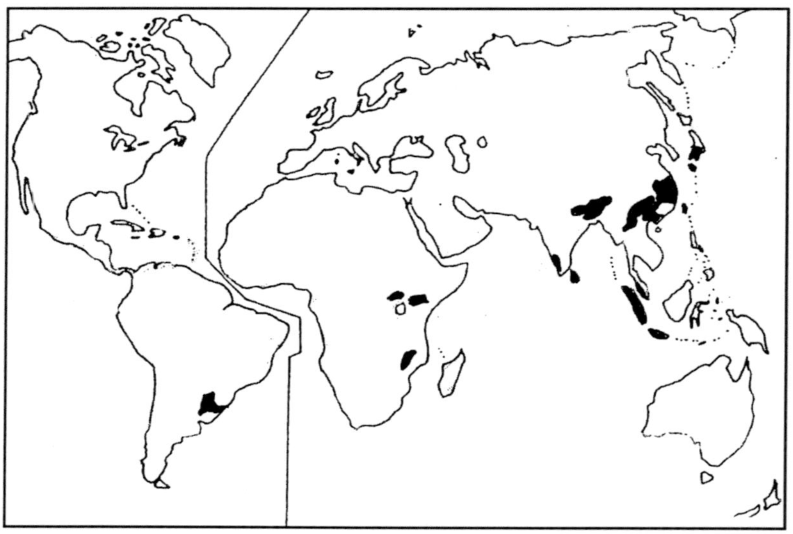

China

China is the largest producer of tea in the world. Its production in 2013 was 1924.5 thousand metric tons, which is 34 per cent of the world tea prodution.

Tea cultivation is a 2,000-year-old practice in China. But, unlike India and Sri Lanka, it is less commercial in nature due to small scale and scattered nature of the enterprise. Individual farms are very small and isolated from one another. Unlike other South-East Asian countries, here plantations were not organised by colonial rulers.

Most of the tea estates in China are located in the south-eastern part of the country. The major tea-producing states are Hupeh, Hunan, Sichuan, Fujian, Kiangai, etc. In further north, due to harsh winter, cultivation is restricted.

China is the largest producer of 'green tea'. Apart from green tea, China also produces jasmine tea, wulong tea and brick tea.

India

India is the second largest producer of tea in the world. In 2013, India produced 1200.4 thousand metric tons tea, which was 23.69 per cent of the world's total tea production. The tea-growing areas of India are as follows:

The Darjeeling Hills

Some of the best quality tea in the world is produced in the Darjeeling tea gardens. The well-drained hilly slopes (above 500 metres) produces best variety of tea. Here, tea estates are situated between Mechi-Balasan and Mahananda rivers. Despite high quality, Darjeeling tea production suffers from unpredictability of production. It contributes roughly 15 to 20 per cent of the national output.

The Brahmaputra Valley

It is the largest tea-producing region in India. Plantations are widespread in the districts of Kamrup, Darrang, Goalpara, Sibsagar, Lakhimpur, etc. Socio-political tension, ageing problem of estates and other problems have disrupted tea production here in the late 1990s.

The Dooars

The foothills of eastern Himalayas – comprising large areas of Cooch Bihar and Jalpaiguri districts – have been devoted to tea production. Here, some of the notable tea estates are Madarihat, Nagrakata, Kalchini, etc.

The Surma Valley

Surma valley in Assam is a significant producer of tea, having more than 100 tea estates.

Tea Estates in South-West India

South-West Indian region – comprising areas of Karnataka, Tamil Nadu and Kerala – are spread over vast tracts of Palni, Kardamom and Annamalai hills. Here – compared to North Indian gardens – tea estates are smaller, discontinuous and yielding low production.

Generally speaking, the best tea comes from the Darjeeling area but the greatest yields come from Assam. Here the estates are huge, covering thousands of hectares. Each estate is an almost self-contained community with staff quarters, labour lines, schools, factory sites, shops and temples. The factories are equipped with up-to-date machinery for processing and grading the tea. Most of the exports go by rail to Calcutta for shipment to London, Rotterdam, Marseilles or New York. Production in the Nilgiri Hills of southern India is less important but of high quality.

Kenya

The African country Kenya ranks third in the tea-producing countries of the world. Its annual production in 2013 was 436.3 thousand metric tons, i.e. 8.6 per cent of the world production. The plateau region of Kenya having tropical climate is the principal tea-producing area. The tea is exported form the port Mombasa.

Sri Lanka

Sri Lanka is the fourth largest tea-producing nation in the world. In 2013, the country produced 343 thousand metric tons of tea, contributing 6.77 per cent of the global total.

Turkey

Turkey is the fifth largest producer of the tea in the world. In 2013, the tea production of Turkey was 227 thousand metric tons, which was 4.48 per cent of the world tea production respectively.

Vietnam

Vietnam is another important tea-producing country, which ranks 6th in the world and produced 185 thousand metric tons of tea in 2013.

Indonesia

Indonesia is the seventh largest tea-producing country in the world. In 2013, the country produced 152.7 thousand metric tons of tea, i.e. 3.02 per cent of the global total. The area under tea cultivation is 0.09 million hectares of land.

Most of the tea estates are located in the islands of Sumatra and Java. The mountain slopes of volcanic Gadak and Salak provides excellent favourable conditions for tea cultivation. Indonesia is a tea-exporting country.

Japan

Japan mostly produces green tea. Tea is inseparable with the tradition and culture of Japan. The country roughly produces 1.67 per cent of global production. The slopes of mountains with volcanic soil are very suitable for tea cultivation. Uji and Shizouka Hida districts in S. Honshu and Kyushu island are famous for tea cultivation. Despite huge internal demand, Japan is able to export some of its tea production.

Bangladesh

Bangladesh accounts for 1.3 per cent of the world's tea production. Most of the tea estates are located in Surma valley and Chittagong hills.

Apart from the above, the other tea-producing countries of the world are Iran, Argentina, Malawi, Uganda, Zimbabwe, Tanzania, Cameroon, Brazil, Equador, Bolivia and Malaysia.

COFFEE

Coffee is a popular drink all over the world. The coffee tree is a native of the highlands of southern Ethiopia and the name coffee is derived from that of the highland district of *Kaffa* where it was found. From Ethiopia, it was taken across the Red Sea to Saudi Arabia. The practice of coffee drinking was first started in Middle East and was subsequently introduced in Europe, where it became very popular. In 18th century Dutch recommended the commercial cultivation in East Indies. From here its cultivation spread to many parts of the tropics.

The status of coffee-producing areas has changed from time to time. Arabian Peninsula, the home of *Mocha coffee,* at first had a monopoly in its production. It was then introduced in Jamaica and other West Indian islands, and the *Blue Mountain coffee* became world renowned. Dutch then introduced coffee plantation in Indonesia, brought about the emergence of *Java coffee*, which is highly flavoured. In Sri Lanka also coffee cultivation was started and finally Brazil then rose to prominence and has become the leading producer of coffee in the world.

Cultivation and Types

The coffee tree may grow up to a height of 9 metres, but its height is kept low up to 1.5 to 2.5 metres in commercial cultivation. The coffee is obtained from seeds of berries which are dark red in colour when ripe. Each berry contains two seeds or beans which are dried, roasted and ground into coffee powder.

Coffee cultivation is a technical work. First of all coffee is propagated from seeds or cuttings in a nursery and, after about six months, it is transplanted to the field. Plants are positioned 3 metres apart which grow rapidly. Its harvesting generally began in the third year after planting, but actual profitable production used to start after fifth year. An average tree yields about 1.4 to 2.3 kg of coffee berries in a year. Coffee picking is done by hand.

After picking, the coffee berries go through a number of processes. These are removal of outer cover, fermentation then dried beans are winnowed and graded, afterwards beans are roasted and then ground into coffee powder which is used to make beverage.

There are three types of coffee according to their nature and geographical distribution:

(a) *Coffee Robusta:* Mostly grows on lowlands of African plateaus. It contributes 15–20 per cent of global output.

(b) *Coffee Arabica:* According to volume of production and popularity, it is the most important and contributes 70–80 per cent of global output. It grows in the slopes of the highlands.

(c) *Coffee Liberica:* Inferior grade coffee, contributes only 5–10 per cent of global output and grows in Africa.

Growth Conditions for Cultivation

Climate

Coffee is a tropical plant which is also grown in semi-tropical climate. The coffee tree requires heat, humidity and abundant rainfall. The following temperature and rainfall conditions are necessary for coffee cultivation.

(a) *Temperature:* Coffee requires an average temperature between 20°–27°C. Although it grows in day temperature over 32°C in the Arabian Peninsula. Growth is most rapid during hot rainy season and during cool dry season berries ripen and ready for picking. Bright sunshine and warm weather are necessary for the harvesting.

(b) *Rainfall:* Coffee needs abundant rainfall, i.e. 100 to 200 cm annually. The hill slopes which receive oragraphic rainfall are thus best for coffee cultivation.

Shade

Direct sunlight is harmful for coffee plants, therefore, these are planted under shade of taller trees such as bananas. In Brazil, leguminous plants are used, which not only provide shade but also enrich soil with nitrogen.

Topography

Generally, coffee is grown on slopes having height between 600 to 1,800 metres. The suitability of slopes for coffee is because these are well-drained and also cooler. Water stagnation is very harmful for coffee plants, therefore, hill slopes are best suitable for it.

Soils

Soil is the guiding factor in coffee plantation. The ideal soil is one with a good sub-surface drainage, and one that is easily workable. The presence of humus and other nitrogenous matter in the soil is an advantage. Well-drained volcanic soils like the terra-roxa of Brazil which contain much potash as well as organic material are the best.

Economic Conditions

(a) *Labour:* Coffee cultivation required a large number of labour force because coffee is to be hand-picked, as no machine has so far been developed to do this job. Apart from this, there is much work to be done on plantation all around the year such as field preparation, transplanting, cultivating, pruning, weeding and of course harvesting.

(b) *Capital:* Plantation of coffee is a capital-intensive activity. This is more due to the fact that during first three to four years returns from coffee plantation are nil and expenditure is more. Therefore huge capital is required for coffee cultivation.

(c) *Transport:* For a successful coffee plantation a good network of both internal and external transport is necessary. The internal rail and road transport helps in collection of coffee from producing areas, while distribution is done either by sea and air routs or sometimes by land routes.

(d) *Markets:* Coffee is having international market. It is necessary to maintain international market because nowadays there is much competition in the market. Similarly market fluctuations also have a direct impact on the production and price of coffee.

Production and Distribution

Coffee is mainly produced in tropical countries of the world. The following table indicates the major coffee-producing countries and their production:

Table 6.2

Top ten coffee-producing countries of the world, 2016

Country	*Production (in thousand US tons)*
Brazil	2859
Vietnam	1818
Columbia	829
Indonesia	814
Ethiopia	423
India	385
Honduras	380
Uganda	314
Mexico	257
Guatemala	224

The Total world production of coffee in 2016 was 7,743,000 metric tons. The distribution of coffee-growing areas has been shown in Figure 6.2.

Figure 6.2 shows that there are four major areas of coffee production in the world. These are:

(a) *South America:* Comprising countries like Brazil, Venezuela, Columbia, Ecuador and Peru. This region contributes more than 70 per cent of global production.

(b) *South-East Asia:* Comprising countries like Indonesia, India, etc.

(c) *Africa:* Comprising countries like Kenya, Uganda, Congo, etc.

(d) *Caribbean Region:* Comprising countries like Mexico, Guatemala, etc.

A brief description of the important coffee-producing countries is given below.

Figure 6.2

Coffee-growing areas of the world

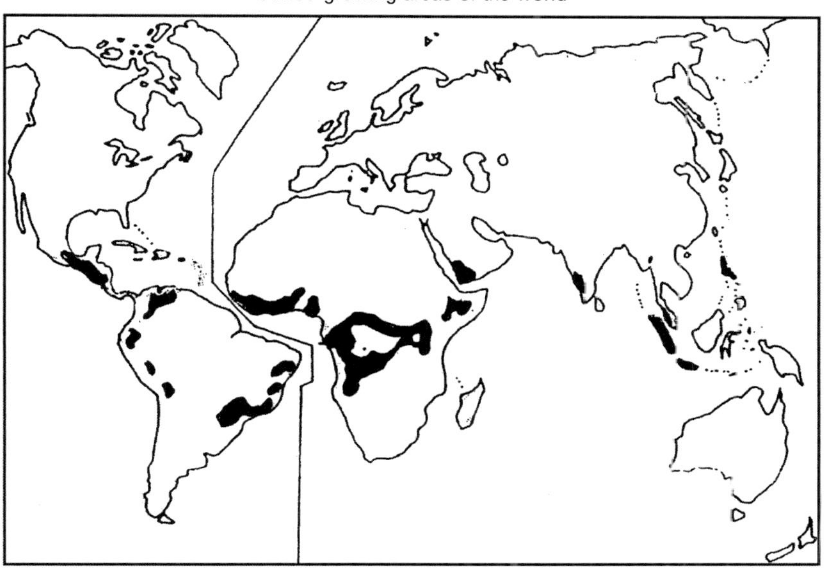

Brazil

Figure 6.3

Coffee in Brazil

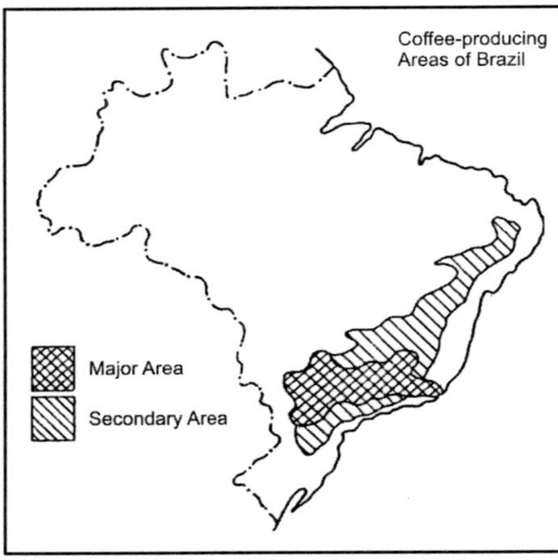

Brazil is the largest producer of coffee in the whole world. The coffee cultivation in Brazil was started in 1870s and one accounted for over 80 per cent of world production. But with the increasing production in other Latin American, African and Asian countries its percentage has now reduced to about 29. In year 2016 Brazil produced 2,859,502 US metric tons of coffee, which is 29.05 per cent of the world's total production and highest in the world.

The coffee is produced in many provinces of Brazil, but its main concentration is in the Sao Paulo state from where about two-third of the Brazilian output comes. The four states of Brazil, i.e. Sao Paulo, Rio de Janeiro, Minas Gerias and Espirito Santo are important and combindly they form a region known as 'Coffee Region' of Brazil. This region is located in south-eastern part of Brazil having all the favourable geographical conditions necessary for coffee production.

The factors responsible for coffee-growing in Brazil are as follows:

Availability of Vast Land for Plantation

In the early days of coffee-growing in Brazil vast areas of the interior remained under virgin forest. These could be quickly and cheaply cleared and prepared for coffee cultivation. When soil fertility in one area was exhausted, new areas were cleared; this wasteful practice was cheaper in the short term because profits were not reduced by the cost of fertilising and rehabilitating the land.

The land around Sao Paulo and extending 400–560 km inland was ideal for coffee-growing. Conditions were better here than in most other parts of Brazil. The rolling plateau between 300 and 915 metres (1,000 and 3,000 ft) in altitude is well-drained and suitable for the development of coffee plantations, known as 'Fazendas' in Brazil.

Climatic Conditions

The south-eastern Brazil has a warm and humid climate, suitable for coffee-growing. The moderate temperatures of 14°–26°C in the uplands mean that shade is not essential. There is adequate rainfall of around 150 cm a year in this region. In coastal region maritime climate is also beneficial to coffee plants.

Soil

The soil here is deep brown silt residual on an old crystalline rock. The two types of soils on which coffee is grown in Sao Paulo are 'terra-roxa' a dark brownish red soil, and the 'Massapee' which varies from yellowish brown to dark red or even black.

Topography

In this region coffee occupies ridge tops and upper slopes. The lower slopes are left out owing to the danger of frost and are devoted to other crops. The escarpment and hilly-undulating topography helps in coffee plantation.

Cheap Labour

In Brazil labour supply is proper that too at a cheaper rate. These workers are also trained because for many years they are doing this work. The agricultural labourers are not permanently settled on the land but move from one estate or fazenda to another. The workers are allowed to grow their own crops, therefore, money wages are low.

Transportation Facility

This region is well-served by road and rail transport. A dense network of railways helps in connecting fazendas with the export ports. Santos and Rio de Janeiro are the main ports, which are well-connected both by rail and roads with coffee-growing regions.

Vast International Markets

For Brazilian coffee vast international market is available. Most of the coffee produced here has been exported to USA and European countries. There is a great demand of coffee in the international market.

Government Patronage

Brazilian government always helps in coffee production, export as well as in solving the other problems related to coffee production. Since coffee is a main source of finance, government is always particular regarding its development. The government has established several coffee research labs and also formulates policies of its export. An 'International Coffee Agreement' has also been signed by the government. In brief, government helps the coffee growers in every way.

Tropical American Coffee Producers

Apart from Brazil, several other tropical American countries are also important coffee producers of the world.

Columbia is the third largest coffee producer in the world. Columbia produced 892,871 US tons of coffee in 2016, which was 9 per cent of the global production. Cultivation techniques in Columbia are very different from those in Brazil. Estates located between 760 and 1,980 metres on the slopes of the Andes are smaller than those of Brazil, being isolated from one another by either mountain ranges or forests. The chief coffee centres are *Medellin, Manizales* and *Tolima*. Transportation from estates to the exporting ports is often a great problem, for the construction and maintenance of roads and railways are difficult and expensive in the mountains. Shade trees are grown and some measures are taken to prevent soil erosion. Harvesting is done more carefully and the berries are only picked when they are ripe. In some areas, however, land too steep for cultivation has been cleared and has been badly eroded. Columbian coffee has an excellent flavour and fetches higher prices than Brazilian coffee. Small quantities of 'mild' Columbian coffee are blended with 'Brazil' coffee to produce the various commercial coffee brands. Columbia produces 60 per cent of the world's mild coffee.

Peru, Venezuela and *Equador* are other important countries of South America which produces coffee.

In Central America coffee is the chief crop. The physical and climatic conditions, especially in the highlands with their rich volcanic soils, are well-suited to coffee cultivation. Annual rainfall is between 1,016 and 3,050 mm (40 and 120 inches) and there are alternate hot, rainy and cool, dry seasons as in Brazil. The coffee trees are regularly pruned and the soils carefully tilled and manured and the coffee beans are of fairly high quality. Yields per hectare are also high – about twice as great as in Brazil. Amongst the Central American states, *Mexico* and *Guatemala* are the most important. Coffee producting countries and rank 9th and 10th respectively in world coffee production.

Most of the West Indian islands produce some coffee, e.g. the Blue Mountain coffee of Jamaica, and conditions of moisture, temperature, soil, labour and market are generally good.

African Countries

During colonial rule coffee cultivation has been started, specially in French and Belgian colonies. In Africa coffee is produced both in East and West African states. *Cote d'Ivoire, Zaire, Cameroun, Madagascar, Kenya, Uganda* and *Ethiopia* produced coffee. Ethiopia ranks 5th in world coffee production and has produced 423,287 US tons of coffee.

Asian Countries

Among Asian coffee-producing countries *Vietnam, Indonesia* and *India* are the main producers. *Vietnam* is the second largest coffee producer in the world in 2016. It produces 1,818,811 US tons of coffee. While *Indonesia* ranks fourth in coffee-producing countries of the world. In 2016, Indonesia produced 814,629 US tons of coffee which was 8.74 per cent of the world production. Java and Sumatra are the main coffee-producing islands.

India is also a leading coffee producer and ranks 6th in world coffee-producing countries. In 2016, India produced 385,786 tons of coffee, which was 3.72 per cent of the world total production. Coffee in India was first cultivated on the Malabar coasts. Soon its cultivation spread to the states of Tamil Nadu and Karnataka. Now coffee is grown on the eastern sheltered slopes of Western Ghats in Coorg, Karnataka and Tamil Nadu. Kadur Shimoga and Hassan of Karnataka, the Nilgiri Hills and Palni Hills are the main coffee-growing areas in India.

Philippines and *Thailand* are also important coffee-growing countries of South-East Asia. Coffee is also grown in West Asia. The world's best coffee, i.e. *Mocha coffee,* is grown chiefly in Yemen.

COCOA

Cocoa is obtained from the beans or seeds of the tropical tree whose botanical name is Theobroma cocoa and is used as drinks as well as for chocolate making.

The cocoa tree, indigenous to *tropical America*, was first found growing wild in lowland Central America, from Panama to the Yucatan Peninsula and in the river basins of the Amazon and the Orinoco. It was used to make *chocolate*, a national drink of the Aztecs for many centuries, and was regarded as the 'food of gods' because of its high nutritional value and its good flavour. But, the drink was not known outside tropical America till the early 16th century when Hernando Cortez, the Spanish conqueror of Mexico, brought some cocoa beans back to Spain. Because of its pleasant taste it soon became a popular drink in many countries of Europe, but in the rest of the world it gained favour much more slowly than either tea or coffee. It was not until the art of chocolate making became known in the industrial west that large-scale cultivation of cocoa began, and only in the 20th century has it become important in the world economy. The consumption of cocoa is more in countries like USA, UK, France, Netherlands, Belgium, Germany and other western European countries. But now chocolates and other cocoa products are popular throughout the world.

Cocoa Cultivation and Processing

The cocoa tree is an evergreen tropical plant which grows to a height of 4.5 to 9 metres (15 to 30 ft). It bears flowers in the third year after planning but only comes into full bearing after five to eight years. It continues to bear flowers for as long as thirty years. There are two major varieties of cocoa: Cocoa criollo from tropical America, which gives superior beans but whose yield is low, and Cocoa forastero from West Africa, which gives abundant crops of slightly inferior quality. Cocoa is extracted from the seeds (beans) embedded in a pulpy pod, which grows from the trunk or branches of cocoa trees.

Cocoa thrives in tropical lowland environment and the plant is propagated from seeds and grows best in forest conditions. The cultivation of cocoa is mostly done in small holdings. The trees are planted close together. Occasional weeding and manuring is necessary to improve the quality of beans. The ripe pods are removed from the trunks and branches and collected at central place.

The cocoa pods are split open with a sharp knife, called a machete, and the beans, which are embedded in the pulp, are scooped out by hand. They are allowed to ferment for a week which removes the unpleasant bitter taste of the fresh beans and stops the seeds from germinating. *Fermentation* is done by piling all the beans in a heap and covering them with large banana leaves for three to seven days so that heat is generated. This *'sweating'* process liquefies the unwanted soft pulp which drains off. The fermented beans are washed and cleaned and then *dried* in the sun. Then the beans are cleaned and roasted and their husks are removed to produce cocoa-nibs. The cocoa-nibs then grinds through machines into powder. This powder is used for making various types of chocolate and other cocoa products.

Conditions of Growth

Climate

Cocoa is essentially a plant of tropical region. The equatorial environment with high temperatures and heavy rainfall is the best. An annual rainfall of 200 to 350 cm is ideal but it will grow in areas with 150 cm of rain. The cocoa farming is best developed in regions having about 27°C of average annual temperature.

Shade

Although cocoa requires much heat but direct sunlight is harmful to it. Some protection is necessary, especially when trees are young. In cocoa plantations, tall banana plants or other shady trees are usually grown to provide shade.

Protection from Strong Winds

Strong winds are harmful for cocoa cultivation because they often blow off unripe pods which will be wasted. Hurricanes also do great damage to the cocoa trees in the West Indies and Central America.

Soil

Cocoa can be grown on a wide range of soils providing they are fairly deep and well-drained. Loamy soils rich in *iron* and *potassium* are ideal but light clays are also suitable. The heaviest crops come from cocoa grown on newly cleared virgin equatorial forest soils with high humus content but manuring in long-established groves enhances the yields.

Labour

Cocoa cultivation and processing are *labour-intensive*. The cocoa tree bears fruit all the year round but beans are usually harvested during the drier season, i.e. from September to February in West Africa, or April to December in Brazil. Cutting down the pods and splitting them, fermenting, drying and sacking the beans all require much manual labour.

Transport

Since much of the cocoa produced is exported, a good network of transport is necessary. The cocoa-producing regions are humid regions, therefore, it is very difficult to maintain the roads and railways. Excessive rain causes great damage to keep roads in good running condition.

Production and Distribution

The total production of cocoa in 2007–08 was 3,664,000 metric tons. The important producers and their production are given in Table 6.3:

Table 6.3

Cocoa production in the world

Country	*Production (in thousand metric tons)*		
	2012–13	*2015–16*	*2016–17*
Cote d'Ivoire (Ivory Coast)	1448	1581	1900
Ghana	835	778	850
Indonesia	770	330	330
Nigeria	238	200	230
Cameroun	275	211	250

Cont'd...

...Cont'd

Brazil	256	140	190
Ecuador	128	252	270
Mexico	82	–	–
Peru	71	–	–
Dominican Republic	68.02	–	–

The world distribution of cocoa-growing areas has been shown in Figure 6.4. There are three cocoa-growing areas in the world: (i) West African Region, (ii) Tropical American Region, and (iii) South-East Asian Region.

West African Region

The West Africa is the largest for producer of cocoa in the world. This region is having best climatic condition for cocoa cultivation. Large areas of long coastal lowlands bordering the Gulf of Guinea are devoted to cocoa cultivation. The cocoa-producing countries of this region are *Cote d'Ivoire (Ivory Coast), Ghana, Nigeria, Cameroun, Liberia, Sierra Leone and Equatorial Guinea* (Figure 6.5).

Cote d'Ivoire (Ivory Coast) is the largest cocoa producer in the world. In year 2016–17 it produced 1900 thousand metric tons of cocoa, which was 39.06 per cent of the total world production. Earlier, Ghana was the top producer of cocoa in the world but during recent years Ivory Coast became number one. In fact, the cocoa-producing belt is continuous from Ghana to Ivory Coast.

Ghana is the second largest producer of cocoa in the world and in 2016–17 it produced 850 thousand metric tons of cocoa, which was 19.92 per cent of the world's total production. In Ghana, cocoa production rose rapidly from less than 45 kg in 1891 to over 4,20,000 tons in 1967, but dropped gradually due to the predominance of old trees. But now it is a leading producer, although second in the world. In Ghana, the greatest concentration is in the *'cocoa triangle'* formed by the towns of Accra, Kumasi and Takoradi.

Figure 6.4

Cocoa-growing regions of the world

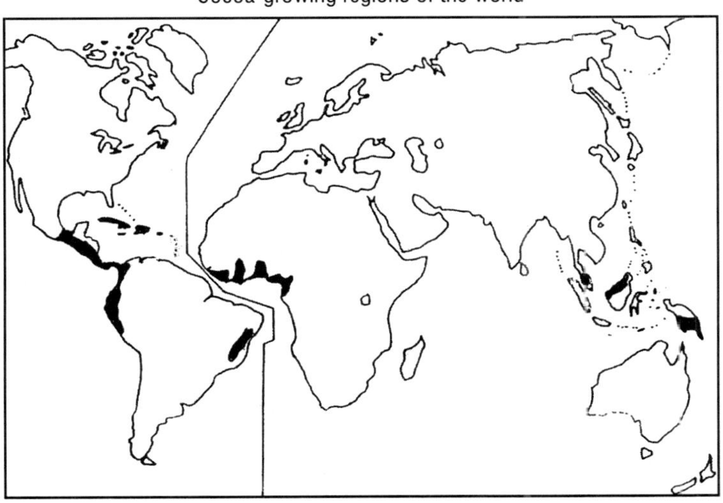

Figure 6.5
Cocoa-growing regions of West Africa

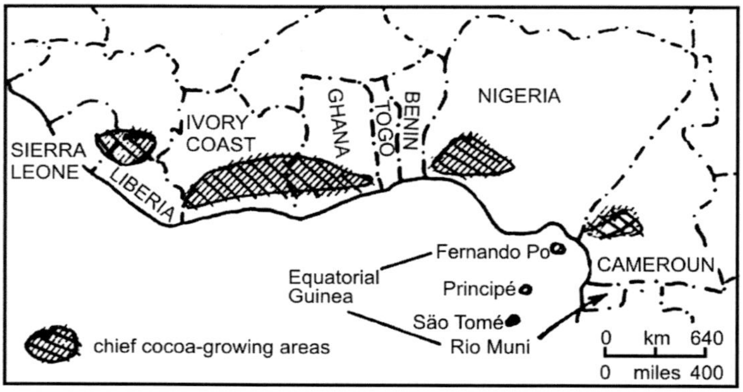

Nigeria is also an important cocoa-producing country of the West Asia. It ranks fourth among the world cocoa-producing countries and in 2016–17 produced 230 thousand metric tons of cocoa, which was 5.46 per cent of the total world production. The leading cocoa region is in south-west, around lbadan.

Cameroun is another producer of cocoa in West Asia, which ranks 5th in the world. In 2016–17, Cameroun produced 250 thousand metric tons of cocoa which was 5.13 per cent of World production.

The other cocoa-producing countries are Liberia, Sierra Leone, Sao Tome and Equatorial Guinea.

Tropical American Region

In this region cocoa is cultivated in *Brazil, Ecuador, West Indies, Mexico, Dominican Republic, Costa Rica* and *Hati*.

Brazil is an important producer of cocoa in the world and ranks 6th in world production. Its production was 190 thousand metric tons in 2016–17. Bahia district in north-eastern Brazil accounts for 90 per cent of the Brazilian output, the remainder coming from around Espirito Santo and Sao Paulo.

Ecuador's production of cocoa was 270 thousand metric tons in 2016–17. In Ecuador cocoa cultivation is concentrated in the Guayaquil lowlands between the Gulf of Guayaquil and the foothills of the Andes.

Cocoa production in rest of South America is small. There are small plantations in *Venezuela, Peru, Columbia,* and islands of *Trinidad* and *Tobago.*

In Central America and the West Indies cocoa cultivation is done on a small scale. Some farms are owned by Europeans but there are many local small holders. Cocoa is grown chiefly for home consumption. In many parts of Central America, cocoa is grown on abandoned banana lands, e.g. in Costa Rica where a disease destroyed most of the banana plants. Amongst the more important cocoa producers are Mexico, Haiti, the Dominican Republic and Costa Rica. The Caribbean region produces excellent cocoa, though limited in quantity.

South-East Asian Region

In comparison to above mentioned two regions this is not an important region in cocoa production, although climatic conditions in some places are suitable.

Malaysia is an important producer of cocoa in this region. Malaysia produce 0.87 per cent of the world cocoa production. The chief area is in eastern Sabah. The Malaysian government is encouraging its cultivation in Peninsular Malaysia. *Papua New Guinea* is another country which produces cocoa.

NATURAL RUBBER

Rubber is an important commercial agricultural product, collected from the latex of the tree *Hevea brasiliensis*. It is an indigenous tree of tropical rainforest of Amazon basin of Brazil. Rubber is useful because of its invaluable qualities such as elasticity, resistance to water and non-conduction of electricity. It is thus a useful substance for waterproofing, insulating and for use in making pneumatic tyres. Rubber is obtained from various tropical trees such as *balata, funtumia elastica* and *gutta percha,* but *Hevea* tree has become the almost exclusive provider of natural rubber.

Rubber was used by the native Brazilians since time immemorial. But was only introduced into Europe in 18th century. Its actual value as waterproofing agent was realised by Charles Mackintosh who used it on cloth to make water-proof material. The use of rubber was possible after the discovery of the *vulcanizing* process in 1839. Charles Goodyear of USA found that, by heating the rubber and mixing it with sulphur a stronger substance could be made. With the development of motor car and use of pneumatic tyres after 1895, the importance of rubber become well-established.

Rubber cultivation had its beginnings in 1876, when Sir Henry Wickham brought Hevea seeds to Kew Gardens in London where he succeeded in germinating trees which he sent to Sri Lanka. Following this experiment, numerous plantations begun in the British and Malay Archipelago, the regions which long supplied most of the world's natural rubber. In early phase of rubber production Amazon basin and African tropics were the main producers, but with the growth of commercial rubber plantation agriculture, the South-East Asian region become its main producer. Today, the South-East Asian countries of Malaysia, Indonesia, Sri Lanka, Vietnam, Thailand and India produce more than 90 per cent of the world's total production of natural rubber.

Cultivation and Processing

Rubber cultivation in plantation is a systematic agriculture in which first seeds have been raised in a nursery. When the rubber seedlings are about 5 cm in diameter buds from high yielding clones are grafted on to the seedlings. This grafted section forms the main part of the tree. The trees are placed at an interval of between 3.5 to 6 metres in regular rows. Rubber tree has a gestation period of 5 to 7 years. Cover crops are usually planted between the seedling trees to prevent soil erosion. The fully grown rubber tree is a large, smooth-barked tree with branches springing out at some height from the ground. The tree yields latex – a white milky liquid which comes out when the bark is cut. *Tapping* is the carefully controlled cutting of the bark to release the latex. The latex runs out into small cups attached to the tree and collected by the tappers. Rubber trees can be tapped for about 35 years.

The collected latex is first *coagulated* into soft, spongy blocks by adding formic acid or acetic acid. This makes it solid and produce sheets which are cut into standard size. There are several other ways of processing the rubber. The latest processing method is to produce *Hevea crumb*. This is done by adding a mixture of chemicals to the rubber to form a mass of crumb like pieces.

Conditions of Growth

Climate

Rubber is a tropical tree. It requires high temperature throughout the year – ranging between 20°–35°C or average monthly mean of 27°C. Less than 20°C temperature is detrimental. Similarly, rubber also requires heavy rainfall. The annual average rainfall of not less than 200 cm is optimum. Rubber tree thrives well when the distribution of rainfall is uniformly high all over the year. The equatorial regions of the world are suitable for rubber cultivation.

Soil

Rubber will do well on a wide variety of soils, some of which would be too poor for many crops. Deep, friable, well-drained soils are ideal as they promote root development, and acidic soils are also suitable.

Land

The plain or gently undulating land is suitable for rubber plantations. This land is generally obtained from clearing of forests. The soil erosion is often a problem in tropical areas, when the original forest cover is removed. Sometimes terraces are used to control soil erosion.

Economic Conditions

Among economic conditions labour, capital, transport and market are necessary for proper rubber plantation.

(a) *Labour:* It is required for maintenance of plantations, collection of latex, preparation of rubber, nurturing of rubber tree, etc. It is a labour-intensive activity.

(b) *Capital:* For cultivation of rubber huge capital is required, specially during first 6–7 years, when income is more or less nil. Capital requirement is necessary for labour wages, plantation cost, processing machines, etc.

(c) *Transport:* Both internal and external transport network is necessary for successful rubber cultivation. Internal transport is required for collection of latex and its transportation up to processing centres, while external transportation network is a pre-requisite for export.

(d) *Market:* Although, rubber is in great demand but with the development of synthetic rubber its demand has decreased. Market demand encourages the rubber plantation.

Production and World Distribution

Asia is the largest producer of the world and produces about 91 per cent of the world production, followed by Africa which produces 6 per cent. The following table indicates the important rubber producers in the world:

Table 6.4

Major rubber producers in the world, 2013

Country	*Production (in thousand metric tons)*
Thailand	4305
Indonesia	3107
Vietnam	946
India	900
China	864
Malaysia	826
Philippines	444
Guatemala	356
Cote d'Ivoire	289
Brazil	185

In 2016, the total world production was 1,24,01,000 metric tons. Thailand is the highest rubber producer in the world, which produced 31.29 per cent of world production. Indonesia is the second largest producer. While Malaysia ranks third in rubber production. There was a time when Malaysia was the highest producer but now its rank is third. The other producers are India, Vietnam, China, Sri Lanka, Cambodia, Nigeria, Cote d'Ivoire (Ivory Coast), Ghana, Liberia, Kenya, Zaire and Brazil.

Thailand

Thailand now ranks first in global rubber output and produced 4.3 million metric tons of rubber – 35 per cent of global total. In Thailand rubber cultivation is a recent phenomenon. In 1990s the country registered a big thrust in rubber cultivation. Most of the rubber plantations are located in the southern part of the country.

Figure 6.6

Rubber-growing areas of the world

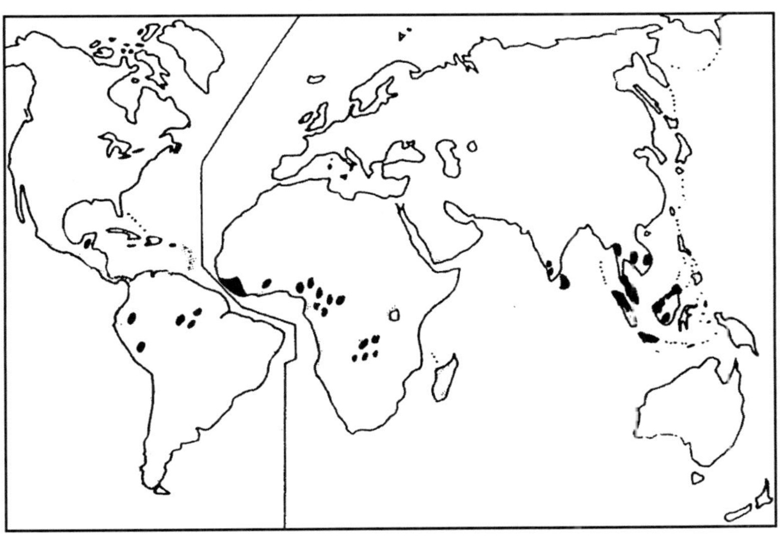

Indonesia

Rubber was introduced into Indonesia at the end of the 19th century by the Dutch. Most of the rubber estates were set up in Sumatra. The remarkable adaptation of rubber trees to the local tropical climate, zeal of the local people and cheap labour availability helped Indonesia to prosper and secured second position in world rubber production and now produce about 25 per cent of the total world production. Most of the rubber plantations are confined to Java, Sumatra and Boroneo islands. Indonesia is now able to export her output.

Vietnam

Vietnam ranks third among rubber-producing countries of the world. It produced 9,46,000 metric tons of rubber, which was 7.79 per cent of the world production.

India

India is in the fourth position in global production. In 2013, the country produced 9,00,000 metric tons of rubber, which was 7.41 per cent of the world production. Rubber plantation was started in 1880 in South India. Kerala, Tamil Nadu, Karnataka, Andaman and Nicobar Islands are the main rubber producers.

China

Recently emerged as a leading rubber-producing country in the world. In 2013, China produced 8,64,000 metric tons of rubber, which is 7.11 per cent of world production, thus ranks 5th in the world.

Malaysia

Rubber has been grown on plantations in Malaysia since the end of the 19th century. There was a time when Malaysia was the largest single producer of rubber in the world. But now it ranks sixth in global production of rubber and has produced 8,26,000 metric tons of rubber in 2013, which was 6.80 per cent of the world production. Rubber is grown mainly on the western side of the peninsula and to a lesser extent or the East Coast of Peninsular Malaysia and in scattered areas of East Malaysia. The rubber plantations in Malaysia have been developed because of suitable climate, government patronage, expansion of rubber-growing areas, new presentation, cheap local, Indian and Chinese labour force, easy transportation facilities, etc. But its production reduced drastically in 21st century. It was also due to the emergence of competitors like Thailand and Indonesia.

Other Countries

Sri Lanka is also an important rubber-producing country. The major producing areas of Sri Lanka are located in the south-western hill slopes.

Philippines and *Cambodia* are other South-East Asian countries which produce rubber.

In African countries *Nigeria, Kenya, Liberia, Zaire* and *Ivory Coast* also produce rubber.

Brazil is the South American country which produces rubber. The Amazon basin was once the important producer of natural rubber. The rubber was collected from the rubber trees located in Amazon forests.

A very small quantity of rubber is also produced in Ecuador and Peru also.

COTTON

Cotton is the main natural fiber accounting for about 50 per cent of the world's fiber supply. Besides being the source of fiber, cotton plant is also the basic raw material for the production of edible oil and cotton seed meal. The latter is one of the world's principle oilseed, one-fifth of the cotton seed is crude protein, yielding 5 to 6 per cent of aggregate world protein supply. The use of cotton fiber to make textiles was known to ancient Egyptians, and cotton has been the major textile in China, India and Central Asia for centuries. But cotton textile remained a luxury in Europe until the 18th century when invention of cotton ginning machines and of mechanised spinning and weaving processes allowed it to be cheaply mass-produced. Thus, in the 19th century, the cotton textile industry was not only started but grew faster in Europe and in other parts of the world, which resulted in the growth of cotton in various parts of the world.

Types of Cotton

Cotton is derived from the hair surrounding the seeds of plants of the Gossypium family. There are many varieties of the plant, some of which originated in Eurasia and some in the Americas, while modern varieties have been developed by breeding and hybridisation. On the basis of staple length of the fiber, there are three main types of cotton:

(i) *Long Staple:* Staple length of this cotton varies between 25 to 65 mm. The major growing areas are Egypt, Sudan, Haiti, Peru, USA etc.

(ii) *Medium Staple:* This is also called upland American cotton. Staple length varies between 15 to 35 mm. Mostly grows in India, China, Brazil, Argentina, etc. This variety comprises maximum production of global cotton.

(iii) *Short Staple:* Mostly varies between 8 to 25 mm in length. It is a low quality cotton and mostly found in China and India.

Conditions of Growth

The following physical and economic conditions are required for the cotton cultivation:

Physical Conditions

(i) *Temperature:* Cotton grows in tropical and sub-tropical warm humid climate. Annual temperature requirement is 20°–28°C. Equitable temperature distribution and bright sunshine is desirable.

(ii) *Rainfall:* Annual rainfall of 55–100 cm is ideal for cotton cultivation. Rainfall during harvesting is harmful.

(iii) *Frost-free Days:* About 180 frost-free days are the bottom-line for cotton cultivation. At least 200 frost-free days are desirable for cotton cultivation.

(iv) *Soil:* Fertile, saline soil with high water-retention capacity is ideal for cotton cultivation. Loamy soil with high calcium carbonate is best for cotton cultivation.

(v) *Relief:* Slight slope of the land drains the soil and is good for cotton cultivation.

Economic Conditions

(i) *Labour:* Cotton cultivation is very labour-intensive, large number of cheap labour is required.

(ii) *Capital:* Mechanised cotton cultivation requires huge capital for machinery, pesticides and fertilisers.

(iii) *Transport/Market:* As it is essentially a commercial crop, for export facilities good transport network and steady demand in international market are pre-requisites.

Production and World Distribution

The total word production of cotton in 2016–17 was 105.99 million bales. The production of main cotton-producing countries is given in the following table:

Table 6.5

Major cotton producers of the world

Country	*Production in million bales (480 lb=one bale)*	
	2015–16	*2016–17*
India	26.40	26.50
China	22.00	22.75
USA	12.89	17.17
Pakistan	7.00	7.70
Brazil	5.90	6.80
Uzbekistan	3.80	1.63
Australia	2.85	4.40
Turkey	2.65	3.20
Turkestan	1.45	1.33
Burkina	1.13	1.30

Source: USDA, June 2017.

The cotton-producing areas of the world are shown in Figure 6.7.

Figure 6.7

Cotton-producing areas of the world

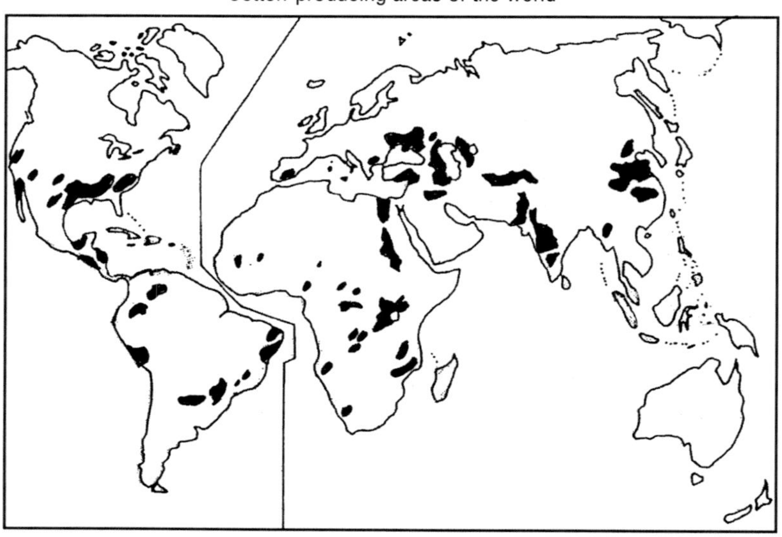

India

India produced 26.50 million bales of cotton in 2016–17, which was 25.47 per cent of the world production. Thus India is the largest producer of cotton in the world. The main cotton-producing areas lie in the western part of the Deccan Plateau, where the soil is black and rainfall is 102 cm and temperature is high. Cotton is also grown in southern part of the Plateau, Madhya Pradesh and Punjab. Much of the cotton produced in India has short staple. Maharashtra, Madhya Pradesh, Punjab, Tamil Nadu, Karnataka and Rajasthan states are important producers. India grows large variety of cotton over a wide range of climate and soil. American cotton has been introduced in Punjab, Maharashtra, Tamil Nadu and Karnataka. Indian cotton has certain local names such as *Wagads, Kumpta, Uppan, Broach, Lalios, Narma* and *Kauvi*. India also exports cotton to European countries and Japan.

China

China ranks second in the world in cotton production. In 2016–17, China produced 22.75 million bales of cotton, which was 21.69 per cent of the world production. Cotton is widely distributed over most of northern and central China, but its intensive cultivation is limited to the Loess region, and only eight provinces grow cotton. The Yangtze valley is the main cotton-growing region, which extends up to Honan, Northern Anhwei to Western Shantung, Chihli and Southern Shansi. It also extends up to the valley of Hwang Ho into Shansi and even to Kansu. The other notable cotton-growing regions are Wei He valley, Sichuan, Hopeh, Shantung, Hunan, etc. In China more and more high-yielding variety of long staple cotton is replacing short staple variety. About 90 per cent of China's cotton crop is grown after the winter crop. Because of high internal consumption of cloth, China cannot export much of its products.

USA

USA remained a leading cotton producer in the world for several decades, until China and India surpassed it in cotton production. Now USA is the third cotton-producing country in the world. In year 2016–17 USA produced 17.17 million bales of cotton, which was 16.98 per cent of the global production.

A large area of south, south-eastern USA is the cotton-producing area known as the 'Cotton Belt of USA'. The cultivation of cotton is to the south of 36th parallel line which coincides with 210 frost-free days and a mean temperature of 25°C in the growing season. The western boundary of the cotton belt is at 50 cm annual rainfall line and the southern boundary is at 25 cm autumn rainfall line. The eastern boundary is in the border between the outer and inner coastal plains where swampy land, more than 25 cm autumn rainfall and infertile soil restrict cotton cultivation. With the cotton belt, there are six major cotton-growing regions:

1. Atlantic Coast and Piedmont
2. Tennessee Valley
3. Mississippi Flood Plain

4. Black Waxy Prairies
5. North-West Texas and Oklahoma
6. Southern Texas Coastal Plain

Pakistan

Pakistan is the fourth cotton-producing country in the world. In 2016–17 it produced 7.70 million bales of cotton, which was 7.54 per cent of the world production. The improvement in the quality of cotton, grown in the Indus basin, by research, irrigation and improved agronomical practices, has indeed been remarkable. A number of varieties have been developed and now cultivated extensively in Sind, Charich Doab and Bari Doab regions of Pakistan. It is one of the most important cotton tracts of Pakistan. The American varieties of cotton are grown here.

Brazil

Brazil is also an important cotton-producing country in the world and rank fifth in the world. In year 2016–17, Brazil has produced 6.80 million bales of cotton, which was 6.60 per cent of the world production. The south-eastern Brazil is the main producer. Sao Paulo province with tropical highland climate is most suitable for cotton production.

Apart from the above, *Uzbekistan, Australia, Burkina, Turkey, Greece, Turkestan* and *Syria* are other important cotton-producing countries, which rank 6th to 10th in the world cotton production. On the other hand the Nile valley of *Egypt* is the best cotton field in the world. The Egyptian cotton is considered as best cotton in the world. The sunny desert type of climate, irrigation facilities and fertile alluvium soil in Nile valley are greatly suited to cotton production.

Figure 6.8
Cotton belt of USA

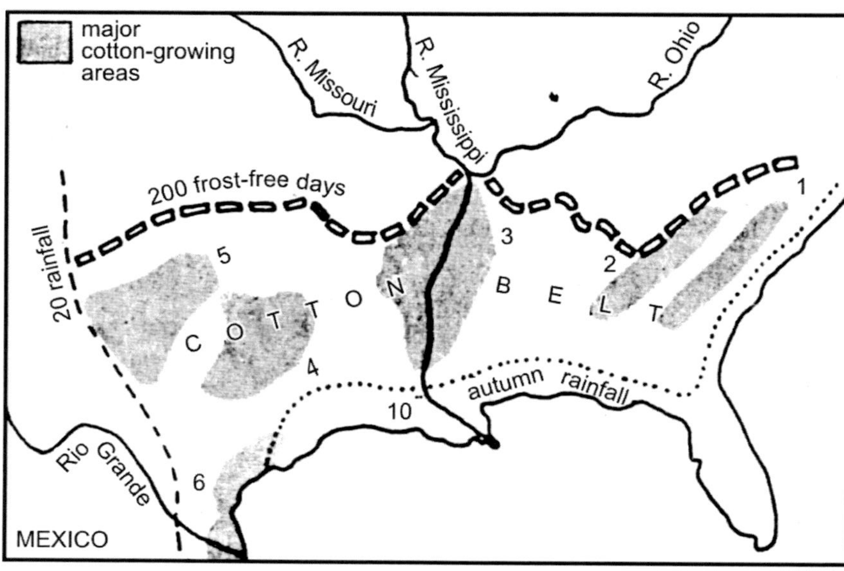

Small quantity of cotton is also produced in *Australia, Peru, Bolivia, Argentina, Sudan, Yemen, Nicaragua, Guatemala, Syrian Arab Republic, etc.*

JUTE

Cultivation of jute was prevalent in the Indian sub-continent even during the pre-historic period. In spite of its long history, jute cultivation did not develop much until the beginning of the 19th century. The fiber was first spun in England in year 1820 at Oxfordshire. Jute is the fiber obtained from certain species of the *Corchorus* family, tall reed-like annuals, which grow to a height of 3 to 3.7 metres. Jute is a course fiber and it is demanded for the manufacture of gunny bags, hessian, carpets, ropes, tarpaulins, rugs and coarse cloth.

Conditions of Growth

Jute is essentially a tropical plant and requires high temperature and high precipitation. It needs a well-distributed rainfall throughout with light showers and ample sunshine in the early stages.

Jute, like other fibers, requires rich soils and thrives on river alluvium, specially where annual floods renew the fertility of the soil. The best quality of jute is obtained from loamy soils, whereas the heaviest yield comes from clayey soils. The alluvial soils of the lower Ganga valley are the ideal. Jute requires so much moisture that it is usually grown under flood conditions.

Jute is a labour-intensive crop. It requires large labour force during growing and harvesting season.

There are two main varieties of jute:

(i) *Corchorus capsularies:* lowland type, and

(ii) *Corchorus olitorius:* upland type.

The production of the second variety is much more expensive and cannot be carried from year to year without heavy manure. On the other hand, the first type can be grown on the flood-plains without fertiliser. The lowland varieties used to flourish even when the land is partly submerged. Seeds are sown in the spring, early enough for the crop to be harvested before the annual floods which follow the monsoon making the water-level rise and harvesting difficult. The plant grows rapidly and is harvested after about 3–4 months. By this time the workers are already waist-deep in water as they cut the long stalks. Jute is piled in boats for transportation to processing centres.

After harvesting, jute is processed. The stems being stripped on leaves and allowed to rot in water to release the fiber. It is loosely spun and woven, for use in making sacks and bags of gunny cloth, for making carpet and other uses. It is also used in making ropes as well as for brown paper used in wrapping and packing.

Production and Distribution

Jute production is very limited and 52.30 per cent is produced by India and another 47.61 per cent by Bangladesh. Other jute-producing countries are Nepal, Myanmmar, China, Ivory Coast (Cote d'Ivaria), Thailand, Brazil, Uzbekistan and Vietnam. The following table indicates the production of jute in the world:

Table 6.6
Jute production in the world

Country	*Jute production (in lakh bales – each bale 180 kg.)*				
	2009–10	*2010–11*	*2011–12*	*2012–13*	*2013–14*
World	143.38	171.58	174.63	162.98	168.68
India	82.71	92.22	94.72	86.33	87.78
Bangladesh	59.45	78.03	74.05	75.72	80.00
Nepal	0.98	0.80	0.80	0.83	0.87
Myanmar	0.24	0.53	0.21	0.09	0.03

Source: www.ijma.org.word.jute.html

Almost all the world production of jute comes from *India* and *Bangladesh.* Most of the jute is grown in the fertile, alluvial, annually flooded area at the mouth of the Ganges and Brahmaputra rivers, where all the geographical requirements are present. The jute-producing areas of the world are shown in Figure 6.9.

India

The largest jute-producing country in the world is India, which produced 52.30 per cent jute of the world in year 2013–14. Its cultivation is restricted to the Ganges-Brahmaputra delta in West Bengal and Assam. Jute is also produced in Bihar and Odisha. West Bengal has the largest acreage under jute in India. Raw jute is grown in the districts of 24 Parganas, Noida, Murshidabad, Malda, West Dinajpur, Jalpaiguri, Cooch Bihar, Howrah, Hooghly and Burdwan. West Bengal raises about 50 per cent of India's total jute production.

In Assam raw jute is grown in the districts of Goalpara, Kamrup, Nowgong and Tejpur. In Bihar jute is produced in the Purnea district, while in Odisha,

Figure 6.9
Jute-producing areas of the world

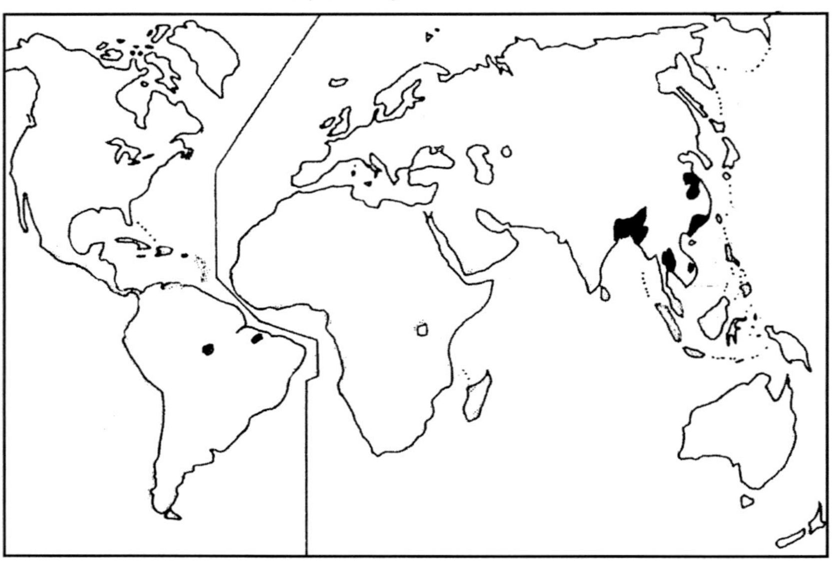

Cuttack district is the only jute-producing area. A little amount of jute is also produced in Uttar Pradesh and also in coastal districts of Maharashtra.

Bangladesh

The districts for jute cultivation are Mymensingh, Dacca, Rangpur, Bogra and Paina all bordering on the Brahmaputra or the Jamuna in Bangladesh, they also provide clear water for retting the jute than the Ganga. The cultivation of jute decreases towards the south in the Ganga Delta where the land is too low for jute and towards west where the rocky ground of the Southern Plateau is more marked than the Ganga alluvium. In year 2013–14, Bangladesh produced 47.61 per cent jute of the world.

Apart from the above, the other jute-producing countries of the world are *Nepal, Myanmar, China, Cote d'Ivoria, Thailand, Brazil, Uzbekistan* and *Vietnam.*

SUGARCANE

The most important commercial crop of tropical countries is sugarcane. Sugarcane is a member of the grass family, and is a tall tropical variety, with a hard, thick stem and sugar is stored in them. It is believed that the plant originated in Eastern Asia and was taken to the Middle East and Southern Europe by Arab trades in the Middle Ages. The Portuguese realised the profits to be made from growing sugar and introduced it to their colonies in Maderia and the Canary islands and later to Brazil in the 16th century. From Brazil it spread to the West Indies and Caribbean countries. It has also been introduced to Africa (especially Netal in South Africa), Australia, Hawaii and Fiji. Now, sugarcane is cultivated in most of the tropical countries.

Geographical Conditions for Growth

Sugarcane is a tropical plant, therefore, requires a year warm weather to reach maturity. The areas having temperature of 20° to 26°C and an average rainfall of 150 cm are suitable for its cultivation. In many areas water is partly supplemented by the canals. Much sunshine is required, particularly at the end of the growing season, to produce cane with a high sugar content.

Sugarcane grows well in alluvium and light-clay soil. Moist clay-loam with good drainage is the best soil for cane. As the crop is a valuable one large amounts of fertilisers are used to increase the yield. Sugarcane cultivation also needs sufficient capital and labour.

Methods of Cultivation and Processing

The native method of sowing sugarcane is to plough the land some three to five times, the plough going round and round the field and forming a fine seed-bed about 10 to 15 cm deep. Next the field is levelled and the cuttings of seed cane are planted. New canes are usually planted by taking cuttings from old plants. These cuttings become established and after a few days buds sprout to form new stalks. Six to ten stalks grow from each plant, and the sugarcane then takes from one to two years to mature.

Little work is done in the field while cane is growing, except in the early stages when plants are kept free of weeds. Before the crop is harvested the field may be fired to burn off dead foliage to get rid of pests from the fields. The crop is then cut by hand. The canes are loaded on to trucks or tractors or by any other fast means of transportation to take them quickly to the mill for the processing as early as possible to preserve the high quality of sugar. Sugarcane is a perennial crop and the same plants could continue to produce cane for many years.

The sugar mills are generally located near producing areas. Because firstly, the sugar deteriorates if it is not quickly processed and secondly, sugar accounts for only between 10 to 20 per cent of the bulky sugarcane and thus it would be prohibitively expensive to transport cane over long distances in its original form. In the mills the cane is crushed, then boiled with lime to form crystallise sugar. By-products of the crushing process also have important uses. *Molasses* is used to make rum and industrial alcohol, while *Bagasse,* the cane residue, can be used as a fuel for the mills, as cattle fodder as well as a source of fiber in the paper and synthetic textile industries.

Production and Distribution

Sugarcane is grown in a very wide range of tropical and sub-tropical countries but the largest producers are from Latin America and Southern and Eastern Asia. In year 2016, the world production of sugarcane was 1,700 million metric tons. The following table indicates the important producers and their production of sugarcane:

Table 6.7

Major sugarcane-producing countries of the world, 2016

Country	*Production (in thousand metric tons)*	*Percentage of the world*
Brazil	739,300	43.47
India	341,200	20.06
China	125,500	7.35
Thailand	100,100	5.88
Pakistan	63,800	3.70
Mexico	61,200	3.58
Columbia	34,900	2.00
Indonesia	33,700	1.90
Philippines	31,900	1.82
USA	27,900	1.64

Source: Food & Agriculture Organisation of United Nations, Economic and Social Department.

The distribution of sugarcane-producing areas is shown in Figure 6.10.

Brazil

Brazil is the leading producer of sugarcane in the world and it ranks first with 43.47 per cent of the world production. Sao Paulo and adjacent regions produce more than one-half of the Brazil's sugarcane. The other sugarcane-producing areas of Brazil are located in coastal districts of north-east. Much of the Brazil's sugar output is used within the country but now it is also exporting sugar to European and other South-American countries.

Figure 6.10

Sugarcane and sugar beet-producing areas of the world

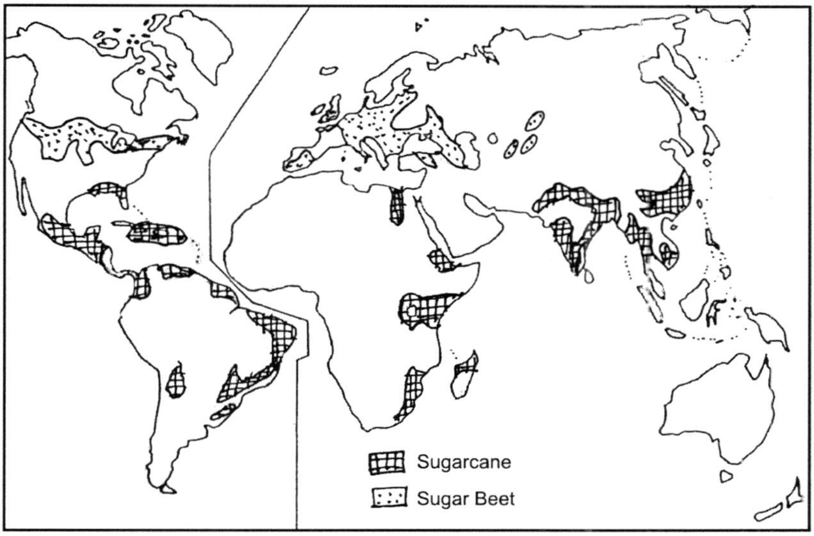

India

Sugarcane in India is mostly grown in the Gangetic Plain. Though sugarcane is cultivated throughout India, the most important states are Uttar Pradesh, Bihar, West Bengal, Maharashtra, Andhra Pradesh, Punjab, Tamil Nadu, Karnataka and Odisha. The most productive belt extends from North Bihar to Uttar Pradesh and Punjab. In year 2016, India produced 20.06 per cent sugarcane of the world and ranks second in the world. Northern India produces about 70 per cent of the total production, in which UP alone used to produce 35 per cent of India's total output.

China

The third largest sugarcane-producing country in the world is China, which produced 7.35 per cent of the world sugarcane production. Kwangtugn, Kwangsi, Fukien, Chekiang, Hunan and Szechwan are the important provinces where sugarcane is produced.

Thailand

The production of sugarcane in Thailand was about 100 lakh metric tons in 2016, which was 5.88 per cent of the world production.

Pakistan

Pakistan ranks fifth in world production of sugarcane and it produced 3.70 per cent sugarcane of the world in 2016. The sugarcane-producing districts of Pakistan are Lahore, Lyallpur, Multan and Sialkot.

Mexico

Mexico is the sixth largest sugarcane-producing country of the world. In 2016, its production was 61 lakh metric tons, which was 3.58 per cent of the world production. In Mexico sugarcane cultivation is mostly concentrated in Nuevo, Leon, Tamaulipas and Vera Cruz provinces.

Columbia

Columbia ranks 7th in the world in sugarcane production. In 2016, its sugarcane production was 35 lakh metric tons, which was 2.00 per cent of the world production.

Apart from the above, the other leading sugarcane-producing countries in the world are Australia, USA, Phillippines, Indonesia, Cuba, Argentina, Egypt, Kenya, Fiji, etc. Among these countries Cuba's position as a sugar producer and exporter is very good. In Cuba, about 50 per cent of the cultivated land has been devoted to cane cultivation. This is because of the existence of favourable geographical conditions for the production of sugarcane.

SUGAR BEET

Beet is the second most important source of sugar. Sugar beet is a root crop of the beet family. Sugar beet is a large white or yellow root which grows in temperate regions. Its sugar content was first discovered in Germany in the 18th century. But its wide cultivation was started in early 20th century in Europe. Its use has spread to most European countries and to North America as well as in Russia.

Conditions of Growth

Sugar beet is a native of temperate climatic regions with moist and mild winters and moderate summer temperature and thus, in wide contrast to sugarcane it grows in mid-latitude regions. It is very sensitive to annual ranges of rainfall which should necessarily be around 60 to 65 cm.

The most suitable geographical conditions for beet-growing are found where the soil is deep, friable, well-drained and contains certain proportion of lime in it. Sugar beet is usually cultivated as a rotation crop on the characteristic mixed farms of Europe and North America. It replaces turnips or other root crops in rotation and is usually alternated with a grain crop.

Economic conditions are also very important for sugar beet. It is a highly capital-intensive crop, its cultivation is limited only to the affluent countries of the world. It also requires cheap and easy supply of labour to perform the works from planting to harvesting the crop.

Production and Distribution

The total production of sugar beet in the world is 242 million metric tons. The following table indicates the production of sugar beet in various countries:

Table 6.8

Major sugar beet producers of the world

Country	*Production (in thousand tons)*	*Percentage of the world*
Russia	45057	18.0
France	33688	13.6
USA	31954	12.8

Cont'd...

...Cont'd

Germany	27891	11.2
Ukraine	18438	7.2
Turkey	15000	6.0
Poland	12349	4.8
China	11469	4.4
Egypt	9126	3.6
United Kingdom	7291	2.8

Source: FAO, Economic & Social Department, The Statistical Division, May 2017.

It becomes clear from the above table that most of the sugar beet-producing countries are located in Russia and European Countries as well as in USA and China. In fact, temperate climatic conditions of Russia, Europe and USA are most suitable for sugar beet production.

Russia

Russia ranks first in the world in sugar beet production. It produces 45 million tons in 2016–17, whichis 18 per cent sugar beet of the world. Most of the sugar beet is produced in lower Volga river region of the eastern European section.

European Countries

Europe produces nearly 80 per cent of the world production of beet sugar.

France ranks first in Europe and second in the world. It produces nearly 13.6 per cent of the total sugar beet of the world. One of the most important productive areas of France is Picardy. The land is rather flat, but dips slightly in the middle, so that the upper Seine, Yonne, Marne and Oise flow down towards the centre.

Germany is the second largest producer of sugar beet in the Europe and fourth in the world. It produces 11.2 per cent of the world sugar beet production. The important producing areas are Schleswig-Holstein, Saarland, Lower Saxony, North Rhine-Westphalia, Hessen, Hamburg, Bremen, Bavaria, Rhineland and Palotinate. The Middle Elbe valley is also a leading sugar beet-producing area of the Germany.

The other important sugar beet-producing countries of Europe are United Kingdom, Italy, Poland and Spain. Sugar beet is also produced in Holland, Belgium, Portugal and Hungary.

USA

USA is the third largest producer of sugar beet in the world and it produces about 12.8 per cent of the world sugar beet. In Western United States the crop is grown quite successfully in numerous irrigated valleys. In US some 22 states grow sugar beet, though more than half of the total output comes from California, Colorado and Idaho states. Other sugar beet-growing states are New Mexico, South Dakota, Nebraska, Iowa, Wisconsin, Ohio, Michigan, New York, Pennsylvania, etc.

Ukraine

Once part of Russia, Ukraine now ranks fifth in the world in sugar beet production. It produces 7.2 per cent sugar beet of the world. In Ukrainian wooded steppe about a tenth of the area is under sugar beet cultivation. The black soil region of Ukraine is best suited to beet production.

Turkey

Turkey is the sixth producer of sugar beet in the world. It produces 6 per cent sugar beet of the world. Apart from above mentioned countries, sugar beet is grown as a rotational crop in China and Japan.

TOBACCO

Tobacco is a commercial crop of considerable importance that provides, directly and indirectly, employment to millions of people. Tobacco has a very wide market as it is consumed by large number of people of the world in some form or other. The tobacco plant is a broad-leaved annual growing to a height of around one metre. It is a native plant of tropical America, but it has been introduced to many parts of the world. It is now grown in almost every country with a warm temperate, sub-tropical or tropical climate.

Geographical Conditions for Growth

Tobacco plant requires moderate rainfall and rich regularly-fertilised soil. Temperature exceeding 18°C in the warmest month is ideal. The plant requires a frost-free period of 120 to 180 days and a warm growing season.

Tobacco is grown mostly wherever the soil is rich sandy loam. The best kind is well-drained, friable, sandy loam, not too rich in organic matter, but rich in mineral salts like potash, phosphoric acid and iron. Light soil which allows a full development of the roots of tobacco is the best for it.

The tobacco farming requires cheap supply of labour in all stages – field preparation, transplantation, harvesting, processing as well as for marketing.

Cultivation and Processing Method

The cultivation of tobacco is a painstaking task. The process involves the sowing of tobacco seeds in small beds. When the plants attain a height of 10 to 12 cm, they are carried to the larger field for transplantation. In most of the developing countries, curing of tobacco is done in a very primitive way. The leaves are not removed one by one when ready for picking, but after few spots have begun to appear on the lower leaves, the entire plant is cut off close to the ground, and is left exposed to the night dew.

The harvesting, grading and cutting of leaves are carried out by hand. The flavour and quality of the tobacco depends on several factors, such as type of soil, variety of tobacco grown, climatic conditions and the method of curing the leaves. The regions having suitable climatic and soil conditions are used to produce high quality of tobacco. The four main types of tobacco are: *Virginia Tobacco,* grown in a number of areas and lightly tobaccos, Turkish or *Oriental Tobacco; Cigar Tobacco,* and other tobaccos, mostly dark-coloured and grown in Asian countries. The quality of tobacco varies according to the part of the plant from which the leaf is taken. Tobacco is usually blended to produce the mixtures used for cigarettes.

Production and World Distribution

Tobacco is produced in several parts of the world. On the continental basis, Asia produce about 63 per cent tobacco of the world followed by Central America (10%), Europe (8%), Africa and South America (7% each), The total world production of tobacco is about seven million tons. Table 6.9 indicates the major tobacco-producing countries in the world.

Table 6.9

Major tobacco producing countries of the world, 2015–16

Country	*Production (in thousand tons)*
China	2997.05
Brazil	862.39
India	720.72
USA	397.53
Indonesia	196.30
Pakistan	129.87
Malawi	126.34
Argentina	119.43
Mozambique	97.07
Bangladesh	85.00

The distribution of tobacco-producing areas in the world has been shown in Figure 6.11.

Figure 6.11

Tobacco-producing areas of the world

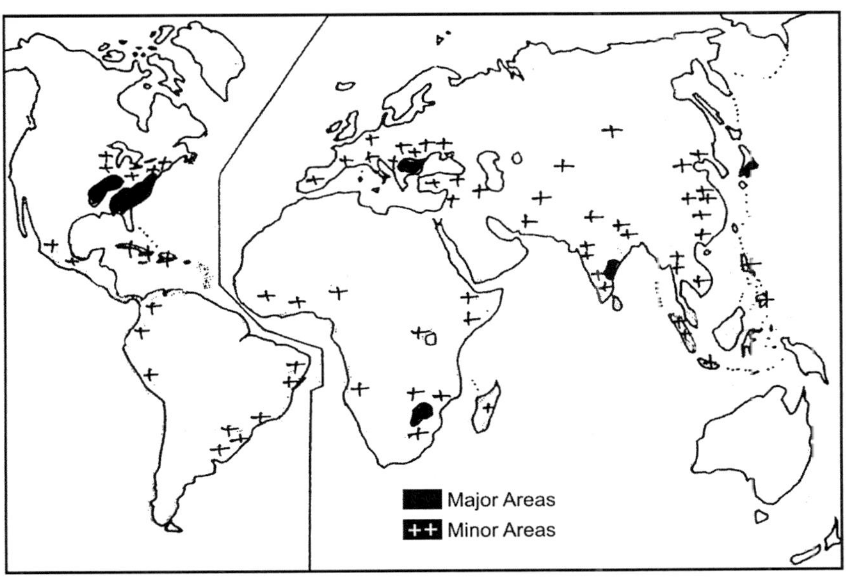

China

China is the largest tobacco-producing country in the world. It produces about 40 per cent tobacco of the world production. Tobacco is produced in the irrigated region of Changtu in the Red basin and in Sikiang valley in the south. Tobacco planting depends on climate. In the southern China the winter is rather a short period of stagnation of growth rather than a true winter. Under such conditions it is possible to grow tobacco as a winter crop and harvesting is done at the beginning of spring. Other areas of tobacco cultivation in China are North China Plain, Fukien, Kwangtung, Kwangsi, Yunkwei, Chekiang and Yunan.

Brazil

Brazil is the second largest producer of tobacco in the world. Its production was 0.86 million tons, which was 11.49 per cent of the world production. Most of the tobacco is produced in south-eastern and north-eastern coastal regions of the Brazil.

India

India produced 0.72 million tons of tobacco, which was 9.60 per cent of the world production. Production of tobacco, is concentrated in the Ganges basin of north Bihar, in the Godavari and Krishna deltas of Andhra Pradesh, in Madurai and in Belgaum, Baroda, Satara and Kaira near Mumbai. Tamil Nadu and Andhra Pradesh produce the bulk of the tobacco production in India. Andhra Pradesh is the leading producer of Virginia tobacco in India. Next in order of importance are Maharashtra, West Bengal, Bihar, Gujarat, Assam, Uttar Pradesh and Odisha.

USA

USA ranks fourth in tobacco production and it used to produce 5.29 per cent of the world production. More than 50 per cent tobacco of USA is grown in Virginia-Carolina Belt. This belt is running from southern Maryland through the middle part of Virginia and north Carolina and on into south Carolina. The second important region is the Kentuky-Tennesse tobacco region.

European Union

In European Union, tobacco is grown in Hungary, Bulgaria and Balkan region. The total production of European union is the 4.6 per cent of the world tobacco production.

Pakistan

Pakistan ranks 6th in the tobacco production of the world. Its annual producation is 130 thousand tons.

West Indies

In Cuba production of tobacco is concentrated in the rolling sandy plains of south-western Pinerdel Rio. The region is noted for cigar filler and wrapper leaf.

The framing of tobacco is done on large plantations and is highly commercialised in nature. Puerto Rico produces high grade filter tobacco in the mountain areas of east central part.

Indonesia

In Indonesia tobacco is produced on small and large holdings and on well-managed plantation lying in eastern Java and north-eastern Sumatra.

Among the other tobacco-producing countries of the world are included Turkey, Philippines, Zimbabwe, Russia, Uganda, Ethiopia, Argentina, Thiland, Tanzania, Kenya, Vietnam, Italy, Equador, Serbia, Algeria, etc.

7

Livestock and Fisheries

LIVESTOCK

The relationships between man and animals is as old as human civilisation. Prior to the domestication of animals man used to practice hunting, which was the major source of food at that time. Men soon realised the importance of animals in their life and started their domestication probably more than 5000 years ago. From man's point of view, animals have many uses. They can provide food in the form of meat or milk, clothing in the form of hides, furs, wool, hairs, many other products such as horn, bones, feathers, transport for men and goods, power for ploughing, traction or driving machinery and manure for fertilising farmland. The importance of livestock remained during all the periods of human history and at present also livestock raising plays an important role in the economy of many countries of the world. This has become possible only after the commercialisation of the pastoralism.

Pastoralism is a worldwide activity prevalent in many forms in different regions of the world. These are:

(i) *Nomadic Herding:* Nomadic herding is still prevalent in arid and semi-arid regions of Africa and Asia. This practice is also prevalent in high altitude areas of Himalaya, as well as in Polar regions. In these areas animals are mostly used as a source of food in form of meat and as a means of transportation.

(ii) *Livestock Ranching:* This practice is performed in areas of hostile climate and where terrain is not suitable for agriculture. They use cattle, goats, sheep, etc. for the commercial purpose. Dairy products, meat, hide, wool are extracted and sold in the market. Such type of subsistence livestock ranching is done in parts of Argentina, Venezuela and Australia.

(iii) *Mixed Farming:* In many regions of the world pastoralism is performed along with agriculture. In some areas of Africa and Asia it is just in the form of subsistence, which supplement the agricultural activity. But on the other hand this practice is performed in a commercial way as is done in Western Europe and in North and South America. The grasslands of Prairie in North America, Pampus in South America, Veld in South Africa are suitable areas for mixed farming.

(iv) *Dairy Farming:* Today, in many parts of the world, dairy farming is an important commercial activity, in which livestock are reared properly for the production of several milk products. Dairy farming is common in Western

Europe, New Zealand, USA, Canada and in some parts of South America. Dairy farming plays a vital role in the economy of the countries like New Zealand, Denmark, Sweden, Norway, Spain, France, England, Germany, Canada, USA, etc.

Geographical Factors Controlling Livestock Ranching

The growth and development of livestock ranching, specially commercial livestock farming always depend upon certain geo-economic factors. These factors are as follows:

(i) *Climate:* Most commercial grazing occurs in dry and moderate climate. Dry climate prevail in five of the largest ranching areas – those of North America, Southern South America, South Africa, Australia and the Central Asia. New Zealand and portions of South Africa are having humid climate. Moderate temperature and medium rainfall favours grassland development which is most suitable for livestock ranching.

(ii) *Topography:* The undulating, flat and rolling plains are favourable for the growth of grassland as well as for livestock ranching. The Savanna in Africa, Steppes in Russia, Prairie in North America, Pampus in Argentina, Veld in South Africa and Downs in Australia, all are having rolling plain topography.

(iii) *Natural Vegetation:* Livestock ranching occurs in regions of grasslands and desert shrub. The type of grass varies regionally. In the low latitudes are the tropical grasslands generally termed as Savannas – such as the Lanos of Venezuela, the Campos of Brazil, the Gran Chaco of Argentina-Paraguay-Bolivia. The mid-latitudes have the best grasslands: Prairies and Steppes. Marginal grasslands are also used, such as desert fringes adjoining Steppes and grassland patches on the edges of forests that adjoin Steppes.

(iv) *Economic Conditions:* Livestock ranching also depends upon the nature of economy. Economic stability is necessary for the successful growth of commercial livestock farming. Among economic conditions, (a) capital, (b) transportation, and (c) market demand are the basic requirements. Nowadays commercial dairy farming, meat processing, etc. need a sizeable capital. Similarly, good and fast transportation facilities are also required because dairy and meat products are perishable. Both internal and external demands enhance the rapid growth of livestock industry. Availability of skilled labour is an additional advantage for the development of commercial livestock ranching.

World Distribution of Grasslands and Livestock

The whole pastoral economy depends upon grasslands. Therefore, spatial concentration of commercial livestock ranching in the world is controlled by grazing grounds or grasslands. General distribution of livestock in the world and grasslands are interdependent on each other. The grasslands of the world are classified into two categories:

1. Temperate Grassland
2. Tropical Grassland

Similarly, commercial grazing is also related to them and their spatial pattern is more or less the same.

Temperate Grassland Areas of Livestock

Temperate grasslands are widespread in temperate regions across North and South America, Oceania and South Africa. These are known as mid-latitude or temperate or intermediate grasslands. These grasslands are known by different names in various continents such as Steppes in Russia, Prairies in North America, Pampas in Argentina, Veld in South Africa and Downs in Southern Australia.

Generally these are found in areas of moderate to heavy rainfall on land once occupied by natural forest. Soils in these areas are well supplied with moisture during much of the year, with some leaching occurring due to the percolation of excess water. They are grasslands that support the intensive, highly developed livestock industry in New Zealand, Western Europe, the United Kingdom, humid regions of North America and other parts of the world.

North American grasslands, provide excellent grazing ground. Vast stretches of land covering the parts of Canada and USA – extending over Alberta, Saskatchewan, Nevada and Texas provinces.

Among all the South American countries, Argentina holds the pride position in commercial livestock ranching. The lush green grasslands Pampas provide excellent grazing facilities to millions of cattle and sheep. The alfalfa grass grows luxuriantly all over the Pampas grassland which enable ranchers to improve their livestock health in such a way that Argentina is the largest exporter of dairy product and wool. Apart from Argentina, Uruguay has also improved livestock farming in a big way.

Australia and New Zealand are famous for livestock ranching. Low density of population, availability of land, extensive grasslands and traditional skill of livestock ranching provided incentives to commercial grazing in a grand scale. New Zealand is famous for its dairy industry in the world and its economy is based on livestock.

South African grassland, known as Veld, is famous for sheep rearing. This region produces sizeable quantity of high quality wool.

Tropical Grassland Areas of Livestock

Intervening between the tropical forests and the dry deserts of the trade-wind belts, occur stretches of warm country with a moderate rainfall only. Here there are very few trees but grasses of various kinds which afford abundant food to herds of grazing animals. Such *Savannas* include the African Sudan, the Venezuelan *Lanos* of the Orinoco basin, the Brazilian Campos or *Selvas* of Amazon and *Shola* of India.

These Savanna grasslands generally occupy those areas between the climatic extremes of humid woodlands and dry desert shrub, the transition belts, therefore, between typical grass Prairie and either of these extremes contain more or less tree growth on the one hand, or desert shrub on the other. Soil moisture, rather than total rainfall, usually determines the extent of natural grassland. If the upper layers of soil are moist during part of the year, but the deeper layers remain dry, tree growth cannot complete with grass. The Savannas of the tropics annually receive substantial total rainfall, but a prolonged dry period each year, combined with high temperatures and evaporation, prevents the development of forests.

Figure 7.1
Grassland of the world

Figure 7.2
Cattle rearing areas of the world

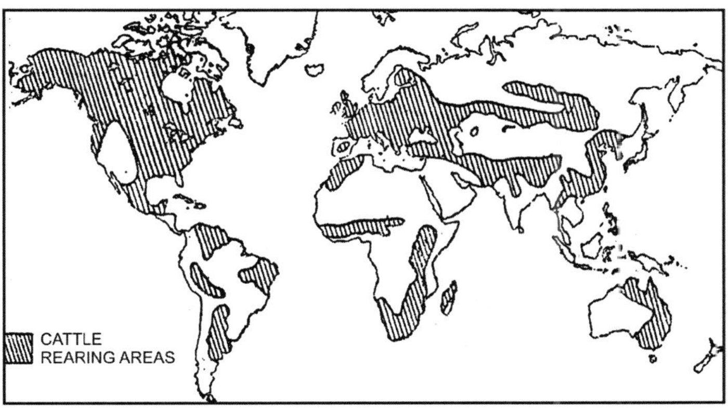

African Savannah

Extends from Indian ocean on the east to Atlantic on the west. This sparsely populated, hostile environment now supports only few aboriginals and large number of wild animals. Most areas still remain virgin as human interference is very low. Tribal people, for example Masai, own a large number of cattle population. Grazing activities are still at its primitive level.

American Grasslands

Compared to its African counterpart, American grassland is not so vast and extensive. The major grasslands include Lanos of Venezuela, Savannah of Bolivia, Campos of Brazil and El Gran Chako of Argentina. Commercial grazing activities in the form of cattle rearing is predominant in the interior part of the grasslands.

Numerical Status of Livestock

According to FAO, the world has 1,467,548,724 cattle (1.468 billion). Table 7.1 shows the top fifteen countries in terms of cattle heads:

Table 7.1
Livestock in the world top 15 countries

Rank	*Country*	*Head (number)*	*Percentage of world total*
1	Brazil	211,764,292	14.43
2	India	189,000,000	12.88
3	China	113,500,000	7.73
4	USA	89,299,600	6.08
5	Ethiopia	54,000,000	3.68
6	Argentina	51,095,000	3.48
7	Sudan	41,917,000	2.86
8	Pakistan	38,299,000	2.61
9	Mexico	32,402,461	2.21
10	Australia	29,291,669	2.00
11	Tanzania	24,531,673	1.67
12	Bangladesh	24,000,000	1.64
13	Colombia	23,141,000	1.58
14	Nigeria	20,000,000	1.36
15	Russian Federation	19,930,354	1.36

Source: FAO stat. org (2013).

It becomes clear from the above table that Brazil is having highest number of livestock, which is 14.43 per cent of the world total. India and China ranks second and third with 12.88 and 7.73 per cent of the world total respectively. Other notable countries are USA, Ethiopia, Argentina, Sudan, Pakistan, Mexico, Australia, Tanzania, Bangladesh, Colombia, Nigeria and Russia. Although, livestocks are common in all the countries of the world.

Commercial Livestock Rearing

The most important aspect of pastoralism or livestock rearing is its commercialisation, which is not only responsible for its systematic and scientific development but also a source of income to many countries of the world. The various livestock products and their marketing is a notable feature of international trade. Therefore, it is necessary to discuss in detail these aspects of livestock rearing which are commercially important. These are:

1. Dairy Farming or Dairy Industry
2. Meat Industry
3. Sheep Rearing
4. Goats and Pigs

DAIRY FARMING OR DAIRY INDUSTRY

The object of dairy farming is to raise cattle to produce milk. For hundreds of years men in certain parts of the world have consumed animal milk. Milk is a highly nutritious food containing all the essential minerals and vitamins for human growth. Earlier most of the milk has been produced on a subsistence level. What little was sold commercially came from general farmers. Only within the past 150 years has there been much specialisation in milk production in the form of dairy farming. Not all the milk produced on dairy farms is consumed in its fresh state. However, milk can be turned into a variety of less perishable products for storage or for export. Such milk products are *condensed* or *sweetened milk, milk powder, butter, cheese, ghee*, etc. The by-product of this process is skimmed milk, which makes an excellent feed for pigs.

Most of the world's best known breeds of dairy cows come from Western Europe, especially Britain, Netherlands and Switzerland. The *Ayrshire* breed, originally, from Ayrshire, south-west Scotland is famous for its milk production. The *Guernsey, Alderney, Jersey, Friesion, Swiss Brown* are famous breeds of cows. Several other breeds and now cross breeds are commonly used for milk production in many parts of the world.

Factors of Growth

Dairy farming has developed only in certain parts of the world. This is because of the fact that certain geo-economic conditions are required for its growth and successful development. The factors favourable for the growth of dairy farming are as follows:

(i) *Climate:* Temperate climate is most suitable for dairying. Commercial dairy farming has developed in humid temperate regions. Dairy cattle best thrive in 10°C to 17°C temperatures and 50 cm to 75 cm rainfall. High summer temperature and below freezing winter temperature are harmful for raising cattle. The coastal areas having marine climate and humid continental climate are also suitable for dairying.

(ii) *Fodder:* Dairy cattle require green grass throughout the year. The fodder is also obtained from certain crops such as clover and leguminous crops, which are especially grown for dairy cattle. The good quality of grass available in western Europe, USA, Canada, New Zealand is the main factor of the development of dairy industry in these areas.

(iii) *Water:* On an average 200 liters of water is required for a cow. Therefore, good quality of water and its availability throughout the year is necessary for dairy industry.

(iv) *Urbanism:* There is a close relationship between dairying and urbanism. The concentration of population in cities create great demand of milk and milk products. The two world's main dairy regions, i.e. Anglo-America and Western Europe are located in highly urbanised areas. The specific type of dairy farming in a dairy region depends to a large degree on the distance to urban markets. The milk consumption in large cities is much more than other regions.

(v) *Capital:* Dairy farming nowadays needs capital for the purchase of cattle, their maintenance, for the purchase of machines as well as for marketing of the products. The processing of milk and their preservation requires special type of machines. Similarly packing and marketing also needs capital.

(vi) *Transportation:* Quick and efficient transport network is essential for the dairy industry. The internal transport system helps in collection of milk from production centres, which are generally located away from the production centres. Similarly, external transport system is required for the export.

Nowadays air transport is also in use for the export of dairy products to distant regions.

(vii) *Market:* Since dairy products are in great demand, there is no problem of consumption of these products. But when markets are located in nearby places, problem of transportation is lesser and the production is cost effective. Dairy products are having worldwide market. The dairy products of New Zealand and Denmark are in great demand throughout the world.

Among other factors availability of good quality of milk-producing cattle, skilled labour, government policy, prevention of cattle diseases, etc. are also important. Regular researches and constant experiments with regards to breeds, health, forage, etc. are also necessary.

World Distribution

The spatial distribution of dairy farming in the world is widespread. But three main regions of commercial dairy farming are important. The largest is in Western Europe, a belt extending about 3000 km from Atlantic Coast almost to Moscow. The second dairy region, that of Anglo-America, is likewise a belt, this one beginning at Atlantic Coast to the Prairie Provinces of Canada. The third region is the Australia-New Zealand region. The other dairy regions are smaller and located in South Africa and South America. In Asia, dairying has developed in Japan, South Korea, China, India, Pakistan, etc. but most of the production is consumed locally. Figure 7.3 depicts the world distribution of dairy farming.

Figure 7.3
Dairy farming areas of the world

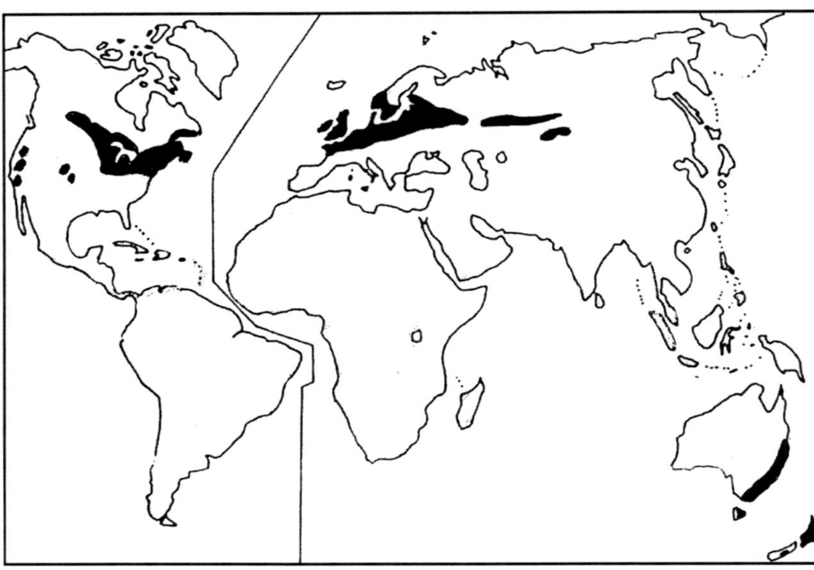

A brief description of the countries having developed commercial dairy farming is as follows:

United States of America

The United States is the largest milk and butter producer in the world and also leads in cheese production. It has a large domestic demand for dairy products and has only a small surplus for export. Exports, mainly in the form of canned milk, are sent to the Far East. The chief dairying regions are Hay and Dairy Belt south of the Great Lakes in the states of Wisconsin, Minnesota and parts of Dakota. Along the Atlantic seaboard dairying is widely practised in the states of New York, New Jersey, Pennsylvania and some of the New England states.

Canada

The dairy region of Canada is a continuation of the US region. Dairying activities are also important in the Lake Peninsula and the St. Lawrence lowlands of Canada. The heavy concentration of population and industries in this part of north-east North America creates a huge demand for fresh milk and other dairy products. Nowadays Canadian dairy industry has experienced a massive improvement. Ontario Peninsula and Maritime provinces now produce the bulk amount of milk and milk products.

Europe

Almost all the European countries have important dairying industry. But the leading producers are France, Germany, Denmark, Netherlands, UK, Switzerland, etc.

France leads in the production of milk, butter and cheese. The main dairying regions are Normandy, Flanders, the Paris basin, Brittany, the Rhone delta, and the Vendee. Dairy cattle are also kept in upland areas such as the Vosges, Jura, Alps and Central Massif. However, there is not a large demand for milk, wine being preferred, and most of the production goes to make butter, specially in Normandy, and as many as 300 different types of cheese, some of which are world famous.

Germany is a leading producer of milk and butter, the chief dairy farming regions being in the marshy lands of the north, the Bavarian Foreland, and in upland regions such as the Central Uplands and the Alps.

In *Denmark,* dairy farming is the main agricultural occupation and it is one of the world's leading butter exporters. Denmark combines dairy production with pig rearing and is also a major exporter of bacon. The highly developed co-operative farming system in Denmark has helped farmers to take advantage of new techniques and output is of very high quality. Danish milk yields per cow are amongst the highest in the world.

The *Netherlands,* with its lush polderland pastures is also an important producer of dairy goods and has very high milk yields. It is the leading exporter of condensed, evaporated and powdered milk.

In *Switzerland* about 70 per cent of available agricultural land is used for dairy farming, and transhumance is practised in the rugged mountain valleys. Butter, milk and cheese are all important and the dairy products are also used in the important chocolate industry.

UK produces about 4 per cent of the world's milk and is an important producer of cheese.

The major dairying regions are the Central Lowlands of Scotland, the Lancashire and Cheshire plain, the lowlands of Herefordhire and Gloucestershire, the Vale of York, the Hampshire basin, south-west England, coastal areas in South Wales, and many parts of Northern Ireland. Milk yields are high, and apart from fresh milk production, the making of cheese, condensed and evaporated milk and chocolate is well-developed. Dairying is often combined with pig and poultry rearing, and the UK is a major pork and egg producer.

Other European dairying countries include southern Sweden, Austria, Czechoslovakia and Italy. In Italy the main dairy-farming region is the Lombardy Plain. Milk and butter are less important than cheese production. Butter is replaced by olive oil, and wine is preferred as a drink to milk. Other countries such as Bulgaria and Greece are also noted for cheese production.

Russian Belt

Earlier, USSR was the largest producer of milk and butter, but because of its disintegration the production of dairy products have been reduced. Now apart from Russia other countries of this belt like Estonia, Lithuania, Latvia, Byelorussia have also become dairy-producing countries. Kazakhstan also has dairy industry. But the production of milk and other dairy products of all these countries is limited to their own consumption.

New Zealand

New Zealand is a major dairy-farming country with more than 2 million dairy cattle, but owing to the smallness of its population more than half of the milk produced is processed into butter or cheese for export. New Zealand is the world's leading butter exporter. The leading markets for New Zealand butter are Britain, the USA and Japan. The main dairying regions are on the wetter west of the North Island: the Auckland Peninsula, the Taranaki Lowlands, the Waikato Hauraki District, and in scattered areas of the Eastern Lowlands (Figure 7.4).

Figure 7.4

Dairy farming and cattle rearing areas of New Zealand

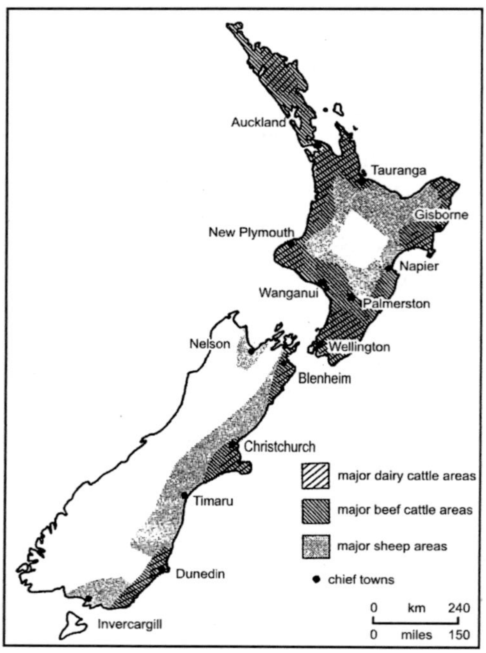

Dairying is modelled on the Danish co-operative system with more than 200 central dairies, creameries and bacon factories. New Zealand has over 600,000 pigs that are fed mainly on the residual skimmed milk from the many creameries. New Zealand has all the ideal conditions for dairy farming: (i) a mild oceanic climate, (ii) well-drained ground, (iii) rich pastures, (iv) good communication lines, (v) scientific farm management, and (vi) government-sponsored research centres in dairy science and animal breeding. All New Zealand dairy products are of high quality and in great demand throughout the world.

Australia

Australia is more noted for ranching than for dairying because much of the country suffers from unreliable rainfall, and 70 per cent of the continent receives rainfall less than 510 mm (20 inches) per year. Commercial dairy farms are thus restricted to the more humid south-east in the states of Victoria, New South Wales, and parts of Queensland. Much of Australia's milk output is required for use in the large cities but a large proportion is converted into butter for export.

South America

In south America Argentina and Uruguay are the main producers of dairy products. But their production is limited for local consumption. In Argentina dairy industry has developed in the La Plata region. Uruguay also has small dairy output. The dairy cows in this region graze on sown alfalfa and fodder crops.

Africa

In Africa, only South Africa and Zimbabwe have significant dairy farming output, but this is very small by world standard.

India

India is an important country in terms of milk production. India accounts for 7.2 per cent of the world's milk production. Although, India has the largest number of dairy cattle in the world, but their yield is very low. Dairy industry in India is not done scientifically and most of the milk produced is consumed locally. Punjab, Haryana, Gujarat, Maharashtra, western Uttar Pradesh, Rajasthan and Madhya Pradesh are the important milk-producing states in India.

BEEF CATTLE REARING (MEAT INDUSTRY)

One of the main objectives of cattle rearing is to obtain meat or beef. Beef cattle are much more widely distributed than dairy cattle because they are more hard and can tolerate wider range of physical and climatic conditions. They can survive on sparse pasturage. Beef cattle rearing is also the means of livelihood for thousands of people in many areas of Asia and Africa. While in many countries like Argentina, Australia, New Zealand it is done for the commercial purpose. Due to the introduction of refrigeration in the 1880s, the international trade in beef expanded rapidly. Chilled meat is transported in cold storage chambers at a temperature just below freezing point, so that it arrives in the consuming countries in fresh state. There is a considerable trade in corned beef (canned, cooked meat), beef extracts, ox-tongues and other prepared and cooked canned beef products.

There are several breeds of beef cattle. Western Europe is the home of many beef cattle breeds. The *Aberdeen Angus* breed originated in Abesdeenshire, Scotland. It was first imported into the USA in 1850 and now a new breed, the *Red Angus* become important. The *Hereford* breed now cross-breed called *Polled Hereford,* developed in US and Canada. The Scotland breed of north-east England, the *Galloway* of south-west Scotland, the *Devon* of south-west England, the *Highland* of Scottish highland are some of the very important breeds of beef cattle, now widespread in many countries. There are several other local and regional breeds of beef cattle found in various countries of the world.

World Distribution of Beef Cattle

The spatial distribution of beef cattle in the world is quite widespread but there is concentration in certain areas. USA, Brazil, China, Argentina, Russia, France, India, Mexico, Germany, Canada, Italy, Ukraine, UK, Columbia and New Zealand are important beef-producing countries. Figure 7.5 shows the distribution of cattle in the world.

A brief analysis of the beef cattle and meat industry in important countries of the world is as follows:

Figure 7.5
World distribution of cattle rearing

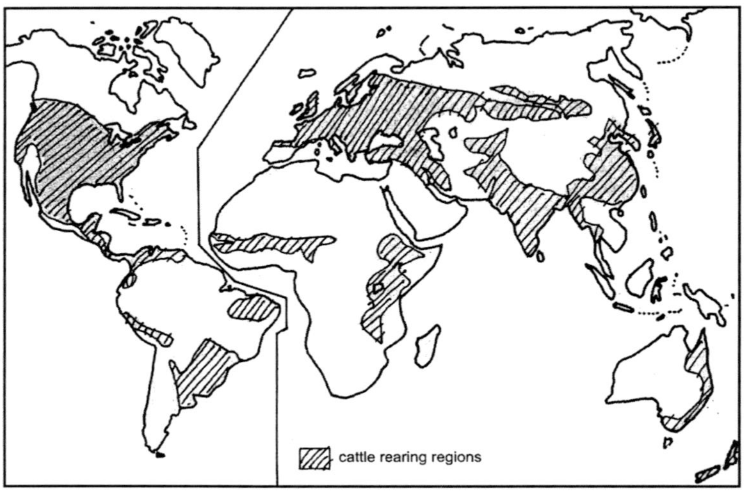

United States of America

The USA is the largest beef producer in the world and produces more than 20 per cent of the world's beef production. But because of large local demand for beef it has little surplus for export. Western Prairie region is the largest one where cattle for beef are reared and when they reach maturity they are taken to the cattle-fattening areas. Traditionally cattle were fattened in maize field of the Corn Belt. The grassland of west are extensively utilised for grazing cattle. Large concentration of beef cattle occur in the corn-producing states of Iowa, Illinois, Nebraska, other north-central states and Texas. Chicago is the largest meat-producing centre of the USA. Now production of beef has also developed in southern part, particularly in Florida.

Argentina

Argentina has about 5 per cent of world's cattle population, but majority are kept for beef. In spite of large beef consumption, Argentina has surplus for export.

Argentina exports about 15 per cent of its production mostly to USA, European and Arab countries. The vast Pampas grassland provides excellent facilities for ranching. Improved cattle variety – Aberdeen, Angus and Herefords were introduced in the last century. The vast cattle farms or *estancias* may be 10,000 hectares in extent and are manned by gauchos (cowboys). Small estates are called *chacras*. The fodder used for cattle is *alfalfa grass* and maize. The maritime climate allows grazing to go on all round the year. The cattle are rounded up and sent by rail to *frigoificos* or slaughter houses of the major towns such as Buenos Aires and Rosario. The meat is exported in chilled or frozen form.

Figure 7.6
Livestock rearing in Argentina

Brazil

In Brazil beef cattle are found on the plateau lands extending from southern Goias to Minas Gerais to the southern part of the country. Brazil produces nearly 13 per cent of the world's beef. The best beef is produced in Rio Graude do Sul.

Australia and New Zealand

Australia is also a major exporter of beef. Beef cattle are kept mainly in the north of the country on the Savanna grassland and it is more successful than in many tropical areas.

Cattle are also kept in the more humid south-east. More than a third of Australia's cattle (mainly for beef) are found in Queensland and another third in New South Wales and Victoria (for both beef and milk).

In New Zealand, as in Europe, the cattle are kept not on huge open ranges but on fairly small farms, and are carefully fed to give high quality meat. Dairy farming is much more important than beef production but New Zealand is nevertheless a major beef exporter.

European Countries

Although dairying is more important in Western Europe, but beef production is also significant in some countries. In some areas rich pasture lands are available for beef cattle, as in Ireland, the Cornish Peninsula of England, and the Brittany Peninsula in France. France, Germany, Italy and Great Britain are leading beef producers in western Europe. Since demand of beef is more, most of the beef demand is fulfiled through import from other countries.

Asian Countries

In Asia, China, India, Pakistan and Japan cattle rearing is done both for dairy as well as for beef. In India, the number of cattle are largest in the world, but production of beef is limited due to religious consideration. The beef produced in Asian countries is consumed locally.

Apart from the above, other beef-producing countries of the world are Russia, Mexico, Italy, Ukraine, Columbia, Uruguay, Venezuela, South Africa, Ethiopia, Tanzania, Kenya, Uganda, etc.

SHEEP REARING

Sheep are reared either for wool or for meat (mutton or lamb). Apart from wool and meat, sheep may also yield milk, but they are rarely kept for this purpose.

Generally speaking, sheep are less valuable animals than cattle. They are smaller and yield less meat. Moreover mutton and lamb are not popular in many countries so that markets are more restricted. However, sheep can live in much more rigorous climatic conditions than cattle. They can live on the scanty pasturage of semi-arid regions, in rocky, exposed upland areas and even in very wet regions such as North Wales. They do not do well in tropical regions, but even in Malaysia, a few are found. Sheep are very often not economic to keep in well-favoured agricultural areas but are of some importance in marginal agricultural regions, where huge flocks are kept. Sheep farming is therefore associated with regions of sparse population. The use of marginal land for sheep rearing sometimes leads to overgrazing with consequent soil erosion and impoverishment, as for example in Mediterranean and semi-desert areas. Sheep farms, especially in Australia, are often badly affected by drought.

Although sheep can thrive in poor areas and often produce fine wool in such conditions, sheep kept for meat require *better pasturage* if the quality of the meat is to be good. They are therefore kept in rich lowland pastures, or animals raised in the marginal lands are brought to the better areas for fattening and conditioning before slaughter.

The main wool-bearing sheep breed is the Merino. The *Blackface* of Scottish Highland yields better meat but poor wool. The *Cheviot* breed is used both for meat and wool. *Leicester, Lincoln, Romany March, Black Welsh, Rough Fell* and *Swallowtail* are other important breeds of sheep.

World Distribution of Sheep

Sheep are more widely distributed than any other domesticated animal, but majority are kept for wool rather than meat, especially in semi-arid regions. Mutton and lamb are not consumed so widely as beef and the main regions where they are eaten in large quantities are Britain, the drier parts of Eurasia and North Africa. While the sheep-raising regions are mostly located in the southern continents, China, Russia and some of European countries. The world distribution of sheep is shown in Figure 7.7.

Australia

Australia is the largest wool-producing country in the world and produces about 32 per cent of the total world's wool. Production is partly because the climatic and vegetation condition are well-suited to sheep. The *dry climate* of much of Australia is ideal for wool production, though temperatures are too warm in the northern part of the country. The poor grassland vegetation is also suited to sheep, though the farms must be very large to provide adequate pasturage for the large numbers of animals kept. In the drier parts of the country sheep are kept mainly for wool and Australia is the world's leading wool producer and exporter. Australia is also

Figure 7.7
World distribution of sheep

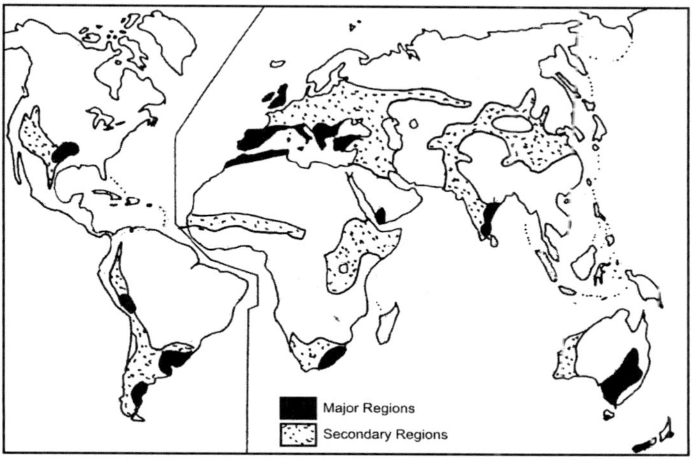

the second largest producer of lamb and mutton and is a major exporter. The sheep raised for lamb are kept mainly in the south-east of the country, where the climate is more humid and where the pasturage is better. They are fed on improved pastures or kept on arable farms where they graze the wheat stubble or graze on ley pastures. The states of New South Wales and Victoria have the largest numbers of sheep and produce most quantity of meat.

They have the advantage not only of better natural conditions but also of the nearby markets in the large towns and cities, such as Sydney and Melbourne. While Merino is the major breed kept in Australia as a whole, increasing numbers of such breeds as Leicester, Lincoln and Romney Marsh are kept for meat, with wool as a by-product. Australians eat much lamb and mutton but also export large quantities in chilled or frozen form.

New Zealand

New Zealand is the second largest producer of wool in the world and produces 16.4 per cent of the total wool production of the world.

Despite its small size, New Zealand has the fourth largest number of sheep in the world, most of them kept primarily for lamb production. New Zealand is by far the largest lamb and mutton *exporter*. The main markets for New Zealand lamb are Britain and the USA. This situation is made possible by the large-scale use of refrigerated ships to transport the meat round the world. The mild, maritime climate; the predominance of a type of mixed farming geared especially to animal fattening; the use of fertilisers and sown pastures and the proximity of the farming areas to ocean transport routes, are the main advantages which have given New Zealand a lead in lamb production. Meat production is highly efficient and the lamb is of high quality.

The main area of sheep rearing is located in southern Island, especially the Canterbury Plains and its adjoining of areas. The other regions, where both meat and wool sheep are kept are Auckland Peninsula, the Hawkes Bay region, Tarauaki and Wangarui of the North Island and Otago region of South Island.

Argentina

In *South America,* sheep rearing is most important in the direr parts of *Argentina* including the whole of Patagonia, Tierra deal Fuego, western Argentina and the eastern foothills of the Andes. The low and variable rainfall, the poor pasturage, the severe winter and the sparse population, all make the region more suitable for sheep grazing than for cattle rearing. The sheep ranches are extremely large in Patagonia, covering several hundred thousands of hectares each, because it needs many hectares of this semi-arid land with its bunchy grasses to support a single sheep. Argentina is an exporter of both wool and mutton and Patagonia alone contributes between a third and half to the national output.

South Africa

South Africa has about 31 million sheep, almost all of which are kept for wool. The large majority are merinos and South Africa is therefore the second largest producer of high-quality of merino wool. Sheep are mostly kept in eastern Cape Province, in Transvaal, and in Orange Free State. The dry climate of Veld, its grassland vegetation and plateau relief are ideal for sheep. The sheep reared are almost exclusively merino breeds kept for wool, of which South Africa is a major exporter. Most of South Africa's output of mutton or lamb is consumed locally.

China

China is the third largest wool-producing country in the world and produces about 11 per cent wool of the total world production. In China sheep rearing is mostly done in the large 'empty' areas of the west.

United Kingdom

Sheep rearing is a major occupation in the United Kingdom either by itself or as part of the mixed farming system. Sheep kept on mixed farms graze on arable stubble or ley pastures. Britain has for centuries been a sheep raiser and an exporter of pedigree sheep. It is on British sheep breeds that most of the world's commercial flocks are founded. Mutton and lamb are such popular meats in Britain that despite its own considerable production the UK also imports large quantities. The principal British sheep areas are generally those where crops cannot be grown or where cattle cannot be kept. They include the rough pasture lands of the Scottish Highlands, the Southern Uplands of Scotland, the Cheviot Hills, the Pennines, the Lake District and the Welsh mountains.

USA

Sheep are relatively unimportant in the USA, since they give much small returns than cattle. Some sheep are kept in most parts of the country but majority are kept for meat. Lamb in not a favourite in the USA. Local wool supplies are supplemented by imports.

In addition to the above, other sheep-rearing countries in the world are India, Uruguay, Pakistan, Sudan, Russia, Turkey, Spain, Romania, Algeria, Portugal, France, Iran, Afghanistan, Ethiopia, Kenya, Nigeria, etc.

GOATS

Goats are kept as a source of milk, meat and hides. Goats are able to survive on very poor pastures and, in fact, will eat almost anything including farm or household refuse, grass, the leaves of trees and so on. They are extensively kept in the *drier* and more *densely peopled* parts of the world, where the pasturage is too poor or too restricted in area for cattle farming, and where the climate is too warm for large-scale sheep production. The main areas in which they are reared are North Africa and the Sahara, the Middle East, Central Asia, India and Pakistan, China, South-East Asia and East Africa, but generally speaking, fewer goats are kept than either sheep, cattle, or pigs. Goats, like sheep, are voracious grazers and eat down the grass to ground level. Where too many are kept in semi-arid areas, the result is often overgrazing and soil erosion.

Certain types of goats, specially those with long silky hair are also kept for their hair which is used for making things in the same way as wool. The most important goats of this type are Angora goats of South Africa and Turkey and the Kashmir goat which is found in Kashmir and the western Himalayas.

PIGS

Pigs are reared for their meat known as pork. Pork is an important foodstuff and large quantities of processed pork, e.g. bacon, ham are produced in many parts of the world. Pig is an animal which can survive on anything that is given, including domestic and farm wastes, roots, leaves and rice bran. But the best forage crops for pigs are maize, barley, rice, oats, sorghum, alfalfa, clover, soya beans, etc. In USA largest number of pigs are found in Corn Belt. Pigs are easily kept indoor or outdoor and their growth is also rapid. The pigs are easily fattened and reach peak condition within 4–6 months. The quality of pork is very high and therefore fetches a good price. The pigs are also reared even in most densely populated parts of China where pasturage is too scarce for much animal farming.

The world distribution of pig is not restricted by climatic conditions. It can be reared anywhere either indoors or outdoors. But pigs are not domesticated in many areas due to religious considerations.

China is the most important pig-rearing country, accounting for more than a third of world's swine. In countries of eastern and south-eastern Asia pig rearing is done. *Korea, Hong Kong, Japan* and the *Philippines* are important pig-rearing countries.

In Europe, *UK, France, Italy, Germany, Denmark, Poland* and *Netherlands* all have large number of pigs. The greatest bacon specialists and leading world bacon exporters are Denmark, France, Netherlands and Poland.

USA and *Canada* are also having large number of pigs. The main concentration of pigs is in the Corn Belt, especially in the states of Iowa and Missouri. Large numbers of pigs are also found in dairy region of Southern Wisconsin.

Brazil, Russia, Argentina, Vietnam, Australia, Spain, etc. are the pig-rearing countries.

FISHERIES

Fishing is a primary economic activity and an ancient occupation in many of the coastal parts of the world. At present also fishing is a common activity in all parts of the world where suitable conditions exist. Fishing is practiced in those waters which afford at the same time a suitable land base for fishery and abundance of fish of the species in demand for human consumption. Fish provides an important source of protein in the diet for much of world's population. In many parts of the world, both developed and developing, fish is a predominant source of high-quality animal food. Over the long period of development of human civilization, fishing has been changed almost completely from what it used to be in their earlier period. Large fishing vessels carrying nets capable of harvesting large areas of sea have replaced the traps and arrows of the yesteryears. These ships can fish for several days and process and preserve fish. Today fishing has become a modernised and commercial industry in the world.

Types of Fishing/Fisheries

Fisheries are commonly divided on the basis of their volume or economic importance and according to their location. When fishing is done for the own consumption or for limited local consumption, it is known as *subsistence fishing.* This form although more prevalent in earlier time, is still seen in many parts of developing countries where fishing is done for the use of family only. This practice is common in South-East Asian, South Asian, African and Latin American countries, where small quantity of fishing is done either in local ponds or in small rivers. Contrary to this, another type of fishing is the *commercial fishing.* Commercial fishing is largely done in the oceans and in big lakes and its main objective is trade, i.e. to supply in various regions/ parts of the world. The largest areas of commercial fishing are the coastal margins in the temperate regions which are rich in fish that are most desirable for human consumption.

Another classification of fisheries is according to their habitat. There are two broad categories of fisheries:

(i) Freshwater fish

(ii) Marine fish

(i) *Freshwater fish:* This is also known as *inland water fish* and grown in the lakes, ponds, rivers, canals and, sometimes, even in paddy fields of south-east Asia. Due to low income and easy availability, inland fishing is very common in Afro-Asian and Latin American countries. Even in Europe and America, inland fishing is done as a part of commercial fishing.

The total quantity of inland fish in the world is million tons. A rare type of inland fish is the *Catadromous* fish, which migrate from fresh water to marine saline water for breeding purpose.

(ii) *Marine Fish:* There are two types of marine fish, first *coastal fisheries* and second *open-sea fisheries.* About ninety per cent of the world fish production come from marine or sea-water fisheries. The coastal fishing depends on the favourable geo-economic conditions, i.e. population of adjacent lands, the number and location of shallow coastal indentations, variety of species of fish, available means of transport, etc. The coastal fishing is common in low-latitudes and low-middle latitudes. The *open-sea fishery* areas of the world are wide spread in ocean water, but the most important areas are:

(i) European North Atlantic from Northern Spain to the White Sea in Northern Russia,

(ii) American North Atlantic from southern New England to northern Labrador, and

(iii) Asian Pacific from southern China to northern Kamchatka.

Marine fish includes *Pelagic fish, Demershal fish* and *Anadromous fish*. *Pelagic fish* are smaller in size and breed in shallow water. Major pelagic species include Herrings, Mackerel, Sardine, Pilchard, Brisling, Manhaden, Anchovies, etc. *Demershal fish* is larger in size and generally obtained down to a depth of about 200 metres. It's major species are Cod, Halibut, Sole, White Fish, Hake, Tuna, etc. *Anadromous fish* is mostly found in shallow and marginal sea as well as in inland water river for breeding purpose. Salmon and Hilsa are two main species of anadromous fish.

Production of Fish

The world fish production is given in Table 7.2. It becomes clear from this table that in 2014 the total fish production was 93.4 million tons. Of this total 81.5 million tons, i.e. 87.25 per cent was marine fish and remaining 18.5 was inland fish. There is not much variation between 2009 and 2014 fish production. In 2009 the total fish production of the world was 90.2 million tons, which becomes 93.4 million tons in 2014. The top ten producers of the fish in the world and their production is given in Table 7.3.

Table 7.2

Fish production in the world (2009 to 2014)

Category	*Production (in Million Tons)*					
	2009	*2010*	*2011*	*2012*	*2013*	*2014*
Inland	10.5	11.3	11.1	11.6	11.7	11.9
Marine	79.7	77.9	82.6	79.7	80.0	81.5
Total	90.2	89.1	93.7	91.3	92.7	93.4

Source: FAO – The State of World Fisheries and Aquaculture, 2016.

Table 7.3

Top ten fish producing countries of the world

Country	*Production in Thousand Tons*
China	14,811
Indonesia	6,016
USA	4,954
Russian Federation	4,000
Japan	3,630
Peru	3,548
India	3,418
Vietnam	2,711
Myanmar	2,707
Norway	2,707

Source: FAO – The State of World Fisheries and Aquacultures, 2016.

China is the largest fish producing country in the world. It's production in 2014 was 14,811 thousand tons. Indonesia and USA are second and third largest fish producers respectively followed by Russia, Japan and Peru. India is at the seventh rank in word's fish production with 3,418 thousand tons of fish production in 2014.

Factors Favourable for Commercial Fishing

In the world there are certain areas which are suitable for commercial fishing. Temperate regions are more favourable for fishing in comparison to tropical regions. The geo-economic factors responsible for the development of fishing are as follows:

Plankton Availability

The basic food supply for fish is the plankton. The tiny unicellular marine organism is known as plankton. These are of two types – phytoplankton and zooplankton. The growth of plankton requires: (i) *Shallows seas* are suitable for phytoplankton, therefore, ideal commercial fishing grounds develop within 200 metres depth of continental shelf, where planktons are plentiful (ii) *Temperature difference* – Planktons grow in abundance where cold and warm currents meet. The famous fishing ground is located where Gulf Stream (warm) and Labrador (cold) currents meet. Similarly in Pacific Ocean, Kuroshio (warm) and Kurile (cold) current meeting place is the major fishing ground.

The other major areas of phytoplankton growth are the water over continental shelves. These areas receive additional supplies of nutrients from rivers discharging into the sea.

Climate

As described earlier, temperate climate is more suitable for fishing than the tropical climate. Although, fishing is also done in tropical areas but tropical fish lack taste. Infact, commercial fishing is mostly done in temperate areas.

Nature of Coastline and Fishing Ports

The type of coastline, the nature of the land behind the coast, the transportation facilities in the area, and the size of market all contribute to the importance of a fishing port in a region. The absence of sheltered deep-water harbours, and the formation of sea ice in winter tend to limit commercial fishing. Most countries with a commercial fishing industry have a few large fishing ports with quick access to the densely populated areas. Larger catches and expanding markets necessitate better handling facilities at the ports. Modern fishing ports have good transportation facilities to nearby urban areas, plants for freezing, filleting, curing, and processing fish.

Rates of Carbon Fixation

As per expert opinion, rate of carbon fixation is important to attract fish community. Marine biologist said that, per day reach cubic metre of water should not have more than 0.3 gram calorie fixation rate. Most of the upwelling systems in temperate region have optimum carbon fixation rate.

Market

Fish is a perishable product. It needs to be moved quickly to the market before it spoils. Large catches from distant places need to be kept in good condition for longer periods of time. Nowadays, bit fishing vessels have freezing plants on board for storing large quantities of fish. Freezing and canning allow the fish to reach the consumer in a comparatively unaltered from. The demand for fish and nearby market are an added attraction for fishing. The problems of a lack of local demand, and remoteness from markets have inhibited commercial fishing in the southern Hemisphere.

Other Factors

Some of the other factors favourable for fishing are:

(i) Preservation facilities
(ii) Cheap labour
(iii) Skilled fishermen
(iv) Food habit
(v) Transportation
(vi) Lack of agriculture and other occupations
(vii) Lack of alternative protein source
(viii) Financial support, and
(ix) Government patronage and research facilities.

Major Fishing Areas

Fishing areas of the world can be divided into two groups:

1. Temperate Fishing Areas
2. Tropical Fishing Areas

Temperate Fishing Areas

Most of the temperate fishing areas are located in the northern hemisphere, although, in southern hemisphere also temperate fishing areas exist. The major fishing ground are:

(i) The north-east Atlantic region
(ii) The north-west Atlantic region
(iii) The north-west Pacific region
(iv) The north-east Pacific region
(v) Temperate fishing ground of southern hemisphere

The North-East Atlantic Region

Northeast Atlantic and the adjacent water of the Arctic, extending from Norway to Great Britain and Iceland, constitute a major fishing region of the world. The region is known as the world's best cod-fishing grounds. Besides Cod, Herring and Haddock are the other important contributors to the catch. Norway, Great Britain, Denmark, Iceland and Greenland are the important fishing countries of this region. The important fishing banks in this region include the Grand Bank and St. Pierre Bank.

The North-West Atlantic Region

This region extends along the eastern coast of Canada and US and includes the famous Grand Banks and the Georges Bank. Canso Bank, Sable Island Bank, la Have Bank, Brown's Bank and Middle Bank are also situated in this region. Convergence of the Labrador Current and Gulf Stream near the New Foundland enhances fish productivity in this region. *Cod* is the most important fish of the region. Other important varieties caught in this region include halibut, squid, flounder and red fish. Menhadden and shrimp are important varieties caught in the Gulf of Mexico. In terms of the total catch, *menhadden* is the most important fish caught in the United States. Canada and US are the most important fishing nations in this region.

The Northwest Pacific Region

This region extending from the Aleutian Islands in the north to south-eastern Asia, contribute nearly one-third of the world's fish catch. The seas are fished in varying degree of intensity by all the bordering countries, i.e. Russia, Korea, Japan, China, Philippines, and Indonesia. A wide continental shelf and the meeting of the warm Kuroshio current from the south and the cold Oyashio current from the north cause a dense fish population. Salmon leads the output from the area. Herring and cod are the other varieties of fish of great commercial significance in the northern part. In the warmer waters of the south, Tuna, Mackerel, Sardines are caught in large numbers.

The North-East Pacific Region

The region extends from Alaska to California and owes its importance to the large quantities of Salmon and Tuna as well as significant amounts of halibut and sardine. Salmon dominates in the north near the mouths of the Columbia and Fraser rivers and Bristol Bay in Alaska. Halibut and herring are caught in the cool Pacific waters. Southward in the California current, tuna is abundant, followed by pilchards and mackerel. Salmon canning was first established in California, Oregon, Washington and British Columbia (Canada). Canned salmons are exported to many parts of the world. More than half of the world's Halibuts are caught between Cape Blanco (Oregon) and Dutch Harbour in the Aleutian Islands of Alaska. Most of them are landed at Pouget sound ports and at Prince Rupert in British Columbia. A thriving Oyster industry has been developed in Puget Sound, Gray's Harbour, Willipa Bay, and Chincoteague Bay of Maryland and Virginia.

The Temperate Fishing Grounds of Southern Hemisphere

In southern hemisphere temperate fishing areas are located in two major regions, first south-east Pacific region and south-east Atlantic region.

South-East Pacific Region

This is also one of the major fishing ground of the world and the percentage share of this region in global fish production is now over 15 per cent. This region extends over Peru and Chile Coastal areas. Various species of fish-cod, herring, sardine, etc. are abundantly available in this area.

South-East Atlantic Region

This region extends along coast from Angola to South Africa. This region is comparatively a new commercial fishing ground which produces nearby 5 per cent of global fish production. The major fish species available in this area are herring, haddock, halibut, cod and mackerel.

Tropical Fishing Areas

Tropical fishing is limited in comparison to temperate fishing. It is mostly confined within tropical regions. China, India, Indonesia, Peru, Chile, Thailand, Sri Lanka, etc. are the tropical countries which are leading fish producing countries. Inspite of climatic and other physical disadvantages these countries are now producing large quantity of fish. This is possible because of their vast market, skilled human labour, use of technology, existence of open shallow seas, lack of alternative occupation and abundance of fish species.

Figure 7.8

Major fishing areas of the world

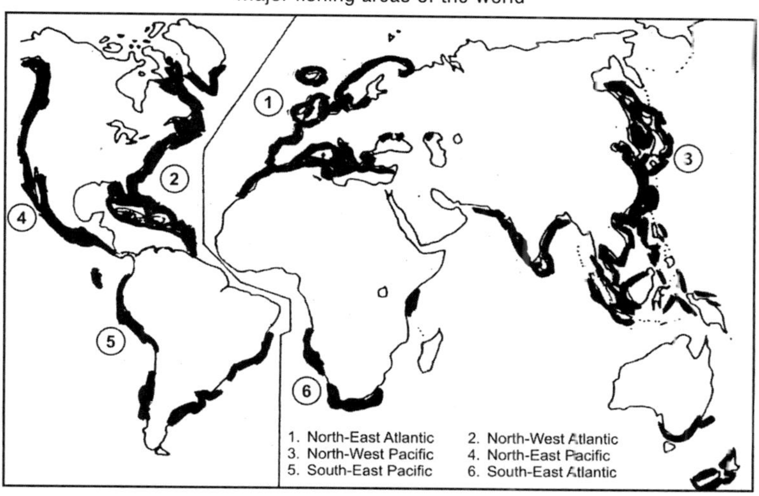

Problems and Management of Fisheries

Fisheries, now has become an important activity and after 1990s, witnessed tremendous increase of fishing activities all over the world. Like any other economic activity, fisheries are also now facing several problems and need proper management for sustainable development. Some of the problems of fisheries are as follows:

(i) Too much exploitation of certain specific fish species, therefore, danger of their depletion now has become a problem in some fishing areas.

(ii) Fishing areas like north Atlantic and north-east Pacific suffered badly by over exploitation of fish.

(iii) With the increase of population in coastal areas and development of other infrastructure has adversely affected the number of fisherman and total fish harvest.

(iv) Current fishing practices are neither foolproof nor earning much profit, unless greatly subsidized.

(v) Fishes are being exploited for industrial purpose than as a protein source.

(vi) Coastal pollution, promotion of tourism and industrial development in coastal areas is a great threat to the fishing activity.

(vii) A sizable amount of fish has been discarded for one reason or other and turned into wastage. This waste material is also responsible for land, water and air pollution.

(viii) The fishermen are now facing several socio-economic problems, specially the conditions of labour class is not upto the standard.

A proper management is required for the sustainable development of fishing industry. Some general suggestions for the management of fisheries are as follows:

(i) Fish harvesting quota be reduced to at least 25 per cent of present level.

(ii) Through international treaty and agreement, maximum limit should be fixed for each country.

(iii) Wastage in fishing industry should be minimised by adopting modern technology.

(iv) Policy for the betterment of fisherman and their families should be adoped by each country.

(v) Modern equipments, boats, etc. should be provided to fishermen.

(vi) Policy of co-operative or community management by adopted.

(vii) Strict checks are necessary to control the water, land and air pollution in coastal areas.

(viii) Planned development is necessary for the sustainable coastal development in areas where fishing is done.

(ix) To conserve the endangered fish species, policy of sustainable development be introduced

(x) Plan for long-term and short-term development of fishing should be prepared.

(xi) There should be a common international policy for fishing and trade.

(xii) Research in the field of aquaculture should be a part of the development of fishing industry.

8

Mineral Resources

Minerals are of vital significance to every country because it is the minerals which make possible the power and machine. The tools and machines which modern man uses are fashioned primarily from minerals taken from the earth. Modern civilisation is in many respects, dependent on mineral products. The development of fundamental science, engineering and technology has made it possible to extract and use a great variety of minerals in increasing proportion. Mineral resources are, however, fixed in quantity; they cannot be increased or replaced. Once minerals are extracted from the earth, they are gone forever. It takes probably millions of years for nature to turn earth substances into minerals. From a practical viewpoint, therefore, mineral deposits are exhaustible and mining is considered as a 'robber industry'. In fact, minerals are decreasing rapidly and in future, civilisation may be threatened by their shortage unless it is counteracted by new discoveries. Owing to the difficulties of renewing supplies, their conservation demands high priority, particularly of those minerals which are available in small quantity and also of those, supply of which is being exhausted rapidly due to great demand.

Minerals occur in three states according to the geological conditions under which they have been formed. The greater number, including most of the non-ferrous metals, have been introduced into the crust of the earth in a fluid condition, have solidified and have been exposed either in mines or on the surface of the earth by the natural forces of denudation. Minerals thus accumulated have been redistributed in some instances by percolating waters or ascending gases and solutions. Chemical changes may have taken place in the ores; they have either become enriched or impoverished and the actual deposits have assumed forms often of indescribable and indecipherable complexity. Minerals have, lastly, been laid down on the surface of the earth by normal agents of deposition.

The distribution of minerals is governed by well-defined geological conditions. Their distribution is the outcome of geological action in the past. Generally, three groups of rocks are associated with the recurrence of minerals. These are:

(i) *The Pre-Cambrian Rocks:* These are oldest igneous rocks composed of basement complex in its most contorted or compressed form. These rocks contain rich metallic minerals, e.g. gold, silver, copper, nickel and iron ore.

(ii) *Sedimentary Formations of Cambrian and Post-Cambrian Period:* These rocks contain resources like coal, petroleum, potassium and magnesium and some non-ferrous metals.

(iii) *The Geological Structures Associated with Volcanic Activity:* Some of the world's most important reserves of minerals like copper, lead and zinc, tungsten, vanadium, molybdenum and manganese, etc. are found in rocks, especially those of tertiary age and are the result of volcanic activity.

Factors Affecting Exploitation of Mineral Resources

The possession of minerals cannot decide the prosperity of a country, because existence of a mineral ore is no guarantee that it will be exploited. Often they are found in such a small proportion as to be almost unavailable and, hence, not useful for man. Before a mineral can be worked it must be ascertained whether its value is greater than the costs of working, transporting and concentrating the ore. The main factors influencing their exploitation are as follows:

(i) *Richness or Grade of the Ore:* The abundance or otherwise the absence of minerals determines in a large measure their commercial exploitation. Ores vary in their metal content. Generally the higher-grade ores are more economic to work, not only because they yield large amount of metal but also because their higher metal content makes them easier and cheaper to smelt. Minerals of high value such as gold, diamonds, copper, uranium, can often be mined at very high cost, because they are in great demand and fetch high prices.

(ii) *Size of Deposit:* The size of deposit is important because mining requires a large amount of expensive equipment. It will not be worthwhile to provide such equipment to work a deposit which will run out in some months. Small-scale working is only profitable for precious minerals. Sometimes, small deposits may be worked out profitably where transport cost is low.

(iii) *Method of Mining:* The method of mining depends on the mode of occurrence of the ores. The open-cast mining is the cheapest, while shaft mines are very expensive. The cost of mining also depends on the scale of operations. If the mining has been done at a large scale, the capital and running costs can be offset.

(iv) *Accessibility:* The accessibility of a region where the particular mineral deposit occurs is of great significance. The terrain and climate determine accessibility which helps or hinders the mining operations.

(v) *Transportation Facilities:* For a successful mining transportation facilities are very essential. Not only for the mining but it is also necessary for mined ores to be transported at the sites of their use. Ores are relatively bulky and heavy. They are thus costly to transport and the shorter the distance to be covered the better. The deposits having coastal location or located near industrial sites have an advantage over those far inland.

(vi) *Stage of Industrial Development:* The stage of industrialisation of a country is the general index of the exploitation of her mineral wealth. In fact, mineral exploitation is cumulative in the industrial cycle. The vast mineral resources of China, India and Brazil almost remained neglected till they marched on the path of industrial development.

(vii) *Technology:* Technological changes pertaining to mining methods, manufacturing processes and the like may change once worthless deposits are converted into esteemed commercial ores. The techniques of geological survey has now been changed. With the help of remote sensing techniques, one is able to estimate the reserves of mineral resources of a region. Other technological changes have changed the pattern of exploitation of mineral resources.

(viii) *Other Factors:* Among other factors (a) cheap labour supply, (b) competition from other sources, and (c) economic system and tariff policies are notable.

Classification of Minerals

There are several types of minerals, but according to their general characteristics and commercial use, they are classified as follows:

1. *Metallic minerals:* Metallic minerals are being used for a very wide range of purposes. These are sub-divided into the following groups:
   (a) Iron.
   (b) Base metals such as tin, copper, aluminium, lead and zinc.
   (c) Ferro-alloys such as manganese, chromium, nickel, cobalt, tungsten, molybdenum and vanadium can be alloyed with iron to produce better steel.
   (d) Precious metals like gold, silver and platinum.
   (e) Others include uranium, which has specialised uses.
2. *Non-metallic minerals:* These minerals are used for structural purposes, chemicals and various industries. The more common non-metallic minerals are asbestos, mica, graphite, fluor spar, sulphur, diamonds, phosphate rocks, gypsum, etc. Certain precious stones, e.g. diamonds are also non-metallic minerals.
3. *Mineral fuels:* Coal, petroleum and natural gas are the mineral fuels. These three are also known as *fossil fuels.*
4. *Rocks:* Rocks are also aggregations of minerals. Those commercially exploited include granite and other crystalline igneous and metamorphic rocks. These are used as building stones, road-metal, brick making, cement making, etc.

Production and distribution of important minerals like iron ore, manganese, copper, aluminium, tin, lead, zinc, nickel, chromium, tungsten, etc. the world over, is described below:

IRON ORE

Iron is a basic mineral and the most useful of all the metals. The success of almost every industrial enterprise depends upon the extensive and efficient use of machinery and other economic equipment made wholly or in part from iron and its alloys. Iron ore has unique importance in the modern world. It provides steel which is the basis of all industrialisation. It has been worked since pre-historic times. Though iron is a newcomer compared with copper and bronze, more than 3,000 years ago it was used to make implements and weapons. Today, it is an essential metal in the structure of civilisation. Without it, there would be no railways, steamships, or machinery. Apart from its use in the construction of chemical plant, iron and some of its compounds are vital in certain chemical processes. Iron is also used as a catalyst in the production of synthetic ammonia and iron pyrites – a sulphide of iron in sulphuric acid manufacture. But its main use is in making the steel. Iron ore smelted in a blast furnace with coke and limestone becomes pig iron, the raw material from which cast iron, wrought iron and steel is made.

Types of Iron Ore

There are four types of iron ore, viz., Magnetite, Haematite, Limonite and Siderite.

(i) *Magnetite* (Fe_3O_4): This is the finest type of iron ore with a very high content of iron up to 70 per cent. Magnetite is black in colour and formed in igneous or metamorphic rocks. It has excellent magnetic qualities.

(ii) *Haematite* (Fe_3O_3): The iron content in this ore is between 50 to 65 per cent and is the most important industrial ore in terms of quantity used. Haematites are red ores derived from sedimentary rocks and occur in crystalline or in powdery forms.

(iii) *Limonite* ($2Fe_2O_3H_2O$): The iron content in this ore is less than 50 per cent. This is a brown ore occurring in sedimentary rocks over large areas of the world. It also sometimes occurs in swamps, where it is known as bog iron.

(iv) *Siderite* ($FeCO_3$): This is a carbonate of iron, ash-grey in colour, and is found interbedded with sedimentary rocks. Its iron content is usually between 20 to 30 per cent.

Production and World Distribution

Iron ore-producing areas are widely distributed in the world. There are about 60 countries in the world, which produce iron ore. China, Brazil, Australia, India, Russia, Ukraine, USA, South Africa, Canada, Sweden, etc. are the main producers of the iron ore. The total world production fo iron ore in 2015 was 3,320 million metric tons. Table 8.1 indicates the iron ore production in important countries of the world.

Table 8.1

Iron ore production of important countries 2015

Country	*Production (in thousand metric tons)*
China	1,380,000
Australia	824,000
Brazil	428,000
India	129,000
Russia	112,000
South Africa	80,000
Ukraine	68,000
USA	43,000
Canada	39,000
Sweden	37,000
Iran	33,000
Kazakhstan	25,000

Source: www.worldatlas.com.

The world distribution of iron ore-producing areas is shown in Figure 8.1.

Figure 8.1
World distribution of iron ore-producing areas

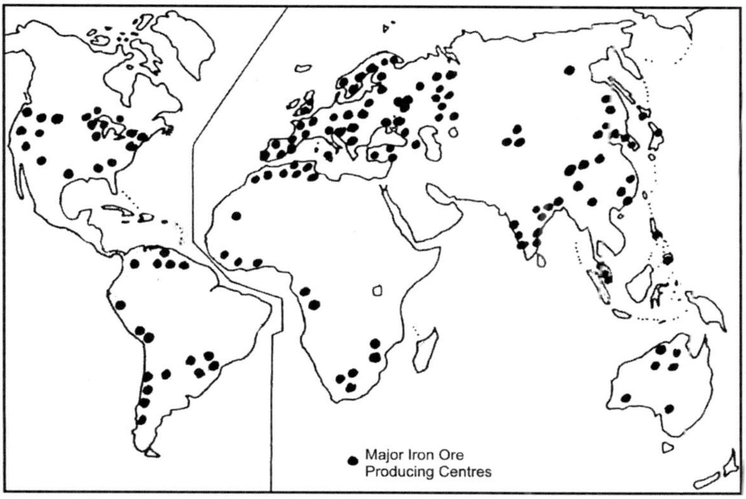

China

China now emerged as a leading iron ore-producing country in the world. Till 1975, its production of iron ore in the world was only 6.5 per cent, but in year 2000, China produced 24.3 per cent iron ore of the world. This percentage further increased to 30.77 in year 2006–07 and 41.56 per cent in 2015, accordingly China is now first in iron ore production in the world. Its production of iron ore is 1380 million tons in 2015 . China has large iron ore deposits, of which the Manchurian deposits are the most actively mined. Other important regions are the Lower Chang (Yangtze) at Ma'anshan and Tayeh, the Chungking area, and around Taiyuan. Scattered deposits occur in the peninsula, north of Baotou (Paotow), border of Xinjiang (Sinking), at Kiuchure, in the lower Xi Jiang (Si Kiang), near Guangzhou (Canton), and on the island of Hainan in the south.

Australia

Australia produced 824 million metric tons of iron ore in 2015 and ranks second in world production with 24.81 per cent production. Australia has widely distributed iron ore deposits and reserves which are very large. The recent working of vast iron ore fields in Western Australia at Mt. Goldworthy, Mt. Whaleback, Mt. Bruce, Mt. Tom Price, and at Yami Sound has greatly increased production. In Southern Australia, the largest deposit occurs in Iron Knob, Iron Monark, etc. Australia exports most of its iron ore to Japan and European countries.

Brazil

Brazil is the world's third largest iron ore-producing country contributing 12.89 per cent of the world's total production. Till 1975 its percentage in world production of iron ore was 9.2. The main iron ore-producing areas are located in Itabiria in south-east Brazil. Itabiria is believed to be the richest iron ore reserves in the world – estimated reserves of 35,000 million metric tons. Brazil's other important areas of iron ore are: Urucum (Mato Grosso), Catalao (Goias) and Ipanema (Sao Panto). The Carajas iron ore reserve is now identified as one of the main reserves of Brazil. Largely due to the output of this region, Brazil now leads the world in iron ore exports.

India

In 2015, India produced 129 million metric tons of iron ore, also the fourth largest producer of iron ore in the world. On an average, India produces about 3.88 per cent of the world production. It has about 2.6 per cent iron ore reserves of the world. The leading states and their iron ore-producing areas are as follows:

1. *Chhattisgarh:* Arindogi, Raoghat and Bailadia (Bastar), Dhalli – Rajbara (Durg), etc.
2. *Odisha:* Keonjbar, Mayurbhanj and Diringburi districts.
3. *Karnataka:* Babudan hill, Hospet, Chitradurg, Tumkur, Sandur and Bellary districts.
4. *Jharkhand:* Noamundi, Notaburu, Pansiraburu, Budaburu, Guo, Barajamada, Meghahataburu in Singhblim district.
5. *Andhra Pradesh:* Anantpur, Kurmool, Adilabed, Karimnegct, etc.
6. *Goa:* Bicholim, Sirigao, Mapusa, Netarlim, etc.
7. *Maharashtra:* Pipalagoon, Asola, Lohara in Chandrapura district.

Mostly India's ore deposits are concentrated in the north-east of peninsular India in the states of Jharkhand, Chhattisgarh and Odisha. Other fields have been discovered in many parts of the country, among them Andhra Pradesh and Karnataka iron ore mines are notable. India also exports large amount of iron ore through Paradip, Muruagao and Vishakhapatnam ports to Japan, Poland, UK, etc.

Russia

The undivided USSR was the leading iron ore-producing country in the world. As shown in Table 8.1, in 1960 and 1975, the production of USSR was 21.2 and 25.4 per cent respectively of the world. But, in 2000 and 2006, it was 6.3 and 6.21 per cent respectively. Now, Russia ranks fifth in iron ore-producing countries of the world. In year 2015 the production of Russia was 112 million metric tons.

The three main areas of iron ore in Russia are:

(i) *Ural Region:* This region is having a high-grade ore and produces about 25 per cent of the country's total. Magnitogorsk, Novotrotsk, Zlaloust, Nizny Taghil and Seerow are the main areas of this region.

(ii) *Moscow:* Tula region also known as Kursk Magnetic Anomaly is having large reserve of iron ore. This region produces high-grade iron ore. Orel and Veroneth are two major areas of this region.

(iii) *North-West Russia:* In this region Murmansk and Kovador are significant mining areas of iron ore.

In Russia, most of the iron exploitation and associated industrial development is concentrated near Moscow. Many rich deposits were found in Siberia also.

Ukraine

Ukraine is the sixth leading producer of iron ore in the world and it produced 2.04 per cent of the world production in 2015. Krivoi Rog of Ukraine possesses best iron ore having 68.5 per cent metallic percentage. It contributes 75 per cent production of Ukraine. The estimated reserves of the region are more than 200 million tons. Other regions of Ukraine are Zaporozhe, Zdanow, Lipetsk and Kerch Peninsula.

USA

Once USA was the highest iron ore-producing country of the world. The percentage of world production of iron ore was 18.1 in 1960 and 9.8 in 1975. But now it produces less than 2 per cent of the world's production and ranks 8th. The four main iron ore-producing regions of USA are Lake Superior region, north-eastern region, south-eastern region and western region.

(i) *Lake Superior Region:* In this region haematite iron ore occurs as long low ridge, the most important of which is the Mesabi Range. Other deposits occur in the Vermilion, Cuguna, Gogebic, Menominee and Marquette ranges. This region comprises north-eastern Minnesota, Michigan and south-eastern Wisconsin states.

(ii) *North-eastern Region:* Mainly magnetite ores are mined in the Adirondacks region of New York and the Cornwall area of Pennsylvania. They have the advantage of a central location near the industrial cities of New York and Pittsburgh.

(iii) *South-eastern Region:* This region, centered at Birmingham, Alabama, produces both haematite and limonite ores. It is favourably located near the coalfields of the southern Appalachians and serves the iron and steel industry of Birmingham.

(iv) *Western Region:* This includes many scattered fields in western USA in the states of Utah, Nevada, Wyoming and California. The ores are transported to the steelworks at San Francisco, Los Angeles, Pueblo, Colorado and Provo, Utah.

South Africa

South Africa, emerged as a leading iron ore-producing country of the African continent and ranks 7th in the world iron ore production. In South Africa Transvaal is the main iron ore-producing centre. Transvaal is having high-grade ore with 60 to 65 per cent iron content. The total reserves have been estimated at 10 billion tons in South Africa. The production of iron ore in South Africa was 80 million metric tons in 2015.

Canada

Canada produces 1.17 per cent of the total world production of iron ore in 2015. Canada has iron ore in the Lake Superior region, as does the USA. The main centres are Schefferville and Wabush City. The iron field covers some 51,800 sq km and is estimated to have 400 million tons of iron reserves. Ore is taken by rail to Sept Isles on the Gulf of St. Lawrence and shipped via St. Lawrence Seaway and Great Lakes to Canadian and US steel-making centres.

Sweden

Sweden is a major iron ore producer in Europe and ranks 10th in the world production. It produces 1.11 per cent of the total iron ore production in 2015. The major iron ore mines of Sweden are located at Kiruna, Malmberget, Dannemore, Grangeberg, Falun, Fargesta, etc. The ore is having high grade magnetite iron, in which iron content is 65 per cent. Sweden used to export about 80 per cent of its production to its neighbouring European countries.

United Kingdom

In the 19th century Great Britain was the leading producer of iron ore of the world but now it is no more in prominence and most of its ores have been exhausted. The area of eastern England is the most important in output of iron ore stretching from Yorkshire through Lincolnshire, Rutland, and Northamptonshire. UK is now a major iron ore importing country.

France

The major producing areas of France are Lorraine, Normandy and Pyrenees. The Lorraine district supplies about 95 per cent of country's total. Though the metallic content of the ores is about 35 per cent on the average, it can be smelted at a low cost because of calcium carbonate content in the ore. It is the largest single ore-body reserve in Europe. It helped much in setting up steel plants in France.

Germany

The major iron ore-producing areas of Germany are located in West Germany, these are: Saar Vogelsburg, Erzeburg and Westphalia. Germany has considerable reserves of medium quality of ore located in the eastern part of Rhine valley, Siege and Lahn river valley.

Spain

The main areas of iron ore in Spain are Bilbao, Oviedo and Santander of Iberian Peninsula.

Africa

In Africa, apart from South Africa, other countries having iron ore mining are Tunisia, Algeria, Morocco, Liberia and Mauritania. Mauritania is the 15th iron ore-producing country of the world, which has produced 0.65 per cent iron ore of the world in 2006.

Asia

There are many areas in Asia, apart from China and India, which are having iron ore and also produce a limited quantity. The most notable ones are Iran and Kazakhstan, which rank 12th and 13th respectively in the world. North Korea, Taiwan, Malaysia and Philippines also produce iron ore.

Latin America

In Latin America, Mexico, Venezuela, Chili and Peru are the iron ore-producing countries, other than Brazil. Mexico ranks 14th in world production and its share was 0.77 per cent in 2006. Venezuela has rich iron ore reserve in the Guiana Highlands at Cerro Bolivar and El Pau. Chile exploits deposits around Algarroba in Central Chile and Peru has mines in the Nazca Marcona area.

Iron Ore Reserves of the World

E.W. Zimmermann, in his book *World Resources and Industries* (1972), has explained the difficulty in estimation of iron ore reserve, he states, "A survey of world iron deposits is so great a task that it can be undertaken only once in a great while, in the meantime the world moves on. Demand expands or contracts, the centre of economic gravity shifts, political borders shift and new regimes mean new politics and laws, transportation conditions change, new areas are explored, new processes are invited that turn the dust of the yesteryear into the ore of today, and vice versa." But now new techniques have been developed and reserves can be estimated to a great extent. The following table indicates the iron ore reserves in the world:

Table 8.2

Iron ore reserves of the world

Country	*Estimated reserve (in crore tons)*	*Percentage of the world*
Ukraine	68,000	18.9
Brazil	67,000	15.5
Russia	56,000	15.1
China	46,000	12.4
Australia	40,000	10.8
Kazakhstan	19,000	5.1
USA	15,000	4.1
India	9,800	2.6
Sweden	7,800	2.1
Venezuela	6,000	1.6
Canada	3,900	1.1
Iran	2,500	0.7
South Africa	2,300	0.6
Mauritania	1,500	0.4
Mexico	1,500	0.4
World	37,00,000	100.00

Source: US Geological Survey.

It becomes clear from the above table that Ukraine, Brazil, Russia, China and Australia are having major reserves of the iron ore. The total reserve of iron ore in the world is estimated as 37,000 billion metric tons.

MANGANESE

Manganese is a ferro-alloy metal and essential to the production of steel. Almost all steel contains some manganese from 0.5 per cent to 12 per cent. A little manganese added to iron removes gases, and acts as a 'cleanser' in manufacture of steel. The addition of 2 per cent manganese adds strength and 12 per cent imparts great toughness and resistance to abrasion, as in the making of heavy duty machinery, railway lines, dredge – bucket teeth and jaws by rock crushers, etc. Manganese compounds are used in making disinfecting liquids, as a decolouriser in glass-making and for the manufacture of bleaching powder. It is alloyed with copper to produce a kind of manganese – bronze and with a little nickel 'manganin' which is highly resistant to corrosion. Manganese is also used in making electric batteries, in colouring pottery, tiles and bricks.

There are two main commercially exploited manganese ores: pyrolusite (MnO_2) and psilomelane. The other types are bronite, manganite, hosmanite and polianite.

Production and World Distribution

The main producers of manganese in the world are South Africa, Australia, China, Gabon, Kazakhstan, Brazil, India, Ghana, Ukraine, Georgia and Mexico. The production of manganese in the world is given in Table 8.3.

Table 8.3

Production of manganese in the world – 2016

Country	*Production (in thousand metric tons)*	*World percentage*
South Africa	4700	29.37
China	3000	18.75
Australia	2500	15.62
Gabon	2000	12.50
Brazil	1100	6.87
India	950	5.93
Ghana	480	3.00
Ukraine	320	2.00
Mexico	220	1.37
Malaysia	200	1.25

The total world production of manganese was 16 million tons in 2016, although it is less metric tons 2015 production of 17.5 million metric tons. The world distribution of manganese has been depicted in Figure 8.2.

South Africa

South Africa now emerged as a leading producer of manganese in the world and its share is 29.37 per cent in the world manganese production in 2016. The important manganese-producing area of South Africa is the Cape Province where Krugersdorp, Postonasburg, Manganore are the major mining areas.

China

China once a highest manganese-producing country in the world, but now it ranks second. Its production in 2016 was 3 million metric tons which was 21.6 per cent of the total world production. The major manganese-producing areas of China are Kiangsi, Hunan, Kuangsi, Kwangtung, Kuangsi and Kwichou.

Figure 8.2
World distribution of manganese

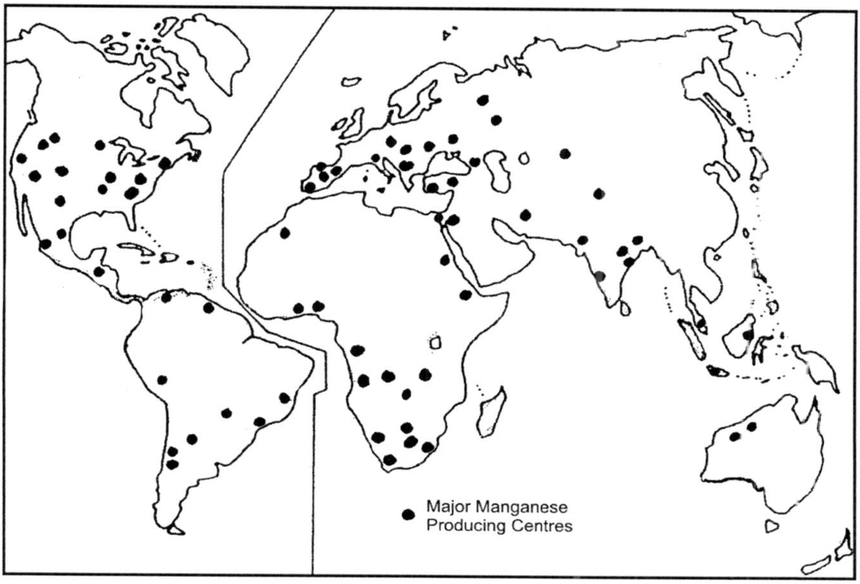

Australia

The manganese production of Australia is 15.62 per cent of the total world production. The manganese-producing areas are located in Leonara, Victoria, Queensland and Woodie Woodie in western Australia.

India

Although India ranks 6th in the production of manganese in the world, but its reserves are of considerable importance because it possesses the largest manganese reserves in the world. At present, manganese is produced in Odisha, Madhya Pradesh, Chhattisgarh, Maharashtra, Jharkhand, Andhra Pradesh and Karnataka. It produced 5.93 per cent manganese output of the world. The main manganese reserves exist in a 1,250 km long belt stretching from Vadodara (Gujarat) in the west to the Damodar valley (Jharkhand) in the east.

Gabon (12.5%), Brazil (8.9%), Ghana (3%), Ukraine (2%), Mexico (1.37%) and Malaysia (1.25%) are other important manganese-producing countries of the world. Brazil's reserves of manganese are very large. Large deposits occur in Minas Geras and Mato Grosso provinces. Limited amount of manganese is also available in Angola, Zairia, Zambia, Egypt, Chile, Japan, Malaysia, Indonesia, Iran, Turkey, etc.

COPPER

Copper is a soft brown metal found almost solely in igneous and metamorphic rocks. It was one of the earliest metals used by man because it often occurs in a pure state and because it is very easily worked. The use of copper was recorded in Egypt as early as 5000 BC, and in the Far East around 2500 BC. It was also very extensively used in Cyprus giving the island its name. Copper is unfortunately very soft, but by mixing tin with copper, bronze can be obtained, which is harder and tougher than pure copper and more suitable for weapons and tools. The Bronze Age in history thus marked a significant milestone in the progress of human civilisation for metals began to be widely used. The present-day industrial significance of copper began only with the invention of electricity.

Copper is useful because of its various advantages. Copper is used in:

(i) Electrical engineering
(ii) Metallurgical industries
(iii) Making of alloys
(iv) Others such as for making tubes, pipes, pumps, radiators and boilers. It is also used in soldering, welding and brazing as well as for attractive appearance in wide range of ornamental uses.

Copper occurs in three forms: (i) as native metal in its pure state, (ii) as oxides, and (iii) as sulphide. Commercial copper ores are not obtained from copper oxides or copper sulphides with a copper content of 2 to 6 per cent. Most copper mines are operated by the open-cast method and are highly mechanised.

Production and World Distribution

Copper is found in every continent and produced in more than 40 countries of the world. The main producers of copper in the world are Chile, Peru, USA, China, Australia, Indonesia, Russia, Canada, Zambia, Poland, Kazakhstan and Mexico. The world production of copper is given in Table 8.4.

Table 8.4
Production of copper in the world

Country	*Production in thousand tons*	
	2014	*2015*
Chile	5,750	5,760
China	1,760	1,710
Peru	1,380	1,700
USA	1,360	1,380
Congo	1,030	1,020
Australia	970	971
Russia	742	732
Zambia	708	712
Canada	696	697
Mexico	515	594
Others	–	3800

Source: US Geological Survey.

The world distribution of copper is shown in Figure 8.3.

Chile

Chile is the largest producer of copper in the world. It produces 30.15 per cent of the world copper and its production in 2015 was 5760 thousand metric tons. In

Figure 8.3
World distribution of copper

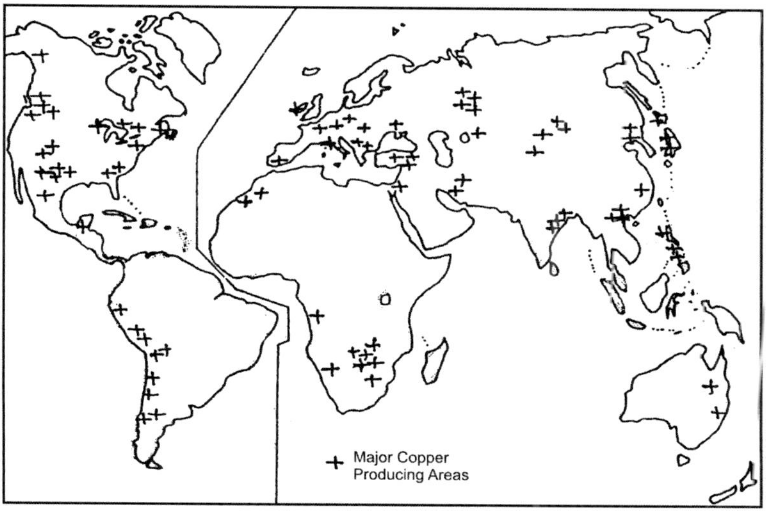

Chile most of the copper mines are located on the western side of the Andes. The important copper-producing areas of Chile are Chuquicamata, El Teniente, El Salvador and La-Africana. Chuquicamata is the largest copper mine in the world.

China

China is the second largest copper producer in the world and produces 8.95 per cent of the world's production in 2015. Yunnan, Czechoau and Tangshan are the main copper-producing provinces.

Peru

The third largest producer of copper in the world is Peru. It produces 8.9 per cent copper of the world in 2015. The important copper mines in Peru are located at Cerro de Pasco, Morococha, Casapalca and Toquepala.

USA

In 2015, USA was the fourth largest producer of copper with 7.22 per cent of the world production. In USA five states are the main copper-producing states, these are Arizona, Utah, Montana, Nevada and New Mexico.

Canada

Canada accounts for 3.76 per cent of the world's copper production. Its main copper-producing areas are Ontario, Manitoba, Quebec and Saskatchewan. More than 80 per cent of Canada's copper production comes from Ontario and Quebec.

In Asia, apart from China, Indonesia, India, Malaysia, Iran, Turkey, Philippines and South Korea produce copper.

India produces only 0.4 per cent of the world's copper. India's copper ore reserves have been estimated at 40 crore tons, with a metal content of 51 lakh tons. The principal copper belt of India lies in Singhbhum and Hazaribagh of

Bihar. The mining centres are located at Mosabani, Ghatsila, Thobani and Badia of Singhbum, Hazariabgh of Bihar, the Khetri and Dariba area of Rajasthan and Agnigundala of Andhra Pradesh. Copper also occurs in the foothills of the Himalayas, Karnataka, Sikkim and Gujarat. Chitradurga, Kalyadi and Thinthuni are copper-bearing areas of Karnataka.

In Africa, Zambia, South Africa, Congo, Botswana, Morocco, Zimbabwe and Namibia are the copper-producing countries. Among them Zambia is the largest producer. Zambia produces 3.72 per cent copper of the world and ranks 9th among the copper-producing countries of the world. In Africa, a 480 km long belt extending from the northern part of Zambia north west across Katanga province of Congo Republic is the world's largest copper region. Democratic Republic of Congo ranks 5th in world's copper production and produce 5.34 per cent of the total copper production of the world.

In *Europe,* Poland, Spain, Portugal, Bulgaria, Sweden, Romania are having copper deposits. *Russia* is a leading copper producer and ranks 7th in the world copper production. It's percentage in world production is 3.83.

Australia is the sixth largest copper producer country in the world. It produces 5.08 per cent of the world production. Most of the copper mines are located in central Australia.

ALUMINIUM (BAUXITE)

Aluminium is not found in the native state as a pure metal. It generally occurs as an ingredient of chemical compounds in highly complex minerals. The following four are the natural compounds of aluminium:

(i) *Cryolite* is a double fluoride of aluminium and soda. It was first used as an ore and later in the electrolysis of alumina as a solvent. The west coast of Greenland is the only place where it is found in large quantities. Now, of course, it can be produced synthetically.

(ii) *Corundum* is a native alumina (Al_2O_3), i.e. aluminium oxide. It is used as an abrasive.

(iii) *Kaolin,* the alumina content being too low and silicate content being too high, is not used in aluminium extraction.

(v) *Bauxite* is the ore containing hydrated aluminium oxide as its important mineral and this is the only source from which aluminium is extracted commercially. Commercial bauxite should contain at least 50 per cent alumina (Al_2O_3) and less than 7 per cent silica. Bauxite is found chiefly in the tropics or in regions of tropical climate. Tropical climates favour the formation of bauxite.

Aluminium is the most abundant metal, making up to 8 per cent of the earth's crust, but its commercial use was not possible until 1886 when a young American chemist, Charles Martin Hall, and a Frenchman, Herault, perfected the Hall-Herault process of separating the metal from its ores. Before the 1890s aluminium was a relatively unknown metal and was very highly priced. With the large-scale smelting of bauxite into aluminium by the Hall-Herault process, the price of aluminium dropped drastically to a mere fraction of the former cost. Today, more than 14 million tons of aluminium are produced annually from almost 80 million tons of bauxite for use in a great range of industries.

Bauxite occurs quite near the surface and is generally mined by highly mechanised open-cast methods. Bauxite is first crushed, washed and dried in a rotary kiln at a temperature of 982°C and is chemically treated by the Bayer process, which removes the silica and concentrates the bauxite into aluminium oxide or alumina, a washed power. Then in a smelter, aluminium is separated electrolytically from the oxygen in the alumina. Once smelted, the aluminium is made into ingots and casts or sheets for the various uses.

Aluminium is an important metal because it combines strength, lightness and also has conductivity and great malleability. It has a wide range of uses. These are:

(i) *Structural uses:* Such as for constructional purposes, in making aircrafts, automobiles, rail wagons, coaches, ships as well as several household appliances.

(ii) *Electrical engineering:* Aluminium is used in making electrical cables because it has conductivity of electricity.

(iii) *Protective uses:* Aluminium has a very high resistance to corrosion, therefore, used for anodized aluminium as well as for aluminium paint.

(iv) *Aluminium alloys:* Where small quantity of copper, magnesium or manganese is added to aluminium, the alloys created are superior to aluminium. Another aluminium alloy containing about 12 per cent silicone is highly ductile and shock resistant.

(v) *Other uses:* Aluminium is used for making cooking utensils, aluminium foils, headlight reflectors, mirrors, etc.

Production and World Distribution

The production of bauxite is done in more than 40 countries of the world. The important bauxite producers are (their percentage in world's production is given in bracket): Australia (31.34%), China (18.41%), Brazil (13.93%), Guinea (8.36%), Jamaica (3.98%), Russia (1.64%), Venezuela (2.39%), Surinam (1.99%), Kazakhstan (2.44%), Greece (1.09%), Guyana (0.60%) and Vietnam (0.01%). The production of bauxite in top fourteen countries is given in Table 8.5.

Table 8.5

Major bauxite producers in the world

Country	*Production in thousand tons*	
	2014	*2015*
Australia	81,000	80,000
China	47,000	60,000
Brazil	32,500	35,000
Guinea	19,300	17,700
India	19,000	19,200
Jamica	9,600	10,700
Kazakhstan	5,500	5,200
Russia	5,300	5,600
Surinam	2,700	2,200
Venezuela	2,200	1,500

Cont'd...

...Cont'd

Greece	2,100	1,900
Guyana	1,800	1,700
Vietnam	1,000	1,100
Indonasia	500	1,000
Others	4,760	8,500
World	234,000	274,000

Source: US Geological Survey.

The world distribution of bauxite-producing areas is shown in Figure 8.4.

The world's greatest bauxite producers and exporters are the countries located in tropical and sub-tropical regions.

Australia is the largest producer of bauxite in the world. It accounts for 29.19 per cent of the world's production of bauxite and also has about 40 per cent of the bauxite reserves. The Cape York peninsula, New South Wales and western Australia are the main bauxite-producing provinces.

China accounts for 21.89 per cent of the world's total bauxite production in 2015 and ranks second in production. Hunan, Guichou and Sichuan are the main bauxite mining provinces.

Brazil is the third largest producer of bauxite in the world and contributes 12.77 per cent to world production. The central region is the main producing area.

India ranks 4th in bauxite production in the world and produces 7 per cent of the world production in 2015. Madhya Pradesh, Chhattisgarh, Jharkhand, Odisha, Maharashtra, Andhra Pradesh, Tamil Nadu and Gujarat are the major producers of bauxite.

Figure 8.4

Bauxite-producing areas of the world

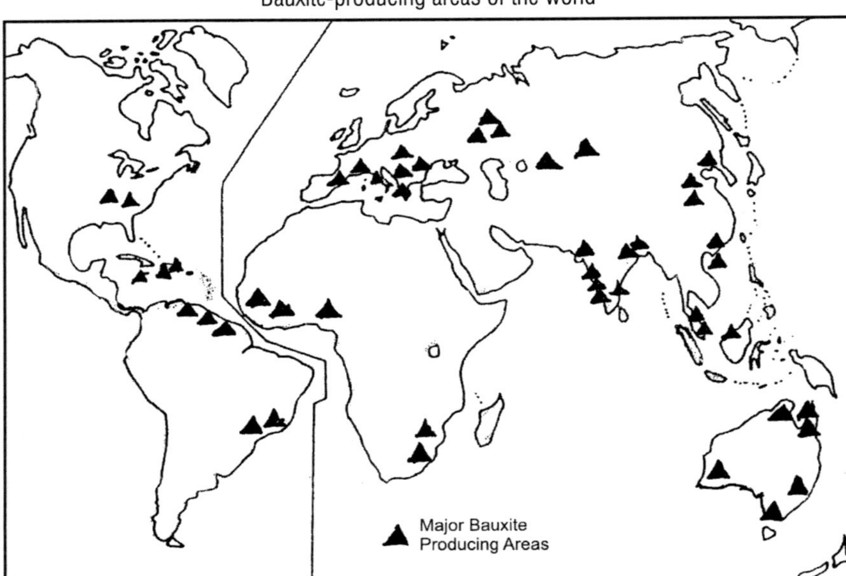

Guinea produces more than 6.45 per cent bauxite of the world and ranks 5th in the world.

Jamaica is also a leading producer of bauxite, contributing about 3.9 per cent of the world's output. Jamaica is also having large reserves of bauxite.

The other bauxite-producing countries are Venezuela, Surinam, Kazakhstan, Russia, USA, Greece, Guyana, Indonesia, Hungary, France, Turkey, Malaysia, Ghana, Sierra Leone, etc.

TIN

Tin was found and used in early times but it has only attained its present importance since the invention of tin cans. Tin is extensively used in the canning industry and as an alloy with copper in bronze. It is also used for coating thin sheets by steel as it is corrosion-resisting. Tin plating consumes about 40 per cent of the world's tin output. An electrolytic process is used to coat thin steel plates with a very fine layer of tin.

The principal ore of tin is cassiterite or tinstone (SnO_2) which contains as much as 75 per cent of tin. It occurs in veins and lodes in igneous and metamorphic rocks. Much tin is weathered out of the original rocks and carried by streams and rivers to be deposited in valley and plain alluvium. As much as 80 per cent of the world's supplies come from alluvial deposits. Mining is thus usually done by placer methods. Several methods are in use in Peninsular Malaysia and other parts of South-East Asia.

Production and World Distribution

The tin-producing areas of the world are limited in certain pockets and very unevenly distributed around the world. Nearly 75 per cent of the total output comes from China and Malaysia. The major producers and their percentage share in the world is given in Table 8.6.

Table 8.6

Important tin-producing countries in the world – 2016

Country	*Production (in thousand tons)*	*Country*	*Production (in thousand tons)*
China	125	Malaysia	3.5
Indonesia	84	Congo	3.0
Peru	23.7	Rwanda	2.0
Bolivia	18	Laos	0.8
Brazil	12	Russia	0.6
Myanmar	11	Nigeria	0.5
Australia	6.1	Thailand	0.2
Vietnam	5.4		

China

China has now emerged as a leading tin-producing country of the world. Now China produces 42.22 per cent of the world's output of tin in 2016. The main areas of tin mining in China are Yunnan, Nanking mountains, Kiangsi and Hunan. Apart from production China also has huge reserves of tin.

Indonesia

Indonesia is the second largest tin producer and produces 29.05 per cent of the total world's production. In Indonesia tin comes from islands of the northern coast of Sumatra including Bangka, Billiton and Singkil and there are also marine deposits in the strait of Malacca.

Peru

Peru is the third largest producer of tin in the world and contributes about 8.00 per cent to the world's total output. San Antonio de Palo is the main tin-producing area in Peru.

Bolivia

Bolivia is another South American country, which contributes about 6.08 per cent of the world's tin production. The high plateau of Bolivia is the main tin-producing area. On this plateau tin mines are located at high elevations, therefore, due to transportation cost, the production cost becomes high.

Brazil

Brazil is another South American country which produces about 12 thousand metric tons of tin in 2016. Its share to world production of tin is 4.05 per cent. Most of the tin is mined in north-eastern part of Boreborema plateau.

Malaysia

Malaysia was the leading tin-producing country in the world but due to increase of production in other Asian and South American countries its share in world production is only 1.18 per cent. All the tin fields are in Peninsular Malaysia and the Kinta valley alone accounts for half the annual output. Other major areas are the Larut Plain around Taiping, the Kelang valley around Kuala Lumpur, the Jelebu valley, Jemaluang and Kota Tinggi in southern Johor and Sungei Lembing.

Other tin-producing countries are Congo Democratic Republic, Rwanda, Nigeria, South Africa and Zimbabwe in Africa. Australia, Russia, Myanmar, Laos, Portugal, Spain, Thailand and Myanmar are other tin producing countries of the world.

LEAD

Lead is a useful metal because of its properties of softness, resistance to corrosion and malleability. Lead was one of the earliest metals used by man. It is very easily shaped into pipes or rods. The Romans used considerable quantities of lead to make pipes. Lead is a dull grey metal. The ore galena or lead sulphide, with a lead content of 85 per cent is commercially the most important source of lead. Lead seldom occurs in its native form and invariably contains some zinc or silver.

Lead is used for various purposes such as protective, plumbing, paint and lead alloys. It is widely used as a protective metal cover for undersea cables, roofing, as a lining in tanks containing acid. It is also used for making plates in storage batteries. Large quantities of lead are used in making pipes, tubes and joints. Another use of lead in making industrial paints such as white and red lead. Similarly lead is useful for alloying with other low melting-point metals such as zinc and tin. The other uses of lead is in making oxides which are used in glass-making, pottery, glazing, etc.

Production and Distribution

The world's total production of lead in year 2009 was 3,900 thousand metric tons. It was 3,143 thousand metric tons in 2003 and 3,280 thousand metric tons in 2005. According to an estimate the total reserves of lead in the world is 35 crore metric tons. The main producers of lead in the world are China, Australia, USA, Peru, Mexico, Canada, India, Bolivia, Poland, Russia, Sweden, Ireland and South Africa.

The production of leading lead producing countries is given in Table 8.7.

Table 8.7
Leading lead producing countries of the world – 2016

Country	*Production in thousand tonns*
China	2400
Australia	500
USA	335
Peru	310
Mexico	250
Russia	225
India	135

Source: US Geological Survey Report, 2010.

- *China:* China has now emerged as a largest producer of lead in the world. It produces more than 43 per cent of the world's lead. The main areas of lead production in China are Hunan, Kiring, and Lieaoning region.
- *Australia:* Australia is the second largest lead producer and contributed 13.23 per cent of world's production. Queensland and New South Wales are the main areas of lead production and also have large reserves of lead.
- *USA:* USA is the third largest lead producer in the world. Its share in world production is 10.26 per cent. Missouri state is the leading producer. Other lead-producing states are Idaho, Utah, Colorado, Washington and Arizona.
- *Peru:* Peru ranks 4th in lead production of the world. It produces 7.82 per cent of the total world's output of lead. The lead mines of Peru are located in the Andes at high altitudes.
- *Mexico:* The fifth largest lead producer in the world and produces about 4 per cent of the world's lead.
- *Russia:* Russia is the sixth largest lead producing country in the world and produces 3.2 per cent of the world lead production.
- *India:* India produces 2.26 per cent of lead in world's production. Rajasthan state is the only state where lead is produced. Lead ore deposits are known to exist in Agnigundala in Andhra Pradesh and Sargipalle in Odisha.

- *Canada:* Canada contributes 2.4 per cent lead to world's output. Most of the lead-producing areas are located in the mountains of south-eastern British Columbia. Other areas are located in Yukon and New Foundland.

Other lead-producing countries are Bolivia, Poland, Sweden, Ireland, South Africa, Korea, Japan, Myanmar, Iran, Turkey, Thailand, Brazil, Greece, Spain, Romania, Morocco, Namibia, etc.

ZINC

Zinc used to occur in various minerals. The ores of commercial value are chiefly sulphides, of which Sphalerite is the most important. It is used in galvanised roofing and siding sheets, wire fence, pails, etc. It is corrosion-resisting. It is found in association with ores of other metals, especially lead. So zinc-producing districts coincide with lead-producing areas. Its earliest use is said to have been in China and Sumatra and it was imported into Europe only in the 18th century.

Zinc comes from two main sources: zinc blende or zinc sulphide and calamine. It is often found with lead, silver and some other minerals. The ore is found close to the surface, therefore, open-cast method is generally used for mining. Zinc ore is crushed, and concentrated by the selective flotation process to separate it from lead, silver or copper with which it is combined. Sulphuric acid is an important by-product of zinc smelting.

Zinc is extensively used as a protective sheath for metals. Zinc plating is done on several metals. Zinc-plated sheets, zinc-covered bolts, nuts, screws, wires, fences, pipes, tanks and household utensils are also very important. Zinc is also used as alloys because it melts at very low temperatures and is used mainly with tin

Figure 8.5
Distribution of lead and zinc in the world

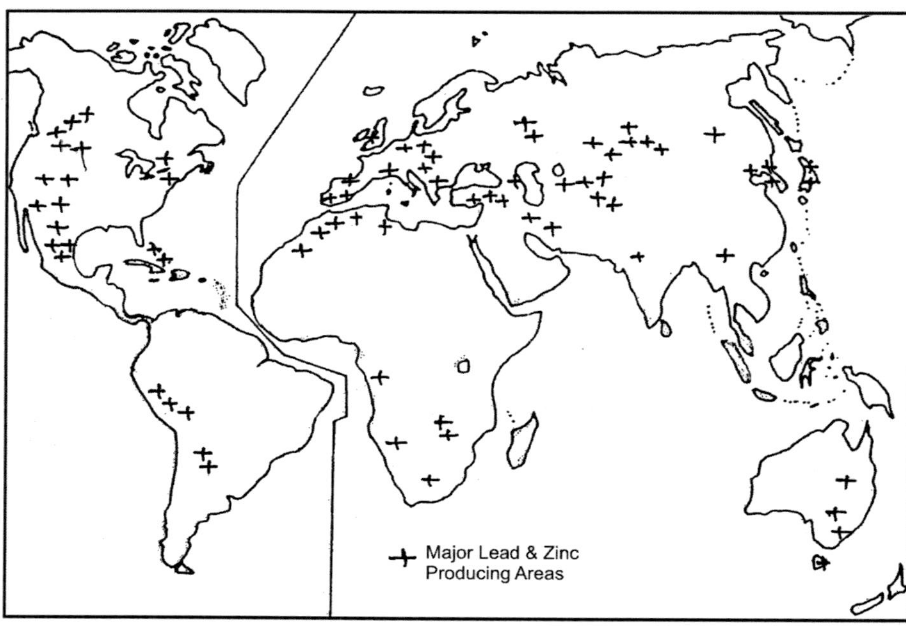

to produce brass, popular in the making of kitchen utensils, ornamental wares, etc. Zinc is also used to manufacture paints, dry batteries, boiler plates, cartridges, pipes, etc.

Production and Distribution

Since lead and zinc so often occur together, the major zinc producers are much the same as for lead. The main producers of zinc in the world are China, Peru, Australia, USA, Canada, India, Kazakhstan, Ireland and Mexico.

The distribution of Zinc-producing areas along with lead has been depicted in Figure 8.5, and production of leading zinc producing countries in the world is given in Table 8.8.

Table 8.8

Leading zinc producing countries of the world – 2016

Country	*Production*
China	4.5 million metric tons
Peru	1.3 million metric tons
Australia	850000 metric tons
USA	780000 metric tons
Mexico	710000 metric tons
India	650000 metric tons
Bolivia	460000 metric tons
Kazakhstan	340000 metric tons
Canada	310000 metric tons
Sweden	250000 metric tons

China

China is the largest zinc-producing country and produces about 45 lakh metric tons of zinc in 2016. Most of the zinc is produced in Yunan Province.

Peru

Peru is the second largest producer which contributes 13.79 per cent zinc in world's production. In Peru, Cerro de Pasco, Huaras and Ayacacho are the main zinc-producing areas.

Australia

Australia ranks third in zinc production and produces 12.59 per cent output of the total world's production. The main zinc-producing areas of Australia are Broken Hill in western New South Wales, Reed Elsevier, Western Queensland and Captains Flat also in New South Wales.

USA

The fourth largest producer of zinc in the world. It accounts for 6.71 per cent of the total world production of zinc. Arizona, Idaho, Colorado, Missouri, Oklahoma, Kansas, New Jersey, Tennesee, Virginia, Illinois and New York are having zinc mining areas.

Canada

Canada produced 310,000 metric tons of zinc in 2016 in total world output. British Columbia is the largest mining area not only in Canada but also in the world. Kimberley in British Columbia, Flin-Flon in Manitoba and Saskatchewan are the main areas of zinc mining.

India

In India, Rajasthan state is the leading producer of zinc. India ranks 6th in world production and it produces 5.86 per cent of the world's total zinc output.

Bolivia, *Kazakhstan* and *Sweden* are also leading zinc producing countries of the world.

Some other zinc-producing countries are:

(i) In South America: Brazil and Argentina.

(ii) In Asia (other than China and India): South Korea, Iran, Japan and Myanmar.

(iii) In Europe: Ireland, Spain, Greece and Ukraine.

(iv) In Africa: Morocco, South Africa, Namibia, Tunisia and Algeria.

NICKEL

Nickel is a hard and silvery metal, used in making stainless steel and for electroplating. It is one of the hardest, most malleable and least fusible metals known. It is less magnetic than iron and is thus useful for constructing metal parts located near compasses. The main ore of nickel is pentlaudite, a complex mixture of nickel, iron and sulphur. It is also often found in association with copper.

Most of the nickel is used in steel-making. An addition of 6 per cent nickel to steel increases its strength, stiffness and ductility, and this alloy is extensively used in making constructional machinery and transport equipment. While an addition up to 35 per cent makes steel highly resistant to heat and acid, which is used in manufacturing turbine blades, marine fittings, tools and machinery parts. Other alloys of nickel are nickel-copper and nickel-silver. Nickel is also used in making coins, marine cable, radio transponders, flame tubes, batteries, etc.

The total production of nickel in the world was 2.53 million metric tons in 2016. The important nickel-producing countries and their percentage in world's production is as follows: Philippines – 19.76 per cent, Russia – 10.11 per cent, Canada – 10.07 per cent, Indonesia – 13.11 per cent, Australia – 11.18 per cent, New Caledonia – 8.10 per cent, Australia – 8.14 per cent, China, Brazil, Cuba and Indonesia are other producers.

Some nickel is also produced in South Africa, Dominican Republic, Norway and Germany. In India nickel ore is found in Cuttack and Mayurbhanj districts of Odisha.

CHROMIUM

Chromium is a hard, silvery metal, essential in making stainless steel, cutlery, kitchenware, household fittings, surgical apparatus and chemical equipments. Chrome Steel is a superior steel used for marine and aircraft parts. Chromium is also used in making nickel-chromium alloys and chromite (chrome ore).

Similarly, chromium plating is done by electro-deposition of chromium on nickel or steel plates to improve their durability and resistance to corrosion and rust. Chromium salts and compounds are used in the manufacture of paint pigments and in the chemical industry.

The total production of chromium in the world was 30400 million metric tons in 2016. *South Africa* is the largest producer of chromium in the world. It produced 46.05 per cent of the total world production of chromium. *Kazakhstan* is the second largest producer, which contributes 18.09 per cent of the total production of chromium in the world.

Turkey is the third largest producer of chromium and its percentage in world production is 11.5 per cent.

India is the fourth largest producer of chromium in the world and its percentage in world production is 10.52. In India deposits of economic significance occur in Bihar, Karnataka, Maharashtra, Odisha and Tamil Nadu.

Other chromium-producing countries are Philippines, Albania, Brazil and Finland.

TUNGSTEN

Tungsten is a heavy metal, with a melting point higher than any other metal. Tungsten is widely used in steel alloys for the manufacture of high-speed cutting tools. Tungsten carbides are very hard than any other metal and employed in the cutting edges of machine tools, razor blades, armour plates, jet engines, rockets and missiles. While pure tungsten is used in making filaments of electric light bulbs. The chief source of tungsten is *Wolfarm* or *Wolframite,* often found in association with tin cassiterites in quartz veins.

In year 2016, the total output of tungsten in the world was 86,400 tons. *China* has a monopoly in tungsten production. China produces 82 per cent of the world's tungsten. The majority of the deposits occur in the Nanking Mountains of Southern China. Hunan and Kiangsi provinces are also important in tungsten production.

Vietnam is the second largest producer in the world and produces 6000 metric tons, i.e. 6.9 per cent of the world total in 2016.

Russia is the third largest producer and produces 3.02 per cent of world's tungsten.

Other tungsten-producing countries are Canada, Bolivia, Portugal and North Korea. The minor producers of tungsten are Kazakhstan, USA, Brazil, Zaire, Rwanda, Burundi, Australia, Spain, France and Sweden.

ANTIMONY

Antimony is obtained from stibnite and it also occurs in very small quantity along with copper, silver, gold and lead ores. Since antimony has a low melting point, it is used as alloys with lead. Lead-antimony alloys are used in making electric cables, pipes, bullets, foil and battery plates. Its chemical compounds are used in fire proofing materials, glass, rubber, paint pigments, etc.

The total world production of antimony is 1,500,000 metric tons. China is not only the largest producer but it also produces about 76.92 per cent of the world's antimony in 2016. Hunan and Kwangsi provinces are having large deposits of antimony.

South Africa produces 4.2 per cent of the world's production of antimony. Here antimony occurs as a by-product from gold mine in the Transvaal.

Russia produces 5.0 per cent and *Tajikistan* produces 6.15 per cent of world's antimony.

Bolivia and *Australia* also contribute 3.0 and 2.6 per cent of world's antimony respectively. Other antimony-producing countries are Peru, USA, Guatemala, Turkey, Mexico, Vietnam, Myanmar, Brazil and Kazakhstan.

VANADIUM

Vanadium is a hard silvery metal named after a Scandinavian goddess of beauty by its discoverer Sefstorm in 1830. The principal use of vanadium is in making alloy steels and iron. It acts as a 'scavenging agent' removing the non-metallic impurities. It also increases strength, ductility and resilience. The vanadium compounds and salts are used in making paints and dyes, coloured glasses and glazes and also used in chemical industry.

China is the largest producer of vanadium in the world followed by Russia with 58.33 and 21.05 per cent respectively in the world. The world total vanadium production in 2016 was 76,000 metric tons. *South Africa* is the third producer of vanadium. It produces nearly 15.78 per cent vanadium of the world. The other producers of vanadium are Finland, Chile, Namibia and Norway.

MOLYBDENUM

Molybdenum is a silvery metal having many properties similar to those of chromium. Molybdenite (MoS) is the principal ore, the production of which is given in terms of concentrates ranging from 48 to 49 per cent metallic molybdenum. Som molybdenum is also derived as a by-product of copper smelting.

The main use of molybdenum is in making alloyed steel for the manufacture of high-speed tools and machine parts. It is also used for making gas turbines and jet engines, because of its toughness and tensile strength. Pure molybdenum is used in the manufacture of electric lamps, valves, X-ray tubes, electrical contact points as well as in equipments used in space engineering.

The world production of molybdenum in 2016 was 225,200 metric tons. *China* is the largest producer with 90,000 metric tons production, followed by *USA*. It produces more than 31,600 metric tons. In USA, Colorado, Utah, Nevada, Arizona, California and New Mexico states are having molybdenum mining areas. The other molybdenum-producing countries in the world are Canada, Russia, Armenia, Iran, Mexico, Norway, Mangolia and Japan.

Apart from the above discussed minerals, there are also some precious metals like gold, silver and platinum. The production and distribution of these metals is described as under:

GOLD

Gold is regarded as a symbol of prosperity and has been used from the earliest days because of its high metallic luster and its attractive yellow-reddish colour. It is used in jewellery and in the manufacture of luxury articles. Because of its rarity, value and durability, it has always been highly prized as a medium of exchange. It was also used as coins in the past in few areas of the world. Today, the international system is backed by gold.

Gold occurs either in alluvial or placer deposits as in California and Alaska, or as reeps or lods underground, as in South Africa. It is difficult to recover but its value makes very lean ores worth working. Pure gold is too soft to use in jewellery or ornaments and has to be alloyed with, e.g. copper, silver, zinc and nickel. The purity of gold is expressed in terms of carat, pure gold being 24 carats.

Although gold is produced in many countries but the important gold-producing countries of the world are China, South Africa, Australia, USA, China, Peru, Russia, Canada, Uzbekistan, Indonesia, and Papua New Guinea. The production of gold in 2016 is shown in Table 8.9:

Table 8.9

Top gold producing countries of the world

Country	*Production metric tons*
China	455
Australia	270
Russia	245
USA	211
Canada	160
South Africa	150
Peru	150
Uzbekistan	102
Mexico	92
Ghana	90
Brazil	70
Indonesia	65
Popua New Guinea	60
Chile	50

Source: World Atlas.com, Feb. 2017 and U.S. Geological Survey.

China has now become largest gold-producing country in the world. Its main gold-producing areas are Yunnan, Manchuria and Tsinling Shan.

Australia is the second leading gold producer in the world. Kalgorlie and Koolgardie in Western Australia are the famous gold mining areas. The other gold mining areas of Australia are Bendigo and Bellwort in Victoria, Mount Morgan in Queensland and New South Wales.

In *Russia*, the Yakuts region of north-eastern Siberia is the main gold-producing area.

USA is the third leading producer of gold in the world. In USA, California, Colorado, Nevada, South Dakota are the main gold-producing states.

In *Canada*, Porkupine, Kirkland, Larder lake, Pikil lake, Red lake, Yellow Knife and Clondyke are the main gold-producing areas.

South Africa now 6th largest producer of gold in the world. The Witwersand district in Transvaal is leading gold-producing area of South Africa. Another area is the Odendabsrust in Orange Free State. Johannesburg, Germinston, Benoni, Booksburg, and Krugersdrop are other gold-producing centres of South Africa.

The other gold-producing countries are Peru, Uzbekistan, Mexico, Ghana, Brazil, Indonesia, Papua New Guinea, Chile, Mali, Tanzania, Philippines, Zimbabwe and Ghana. A little amount of gold is also produced in India in the Kolar mines of Karnataka.

SILVER

Silver is a lustrous white metal, though much less valuable than gold. Only a small quantity of silver is mined as argenite (silver ore). Most of the silver is derived from ore of lead, zinc, copper and gold. In fact, most of the silver is obtained as a by-product.

Because of its beauty and resistance to corrosion it is useful in jewellery and other ornamental articles. Silver was once widely used in making coins. Silver is also used in wide range of industrial applications. Silver is used in electroplating, soldering and alloying, the manufacture of silver ware, and for silver lined steel tanks and beer vats. Due to its high thermal and electrical conductivity, it can be used as an electrical conductor. It is also used in photography and cinematography. Silver nitrate is used as an antiseptic and silver iodide powder is used to alter the weather by cloud seeding. Similarly silver salts are used in backing mirrors.

Mexico is the largest producer of silver in the world and produced 5,400 tone of silver in 2013.

China is the second largest silver-producing country in the world, and produced 4,000 tons silver in 2013.

Peru is the third largest producer of the world. Its production of silver in 2013 was 3,500 tons.

Russia, *Australia, Chile* and *Canada* are also leading producers of silver in the world.

The other silver-producing countries of the world are USA, Korea Republic, Kazakhstan, Bolivia, Sweden, Indonesia, Morocco, Turkey, Uzbekistan, Myanmar, Germany and Spain.

PLATINUM

Platinum is included among the rare metals. It is a white metal having lustrous appearance and a very high melting point. Platinum is found with other rare metals such as osmium, palladium, iridium and rhodium. Apart from its use in jewellery, platinum is also used in industrial applications, especially in the chemical, electrical and metallurgical fields. It is also used as a catalyst in petroleum refining.

The top five platinum producing countries of the world in 2016 are South Africa – 68.32 per cent, Russia – 15.52 per cent, Zimbabwe – 6.83 per cent, Canada – 4.47 per cent and USA – 2.26 per cent of the world.

OTHER INDUSTRIAL MINERALS

Mica

Mica is used in the electrical industry, in condensers, insulators, heating elements, radio components, etc. Mica is a transparent material (sheet) and found in white, black and brown colour. Mica is occurred in igneous rocks and its commercial types are Muscovite (white) and Phlogopite (brown). Powdered mica is used in coating and roofing.

China is the largest produces of mica in the world and produce 69 per cent of the total world mica production.

Russia is the second largest mica producer in the world amounting 9 per cent of the total world production.

Finland ranks third in the world and its production is 6.4 per cent of world's production. *USA* and *Canada* rank fourth and fifth in world's mica production.

Other mica producing countries are Czech Republic, Slovakia, France, Sweden, India, Norway, Australia, Argentina, South Africa, Tanzania, Zimbabwe and Malaysia.

Asbestos

Asbestos is found in the veins of igneous rocks and is a silky and fibrous mineral. Its main ores are Chrysolite and Actinolite. It is used to make fireproof material, industrial cloths, protective clothing, etc. It is also used for brake-linings, safety sheets, roofing sheets and tiles, insulating boards, firemen's ropes, special papers and asbestos cement. Russia, Ukraine, Canada, South Africa, Zimbabwe, China, Italy and Brazil are the main producers.

Phosphate

Phosphate occurs in sedimentary rocks or as phosphatic nodules. Another source is bird droppings or guano. The phosphate is the most important source of phosphorus and is mainly used in fertiliser. It is also used in chemical, drug and food industry. But its primary use is in fertiliser and world's more than 80 per cent phosphate fertiliser is made by it.

USA is the largest producer of phosphate rock. It is mostly found in western states of Idaho, Montana, Utah, Wyoming and Florida. The other phosphate-producing countries are Russia, Kazakhstan, Morocco, Tunisia, Togo, South Africa, Algeria and Egypt. Some Pacific and Indian Ocean islands also produce phosphate such as Carolinas, Mariana, Ruckus, Marshall, Naru, and Society islands. The Guano deposits are found in Peruvian and Chilean desert in South America.

Sulphur

Sulphur is used mainly to manufacture sulphuric acid, which is important in the heavy chemical industry. Its other uses are in manufacture of fertilisers, insecticides, explosives, pulp and paper. There are three sources of sulphur, i.e. native sulphur, sulphide of metals mainly iron (pyrites) and sulphide ores such as copper, zinc and silver bases emitted from volcanoes are highly sulphurous and sulphur thus deposited in volcanic regions. The main sulphur-producing countries are USA, Mexico, Ukraine, Turkmenistan, Kazakhstan, Uzbekistan, Russia, Italy, Norway and Germany.

Potash

Potash or potassium is a salt, similar to common salt and usually occurring within beds or domes. The potassium minerals commonly occur in association with other soluble minerals, such as halite, gypsum and anhydrite, all of which have been precipitated from solution in ancient sea. Potash is used to manufacture soaps, explosives, medicine, glass, paper, dyes, photographic materials as well as in fertilisers.

In the world potash-producing countries are Germany, France, USA, Kazakhstan, Turkmenistan, Russia, Spain, Canada and Israel.

9

Energy Resources

Power or energy resources are the basic components of economic development and the amount of energy production is often considered as an index of any country's economic development. The importance of power resources is increasing day by day and development has nowadays become synonymous with energy use. In primitive days all production processes which were necessary for existence of man, depended to a large extent on human muscular energy. Gradually, man used to adopt wood, wind, water, etc. for exploiting power. It was with the onset of industrial revolution that steam engine came to be developed as a practical power plant. By 1860 coal and steam were unchallenged in their supremacy in the realm of applied power. The introduction of petroleum as a source of power was another step in development of energy resource. Meanwhile the generation of electricity had been placed upon a commercial footing. Electricity generated through the medium of the steam engine and steam turbine and then hydroelectricity power have come to replace to an increasing degree the direct use of mineral fuel. The development of atomic energy and its use as power resource now has become an important source of energy in many countries of the world. Now some non-conventional sources of power have also been developed to a limited extent, such as solar energy, wind energy, tidal energy, etc.

Types of Energy Resources

On the basis of the nature of availability and sustainability, energy resources can be classified into two types as under:

Non-renewable or Exhaustible Energy Resources

Once these resources are used, they cannot be regained again; in other words, these resources are exhaustible. Such resources are coal, petroleum, natural gas and atomic fuels.

Renewable or Non-exhaustible Energy Resources

These resources can be used repeatedly, e.g. running water, wind, tidal waves, solar energy, geothermal energy, biomass energy. The principal renewable resources are water, sun rays and wood.

Depending on the nature of energy, the three types are:

(a) Electrical energy
(b) Mechanical energy
(c) Nuclear energy

Another classification of energy is based on nature of use and its contribution. The types identified are:

(i) Conventional or traditional
(ii) Non-conventional or non-traditional

The conventional or traditional sources of energy are those which are old forms and their uses were known to man for long, such as coal, petroleum, electricity, natural gas as well as nuclear power. While non-conventional energy sources are solar energy, wind energy, geothermal energy, tidal energy, etc. The present chapter deals with both conventional and non-conventional sources of energy.

COAL

Coal is a black or brown rock, consisting mainly of carbon, which is formed by the compressed vegetative remains of past ages. Much of the present-day high quality coals were deposited during carboniferous era, i.e. about 300 million years ago. More recent deposits of Tertiary age are usually composed of lignite or brown coal. Several reasons might be responsible for that large-scale deposition of vegetal cover. Some possible reasons include increase of sea level due to deglaciation – leading to burial of extensive forests under thick alluvium; or, tectonic movements resulting in submergence of large forest cover or any other series of earth movements and resultant decaying and chemical decomposition of buried vegetation. As coal is transformed from vegetation and deposited by alluvium, it is only found within sedimentary rock structures. Coal is considered a sedimentary rock. Most of the present-day coal reserves are found in the peneplain or low dip foldings of sedimentary formation.

Types of Coal

Coal has been classified according to chemical composition, heating value or physical characteristics. The following types of coal have been identified according to their physical properties:

(i) *Peat Coal:* This is the first stage in the change of wood to coal. It is light brown and friable. Producer gas is manufactured from peat. It is also known as brown coal.
(ii) *Lignite Coal:* Lignite burns with much smoke and flame. The first product is lignite coal which ranges in colour from yellow to dark brown, and is still rich in volatile constituents. About half of the world's lignite is mined in Germany. It is also an important raw material for German chemical industries. Lignite coal has the lowest carbon content about 45 per cent and the highest powder content.
(iii) *Bituminous Coal:* Bituminous coals are subdivided into coking and non-coking coals and each one of them in turn is divided into gas coal and steam coal. Coking coal is used for coke-making domestic fuel, the soft coke. It contains a higher percentage of carbon (70–75%) and less water and oxygen than lignite.

(iv) *Anthracite Coal:* Anthracite coal is the last stage in coal formation. It is extremely hard, and has a brilliant black lustre. It has the highest carbon content (80–90%) and produces practically no smoke or flame. Among the nations of the world, only China and the United States have appreciable deposits of anthracite.

Uses of Coal

Man has used coal for hundreds of years, though wood and charcoal were used long before coal was even known to exist. The Romans and Greeks were probably the earliest users of coal as a domestic fuel. But it has gained importance only after Industrial Revolution. Since Industrial Revolution coal has enjoyed complete dominance in the world energy scenario till the discovery of petroleum and other sources of power. But still coal contributes about 25 per cent of global energy demand. Coal is used for various purposes, its major uses are:

(i) *Coal as a source of steam energy:* Coal is the major source of steam energy since Industrial Revolution. At that time, most of the machines were run on coal-based energy. Railway locomotives and ship engines used coal as the only source of energy. Factory boilers also used coal as a source of fuel.

(ii) *As a source of electrical energy:* In developing countries like India, China, Malaysia, etc. coal produces thermal power. Coal gas – an important product of coal – is widely used to produce electricity. Among the various uses of coal, thermal power generation is the most important.

(iii) *Domestic fuel:* In cooler regions, where room heating is necessary, coal is very useful. In under-developed and developing countries of Asia and Africa, coal still provides bulk of the fuel in domestic cooking. Use of coal for this purpose is now being reduced.

(iv) *Metallurgical coke:* Coke is a prime requisite in iron and steel industry. Location of iron and steel plants were earlier guided by the presence of coal mines as huge amount of coal were required in the plants. Despite growing use of electricity in place of coal, coal is important in many steel-based industries – even today.

(v) *Chemical industries:* Coal provides numerous raw materials to chemical industries. Important chemical raw materials include benozle, sulphate of ammonia, coal tar, coal gas, creozote, etc.

(vi) *By-products of coal:* Coal is also a source of several by-products, such as ammonium sulphate, coke, tab, saccharin, authrancene, naphthalene, benzene, toluene, praxylene, phenol, pyridine, etc. All these products are useful in chemical industry as well as for other purposes.

Production and World Distribution

Coal is produced in many countries of the world but its important producers are China, USA, India, Australia, South Africa, Russia, Indonesia, Poland, Kazakhstan, Columbia, Canada, Germany, Greece, Czech Republic and Turkey. The following table indicates the coal production in the world:

Table 9.1

Major coal producing countries (in million tons)

Country	*Production*	
	2014	*2015*
China	3874.0	3747.0
USA	906.9	812.8
India	648.1	667.5
Australia	503.2	484.5
Indonesia	458.0	392.0
Russia	357.6	373.3
South Africa	260.5	252.1
Germany	185.8	184.3
Poland	137.1	135.5
Kazakhstan	108.1	106.5
Columbia	88.6	85.5
Canada	68.8	60.7
Greece	49.3	47.7
Czech Republic	46.9	46.2
Turkey	70.6	46.2
World Total	8,164.9	7,861.1

Source: Statistical Review of World Energy, 2015 and 2016.

The world distribution of coalfields is shown in Figure 9.1 whereas Figure 9.2 depicts the coalfields in China.

Figure 9.1

World distribution of coalfields

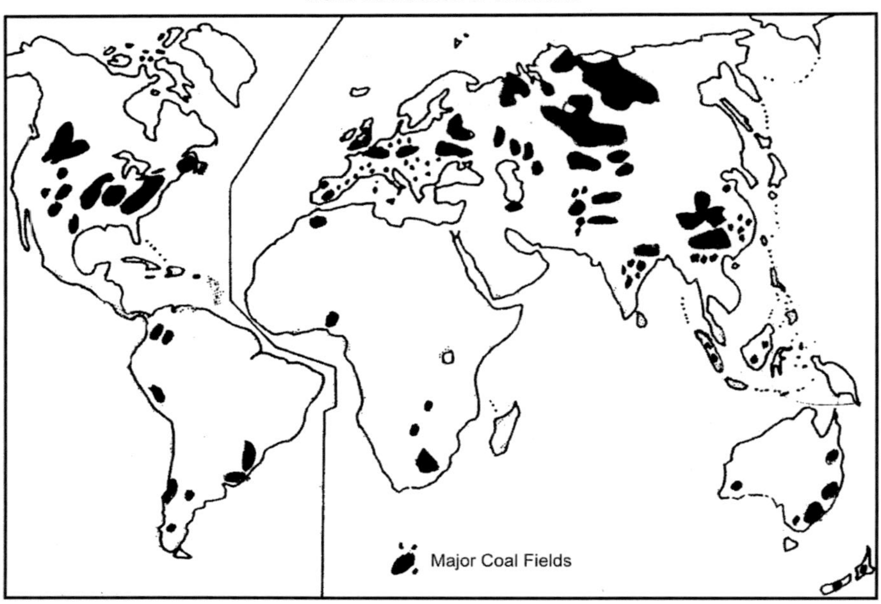

Figure 9.2
Coalfields of China

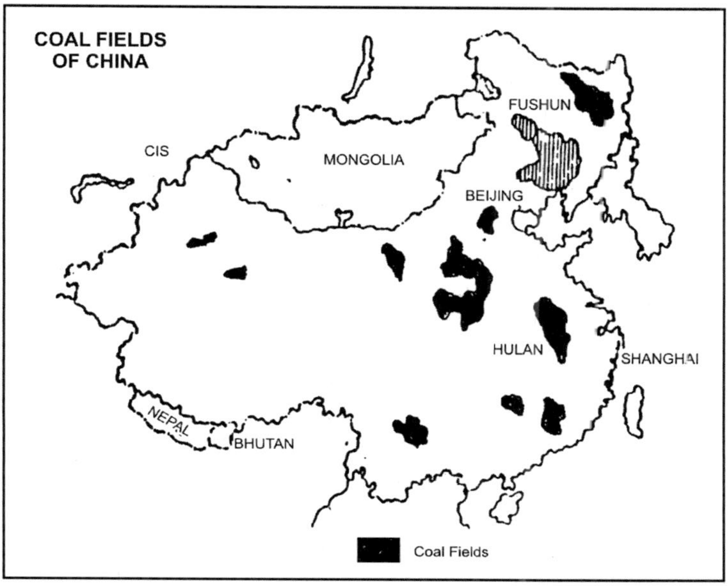

China

China ranks first in the world in coal production. Its production in 2015 was 3747 million tons, which is 87.66 per cent of world's coal output. All types of coal are found, including anthracite, bituminous coal and lignite. Although coal occurs in every province of China, but its greatest concentration is in Shanxi and Shaanxi (Shansi and Shensi). The following are the main coalfields of China:

1. *The Shansi Shensi fields:* The largest coalfields of China, which produces about 40 per cent of China's coal. The good quality of coal seams in this area are more than 10 metres thick.
2. *The Shantung-Hopei fields:* Around Shantung and Hopei medium grade coals are found.
3. *The South-Eastern coalfields:* This coalfield extends from Hupei to Fukien. This area produces some inferior variety of coal.
4. *The South-Western coalfields:* Several small and isolated coal mines are distributed over Sikiang and Yunan region.
5. *The Manchurian fields:* These coalfields are scattered in the north-eastern region of China. The coalfields are located in the provinces of the Liaoning, Heilungkiang, Kirin and Chosen areas. This coal is of inferior grade but reserves are substantial.

USA

The United States of America is the second largest producer of coal in the world. It produces about 10.32 per cent coal of the world. The coal regions of USA are distributed in whole of the country as shown in Figure 9.3.

Figure 9.3
Coalfields of the USA

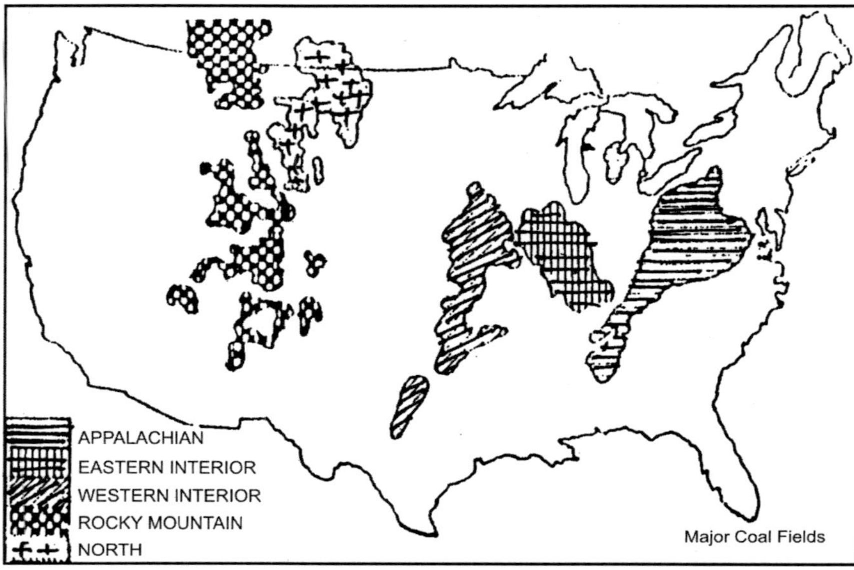

The main coal-producing areas of USA are as follows:

The Appalachian Coalfields: The Appalachian Coalfields, reaching almost without a break from northern Pennsylvania into northern Alabama, contain the finest bituminous coal lands of the world. On this basis this coalfield is also known as Eastern Interior bituminous coalfield. This coalfield falls into three groups:

The Northern Appalachian Coalfield: Pittsburgh is the most important mining centre in north Appalachian Coalfield. The Pittsburgh Coalfield has an area of about 1200 sq km with many workable seams which are 2 to 4 metres thick.

The Central Appalachian Coalfield: The Central part of this Appalachian Coalfield in West Virginia, eastern Kentucky, Tennessee, and part of Virginia was not developed so early because it was more difficult to access, but many mines were opened there after 1915. The Central Appalachian Coalfields have several fairly thick seams.

The Southern Appalachian Coalfield: The Southern most of these Appalachian Coalfields is in Alabama near Birmingham. This coalfield and the nearby deposits of iron ore and limestone are the basis of Birmingham's steel industry. This Coalfield is very accessible to adjacent markets and hence has greater development than any other field South of Kentuky.

Eastern Interior Coalfields

The Eastern Interior Coalfield is situated in Southern Illinois, Southern Indiana and Western Kentuky of USA and is famous for bituminous coal. The bituminous coal is not of as good quality as that of the Appalachian fields, but it is useful for steam and domestic purposes.

Northern Interior Coalfields

Michigan state is now the centre of coal mining in the interior province, but Chicago remains the organising centre of the iron and steel industry, not only of the Lake Superior region but in north America as a whole. Gary is another iron and steel town in Michigan coalfields.

Western Interior Coalfields

This field, like its counterpart, the Eastern Interior field across the Mississippi, has important coal deposits of bituminous and subbituminus. The coal in Western Interior field is below average in quality. The Principal Coalfields being worked in Western Interior are Arkansas, Oklahoma, Kansas, Missouri, Eastern Nebraska and south western Iowa.

Southern Interior Coalfields

The Southern Interior Coalfield is of little importance even locally because of the poor quality. Southern Interior is the extension of western fields in Texas. In the western interior and south western fields extending from Central Iowa to Central Texas are beds of bituminous coal that crop out along the eastern margin, where small quantities are mined for local consumption. It is traversed by the Mississippi and its tributaries, in the bed of which the coal crops out in numerous places.

Rocky Mountain Coalfields

Most of the lignite coal is found in Rocky mountain field, which occurs in various scattered localities. Only two-thirds of the United States coal comes from western fields, along the eastern rim of Rockies in Colorado, Wyoming, Idaho, Arizona, Utah and Montana. The reserves of the Rocky mountain province are enormous, but actual production is small.

Pacific Coast Coalfields

In the extreme far west of the United States between Sierra Nevada and Ellenburg in California, Oregon and Washington, are the most extensive fields, covering more than 2000 sq km and producing low grade coal.

India

India is the third largest coal-producing country in the world. Its production is 8.48 per cent of the total world production of coal. The Indian coalfields can be broadly grouped as follows:

Gondwana Coalfields

1. The Damodar Valley Coalfields: (i) Jharia, (ii) Ranigang, (iii) Bokaro, (iv) Giridih and (v) Karanpura
2. The Mahanadi Valley Fields
3. The Godawari Valley Fields (Singareni)

Tertiary Coalfields in Assam and Rajasthan

Practically 97 per cent of the coal supplies of India are derived from the Gondwana rocks. Among the states, Madhya Pradesh, Chhattisgarh, Jharkhand, Bihar, Odisha, Andhra Pradesh, Maharashtra and West Bengal are the main producers of coal.

Australia

Australia ranks 4th in coal production in the world and its contribution in world's production is 6.1 per cent. In 2015, it produced 484 million metric tons of coal. The largest coal producer in Australia is New South Wales, which contributes more than half of the Australian production. The other notable coal-producing regions are Queensland, Victoria and Tasmania. Both bituminous coal and lignite are produced in Australia.

Indonesia

Indonesia is the 5th largest producer of coal in the world and its production in 2015 was 392 million tons, which is 4.98 per cent of the world total coal production.

Russia

Russia is the sixth largest coal-producing country of the world. Its share in world production is 4.7 per cent. The main coal-producing areas are Kuznestsk basin, Ural-region, Moscow-Tula region, Pechora basin, Eastern Siberia and Northern Siberia.

Kuznestsk basin is a coal region of southern Siberia and produces about 25 per cent of the country's bituminous coal.

Moscow-Tula region produces about 22 per cent of country's output. But most of the coal produced in this region is of low grade.

Pechara basin is having limited quantity of coal but it is of high grade.

Eastern Siberia is a vast coal region. In this region Kansk-Achinsk, Minusinsk and Irkutsk are the main coal-producing areas.

Northern Siberia is also having large coal deposits. The coal deposits are found in Tunguska, Lena and Taimyar basins located in the Northern Siberia.

Ural Region is also an important coal-producing region.

Europe

In Europe coal-producing countries are Poland, Germany, United Kingdom, France, Belgium and the Netherlands.

Poland

Poland is now an important coal-producing country not only of Europe but also of the world and ranks 9th in the world. It produces 2.5 per cent of the world's coal output. The major coalfields of Poland are Upper Silesia, Krakuw and Dombrawa. Anthracite coal is mined in Walbrzych of Oder basin.

Germany

Germany rank 8th in world coal production and produce 2.34 per cent of the world's coal production. Ruhr, Saar, Sexony and Silesia are the main coalfields of Germany.

The Ruhr Region is having good quality of coking coal. The coal belt of this region is 65 km long and 16 km wide and it extends in the east and west of Ruhr.

Saar Region is having bituminous coalfields. Its main deposits are in Rhineland.

Saxony Coalfield is located in eastern part of Germany. Halle, Magdeburg and Leapzig are the main coalfields.

United Kingdom

There was a time when UK was the largest coal producer in the world. But its production declined gradually due to high production cost, low productivity, competition with other energy sources and other countries and also due to great depth of coal mines. The main coalfields of UK are:

(a) *The Scottish Lowlands:* Situated between Grampian highland and Southern highland, this Clyde basin is one of the oldest and consistent coal-producing regions. The major sub-regions are: (1) Ayreshire, (2) Glasgow, and (3) Fifeshire. The coal of this region has helped immensely in the development of the numerous industries nearby.

(b) *Northumberland-Durham Region:* Situated in the eastern slope of Penine range, this area still contributes significant amount of good quality coal.

(c) *South Wales:* High quality coal is sent to the industries in Bristol and Somerset region.

(d) *Lancashire:* Huge amount of bituminous and coking coal is produced.

(e) *Yorkshire:* Scattered coal deposits are found in Warwickshire, Nottingham region.

(f) *West Midland:* Here important coalfields are South Staffs, Potteries, etc.

Belgium

Besides Franco-Belgian coalfields, Kempenland mines also contribute some coal. Belgium was a major producer of coal but presently production is suffering due to depletion of deposits.

France

France is self-sufficient in coal-production. Most of its coal is extracted from Central Massif Nord, St. Etienne region.

Kazakhstan

Kazakhstan is now considered to be an important coal-producing country and rank 10th in world coal production. In 2015, its produced 1.34 per cent coal of the world. This country is believed to have huge reserves of unexploited coal. It is now the 9th largest coal-producing country in the world. Major coal deposits here are:

1. *Karaganda Basin:* It is comparatively a new field where production started only in 1970. Most of the mines are located conveniently, so cheap transportation of coal to industrial regions of Ukraine is an added advantage.

2. *Ekibastuz Basin:* Coal mining started here in the 1950s. It is, practically, a continuation of Karaganda coal mines, situated in the north-eastern part of Kazakhstan. The output of this coal-field is increasing significantly.

Ukraine

Ukraine is also an important coal producing country of the world. After separation from former USSR, coal production has suffered badly but, again, after some government assistance, coal production started increasing. The major coalfield is *Donetsk basin* or *Donbas*. It is one of the oldest mining region and has been contributing significantly since 18th century. These mines produce 90 per cent of the Ukraine coal production. The mines are however, very deep and production cost is significantly high.

South Africa

South Africa is the leading coal-producing country of the world and ranks 7th in the world. During the last few years coal production in South Africa has witnessed a significant increase. Much of its coal production comes from Transvaal, Netal and Cape Province. The major coal mines are Middleburg, Withbank and New Castle.

Apart from above mentioned countries other significant coal-producing countries are South Korea, North Korea, Vietnam, Indonesia, Philippines, Thailand and Malaysia in Asia; Canada in North America, Zimbabwe, Zaire, Mozambique, Zambia and Nigeria in Africa; Chile, Peru, Columbia, Brazil and Argentina in South America.

Coal Reserves of the World

According to an estimate the total coal reserves of the world is 90,906 crore metric tons and its largest share exists in Europe and Asia, but USA is the single largest country having more than 27 per cent of the coal reserves. The following table indicates the coal reserves of the top ten countries of the world:

Table 9.2

Coal reserves of the world

Country	*Total reserves (in crore metric tons)*	*World's percentage*
USA	24,664	27.1
Russia	15,701	17.3
China	11,450	12.6
India	92,445	10.2
Australia	78,500	8.6
South Africa	48,750	5.4
Ukraine	34,153	3.8
Kazakhstan	31,279	3.4
Poland	14,000	1.5
Brazil	10,113	1.1

It becomes clear from Table 9.2 that USA is having 27.1 per cent of coal reserves of the world followed by Russia and China having 17.3 and 12.6 per cent coal reserves respectively. India is also significant in terms of coal reserves with 10.2 per cent. Other important countries having coal reserves are Australia, South Africa, Ukraine, Kazakhstan, Poland and Brazil.

PETROLEUM (MINERAL OIL)

Petroleum, nowadays, is a main source of energy in the world. This is also due to its multiple usability in different fields of machine civilisation. Every aspect of day-to-day life of man is somehow influenced by the use of petroleum. Transportation, defense, technology, industry, commerce, research and development and many other facets of human activities are directly or indirectly linked with the use of petroleum or its sub-products. It provides fuel for heat and lighting, lubricants for machinery and raw material for a number of manufacturing industries.

The word 'petroleum' is derived from Latin words *petra,* meaning rock, and *odeum* meaning oil. It is so called because it is derived from the rocks, like many other minerals, therefore, also known as 'mineral oil'. Samuel M. Kier was the first man who in 1848 found it by chance in wells on the banks of the Allegheny river of Pennsylvania. The first oil well was first drilled on 27th August, 1859 by Colonel Edwin L. Drak at Titusville, Pennsylvania in USA. Since than this 'black gold' has become a main source of energy in the world.

Petroleum is useful for various purposes. Its main uses are:

(i) *Transportation:* The entire transport system of the world depends upon petroleum. It has revolutionised the entire transport system be it road, rail, water or air transport. Petrol and diesel are the main sources of energy for all types of modern transport vehicles.

(ii) *Industrial power:* Oil is the major source of industrial power. Diesel and gasoline are used in gas turbines to produce electricity.

(iii) *Heating and lighting:* Heavier oils are used in central heating plants for shops, offices as well as homes. Oil is also used to produce electricity for industrial and domestic use. The lighter grades of oil such as 'kerosene' are still used for domestic purposes.

(iv) *Lubricants:* Lubricants are very useful for all types of machines specially for the machines used in transport and industries. All types of lubricants and greases are produced from petroleum. Vehicles of all kinds and the vast range of sophisticated machinery in use in factories and offices rely on lubricants and would grind to standstill if they were not available.

(v) *Petro-chemical industry:* Both petro-chemical and chemical industries use petroleum by-products as raw material. Petro-products are used to produce: chemical fertiliser, synthetic fiber, synthetic rubber, nylon, plastics, pesticides and insecticides, perfumes, dyes, paints, carbon black and sulphur, etc.

(vi) *Use of by-products:* The crude oil is a mixture of carbon, hydrogen, impurities and few other components. The refining process separates various fractions of hydrocarbons and several by-products have been produced. The most important products and by-products are: petrol, paraffin, diesel, gas oil, petro-chemical by-products – plastic, detergents, aviation gasoline, neptha, mobil, grease, vaseline, wax , butadine, asphalt, etc. In fact, nowadays thousands of products are produced by petro-chemical combinations.

Formation and Occurrence of Oil

Petroleum is a natural or mineral oil, which mainly occurs in well-defined areas. Now it has been proved that oil is formed by slow chemical and biochemical decomposition of the remains of organic matter entombed in sedimentary rocks. These rocks are marine or estuarine in origin. This means that these organic remains, whether seaweeds, marine animal elements, or plant life such as diatoms, are entombed in the bottom sediments of shallow seas or estuaries under stagnant bottom, conditions which prevent complete decomposition before burial. Subsequently, this organic material is transformed, perhaps by bacterial action and by age-long chemical change, into small globules of oil and gas. In course of geological time, as the original muds are being compacted into snales or marls, these globules, together with a much greater quantity of original water, are squeezed out and are lodged in any convenient porous layer, such as sand or porous limestone.

In this way a water-bearing porous layer may carry globules of oil and bubbles of gas. The next phase is the concentration of this oil into oilfields. This concentration is primarily brought about by the force of gravity. Oil being lighter than water floats, and so the globules trickle up to the top of a given layer of sand, say 50 feet in thickness, until their further upward progress is checked by an impervious cover of rock, such as shale. If this rock layer were itself horizontal, further movement of the oil would then stop. But this is seldom the case. In course of geological time, the layers of rock become tilted by processes of mountain building, and in front of the major mountain ranges of the world the stratified rocks are thrown into a series of folds or anticlines. These anticlines become oil-traps for oil and gas which float up within a porous layer from the adjacent troughs or synclines. The oil thus concentrated along the summits of such an anticline is actually floating on water within its porous rock. If gas is present in greater quantity than can be kept in solution in the oil, the excess gas fills the highest part of the anticline, forming a 'gascap'. The most usual type of oil accumulation is in such anticlines.

Other types of oilfields are (i) where the oil is concentrated in the higher edge of a tilted sandstone wedge. Such an occurrence is called a stratigraphic trap or shoreline oilfield, (ii) where an intrusive body of salt gives a domed structure to the adjacent strata, (iii) where the sealing of a sandstone layer is caused by a fault.

The geologists have found that marine sedimentary deposits of Mesozoic and Tertiary times are highly favourable for the occurrence of petroleum. The search for oil has thus been, though not always, correlative with the search for these deposits. Workable deposits of petroleum are confined entirely to sedimentary rocks which have suitable structures.

Figure 9.4 illustrates the formation and occurrence of oil. Figure 9.4(A) shows how the warping and folding of rocks, connected with mountains building create anticlines, synclines and faults which trap oil-forming organic material. Figure 9.4(B) shows how oil and gas accumulate in the dome of the anticline where they are tapped by wells.

Figure 9.4 A-B

Sketch showing occurrence of petroleum

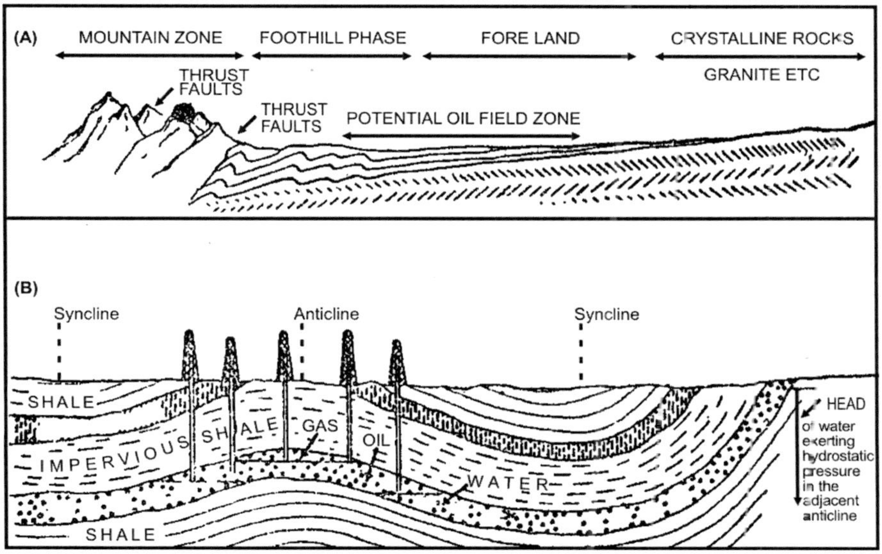

The oil in the rocks is tapped by sinking bore-holes. Oil usually spouts under the pressure of age or water underlying it. If spouting does not occur or ceases, pumping is resorted to until sufficient supplies of oil are given. When pumping has exhausted the well it is abandoned.

Petroleum Reserves, Production and World Distribution

The West Asia or Middle East is having the largest petroleum reserves of the world, which is about 60 per cent of the world's oil reserves. The countries having large petroleum reserves are Venezuela, Saudi Arabia, Canada, Iran, Iraq, Kuwait, UAE, Russia, Libya, Nigeria, Kazakhstan, USA, China, Qatar, Algeria, Brazil and Mexico. Table 9.3 indicates the oil reserves and production of the important countries:

Table 9.3

World's largest oil reserves

Countries	*Oil reserves*
Venezuela	298.4 billion barrels
Saudi Arabia	268.2 billion barrels
Canada	171.0 billion barrels
Iran	157.8 billion barrels
Iraq	144.2 billion barrels
Kuwait	104.0 billion barrels
Russia	103.2 billion barrels
United Arab Emirates	97.8 billion barrels

Cont'd...

...Cont'd

Libya	48.36 billion barrels
Nigeria	37.07 billion barrels
USA	36.52 billion barrels
Kazakhstan	30.00 billion barrels
Qatar	25.24 billion barrels
China	24.65 billion barrels
Brazil	15.31 billion barrels
Algeria	12.20 billion barrels
Mexico	9.81 billion barrels
Angola	9.01 billion barrels
Equador	8.83 billion barrels
Azerbaijan	7.00 billion barrels

Source: World Atlas.com, February 2017. Although, reserves estimate of oil varied in quantity.

Figure 9.5

Distribution of petroleum in the world

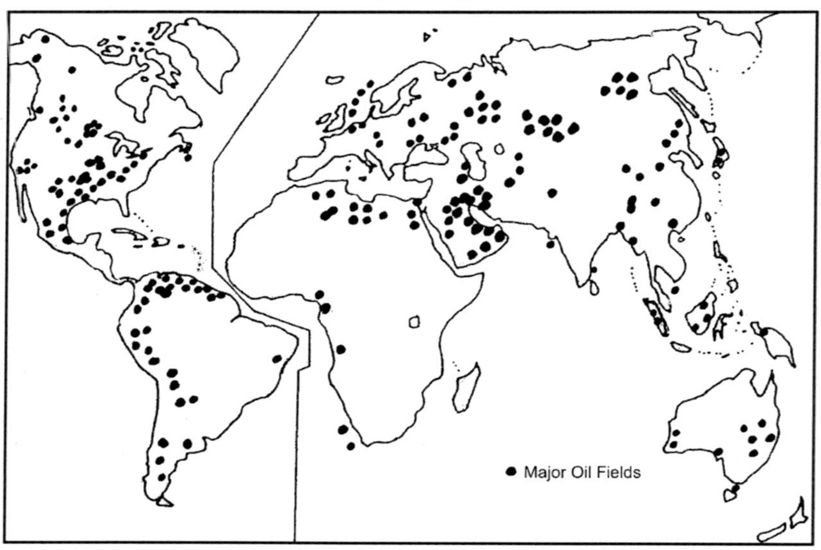

The total world oil production in 2016 averaged 80,622,000 barrels per day. The major oil producing countries and their production given in Table 9.4.

The petroleum-producing countries of the world can be grouped into five geographical regions:

1. West Asia or Middle East Region
2. American Region
3. Russian Region
4. Eastern and South Asian Region
5. African Region

Table 9.4
Major petroleum producing countries of the world

Countries	*Oil production (bbl/day) 2016*
Russia	10,551,497
Saudi Arabia	10,460,710
USA	8,875,817
Iraq	4,451,516
Iran	3,990,956
China	3,980,550
Canada	3,662,694
United Arab Emirates	3,106,077
Kuwait	2,923 825
Brazil	2,515,459
Venezuela	2,276,967
Mexico	2,186,877
Nigeria	1,999,885
Norway	1,647,975
Kazakhstan	1,595,199
Qatar	1,522,902
Algeria	1,348,361
Oman	1,006,841
UK	939,760

Source: US Energy Information Administration, May 2017.

West Asia or Middle East Region

The West Asian region is the largest petroleum-producing region of the world. It also has the largest oil reserves of the world, which is more than 60 per cent of the total world reserves. The main oil-producing countries of this region are Saudi Arabia, Iran, Iraq, Kuwait, UAE, Qatar, Bahrain, Oman and Abu Dhabi, etc. (Figure 9.6)

Saudi Arabia: The largest oil producer of the Middle East and also second in the world and it produces 13 per cent of the total world output of oil. The first oil well in Saudi Arabia was started in 1938 at Dammam. The major oilfields of Saudi Arabia are Ghawar, Abquiaq, Qatif, Dammam, Ain Dar, Abu Hadriya, Kharsaniya, etc. Ghawar is the largest oilfield in the world which spreads over 10,000 sq km area. The crude oil is refined at Ras Tanura and sent through 1,700 km long pipeline to Sidon for further export.

Iran: Iran is the second largest oil producer of the Middle East and ranks 5th in the world. It produces about 5.1 per cent of world oil production and its oil reserves are 8.6 per cent of the world. The main oilfields of Iran are Masjid-i-Sulaiman, Najt & Shah, Aghajari, Lali, Bahregan, Eyden & Naftun, Gach Saran, Hajt & Kel, etc.

Kuwait: Kuwait is having about 8 per cent of oil reserves of the world and produces 4 per cent of the world's total oil production. The oilfields are situated almost over entire Kuwait. The Burghan field is the richest oilfield. The other major oilfields are Mina-al-ahmadi, Wafra, Burgan, Magwa, Sabriya, Mingish, etc.

Figure 9.6
Major oilfields of West Asia

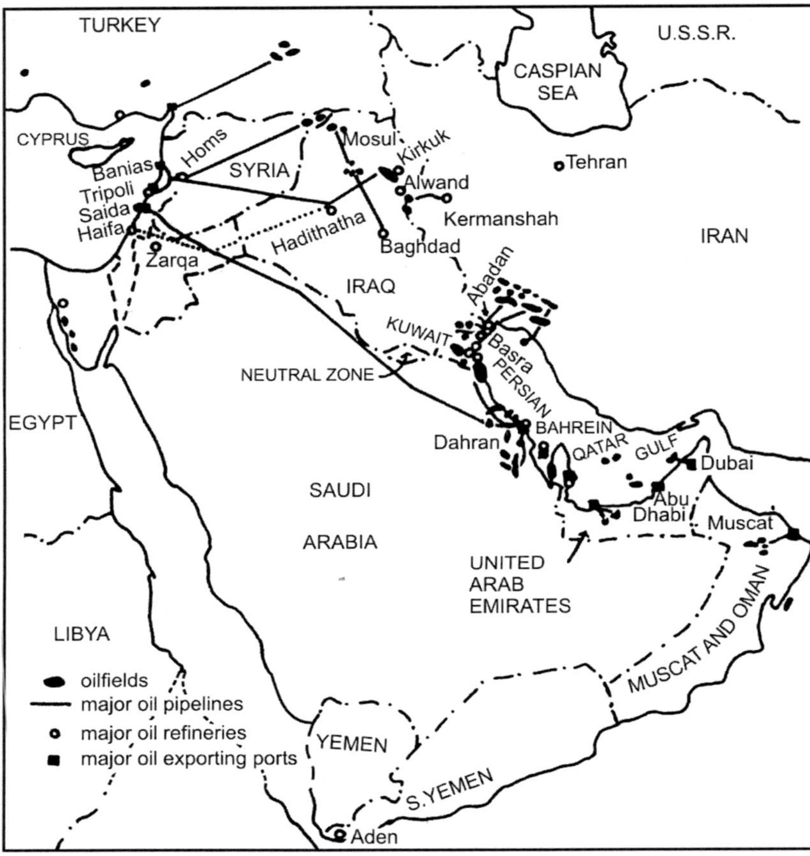

Iraq: Iraq has more than 4.54 per cent of the world reserves of petroleum and ranks 4th in oil production in the world. Major oilfields in Iraq are Kirkuk, Mosul, Daura and Az Zubayr.

United Arab Emirates: UAE, which is comprised of Abu Dhabi, Dubai, Sharjah, Ajman, etc. has about 10 per cent of the world reserves. The leading oilfields are Fateh, Bumusa, Al Bundag, Murban, Bu-hasa, etc.

The other oil producers of the Middle East region are Qatar, Bahrain and Oman.

American Region

American petroleum-producing region is having three distinct areas, i.e. (i) North America, (ii) Central America, and (iii) South America.

In North America, USA and Canada are the petroleum-producing countries. On the other hand, Mexico is the major producer of petroleum; while in South America, Venezuela, Brazil, Columbia, Peru and Argentina are the main producers.

United States of America

USA is third largest oil producting country of the world. It also possesses 5.4 per cent oil reserves of the world. The six important oil-producing regions of USA are:

- *The North-eastern Region:* This is the oldest of the crude oil regions on earth, stretching from Tennessee to New York in the north east. The oil wells are scattered over the states of Tennessee, Kentucky, Ohio, Illinois, Indiana, West Virginia, Pennsylvania and New York.
- *The Central Region:* The central oil-bearing region covers the states of Oklahoma, Kansas, Texas and Missouri.
- *The South-eastern Gulf Region:* In this region oilfields are located in Texas, Louisiana, Mississippi, Alabama, Georgia and Florida provinces.
- *The Rocky Mountain Region:* The Rocky Mountain region contains an enormous amount of petroleum reserve. North Dakota, Montana, Wyoming, Utah, Colorado and New Mexico have several small oilfields.
- *The South-western Region:* In the south-western part of the United States, from just the Gulf of California, considerable amount of crude oil is extracted from the wells.
- *The Kuparuk Oilfield in Alaska:* This is a new oilfield where production started in the 1980s. The production from this oilfield is now gaining momentum. It has been estimated that the total reserve of this field may exceed the reserve of even the north-eastern region.

Canada

Canada is having the third largest oil reserves in the world. Its estimated reserve of oil is 171 (10^9 bbl). In terms of production Canada accounts for about 12 per cent of the world's oil output. The first oil well in Canada was drilled at Leduc near Edmonton in 1947. It is a surplus oil-producing country and exports some of its production. Alberta province provides three-fourths of its production. The other oil-producing states are Saskatchewan, British Columbia and Manitoba.

Mexico

Mexico produces about 4.8 per cent of the world's total petroleum. Tampico and Tuxpum are the two oilfields where oil production was started first in year 1901. At one time (in 1930s) Mexican production touched 30 million tons – nearly one-third of the then world's production. But, since then, because of depletion and other reasons its production has declined. The other oilfields of Mexico are Tehuantepec in the South and Campeche Sound in the Gulf of Mexico.

Caribbean Countries

In Central America apart from Mexico, Caribbean countries also have oil reserves and produce limited quantity of oil. Trinidad has proven reserves of over 600 million barrels of oil and sizeable quantities of natural gas.

South America

In South America, Venezuela, Columbia, Peru, Argentina and Chile are the oil-producing countries.

Venezuela has now become the largest oil-producing country of South America. Its rank in world production is 11th. In terms of oil reserves, it has 3.3 per cent of the world's total oil reserves. The major oil-producing areas of Venezuela are Maracaibo Bay and Orinoco basin.

Columbia is self-sufficient in oil production. Maracaibo basin and Magdalena valley are the important oil-producing areas.

Peru, Argentina and *Chile* are also producing limited quantity of petroleum.

Russian Region

Russia is the largest petrolium producing country in the world. In 2016, its production was 10,551,497bbl/day.

In undivided USSR oil production was started as early as in 1870, around the shores of the Caspian Sea. In the 1930s three-quarters of the oil production came from the Baku fields and another 15 per cent from the Grozny and Maikop fields. The new centres have been discovered in Volga and Urals. Presently, the main oilfields are:

(i) Volga-Caspian Region
(ii) Kamchatka-Sakhalin Region
(iii) Ob-Lena Basin
(iv) Pechora Region

Kazakhstan is having 30 (10^9 bbl) oil reserves and ranks 11th in the world oil reserve countries. Its annual production was 220 m^3d in 2008.

Ukraine is also having petroleum. Much of the oil is extracted from Dnieper basin and Crimean Peninsula.

The Eastern and South Asian Region

China

In recent years, China has increased its oil production and its position in world oil production was 6th in 2016. Since 1963 China has been self-sufficient in oil. This was possible due to the discovery of several new oilfields. The Taching oilfield was discovered in 1958 which went into large-scale production in 1963. The Chinchou oilfield is also located in the same area. The major oilfields of China are situated at Karamai and Lengue in Sinkiang, Taching or Dakang in Hairlungkiang, Yumen oilfields in north-west Kansu, etc. China has struck an oil bonanza in the north continental shelf of the South China Sea. The reserves may be one of the world's largest found through seismic surveys over 320,000 sq km of the South China Sea. Oil deposits are also being worked near Zhanjiang in Gulf of Tonkin in Southern Guangdong province.

Japan

In Japan oilfields are situated in two different areas. These are:

(i) *North-Western Honshu Oilfields:* In this area Negate and Akita are important oil-producing centres in north-western Honshu, which produces about 90 per cent of the Japan's oil.
(ii) *Hokkaido Oilfields:* There are several oilfields situated in Hokkaido especially in south-western coastal region. The notable oilfields are Ishihara, Rumoi, Iburi and Atsuma.

However, Japan is deficient in petroleum resources and only about 0.3 per cent of the nation's entire oil requirement is produced domestically. In other words, Japan depends almost completely on imported crude oil.

Malaysia

Malaysia is one of the main oil-producing countries of South-East Asia. The petroleum industry is becoming significantly important to the economy of the nation. Four oil strikes have been made of the coast of Peninsular Malaysia, three of Sabah and one of Sarawak. Malaysia used to export petroleum to Japan, Australia, Philippines, Thailand and New Zealand.

Indonesia

Indonesia is one of the important oil-producing countries of the South-East Asia. Its oilfields are located in Sumatra, Djambi, Periklanan, Balik, Papan, Rantau, etc. Indonesia is an active member of OPEC and exports oil to many countries.

India

In South Asia, India is a leading oil-producing country. This is possible due to the exploration of the several new oilfields during the last 30 years. The main oil-producing regions are as follows:

North-East Region: The oldest oilfield in India is located at Digboi field in Assam. Digboi opened up Indian oil production in 1889. After some years, several oil wells were opened up. At present, at least 750 oil wells produce oil in this area. Important amongst these are: (1) Nahar Katia, (2) Moran, (3) Hugrijan, (4) Badarpur, (5) Mashimpur, (6) Patharia, (7) Bappa Pang, (8) Hassa Pang, (9) Paintola, (10) Rudra Sagar, (11) Lakwa, (12) Galeki, (13) Barholla, (14) Anguri, and (15) Ampi.

Western Region: Major oilfields are: (1) Ankleswar, (2) Kalol, (3) Kosamba, (4) Dholka, (5) Mehesena, (6) Lunez, (7) Kadi, (8) Nandesan, (9) Vadesar, (10) Nawagram, and (11) Sanand.

Bombay High: Discovered in 1974, situated at 173 km, south-west of Mumbai, it is now considered the largest producer of Indian petroleum.

Other Deposits: Other notable deposits are: (1) Cauvery basin, (2) Godawari basin, (3) Andaman and Nicobar Islands, (4) Barmer–Jaisalmer in Rajasthan, etc.

African Region

In Africa only northern region or Sahara and Sub-Sahara region are having oil deposits. The main oil-producing countries of Africa are: Libya, Algeria, Nigeria and Egypt.

Libya

Since the discovery of oil in 1957, Libya became a consistent producer of petroleum. The total oil reserve of Libya is around 3 per cent of global reserve. Bulk of the product is exported to foreign countries. The leading oilfields in Libya are Dahra, Beda and Zelton at Gulf of Sidra.

Algeria

Algeria is another significant producer of petroleum where much of the national income comes from oil-export. Leading oilfields in Algeria are Edjile, Hassi Messaoud and Hassi R'Mel.

Nigeria

Niger delta in Nigeria contains enormous amount of oil. Boguma, Okrika and Bonny are the leading producers. It also exports a good amount of crude oil.

Egypt

Egypt is self-sufficient in oil production. Major oil wells are confined in Ras Matarma and Ras Gharib in Sinai peninsula.

Apart from the above mentioned petroleum regions/countries, the other oil-producing countries of the world are United Kingdom, Romania, Norway, France, Netherlands, Poland and Germany. All these countries are European countries and produce very limited quantity of petroleum.

NATURAL GAS

Natural gas is the cheapest source of energy, and is generally associated with petroleum. It is a special kind of volatile hydrocarbon which consists of propane, ethane, butane, methane and several other gases. During late 1990s, natural gas has registered the fastest growth as a source of energy and now it contributes about 20 per cent of global commercial energy. The major uses of natural gas are:

(i) It is widely used as fuel in industries and domestic cooking purposes.
(ii) Petrochemical industry uses natural gas as fuel and raw material.
(iii) Different industries, mostly chemical – artificial rubber, plastics, ink, carbon, etc. use natural gas as raw material.
(iv) Natural gas is sometimes used for artificial lighting.

Natural Gas Reserves

The known natural gas reserves in the world are about 6,588.8 trillion cubic feet as per 2016 estimate. Most of these reserves are located in Russia, Iran, Qatar, UAE, Saudi Arabia, USA, etc. The following table indicates the natural gas reserves of the world:

Table 9.5

Top 11 countries reserves of natural gas (2016)

Country	*Reserves in trillion cubic feet*	*Percentage of the world*
Iran	1183.0	18.0
Russia	1139.6	17.3
Qatar	858.1	13.0
Turkmenistan	617.3	9.4
USA	307.7	4.7
Saudi Arabia	297.6	4.5

Cont'd...

...*Cont'd*

Venezuela	201.3	3.1
China	189.5	2.9
Nigeria	186.6	2.8
Algeria	159.1	2.4
Indonesia	101.2	2.9

Source: B.P. Statistical Review of World Energy, 2017.

It becomes clear from the above table that Iran is having 18 per cent natural gas reserves of the world, followed by Russia with 17.3 per cent and Qatar 13 per cent. Turkmenistan is having 9.4 per cent of world natural gas reserves, while Saudi Arabia is having 4.5 per cent reserves, and USA is having 4.7 per cent. Other countries having natural gas reserves are UAE, Nigeria, Venezuela, Algeria, Iraq, Indonesia, Turkmenistan, Kazakhstan, Malaysia and Norway.

Production and World Distribution

The total production of natural gas in the world was 3351.6 billion cubic metres in 2016. The following table shows the production of natural gas in the world:

Table 9.6

Major natural gas producers of the world – 2016

Country	*Production (in billion cubic metres)*	*Percentage in world*
USA	749.2	21.1
Russia	579.4	16.3
Iran	202.4	5.7
Qatar	181.2	5.1
Canada	152.0	4.3
China	138.4	3.9
Norway	116.6	3.3
Saudi Arabia	109.4	3.1
Algeria	91.3	2.6
Australia	91.2	2.6
Malaysia	73.8	2.1
Indonesia	69.7	2.0
UAE	61.9	1.7
Nigeria	44.9	1.3
Egypt	41.8	1.2
World Total	3351.6	

Source: B.P. Statistical Review of World Energy, 2017.

USA

United States of America is the leading natural gas producer and in 2016 produced 21.1 per cent of the world's total production. In USA gas is mostly drilled from the following regions:

1. Appalachian Basin
2. McAlester Basin

3. Anandarko Basin
4. Denver Julesburg
5. San Juan Basin
6. California Area
7. Permian Basin
8. Gulf Embayment
9. Williston Basin
10. Pincher Creek

Russia

Russia is the world's second producer of natural gas and produces 16.3 per cent of the world's total natural gas production in 2016. The country is developing the Saratov deposits of natural gas, which is carried to Moscow by a 835 km long pipeline. Dashava Kiev line supplies gas to the capital of Ukraine. Great deposits of natural gas have been discovered in Stavropol territory. A gasline stretching for 1,280 kilometres has been laid between Stavropol to Moscow. It is the longest gasline in Russia. Other natural gas-producing regions of Russia are Estomia, Volga basin, Sakhalin Island, Pechora valley, etc.

Canada

Canada is a significant producer of natural gas, securing fifth place in the world with 5.1 per cent of the world's production. The major gas fields of Canada are situated at Alberta and British Columbia States.

West Asian Region

In West Asia, Saudi Arabia, Iran, UAE, Qatar and Iraq are the main natural gas producers.

Iran possesses the second position in world's gas reserve (1183 trillion cubic metres). In 2016, it produced 202.4 billion cubic metres of natural gas.

Saudi Arabia is sixth in gas reserves in the world and its natural gas production in 2016 was 109.4 billion cubic metres.

UAE ranks 13th in natural gas production and in 2016 it produced 61.9 billion cubic metres. Bu-Musa, Al Bandus are the major gas fields.

Qatar ranks 4th in natural gas-producing countries in the world and 2016 it produced 181.2 billion cubic metres of natural gas.

Eastern and Southern Asian Countries

China has emerged as a major natural gas-producing country. In 2016, China's production of natural gas was 138.4 billion cubic metres. Thus China ranks 6th in the world in gas production.

Indonesia is another leading gas-producing country with 12th position in the world. In 2016, it produced 69.7 billion cubic metres of gas.

Bangladesh is another leading gas-producing country. Here, huge natural gas reserves have been found in the eastern hilly region.

India also possesses natural gas which is mostly concentrated in Bombay High, Godawari basin, Barmer area of Rajasthan, etc.

Pakistan is also a surplus gas-producing country.

Europe

In Europe *Norway, United Kingdom, Italy, France* and *Netherlands* are the important natural gas-producing countries.

Africa

Algeria is the leading natural gas producer. It contributes more than 70 per cent of the total African output. Reserves of Algeria are the ninth largest in the world.

Egypt, Nigeria, Gabon, South Africa and *Tunisia* are other natural gas-producing countries of Africa.

Some other notable natural gas-producing countries are Turkmenistan, Uzbekistan, Kazakhstan and Venezuela.

HYDRO-ELECTRIC POWER

Electricity is generated in two main ways, i.e. by running water which drives hydro-turbines to generate hydro-electric power and by burning other fuels such as coal or oil to drive turbines to produce thermal power. The present analysis is limited to hydro-electric power only.

Hydro-electric power is the energy harnessed from running water – streams, rivers or any other artificial or natural water flow. The first hydro-power station was started in France in 1883, but soon this power generation system became popular throughout the world and now hydro-power is a very popular system of power generation in whole of the world. This is because of its advantages, such as inexhaustability, ease of use, convenient transportation, industrial importance, etc. Hydro-electricity now contributes about seven per cent of global electricity production, where only 15.3 per cent of the global exploitable hydro-electric potential is being used. Thus, it has great potentialities of development in future.

Factors Affecting the Development of Hydro-electric Power

The growth, development and generation of hydro-power is determined by physical and economic factors. The required ideal conditions/factors are as follows:

Physical Factors

The following physical conditions are necessary for the construction and success of hydro-electric plants:

(i) Regular and abundant supply of water or quantity of water;
(ii) Rugged topography or degree of slope;
(iii) Existence of rapids and waterfalls;
(iv) Solid rock structure or geological stability for construction of dams;
(v) Suitable climate, i.e. temperature above freezing point;
(vi) Presence of lakes; and
(vii) Silt-free water, etc.

Among physical factors two prime factors are quantity of water and degree of slope. The greater the quantity of water available, and steeper or longer the slope, the greater is the energy generated. These two factors, water and slope, are compensatory; that is to say, if a small quantity of water falls from a great height it will yet be able to generate large amount of power or a great amount of water can do the same thing on a slight slope. The power-producing streams may thus be divided into two categories: (a) streams of high fall and small discharge, and (b) streams of low fall and considerable discharge.

However, in the matter of cost the high fall has an advantage over the low fall as it can be maintained at less expense. The advantage thus rests with slope over volume. It is clear from the above statement, water-power can be developed only (i) where there are falls, such falls generally occur in rugged mountainous regions or glaciated areas, whether morainal or ice-scoured; (ii) where the volume of water in the stream is more or less uniform as floods are likely to injure the plant, while the low water flow may cause their stoppage due to insufficiency.

Although with the technological developments condition of natural waterfalls have been overpowered by construction of dams, for which solid rock structure and geological stability is a prime necessity.

Economic Factors

Economic factors play an important role in the development of hydro-electric power. These factors are as follows:

(i) *Demand of power:* In order to compensate the high construction cost of the hydel projects demand for power is necessary. So that the generated electricity should be easily utilised in the nearby area. A densely-populated area is more suitable, where demand for power is more.

(ii) *Lack of other energy sources:* The hydel-power projects are more successful where other sources of power are not available. In countries where coal and petroleum are available in abundance, electricity is also generated with them. Coal and oil deficient countries like Japan, Norway, Sweden, etc. are more dependent on hydro-electricity.

(iii) *Capital investment:* Modern large-scale hydro-projects are expensive involving dam erection, power plant construction, costs of transmission and round-the-year maintenance as well as incidental costs of compensation, etc. The delivery of the power supply from the point of generation to consumers, sometimes hundreds of kilometres away, involves the construction and servicing of pylons, high-tension cables, even undersea cables in some cases, and transmission lines often cross very difficult terrain. Permission has to be sought from the owners and authorities concerned when the transmission lines are laid across private ground, and rental is paid for the land used. A team of engineers, wiremen and administrative staff has to be maintained to run the entire operation. Thus not only initial costs, but also maintenance costs are very high. It is a common misconception, because hydro-electric power is derived from water which is free, that it is always cheap. Once initial costs have been recouped it may indeed be relatively cheap but this will necessarily take sometime.

(iv) *Other factors:* Among other economic factors: (a) location of industrial and commercial centres, (b) improved modern technology, and (c) transport and communication are important.

Potential of Hydro-Power

The total potential hydro-power of the world is estimated at about 657 million horse power, of which only 15 per cent has been developed. The potentialities of hydro-power varies from continents to continents. The following table indicates the potential of hydro-power in the world:

Table 9.7

Potential hydro-power in the world

Continent	*Potential (in million horse power)*	*Percentage of total*
Africa	272	41.4
Asia	151	23.0
North America	87	13.2
Europe	69	10.5
South America	55	8.4
Oceania	23	3.5

It becomes clear from the above table that Africa possesses the highest potential about 40 per cent of the world's total hydro-power. Most of the water resources of Africa are still utilised in terms of hydro-electric production. The Congo river has the greatest hydro-power potential in the world. The water of Zambezi, Nile and several other rivers can also be utilised for power generation.

Asia continent is also having large potentialities of the development of hydro-power. It has 23 per cent potential of the total world's potential of hydro-power.

North America, although has developed more than 40 per cent hydro-power but still has only 13.2 per cent of the world's hydel-power potential.

Europe possesses about one-tenth of the world's potential water-power. Its possibilities of development are more in Norway, Sweden, France, Italy and Switzerland. South America is having 8.4 per cent of the total world's potential of hydro-power. While Oceania is having the least, only 3.5 per cent of the world's total hydel-power potential.

Generation/Production and World Distribution

Most of the countries of the world are now utilising hydro-power as a source of energy. The production or generation of hydro-power in important countries of the world is given in Table 9.8.

Table 9.8

Ten largest hydro-electricity producers of the world – 2014

Countries	*Annual production (Twh)*	*Installed capacity (GW)*
China	1064	311
Canada	383	76
Brazil	373	89
USA	282	102
Russia	177	51
India	132	40
Norway	129	31
Venezuela	87	15
Japan	87	50
France	69	25

China

China is the highest producer of hydro-electric power in the world. In 2014, its production was recorded as 1064 Twh. During the Communist regime, planned efforts were undertaken to develop smaller plants which were considered cost-effective and economically viable. The government sponsored 'Three Gorges Hydro-electric Project' was approved in 1992 on Chang Jiang (Yangtze) river amidst great controversy. This is one of the world's largest hydro-electric projects having capacity of 80 billion Kilowatt.

Hydro-power now contributes 20 per cent of China's electricity consumption. It has, till 2000, been able to tap only 10 per cent of its potential. Some of the potential sites are, however, inaccessible, remote or economically non-viable. China is now concentrating more on micro-hydro projects. At least 60,000 units of micro-projects are already operational – each having less than 25 megawatt capacity. Hydro-electricity in China is now being used mostly for rural electrification. Most of the hydro-power projects in China are located on the Yangtze Kiang, Sikiang and Hwang Ho rivers. Few important projects are San-men, Liu-chia, etc.

Canada

It is the second largest producer of hydro-electricity in the world and produced 383 Twh of hydro-power in 2014. Canada accounts for 12.6 per cent of the world's total hydro-electricity. No other country has more favourable conditions than southeastern and western Canada for the development of hydro-electricity. The bulk of the developed power is located in eastern Canada with dams along the St. Lawrence river and its tributaries, e.g. the Manicougan, Outardes, Peribonka, Saguenay and St. Maurice. Some major hydro-power generating plants include those of the Niagara Falls and the St. Lawrence Seaway, serving the Canadian industrial cities of Toronto, Montreal, Hamilton, Kingston and Windsor. Those at the Sault-Ste-Marie rapids at the outlet of Lake Superior support a thriving steel and lumbering industry. The hydro-power stations on the Nipigon river near Lake Nipigon supply power to Port Arthur and Fort William which handle large volumes of grain, oil and metallic ores obtained from the Prairies and the Canadian Shield. Winnipeg is served by hydro-power from the Winnipeg river. On the Pacific coast, British Columbia is well-endowed with water-power. The Kitimat Scheme on river Nechako supplies electricity for saw-milling and for aluminium smelters that import bauxite from Jamaica, the Dominican Republic and Guyana. Other hydro-power stations are located at Vancouver, Bridge river, Kemano, Arrow Lakes and Duncan.

Brazil

Brazil is the third largest hydro-electricity producer country in the world. Its production in year 2014 was 373 Twh. Brazil produced about 60 per cent of the production of South American hydro-electricity. Brazil's conditions both physical and economic are suitable for the establishment and generation of hydro-electricity.

USA

The United States of America ranks 4th in the production of hydro-electricity. Its production of hydro-power in 2014 was 282 Twh. In USA hydro-power stations have been developed systematically in several regions. The three important regions are: (i) Appalachian Region, (ii) North-West Region, (iii) South-West region, and (iv) Niagara.

(i) *Appalachian Region:* It is the largest hydro-electric-producing region in the rugged topography and swiftly-flowing rivers are conducive to hydel project construction. Tennessee Valley Project is an integrated large project producing huge amount of hydro-power.

(ii) *North-West Region:* Mountainous, rugged terrain and huge water volume of Columbia and Snake rivers provided ideal condition for hydro-power generation.

(iii) *South-West Region:* Colorado river provided excellent favourable conditions for water-power development.

(iv) *Niagara:* It is the largest hydro-power project in the world, jointly developed by USA and Canada. The Niagara river flows from Lake Erie to Lake Ontario and the Niagara Falls and the hydro-electric project forms part of the boundary between USA and Canada.

Russia

Russia has utilised its hydro-power in a planned way and now ranks 5th in the hydro-electricity production. In 2014 its production was 177 Twh. Current production comes mainly from western Russia adjacent to Europe, though several important plants have been built in Siberia in recent years. Among the most outstanding projects is the multipurpose *Dnieper Combine Scheme,* comprising a series of dams along the Dnieper. The power generation schemes have also been established on Volga and Don rivers. There are two huge dams on the river Volga at Volgograd and Kuybyshev. High-voltage transmission lines transmit the electricity to cities as far as Moscow (1,040 km or 650 miles away) and the Donbas. Other large power stations include those of Irkutsk, Bratsk, the largest single hydro-power plant in the world, and Krasnoyarsk in Siberia; and Beloyarsk on the shores of the Caspian Sea.

Soviet hydro-power development accounts for 12 per cent of total electricity and has been hampered by several difficulties. The vast size of the country, with its relatively sparse and dispersed population, means that it is difficult to establish an efficient and economic national grid. The fact that most of the major rivers flow in the north and are frozen for much of the year is another severe disadvantage as river regimes are very varied. Despite these difficulties, a number of very large hydro-power generating dams have been built in Siberia in the hope that the industries they serve will attract settlers to the empty east of the country.

India

After independence, India has developed hydro-electricity generation in a large way. India now ranks 6th in the hydro-power generation in the world and in

2014, its production was 132 Twh. The major hydro-electric power projects of India are:

1. *Jammu & Kashmir:* (i) Barmulla (ii) Salal (iii) Kalakot.
2. *Punjab/Haryana:* (i) Yogindar (ii) Bhakra-Nangal.
3. *Himachal Pradesh:* (i) Sishu (ii) Parvati (iii) Boira Seul.
4. *Uttar Pradesh:* (i) Rihand (ii) Yamuna (iii) Ramganga.
5. *Rajasthan/Madhya Pradesh:* (i) Ranapratap Sagar (ii) Gandhi Sagar.
6. *West Bengal/Bihar:* (i) Maithon (ii) Tilaiya (iii) Panchet (iv) Massanjore (v) Jaldhaka.
7. *Odisha/Andhra Pradesh:* (i) Nijam Sagar (ii) Hirakud (iii) Nagarjun Sagar.
8. *Maharashtra:* (i) Vira (ii) Khopli (iii) Vibpuri.
9. *Karnataka:* (i) Siba Samudram (ii) Sarabati (iii) Joga.
10. *Tamil Nadu:* (i) Papanasam (ii) Mettur.
11. *Kerala:* (i) Pallivasal (ii) Pannica (iii) Idduki.

Besides these, several other hydro-electric projects are producing hydel-power all over India. To cater to local demands, more and more emphasis is being laid on developing micro projects.

Japan

Japan is the only Asian country which has developed its hydro-electric resources on a large scale. Lack of coal and oil, a rugged topography, well-distributed heavy precipitation and an enormous industrial demand for power are some of the obvious factors that have led to Japan's large hydro-power output but Japan's unstable geological situation with frequent earthquakes are a deterrent to the building of really large dams even if the mountain streams were large enough to warrant them. Hydro-power accounts for 14 per cent of the total electricity output. There are ten large hydro-power plants located on the slopes of the Japanese Alps and many smaller ones. Japan now ranks 9th in the world hydro-power production with 87 Twh in 2014.

European Countries

In European countries, Norway, Sweden, Switzerland and France are the leading hydro-power-producing countries.

Norway is not only leading European country but also an important hydel-power-producing country in the world and ranks 7th in world hydro-electric production. The geographical and economic conditions are most suitable for hydro-power generation. Lack of fossil fuel, swift flowing rain and snow-fed rivers coupled with rugged terrain provide ideal conditions for hydro-power development. In 2014, Norway produced 129 Twh of hydro-electricity.

Sweden is another important hydel-power generating country. Nearly two-third of the total electricity is produced from hydel-power in this country.

France is one of the pioneers in water-power production. Some of the old hydel-power projects are La Bathie, Saone and Grenoble. Central Massif and Pyrenees Alps provide favourable conditions for hydro-power generation.

Switzerland has the natural advantage of hydro-power development as most parts are mountainous, rugged and traversed by turbulent short streams. The country produces three-fourth of its electricity from hydro-power. It also exports hydro-power to neighbouring countries.

Apart from above mentioned major European countries, hydro-power generation is also important in Italy and Germany.

South America

In South America, apart from Brazil, other important hydro-power generating countries are Venezuela, Paraguay, Peru, Columbia, Equador, Chile and Argentina.

Venezuela ranks 8th in the world in hydro-electricity production. Its production in 2014 was 87 Twh.

Paraguay also ranks 11th in world hydro-electricity production. It produced 64.0 Twh hydro-electricity in 2009.

Africa

The continent of Africa has the least output of hydro-electricity but its potential is the greatest in the world. Much of Africa is a plateau dropping abruptly to the coast or to the Rift Valley and furnishing natural 'heads' for hydro-power generation. Many parts of Africa lie within the humid tropics where precipitation is heavy and well-distributed, but river fluctuation may be a problem in the savanna regions. The lack of a large market for hydro-power is the main hindrance to development. Some of the more important African hydro-power plants include the Victoria Falls and Kariba Dam on the Zambesi, the Kafue Dam in Zambia, the Owen Falls in Uganda, the Cabora Bassa Dam in Mozambique, the Aswan Dam of Egypt, the Sennar Dam of Sudan and the Akosombo Dam on the Volta river in Ghana. Since independence, many African countries have begun to develop multi-purpose schemes as a basis for national or regional industrial and agricultural development.

Oceania

In *Australia* hydro-power is the least developed because of arid conditions. Only in South-eastern Australia and Tasmania hydel-power is produced to a limited extent.

On the other hand, *New Zealand* is having favourable geographical conditions for the hydel-power generation. In Northern Island of New Zealand water-power is the main source of energy and about 90 per cent of hydel-power of the country is produced in this area.

NUCLEAR POWER

Nuclear power, it is commonly said, holds the key to the future. Atomic or nuclear power is obtained by altering the structure of atoms. When such an alteration is made, much energy is released in the form of heat and this is used to generate electric power. For obtaining atomic power, nuclear fission is required, which takes place in a nuclear reactor containing a heat-producing core and a cooling system. Within the core, atoms of the fuel, usually uranium, enriched uranium or plutonium, are split. The heat released by the reactor is used to generate steam and the steam is used to generate electricity. The first nuclear power station was built in Britain in 1956 at Calder Hall.

In comparison to other traditional fossil fuels as energy sources, nuclear power produces enormous amount of energy. No other source of energy can produce such amount of power from a very small quantity of material. It has been estimated that only 1 ton of uranium produces energy equivalent to the energy produced by 5 million tons of coal. Though, building of nuclear reactor and other installation costs are very high, operative cost and per unit energy production cost and other recurring expenses are very low in nuclear power. But while establishing nuclear power station much care is necessary because not only generation but its waste is also one of the greatest threats to the environment.

The major sources of nuclear power are uranium and thorium. The other minerals like plutonium, barium, zircon, monoxide, etc. are also considered as atomic minerals.

Uranium is the most important mineral widely used for the production of atomic energy. The principal producers of uranium are Canada, Australia, Niger, Russia, USA, Uzbekistan, South Africa, Kazakhstan, Czech Republic, France, China, Gabon and Hungary. India also produces small quantity of uranium.

Canada is the largest producer of uranium contributing about 31 per cent of the world's output. Australia holds the largest reserve of recoverable uranium in the world – over 517 thousand tons followed by Canada, USA, Russia, South Africa, Niger, Brazil and Ukraine.

Thorium is another metal used in atomic power production. Thorium is generally extracted from monoxide sand. Australia, Brazil, Nigeria, USA and Canada are principal producers of thorium. Kerala coast in India is also having monoxide sand.

Distribution

Nuclear energy now has become an important source of energy in many countries of the world. The first nuclear power station was built in Britain in 1956 at Calder Hall and there are now 33 nuclear stations in the UK and nuclear power provides 14 per cent of total electricity output. Britain was rapidly overtaken in this field by the USA, where more than 150 stations of nuclear power provide more than 20 per cent of the USA's electricity supplies. In the world, there are 440 commercial nuclear power reactors operating in 31 countries, with over 390,000 MWe of total capacity.

Other countries with a significant investment in nuclear power are China and Japan, West Germany, Russia, Ukraine, France, Sweden, Canada and Spain. Large increases in nuclear output are planned in some countries such as the USA and France which may produce as much as 70 per cent of its electricity by this means. Other countries have undergone rapid expansion in the past and are now less keen to develop further plants.

The most recent trend for a number of developing countries is to opt for nuclear power as an alternative to conventional forms of electricity production.

Among these countries are Egypt, Brazil, Iran, Iraq and South Korea. India, Pakistan, Taiwan and Argentina already have nuclear plants.

India is developing its nuclear power. The atomic power plants in India are located at Tarapur (Maharashtra), Kalpakkam (Tamil Nadu), Rawatbhata (Rajasthan), Narauru (Uttar Pradesh), Kaiga (Karnataka) and Kakrapara (Gujarat).

In fact, nuclear power is a great source of energy and provides over 11 per cent of world's electricity. If developed and used properly, nuclear power can solve to a certain extent the problem of energy. Therefore, it is considered as a source of power of the future. It is tempting to argue that as nuclear power stations become more economic and supplies of conventional fuels become more difficult to obtain, nuclear power will overtake other forms of electricity generation. It is probably fair to say that nuclear power will play a much more prominent role in future power supplies, but it can never entirely replace conventional generation methods. One reason for this is that nuclear power stations can only be economically operated if they are run at or near full capacity. Although, establishment of nuclear power stations requires special technological skill as well as large capital investment, but its long term benefits are quite economical.

NON-CONVENTIONAL OR ALTERNATIVE SOURCES OF POWER

With the increasing demand for energy, the world is now facing the problem of energy crisis. In future, the energy demand will increase to a level where conventional sources like thermal and hydel power will not be able to fulfil the minimum requirement. The only alternative to solve the energy crisis is the non-conventional sources of power such as nuclear power, solar power, wind power, geo-thermal power, tidal power and biomass energy. Nuclear power has already been discussed; here the world pattern of solar, wind, geo-thermal, tidal and biomass power is being analysed in brief.

Solar Energy

The energy received directly from the sun rays and tapped in photovoltaic cells is known as solar energy. In fact, the energy source based directly on the sun's radiation is the solar energy. Solar heat is trapped by an absorbent material, usually a black metal panel. The heat is then transferred to pipes which carry warmed air or water. Direct conversion systems of solar energy include: (i) *Solar cells,* which convert directly to electricity by thermoelectric and photovoltaic means; (ii) *Flat-plate collectors,* in which a fluid, such as water is heated; (iii) *Focusing collectors,* which concentrate direct radiation on to a small area; (iv) *Chemical and biochemical systems,* which are largely at the experimental stages.

In fact, two processes are considered to be very effective to tap the solar energy, first *Photovoltaic* and second *Solar Thermal Technology.*

Photovoltaic: It is a process of converting direct sunlight into electrical energy through semiconductor devices. For this purpose three types of photovoltaic systems have evolved:

(i) Single-crystal or polycrystalline structure,
(ii) Concentrator structure or module, and
(iii) Thin-film module

Solar Thermal Technology: This system is also known as *Luz System* and consists of trough like mirrors with light-sensing instruments and microprocessors to tap and convert sun rays into energy. The incoming sun-rays are reflected by mirrors to the coated steel pipes. A special variety oil then flows through the pipe and is heated upto 411.6°C. It will create super-heated steam and will start electric turbine generator. In this system, stored power can also be used also during night.

A joint venture was sponsored by Israel and USA. Arnold J. Glodman and Patrick Francois first invented this plant, setup in Mojave Desert in Los Angeles in 1989. This system has some relative advantages over all other non-renewable energy sources. It is cost competitive, eco-friendly, and easy to construct. It is 7 per cent more effective than coal or oil based plants and 10 per cent more effective than nuclear plants. It is more effective in sunny bright areas all over the world.

According to the International Energy Agency's – Trends in Photovoltic Application Report, 2014 the capacity of top countries is presented in Table 9.9.

Table 9.9

Solar energy capacity of top 10 countries of the world – 2014

Countries	*Capacity in Megawatts*
Germany	38,250
China	28,330
Japan	23,409
Italy	18,317
USA	18,317
France	5,678
Spain	5,376
Australia	4,130
Belgium	3,156
South Korea	2,398

While the situation of top ten countries on total PV installed capacity in 2016 is given in Table. 9.10.

Table 9.10

Total PV installed capacity of top eight countries of the world – 2016

Countries	*Capacity in Megawatts*	*Percentage in World's Total*
China	78,100	25.8
Japan	42,800	14.1
Germany	41,200	13.6
USA	40,300	13.3
Italy	19,300	6.4
United Kingdom	11,600	3.8
India	9,000	3.0
France	7,100	2.3

It becomes clear from the above table that leading solar energy users of the world are China, Germany, Japan, USA, Italy, United Kingdom, India, France, Spain, Australia, Belgium and South Korea.

Now many countries of the world are either using or intend to use solar energy because it is clean, cheap and virtually endless. More technological advances in the field of solar energy will definitely boost its use throughout the world.

Wind Energy

Wind energy is generated from wind by using windmills. It is one of the alternative sources of energy that could be used to generate electricity. Wind energy is a pollution free and environmental friendly source of energy in which operational and maintenance costs are minimum. The mechanism of energy conversion from blowing wind is very simple and in this system the kinetic energy of wind is converted into electrical energy.

The use of wind as a force was used in ancient period of the growth of civilization. The earliest known use of wind power of course, is the sail boat. The first wind mills were developed in Persia about 500–900 A.D. to automate grain grinding and water pumping. Although, the first documentation of a Chinese wind mill was in 1219 A.D. by Yehlu Chhu – Tshal. In the beginning of 19th century in USA, Halladay developed advance windmill in 1854. Afterwards, the process of establishment of wind mills has been common in Europe and America as well in other countries of the world. In the field of wind mill development, the first large mill was designed by Charles E. Brush to generate electricity in Cleveland, Ohio in 1888. While in 1891, Dane Poul La Cour developed the first electrical output wind machines used in European tower mills. Several other technologists have also designed and refined the mechanical set up of windmills and now wind energy is considered as an alternative source of power, where conditions are favourable for its generation.

China is the leading country with a capacity of 1,45,362 megawatts in 2015. nearly 80.4 per cent of total installed wind power capacity of the world is housed by eight countries. Table 9.11 indicates the details of these countries:

Table 9.11

Wind power installed capacity of top eight countries of the world – 2015

Country	*Installed Capacity (in megawatts)*	*World's (percentage)*
China	1,45,362	33.6
USA	74,471	17.2
Germany	44,947	10.4
India	25,088	5.8
Spain	23,025	5.3
United Kingdom	13,603	3.1
Canada	11,205	2.6
France	10,358	2.4

It becomes clear from the table that China has 33.6 per cent installed capacity of the total world's wind power. USA and Germany are at second and third places with 17.2 and 10.4 per cent installed capacity respectively. India ranks fourth with 25,088 megawatts of installed capacity in 2015. Other leading countries of the world in wind power field are Spain, United Kingdom, Canada, France, Italy, Portugal, Netherlands, Turkey, Japan, Australia, etc. At present more than 75 countries are using wind power.

Geothermal Energy

Geothermal energy is now getting importance as an alternative source of power. It is generated by natural processing occurring beneath the earth's surface. Below the earth's crust, temperature increases with depth and in inner core it may go upto 4800°C, where all heavy materials like iron, nickel, etc. are converted into molten lava state.

Wherever, fissures or cracks develop in the crust and mantle, then magma and other gases comes out rigorously. This heat energy can be tapped and can be converted in to electric energy. This form of energy is known as 'geothermal energy'. The possible areas where geothermal energy can be developed are geysers, hot spring, volcanoes, etc.

The use of geothermal energy was started in the ancient period of the growth of civilization. The hot springs and geysers are being used since medieval period. But its first successful attempt was done in 1890 at Boise, Idaho (USA), where a hot water pipe network was built to provide heat to the surrounding buildings. In Europe, it was first used in 1904 in Tuscanny district of Italy. In 1958, a geothermal energy plant was established at Waraka, New Zealand. Gradually, in other parts of the world the use of geothermal energy became popular.

Geothermal energy is one of the fastest growing sources of non-conventional renewable source of energy. Its development from 1950 to 2015 is given in Table 9.12:

Table 9.12

Total worldwide installed capacity of geothermal energy (1950–2015)

Year	*Installed Capacity (MWe)*	*Produced Energy (GWh)*
1950	200	
1955	270	
1960	386	
1965	520	
1970	720	
1975	1,180	
1980	2,110	
1985	4,664	
1990	5,834	
1995	6,832	18,035
2000	7,972	49,261
2005	8,933	55,709
2010	10,897	67,246
2015	12,635	73,549

It becomes clear from the above table that in 1950 the installed capacity of geothermal energy in world was only 200 MWe which becomes 12,635 MWe in 2015. In 2015, the production of geothermal energy in the world was 73,549 GWh. The geothermal use data of 2015, for top ten countries of the world are as follows:

Table 9.13

Geothermal use data 2015 (top ten countries)

Country	*Usage (MWt)*
China	17,780.00
USA	17,415.91
Turkey	2,886.30
Germany	2,848.60
France	2,346.90
Japan	2,186.17
Iceland	2,040.00
Italy	1,014.00
New Zeland	487.45
Russia	308.20

Other important geothermal user countries of the world are Philippines, Indonesia, Mexico, Iran, El Salvador, Kenya, Costa Rica, Papua-New Guinea, Guatemala, Portugal, Ethiopia, Australia, Austria, Thailand, Canada, Chile, India, etc. The largest group of geothermal plants in the world is located at the Geysers, a geothermal field in California (USA).

Tidal Energy

Tides are the periodic horizontal motions of the sea, generated by the gravitational attraction of the moon and sun. The flow and ebb of tides can be harnessed to turn turbines for electrical energy and to drive water wheels for mechanical energy. Several efforts were made to use the tidal energy in the 17th and 18th century, but they were not so successful. The first tidal energy project was, perhaps, the brain child of Dr Franklin Roosevelt, at Bay of Fundy (Canada). He estimated that the variation of tidal wave height exceeds 10–15 metres, but this effort went in vain. After 1980, the Canadian government once again took up the project and constructed a 8 km long dam to harness tidal energy. Since then, at least 15 tidal energy projects have been undertaken in the Fundy Bay area. Now many countries of the world are using tidal energy.

According to Ocean Energy Systems–2015 Annual Report, with the total installed tidal power capacity of 511 MW South Korea is the leading country of the world, followed by France (246 MW), United Kingdom (139 MW), Canada (40 MW), Belgium (20 MW), China (12 MW) and Sweden (11 MW)

The notable tidal power stations of the world are:

- Shiwa Lake Tidal Power Station, South Korea

- La Rance Tidal Power Plant, France
- Swan Sea Bay Tidal Lagoon, UK
- Mey Gen Tidal Energy Project, Scotland
- Incheon, South Korea
- Garorim Bay, South Korea

There are certain important potential sites identified for tidal power projects, namely, are Cook Strait and Kaipara Harbour in New Zeland, East River in USA, Pembrokeshire in Wales, Bay of Fundy in Canada, Golden Gate in San Francisco Bay, River Severn between Wales and England, Piscatoqua River in New Hampshire, Sound of Islay – between Islay and Jura in Scotland, the Race of Alderney and the Swinge in the Channel Islands.

Biomass Energy

Biomass is a biological material derived from living or recently living organisms, such as wood, waste, alcohol, fuels, etc. Biomass energy means that can be harnessed from the burning of any natural form of growth. It can be fuelwood, dung and crop residue. Biomass can be converted into electrical energy, heat energy or gas for cooking and fuelling engines. Biomass energy is eco-friendly and very useful for electrification in rural area because it is cheaper and easier. At the same time, it will generate employment in rural areas.

Biomass energy is derived from three distinct energy sources: wood, waste, and alcohol fuels. Wood energy is derived both from direct use of harvested wood as a fuel and from wood waste streams. The largest source of energy from wood is pulping liquor or *'black liquor'*, a waste product from processes of the pulp, paper and paperboard industry. Waste energy is the second-largest source of biomass energy. The main contributors of waste energy are municipal solid waste (MSW), manufacturing waste, and landfill gas. Biomass alcohol fuel, or ethanol, is derived almost exclusively from corn. Its principal use is as an oxygenate in gasoline.

Biomass can be converted to the usable forms of energy such as methane gas or transportation fuels like ethanol and bio-diesel.

The waste recycling and power generating process is very simple. The garbage requires drying, shredding and air filtering to remove moisture and non-combustible particles. The classified biomass can be converted to electrical energy or used as fuel for cooking. Biogas digester has ushered a new hope to combat growing energy demand. The simple fermentation of organic substances through indigenously built gas chambers is yielding required energy for household uses. The cow dung is used as principal fuel. In countries like China and India, more than 10 million bio-gas digesters are in use. Solid waste or refuse is used to produce energy. Denmark and Netherlands are using municipal solid waste as a fuel. Not only developing countries, but developed countries of the world are also using biomass energy. In USA, commercial biomass generating is approximately 1700 MW. The New Hope Power Partnership is the largest biomass power plant in North America. Currently, biomass energy covers approximately 10 per cent of the global energy supply, of which two-thirds is used in developing countries. The leading biomass energy producing countries of the world are Philippines, USA, UK, South Africa, Malaysia, Australia, Canada, India, Germany, China, Netherlands, Malaysia, etc.

10

Iron and Steel and Cotton Textile Industry

IRON AND STEEL INDUSTRY

The iron and steel industry is the fundamental or basic manufacturing industry. The sturdy structure of modern industrial world is made of steel. Most of the subsidiary industries, such as automobiles, locomotive, ship-building, machine-tools, engineering, etc. are directly linked with iron and steel industry. The quality and quantity of the iron and steel industry of a country, greatly influences the nature and type of the industrial development. Iron and steel industry truly forms the basis not only of the industrial structure but of the very way of life in the modern world. The economic growth of both developed and developing country is largely dependent on its steel-making capacity. The usefulness of iron and steel as a metal is because of it's certain qualities such as: (i) great strength and toughness, (ii) great elasticity, (iii) relatively high ductility, (iv) low cost and ease of production, (v) alloyability, etc. Iron can be alloyed with many other metals to produce special steels for diverse and specific needs. Small amounts of chromium in steel improves hardening qualities. When alloyed with nickel it has increased toughness and ductility, and becomes highly resistant to corrosion, so it is used for armour planting. The addition of 12 per cent manganese to steel imparts great toughness and resistance to abrasion. Similarly addition of cobalt, molybdenum, tungsten, vanadium, etc. produce special type of steel useful for various purposes.

Localisation of Iron and Steel Industry

The establishment, development and concentration of iron and steel industry requires many things. It must collect raw material and power resources to produce things. It requires finances, machinery and labour to keep it running. It requires a market to sell its produce and above all it requires transport facilities. At the early period of growth, location of iron and steel industry was entirely governed by the ratio of raw material assembling cost and distribution cost of finished product to the consumer. While considering localisation of iron and steel industry, two sets of factors are important. The primary factor is, of course, availability of raw material, market, energy supply and labour. While second category of factors are the factors of survival, such as (i) establishment costs like taxes, duties, rent, etc. and (ii) production cost, e.g. labour, wage, transport charges, sales tax, income tax, etc.

Basically, iron and steel industry is a resource-based industry; therefore, its location is determined by raw materials as well as by availability of power resources. The capital, market and transport are the other factors influencing the localisation of iron and steel industry.

Raw material and *power resources* are key components of the establishment, development and concentration of iron and steel industry. Many of the world's famous steel centres of today have had their inception during the 19th and early 20th centuries at the places where iron ore and/or coal was available. Although, technology of production of steel now has changed but the factor of raw material still plays a vital role.

Both coal and iron ore are localised raw materials. In earlier days, roughly two tons of coal was necessary for smelting one ton of iron ore yielding, say 50 per cent metal. Thus, two tons of coal and one ton of iron ore produced half a ton of finished steel.

As suggested by 'least-cost location' school headed by Weber, all the raw materials and energy resources used to manufacture iron and steel are localised and impure or weight-losing material. So, the Weberian concept reveals that coal area is the most suitable location, as far as transport costs are concerned. Initially, iron and steel plants had a clear tendency towards coal areas. But, with the passage of time, new technologies were introduced which were, on the one hand, fuel saving, and on the other hand, the requirement of iron ore volume also came down. The LD converters and Oxygen processes need very little fuel. In fact, the continuous casting and introduction of electric furnaces do not require coal as fuel, rather it uses electric energy, may be hydel or nuclear. The continuous casting method is the direct conversion of steel from iron ore. It reduces fuel cost drastically. In this way coal area has lost much of its pre-eminence in the localisation of iron and steel industry.

Both iron ore-based and coal-based sites are common for iron and steel industry. Iron ore based location is not a very rare phenomenon. They occur in Lorraine in France, Duluth in USA, Bhadravati, Vishakhapatnam in India, Corby in UK.

Coal-based plant, in fact, at one time was the most sought after locations. Due to high amount of weight loss during processing, early steel plants were mostly coal-based. The classical examples of coal-based locations are: Ruhr valley in Germany, New Castle in UK , Pittsburgh region in USA, Bokaro, Durgapur and Jamshedpur in India.

The other raw materials required for iron and steel industry are manganese, limestone and dolomite, etc. Metallurgical manganese in the form of alloys with iron and silicon is used in the manufacture of steel. It has a twin action: it acts as a deoxidiser and also as desulphuriser. In the presence of oxygen it produces steel almost free from iron oxides and the ingots thus produced are free from blow holes. It combines with sulphur and thereby prevents formation of iron sulphide. Iron sulphide's presence in steel causes weakness and brittleness of the metal in the hot stage and this is popularly known as redshotness. The manganese requirement for steel making is about 20 per cent. This, even if it is not available locally, the same can be obtained from other areas. The limestone and dolomite are used for purification purposes. In most of the iron and steel-producing centres, there is no dearth of supply of limestone and dolomite.

Capital and *market* are also important factors in localisation of industries, including iron and steel industry. In establishment of iron and steel industry huge capital is required. The requirement of capital is fulfiled either by big corporates or by government and other financial agencies. Similarly, the manufacturer must have access to markets. This market may be of regional, national or international level. Market based location is generally found in the countries where coal and iron ore deposits are rare. As Japan is deficient in both iron ore and coal and almost all raw materials are to be imported from overseas countries, Japanese steel plants are mostly market based. The great 'Tokyo-Yokohama' and 'Osaka-Kobe-Heemeji' iron steel regions are market based.

Transportation is another controlling factor of the location of iron and steel industry. The intermediate location, in some cases, gets distinct advantages in terms of the accessibility with raw materials, market and transportation. The raw material based industries are now facing disadvantages because of depleting reserves of raw material. So, considering long-term survival of the industry, it is desirable for the industries to select a location which can provide sustained growth to the industry. Apart from this, the drastic reduction of coal use and development of fuel economy also attracted industries to the areas where transport is cheaper; for example, cheap water route or break of bulk location, where due to loading and unloading facilities, raw materials are available at a much cheaper rate.

Apart from these locations, another type of lucrative location may occur, where more than one factor is present, i.e. the combination of the three, iron ore, coal and market or the presence of any two among them. The most lucrative location evolves where coal, iron ore and market is present. This region offers maximum advantage from locational point of view. The iron-steel industries of Alabama have all the advantages.

In some cases, after the development of steel industries in coal mine regions, market also developed. The Ruhr valley in Germany and Donetz basin in Russia received this type of locational advantages.

Some steel centres have also developed near the ore-producing centres or at intermediate centres between coal and iron ore. This is because the railway or boats carrying iron ore to the coal areas have to return empty. To avoid this loss the carriers charge lower freight rates for their return journey with coal. The ore-carrying railway or boats therefore, on their return journey carry coal to the ore centres. Iron and steel centres at Metz, Nancy, Longway in Lorraine (France) ore field where trains carrying iron ore to the Ruhr basin steel towns (Germany) come back filled-up with coal.

Nowadays, localisation of steel plants, each of the three factors, i.e. coal, iron ore and the market, has equal importance. The geographic coincidence of any two factors, however, determines the steel plant site. The availability of power has also attracted the establishment of steel plants. Several steel plants now have developed near hydro-electric station. In fact, localisation of iron and steel industry is a result of combination of above mentioned factors along with the theory of 'minimum transportation cost'.

Production and Distribution

The growth and development of iron and steel industry is a reflection of global economy. The iron and steel industry depicts a changing nature in its growth and production pattern. In the mid-1970s, the relatively developed countries of North

America, Western Europe and Japan accounted for nearly two-third of the world's steel production. But gradually the spatial pattern has changed and attention has now shifted to the developing regions. Towards the end of the last century, the growth of steel production in countries like China, South Korea, Brazil and India has changed the entire pattern of steel production in the world. Now main producers of iron and steel in the world are China, Japan, USA, Russia, Germany, South Korea, Brazil, Ukraine, India, France, Italy and Great Britain. The other steel-producing countries are South Africa, Australia, Austria, Netherlands, Czech Republic, Romania, Spain, Belgium, Sweden, etc. Table 10.1 indicates the production of crude steel in major countries of the world.

Table 10.1

Production of crude steel in major countries of the world 2015

Countries	*Production (in million metric tons)*
China	803.83
Japan	105.15
India	89.50
USA	78.92
Russia	71.11
South Korea	69.73
Germany	42.68
Brazil	33.25
Turkey	31.52
Ukraine	22.93

It becomes clear from the table that China is the leading producer of crude steel in the world, which accounts for 50.3 per cent of crude steel of the world's production. Japan is the second largest producer of crude steel followed by India. The other major crude steel producers of the world are Russia, South Korea, Germany, Brazil, Turkey and Ukraine.

The spatial distribution pattern of iron and steel industry in major countries of the world is as follows (Figure 10.1).

China

China is having the oldest system of fabricators of iron, as is evident from its historical records. But until the adoption of her five-year plan in 1953, China had only insignificant iron and steel manufacturing of modern type. Gradually, China has developed the iron and steel industry and now it is the highest producer of iron and steel in the world. Since 1973, growth of steel production in China was spectacular and within a span of 15 years China was able to increase its production of crude steel to 217 per cent. In that period consumption increased 300 per cent. This growth rate clearly reveals the rapid pace of industrialisation, that has been taken in China.

The iron and steel industry is concentrated in Anshan, Wuhan and Paotow triangle. The biggest iron and steel factory was established in the Chinese mainland at Anshan in Manchuria by Japanese, but was greatly expanded by the Chinese with Russian help. Other iron and steel production centres in Manchuria are Fushun, Penki, Shenyang, Harphin and Kirin.

Figure 10.1

Distribution of iron and steel-producing areas in the world

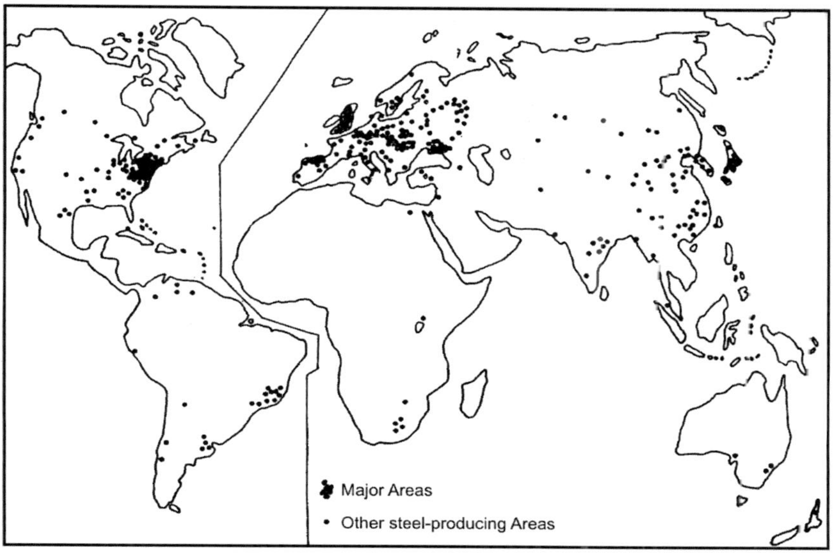

For Wuhan plants, ore is obtained from Taylh, i.e. 130 km away, and coal from Pingtinghan to the north of Yangtze river. The Wuhan steel plant is also in process of expansion. Other less extensive new steel plants are being created in Siangtan (Hunan), Tientsin, Tangshan, Nanking, Shanghai, etc.

At present, China is having following important areas of iron-steel industry:

(i) *Southern Manchuria* is the largest steel plant of China at Anshan and another plants at Pensihu and Mukden.

(ii) *Shansi* is also an old region of iron and steel production. In this region Taiyuan has been developed as a major steel centre.

(iii) *The Lower Yangtze Valley:* In this region Hankow, Shanghai, Hanyang and Chungking are the main centres of iron and steel industry.

(iv) *Other centres* are located at Paotow, Chinling Chen, Canton, Singtao and Huangsih.

The growth of iron and steel industry in China has been spectacular. Since 1973, China has increased its production of steel by 220 per cent, although her consumption of steel has also increased more than 300 per cent.

Japan

In spite of the shortage of raw material (iron and coal), Japan has become one of the leading steel producers of the world. After China, Japan is the second largest producer of pig iron and crude steel in the world.

Yawata, the first steel plant was built in 1901 by government. Yawata is a major centre of heavy industry with about one fifth of Japan's steel capacity. Kamaishi in Honshu and Muroran in Hokkaido are small tidewater plants. The number of large-scale plants directly connected with regional mineral resources and those plants are only in Kamaishi, Kosaka, Osarizawa, Hassei (Akita), Hosokura

Figure 10.2

Centres of iron and steel industry in Japan

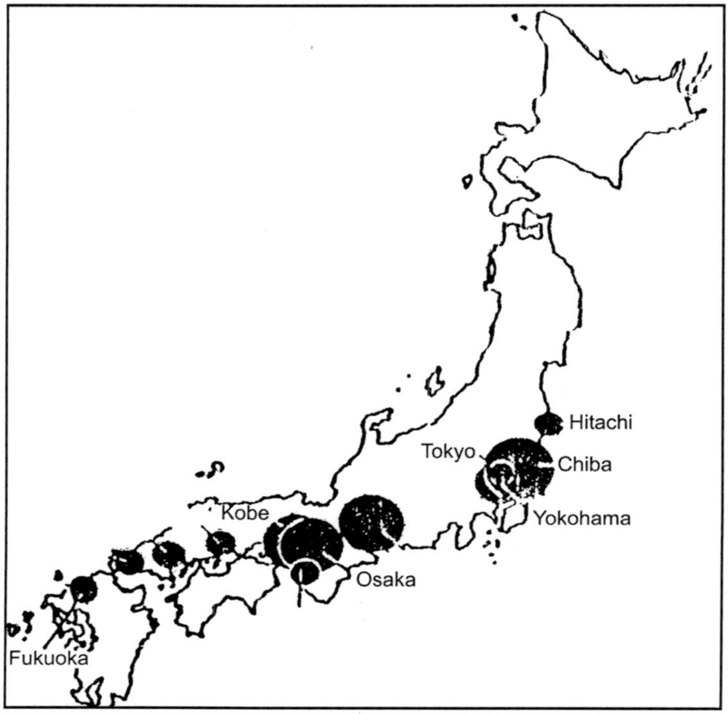

(Miyagi) and Fujine (Iwate). Over half of the Japan's steel capacity is concentrated near the major port cities of Himeji, Kobe-Osaka and Tokyo-Yokohama areas of South Central Honshu. Almost all the iron and steel plants of Japan are situated near tidewater. These steel plants, at or near tidewater, are thus able to draw raw materials from many parts of the world and similarly to ship finished products.

In Japan, large-scale concentration of iron and steel industry has occurred in the following regions:

1. *The Tokyo-Yokohama Region:* It is having all facilities required for the growth of iron-steel industry. The reclamation of Tokyo Bay provided large, extensive plane land for steel manufacturing units. The Tokyo-China region is the main area in which steel industrial units have been developed at Hitachi and North Tokyo.
2. *Nagoya Region:* It contributes about 20 per cent of the Japanese steel production. This region had witnessed a massive growth of industries within the period 1950–60.
3. *Osaka-Kobe Region:* At the head of the Osaka Bay, a highly industrialised area know as the Kinki has developed. The port of Osaka is the main centre. Other centres of this region are Amagaski, Kobe, Hemegi, Sakai and Wakayama.
4. *Fukuoka-Yamaguchi Region:* It is located in the extreme south of Japan within Kyushu and westernmost end of Honshu. The first government steel

plant was established at Yawata in 1901. Kita-Kyushu is another notable iron and steel centre of this region.

5. *Oka-Yamaha Region:* It is a new industrial region situated in between Osaka-Kobe and Hiroshima.
6. *Hokkaido Region:* The main centre of this region is Murroran. A fairly big sized iron and steel industry has developed here depending upon local coal and iron ore.

The most striking feature in the locational pattern of Japan's steel plants is that they are situated either on the Bay-Coast or on some canal or river. This is because of the fact that most of the Japanese steel plants depend upon outside raw material. Another feature is that they are located in the heart of great industrial districts which provide ready market for finished steel. In fact, localisation of iron and steel industry in Japan is market-oriented.

United States of America

Once USA was the highest producer of iron and steel but now its rank is third in the world, next to China and Japan. In the US first iron and steel plant was established in 1629 at Massachusetts. During last 380 years or so the US steel industry has undergone through several changes. This change has not only occurred in growth and production pattern but also in localisation pattern. The major iron and steel regions in the USA are as follows:

(i) *Appalachian or Pittsburgh Region:* The most important of all the regions is the northern Appalachian region of western Pennsylvania and eastern Ohio. This district contains about 42.5 per cent of the blast furnace capacity of the country and its centre, Pittsburgh, is the second greatest centre of steel industry in the world. The mills in this region are located almost exclusively in the narrow valleys of the headwater streams of the Ohio river, including the upper reaches of the Ohio itself.

The region, often known as the Pittsburg-Youngstown region, includes several districts. The Pittsburgh district consists of industries located in the valleys of the Ohio, Monongahela, and Allegheny, within 60 km of Pittsburgh. The Youngstown or the 'valley' districts consist of industries in the valleys of the Shenango and the Mahoning rivers. Wheeling, Johnstown, Stenhenville and Beaver Falls are other important steel-producing centres.

The chief disadvantage of the region is its remoteness from the sources of iron ore supplies, which come from the Lake Superior region partly by rail and partly by water.

(ii) *Lake Region:* The lake region falls into:
   (a) the Lake Erie ports; Detroit, Cleveland and Buffalo, etc.;
   (b) the centres near the head of Lake Michigan, Chicago-Gary or Calument district; and
   (c) the Lake Superior region, Duluth. These districts represent a somewhat different adjustment to the three factors in the localisation of the industry, coal, iron and market. The Lake Erie ports are nearer to the Appalachian coal, but farther from the iron ore than the Duluth region. The Michigan region is midway between the two. One

Figure 10.3
Major centres of iron and steel industry in USA

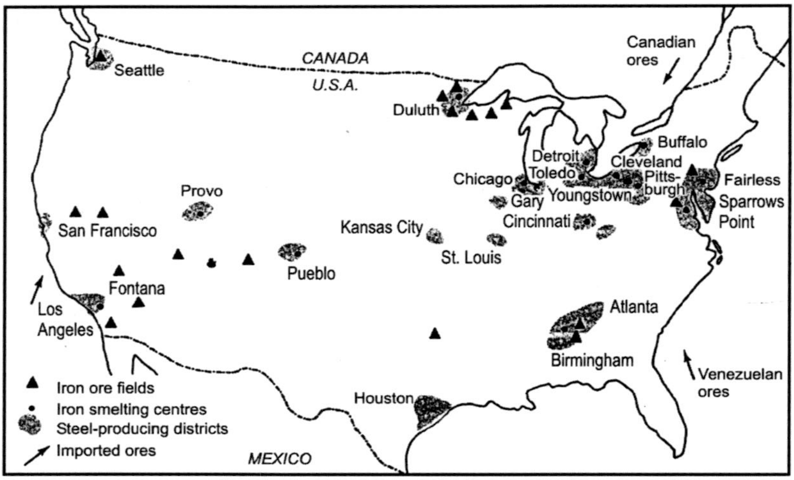

important advantage that all these districts enjoy over the Pittsburg region is that, owing to their location on the lake shores, one extra handling of iron ore is eliminated. On the other hand, these centres are located a little away from the market. Duluth, for example, has in its immediate hinterland the forest, farm, and the ranching country, with little demand for iron and steel goods.

Detroit is the largest steel consuming centre in the USA particularly because of its automobile industry.

(iii) *Atlantic Seaboard Region:* On the Atlantic Seaboard, it is only the Middle Atlantic region (New York, Philadelphia and Baltimore, etc.) that is important. The chief advantage that this region enjoys is in respect of its location, both in relation to the tidewater, and the proximity to the large industrial centres of the East. Its location near the centre of the great manufacturing region of the Atlantic Seaboard, the region of the densest population, and of the most intense industrial development in North America, is the most remarkable.

The Middle Atlantic region is the only major region in which the production of pig iron and steel is notably greater, in proportion, than the iron ore consumed, because of the relatively larger amounts of scrap available in this highly industrialised region. There are many steel mills in this region which operate without blast furnaces, depending both on scrap and pig iron imported from other areas, particularly the Northern Appalachian region.

(iv) *South Appalachian:* In the Southern Appalachians, in Alabama, however, large deposits of these raw materials are found in closer proximity than anywhere else in North America if not the world. While the ore is of low grade and requires shaft mining, much of the rock is lime and the ore is, therefore, self-fluxing. The region lacks, however, large industrial centres in the neighbourhood and has, therefore, a considerable amount of surplus pig iron which goes to the North.

(v) *Western Region:* This region extends from Colorado in the interior to the California on the west. Among the steel region in the USA, this is a new region. The first steel mill, although had been setup in 1882 at Pueblo. Later on steel industries were developed at Fontana in California and Provo at Utah. For these plants, iron ore is obtained from Wyoming and coal from Colorado.

Russia

Prior to disintegration in 1991, USSR was the leading steel-producing country of the world. Now Russia ranks 5th in the production of crude steel.

In the post-revolution period, the Soviet steel industry had achieved a remarkable expansion. During the Second Word War, however, the Soviet iron and steel industry was affected badly. Most of the large production centres were either destroyed or damaged. However, soon the country recovered and by 1975 became the largest producer of iron and steel in the world. The four important iron- and steel-producing regions are:

(i) *Ural Region:* It lies on both sides of the Urals. The major steel centres of this region are – Magnitogorsk, Chelyabink, Nizhnitagil, Sverdlovsk, Serov, Perm, Orsk, etc. Magnitogorsk is the largest steel-producing centre of Russia.

(ii) *Kuznetsk or Kuzbas Region:* It is located in the north of the Alai mountains and south of Tomsk. This steel region is coal-based. The supply of iron ore is from the Ural region. Novokuznetsk is the leading steel centre of this region.

(iii) *Moscow Region:* Important centres of iron and steel in this region are Tula, Lipetsk, Cherepovetsk and Gorky.

(iv) *Others:* Other regions are isolated and developed in various parts. These are Baikal, St. Petersburg, Lower Amer valley and Pacific coastal region.

Ukraine

Now, Ukraine is an independent country and has 10th position in world's production of crude steel. In this region all the raw materials, i.e. iron ore, coal, limestone, manganese are available for steel production. A dense network of railways and cheap water transport facilitate the growth and development of iron and steel industry. The main centres of iron and steel plants are Krivoirog, Kerch, Zhdanow, Tagarerog, Zaporozhye, Pittsburgh, Dniepropetrovsk, etc.

Other notable steel-producing centres of independent countries are Tbilisi, Tashkent and Bogovat in Uzbekistan and Tamir Tan in Kazakhstan.

Germany

Before World War I, Germany was the second largest iron and steel producer in the world. It was the largest exporter of steel goods in the world. In crude steel production Germany ranks 7th in the world and its production in 2015 was 42.68 million metric tons. German iron and steel industry was handicapped since after the war of 1914 by the loss of ore, coal and productive capacity. Germany, however, made a remarkable recovery within a few years, and in spite of her depleted resources she produced in1939 more than the 1913 production of steel.

In 1937 she had established the great Hermann Goering Steel Works at Salzgitter to utilise the grade ores in its Harz Mts.

The division of Germany was the main cause of lower status in terms of iron and steel production. But after re-unification of East and West Germany in 1990, the country is now one of the leading steel-producing countries in the world and ranks 5th in the world with an annual production of 27.3 crore tons of pig iron and 41.7 crore tons of crude steel.

The most important centre of iron and steel industry in Germany is the Rhenish-Westphalia, contributing more than 80 per cent of the steel produced in Germany, and 85 per cent of pig iron. It manufactures a wide variety of specialities. Other regions of importance are the Siegerland Hessen-Nassau, Northern and Central Germany, Saxony, and South Germany. The greatest centre is Essen in the Ruhr valley where the world famous works of Krupp are situated.

South Korea

South Korea is the 6th leading country of the world in iron and steel production. It is the fourth Asian country after China, Japan and India which produces high-grade of steel.

Brazil

Brazil is the 8th ranking country in iron and steel production in the world. Its production was 33.25 million metric tons of crude steel in 2015.

The development of the production of steel in Brazil has been spectacular. Since 1973, production of steel has witnessed more than 300 per cent increase. The consumption of steel within the country is very low. Therefore, Brazil is able to export bulk of her steel production. Most of the steel industries are located around Sao-Paulo and Curumba. Brazil possesses vast amount of iron ore. The largest of these deposit is located near Minas-Gerraes. Another large steel plant is located at Santa Catarina. Most of the mills obtain energy from hydel-power plants.

India

India has a long history of the use of iron and steel. However, it was only after the first decade of the 20th century that manufacture of iron and steel as a modern industry made a beginning in this country. It was in 1911 that India's first iron and steel plant – the Tata Iron and Steel Company Ltd. (TISCO) was set up in Jamshedpur in Bihar in private collaboration with a US firm. Nearly three and a half decades later another plant was launched at Burnpur in neighbouring Bengal – the Indian Iron and Steel Company Ltd. (IISCO) – with British participation.

At the commencement of Five-Year Plans (1951) there were three steel plants located at Jamshedpur, Asansol and Bhadravati. Not only capacity of these plants was increased but six integrated plants in public sector have been established at Durgapur, Rourkela, Bhilai, Bokaro, Vishakhapatnam and Salem. Apart from these more than 140 mini steel plants have also been set up to meet the growing internal demand. India is having the largest iron ore deposits in the world and also having coal, therefore, having very good prospects of the further growth of iron and steel industry.

France

Till 1973, France was the 6th largest producer of steel in the world but now its position is much lower and not included in top ten countries. In France, two regions are notable for iron and steel production. These are: (i) Lorraine, and (ii) Sambre-Meuse. Metz, Briey, Nancy and Longway are notable steel centres of Lorraine region, while Clermount Ferrand, Le Creusot, St. Etienne, Lille, Valenciennes, Le Harre and Marseilles are important centres of Sambre-Meuse region. In Saar basin also, steel industry has developed on local coal deposits and iron ore from Lorraine.

Great Britain (UK)

Great Britain was not only the pioneer but a leading steel-producing country in the world for a long time. But its decline started in the first quarter of the 20th century. Now once again Great Britain has been able to establish itself as one of the important iron- and steel-producing countries and ranks 12th in the world. The main advantage of UK's iron and steel industry is that most of the centres are well-situated in relation to their coal and ore supplies and also have good facilities of importing raw material and exporting finished goods.

The most important steel-producing centres of UK are as follows:

1. North East Coast (Middlesborough, near New Castle, is the largest producing centre, and has the most modern equipment in Britain's industry).
2. Derby, Leicester, etc.
3. South Wales (Cardiff).
4. Lincolnshire.
5. West Coast.
6. Scotland (Glasgow).
7. Sheffield and Birmingham (the oldest, but not the most outstanding).
8. Staffordshire.

Italy

Italy, now has emerged as a leading iron- and steel-producing country not only of Europe but of the world. It ranks 11th in the world's production of iron and steel. Italy's annual production is 10.9 crore tons of pig iron and 26.6 crore tons of crude steel. Although Italy is having shortage of both coal and iron ore but it has developed this industry through well-planned management. The major steel plants of Italy are located at Naples, Genoa, Aosta and Trieste.

Poland

Poland is an important producer of iron and steel in Europe. The main steel plants of Poland are located at Glewitz and Gracow.

Czech Republic

Iron and steel industry is moderately developed in the country. The largest steel plant in the country is Skoda steel plant.

Sweden

Sweden is very rich in her iron ore reserves. Energy is obtained from cheap hydel-power. Swedish steel is of very high quality. The best quality steels are generally exported. This country is not self-sufficient in ordinary steel production.

Holland

This country is deficient in both iron ore and coal. As most of the steel plants are new, productivity rate is very high. The country has to import large amount of steel for domestic consumption.

Australia

Australia is very rich in coal deposits. Most of the steel plants are new in Australia. So, the productivity is very high. The important steel plants are New Castle and Port Keembla.

Canada

The Canadian steel industry is not very old. Most of the iron and steel centres were developed around Lake Ontario, Sydney, Nova Scotia. Canada is self-sufficient in the production of iron ore and coal. Most of the coal reserves are located within Nova Scotia and iron ores are located around Sydney. Apart from that, steady supply of iron ore and coal from adjacent USA has enabled Canada to develop a large steel industry. Some of the major steel plants are Hamilton, Sault Ste, Ontario, Sydney, etc.

Mexico

Mexican steel industry is as old as American steel industry. The largest steel plant is located at Mouterrey. The others are Monclova, Coahuila, Piebras, Negras and Colima. The coal is obtained from Salivas area and iron ores from Durango.

South America

In South America, apart from Brazil, steel plants have been established in Argentina, Chile, Uruguay and Venezuela.

Africa

The largest steel producer of Africa is the South Africa. In South Africa steel plants are located at Transvaal and New Castle. In other African countries, iron and steel industry has not yet been developed properly.

Asia

In Asia, apart from China, Japan, South Korea and India, steel industry has also been developed to a limited extent in Turkey, North Korea, Iran, Taiwan, Malaysia and Vietnam.

COTTON TEXTILE INDUSTRY

Cotton textile industry is the oldest among all manufacturing activities. The sign of existence of cotton textile industry was well-established in all early civilisations like Indus valley, Egyptian, Vedic, Roman, etc. In fact, the history of textile industry is related with the growth of civilisation. Earlier, hand spinning and handlooms were the practices for making the cotton textile. But the real development of cotton textile started in the 18th century after a series of British inventions in the field of ginning, spinning and subsequent inventions of steam engine and cotton gin. All these inventions led to a rapid growth of cotton textile industry in Great Britain followed by USA and Japan in the 19th century. The industry has also developed in former USSR, China, Egypt, Mexico, India, Brazil, Turkey, etc. The cotton textile industry is a combination of ginning, carding, spinning, weaving and dyeing-bleaching activities. Nowadays cotton accounts for about 50 per cent of world's industrial fiber consumption.

Factors of Localisation

The localisation of cotton textile industry depends upon many geo-economic factors. The important factors are: (i) climate, (ii) source of power, (iii) raw material, (iv) labour, (v) transportation facilities, and (vi) market.

Climate

Climate exercises the most powerful influence on cotton industry. Cotton yarn cannot be spun successfully under dry conditions. The humidity of the atmosphere must be considerable, otherwise the yarn breaks constantly during the process of spinning. The localisation of the cotton spinning industry in UK has clearly been determined by climatic factors.

It must be noted that so far as this climatic factor (humid atmosphere) is concerned, it has been overcome by the installation of 'humidifiers' in the cotton mills in dry areas. Thus, places far in the interior with dry climate, like Kanpur in India, in the summer months are able to carry on spinning independent of climate. Only the process of humidification raises slightly the cost of production.

Another climatic factor in the localisation of cotton industry is an abundant supply of water. Water is needed in so many operations connected with the industry. Water is necessary for use in the condensers of the steam engines, and in the numerous washing operations of the industry. The influence of this factor can be seen in the location of cotton mills in Lancashire along streams or canals.

Power

Like any other industry cotton textile industry also requires constant and cheap sources of power. Most of the industries are located near sources of power. Earlier cotton textile industry was based on power obtained from coal, this can be seen in UK where all the cotton textile industry were established near coal mines. But afterwards hydropower has also been used and now all sources of power are being utilised in this industry.

Raw Material

A historical analysis of the locational pattern reveals that, at its earlier period of growth, textile mills were developed near raw material sources, because at that time transportation system was ill developed. Away from the cotton-growing region, availability of raw cotton was also very low. Naturally, due to higher demand, price of raw cotton was high at the distant places. But in its second phase of development, rapid progress of transportation system facilitated easy accessibility within the region. At that time, price of raw cotton became same, both near the raw material source and the market. Naturally, market became the favourite site for plant location. The importance of raw material gradually lost its previous importance.

Labour

Basically, cotton textile industry was a labour-intensive industry. The early history of localisation in any country shows that development of cotton textile industry was a pre-requisite. The need of clothing and requirement of low level of technology enabled the entrepreneurs to set up the industry. Minimum level of training was enough for the labourers to be acquainted with the production system. At that time, wage rate of the labours was also very low. The wage rate of the labour was an important consideration for the location. A slight hike of the wage rate made a lot of difference between one place and another. For example, New England textile centres in USA shifted towards Piedmont because of the prevailing wage rate.

Transport

Easy means of transportation are needed for all industries, and particularly for cotton, the product of which is cheap and for which the market is sometimes situated thousands of miles away. It is an interesting fact that all the leading cotton mill centres – unlike iron and steel industry – cater to distant markets. Lancashire manufactures primarily for India; and the East Japan manufactures for India, China and other Asiatic markets; and the United States manufactures mainly for the West Indies and the South American markets. Even in India, the mills of Mumbai and Ahmedabad produce primarily for inland markets. The effect of cheap transport can be easily seen in the opening of the Manchester Ship Canal. Easy means of communication, in importing machinery and coal by sea, getting raw cotton by rail, and disposing of the finished product to inland and foreign markets, have also been the dominating factors in localising the cotton industry in Maharashtra and Gujarat.

Markets

Markets are a very potent factor in the location of the cotton industry. It has been one of the important factors in the growth of the British cotton industry. Britain's political influence over its colonies, particularly India, and the economic influence through investments, obtained for its large markets, the increasing demand from which naturally gave the British cotton industry an impetus which was denied to others. The weakening of this influence in later years has been the cause of the declining position of the British cotton industry. The cotton textile industry that developed in Japan and China as well as in other countries have both inland and world-wide markets.

The general trend of the location of textile industry reveals that three types of locations are preferred. These are:

(i) the textile industry is located within the market;
(ii) the industry is located within raw material sources; and
(iii) the textile centres have been developed between the above mentioned two regions.

The recent trends in the localisation indicate that in some cases, specialisation in a particular product and the general quality of the product helped a lot to sustain development. In these cases textile industry thrives for export market. The development of Lancashire region in England and Tokyo-Yokohama in Japan depended heavily on foreign markets. Similarly, most of the textile-producing countries, are now concentrating on the production of quality goods rather than coarse fiber production. The import of primary products from producing countries for the production of quality goods now has become a common feature. The automation and high wage rate of the labour forced the countries to adopt a capital-intensive manufacturing activity, rather than the former labour-intensive activity. In brief, the locational factors of cotton textile industry are so complex that it is very difficult to ascertain the reasons liable for concentration of industries in a particular region. The original factors are no more existing but the new factors are also ever changing. The factors responsible for location of cotton textile industry in USA may not be applicable to India. The omnipresent market of cotton textile industries throughout the world is, perhaps, responsible for the dispersed or diffused nature of cotton textile industry.

Production and World Distribution

Cotton textile industry is quite widespread in the world and as many as 90 countries are producing cotton yarn and/or cloth in varying quantity. But the main concentration of textile industry is limited to few countries. There are two types of production related with cotton textile, one is the production of cotton yarn and another is the production of cotton cloth. Although many countries produce both the items. The following table indicates the important producers of cotton yarn and their production:

Table 10.2

Leading producers of cotton yarn in the world

Countries	*Production (in lakh metric tons)*	*Percentage of world production*
China	284.0	26.4
India	226.7	21.0
USA	158.8	14.7
Pakistan	115.0	10.7
Indonesia	75.4	7.0
Brazil	40.5	3.8
Turkey	40.0	3.7
South Korea	23.7	2.2
Italy	21.2	2.0
Egypt	16.4	1.5
Japan	15.8	1.5

Apart from the above countries Germany, Portugal, Greece, Uzbekistan, Syria, France, Bangladesh, Turkmenistan and Iran are also notable producers of cotton yarn.

The leading producers of cotton cloth in the world are China, India, Russia, USA, Japan, Italy, Germany, Hong Kong, Egypt, France and Romania. The production of cotton cloth in these countries is as follows:

Table 10.3
Important producers of cotton cloth in the world

Countries	*Production (in'00 million sq metres)*	*Percentage of world production*
China	2256	25.7
India	1250	14.2
Russia	865	9.8
USA	373	4.2
Japan	177	2.0
Germany	90	1.0
Hong Kong	82	0.9
Egypt	61	0.7
France	81	0.9
Romania	54	0.6

The other producers of cotton cloth in the world are Brazil, Spain, Pakistan, Turkey, Uzbekistan, Bolivia, Vietnam, Korea Republic, Czech Republic, Portugal, Belgium, Poland, South Africa and Syria.

The cotton textile industry is fairly widespread in the world, however, there are areas of concentration. A brief description of the important areas of cotton textile industry is given here to explain the general pattern of distribution.

China

Cotton textile is one of the oldest types of industry in China. Since very old days, weaving and spinning was normal practice of village weavers and most of the output was contributed by cotton industry. Several characteristics of this industry help to explain this locational diversity and concentration. In the first place, there is a ready market for its product. With its vast population, China has a vast domestic market for cheap cotton goods, and its low labour costs, based on its large labour supplies, enable to sell textile abroad. The first modern factory was a textile mill in Shanghai built in 1888. Soon Shanghai had become a major textile centre along with South Manchuria. Besides the advantages of local supplies of raw materials, cheap labour, and regional consumer markets the cotton-growing tracts of Manchuria had an additional advantage of having the remarkable coal mines within the state. The first mainland cotton mill was located outside the coastal China – on the cotton-growing region of Manchuria at Tsing Kiang. Owing to its favourable geographical situation large quantities of cotton are grown in Liao river valley.

The cotton industry retains its pre-eminence here: in 1949 there were 247 factories and by 1957 about fifty more had been opened, engaged in spinning, weaving, dyeing and Calico printing. By 1965 the number of spindles had doubled. Multiple centres of textile production are also being set up at various new sites in the interior of People's Republic of China. The textile industry had previously been concentrated in Shanghai and Tientsin. Production has improved, and new centres have been opened up in the cotton-growing belt in Honan, Hopei, Shansi and Shensi, as well as single factories serving local needs at Lan Chow, Urumchi, Kashgar, Chengtu, Taiyuan, Chengchow, Hongchow, Nanking, Kaiteng, Tientsin, etc. Cloth is now made at Taiyuan and looms are being constructed at Chengchow.

Now, China has emerged as the largest cotton textile-producing country in the world. The Beijing-Hankow industrial conurbation including centres like Paoting, Singtai, Chengchow has emerged as a leading textile centre. Of course, among all the textile-producing centres, Shanghai was the most important. At one stage, this region produced more than 70 per cent of the Chinese textile production. The emergence of different textile centres lowered the relative importance of Shanghai, but it still maintains dominating role in textile industry. The adjacent Hankow region now produces huge amount of textile products. The Wushan integrated textile plants contribute significant amount of cotton products. The Canton textile units were set up very recently. As the plants are modern, output of textile goods per worker is very high in this region.

India

India is the second largest cotton textile producer in the world. The first cotton mill in India was erected in Calcutta in 1818, while first mill in Bombay (now Mumbai) was started in 1854, which was destined to become the home of the cotton mill industry.

The early concentration of the cotton textile industry in Mumbai was governed not so much by natural and permanent factors as by other advantages, such as abundance of capital and credit facilities, the presence of cheap and speedy means of transport and the temporary growth of the demand for yarn from China, which Mumbai was in an exceptionally favourable situation to meet. The year 1877 marks the turning point in the development of the industry from the point of view of its distribution. It saw the beginning of a rapid construction of mills in upcountry centres like Nagpur, Ahmedabad, Sholapur, Kolhapur, etc. situated right in the heart of the cotton-producing tracts. This later distribution was influenced to a very much larger extent by natural factors, such as the vicinity of sources of raw material, plentiful labour and large marketing centres, and was made possible by the development of a railway communication.

The cotton industry received a considerable stimulus from the conditions created by war. The large patronage extended to the mill by the Government in respect of their military requirements in cotton goods in the Eastern theatres of the war, together with the shrinkage in the Lancashire imports into India due to the preoccupation of the Lancashire mills with war work and the sharp rise in the prices of imported cloth due to shortage of shipping, led to a considerable increase in home consumption, though the difficulty of importing machinery prevented speedy development which would otherwise have taken place. Recently, there has been a tendency on the part of the Indian mills to increase the manufacture of finer goods, and a certain amount of long-staple cotton is imported from the USA and elsewhere for this purpose. An improvement in the quality of the home-grown cotton will help the situation. It is significant to note that even within these particular areas or regions, the industry is predominantly localised within a few important industrial centres like Mumbai, Ahmedabad, Sholapur, Vadodara, Pune, Kanpur, Delhi, Indore, Gwalior, Coimbatore, Kalol, Bhagalpur, Warangal, Calcutta, Howrah, Serampur, Konnagar, Sodepur, Panihati, etc.

At present, there are more than 1,220 cotton mills in India; of these, 283 are composite mills and the remaining are the spinning mills. Production wise, Maharashtra tops with 16.4 per cent yarn and 52.3 per cent cloth production in the country, followed by states of Tamil Nadu (30.4% yarn and 8.8% fabric), Gujarat, Uttar Pradesh, Madhya Pradesh, West Bengal, Rajasthan, Punjab, Karnataka, etc.

Russia

Russia ranks third in cotton cloth production in the world and it produces about ten per cent of the total cotton cloth of the world. Although in Russia textile industry has not received priority in its development plans. Before Revolution (1917) the cotton textile industry was localised in Moscow and Ivanovo region but now it has developed in other regions also. The important regions are:

(i) *Moscow-Ivanovo Region* is the oldest and the most important textile region. Ivanovo is having a large number of cotton spinning and weaving centres, also known as 'Manchester of Russia'. The other centres of this region are – Yoroslav, Kostromov, Shuya, Kovrov, Uro-Khavo-Zuyevo, etc. Moscow is another centre, around which Noginsk, Pavlovsky, Yegoryevsk, Serpukhov, etc. have developed.

(ii) *Leningrad or St. Petersburg Region* is also known for cotton textile industry. St. Petersburg, Narva and Tallin are important centres of this region.

(iii) *Kalinin Region* extends west of Moscow. Kalinin, Vishniye, Volochak are important textile centres.

(iv) *Siberia Region* has been developed on availability of cheap hydro-electricity, transport facility and labour. Several centres like Omsk, Novosibirsk, Barnaul, Briansk, Kamarovo, Kansk, Leninsk-Kuznetskiye, Kustney have cotton textile industry.

Volga basin and Ural region also have cotton textile units. The development of textile industry in Russia is due to huge domestic market, hydro-electricity, developed transport system and skilled labour.

USA

USA is the leading cotton textile producer in the world. It ranks third in cotton yarn production and fourth in cotton cloth production in the world. The two factors responsible for its growth and development are: (a) capital, and (b) the local market. In USA cotton textile industry is localised in the following regions:

(i) *New England:* New England used to be the largest centre until a few years ago but the South has surpassed it now. Within New England, the mills are scattered, though a large number of spindles are concentrated within thirty miles of Providence in southern New England. Fall river is the largest centre, with New Bedford, only 30 km away, as the second largest centre. This region has developed earlier because of availability of hydro-power and suitable climate. In this region temperature is less variable and atmosphere more humid than in the neighbouring regions.

The manufactures are characterised by fine goods, and finishing is a feature of the New England industry. A large quantity of cloth comes for finishing, dyeing, printing, etc. from the South and other cotton-manufacturing regions of the USA.

(ii) *Mid-Atlantic:* The Middle Atlantic States cotton factories are located in Pennsylvania, New York and Maryland. But Philadelphia is the only point at which there is concentration. The existence of these mills in Philadelphia, and the character of their output is chiefly due to labour supply, supplemented by machine shops and market facilities. The Mid-Atlantic States are pre-eminent in the production of knitted goods. In both, New York and Pennsylvania, there is localisation of the knitting industry, around Cohoes in the Mohawk valley and at Philadelphia. Philadelphia has been the principal seat of the hosiery industry in the United States ever since the Germans settled in German Town.

(iii) *Southern States:* The growth of cotton industry in the southern states has increased within recent years. The most extensive construction of mills in the South has been in three states – North Carolina, South Carolina, and Georgia.

The Southern States have advantages such as proximity of raw cotton, water-power and cheap labour. The other advantage of the South in comparison with the New England states is its lower operating cost.

Japan

After China and India, Japan is the third leading Asian country in cotton textile production. The first cotton mill in Japan was established in 1862 at Kagoshima, but it was about 15 years later that cotton mills began to be started in quick succession, especially in and around the city of Osaka.

The main geographical factors helping in the establishment of a successful cotton industry in Japan are: (i) a suitable climate, (ii) cheap water-power, (iii) transport facilities, (iv) supply of cheap and skilled labour, and (v) the proximity to the large markets of China and India.

The Japanese industry is said to enjoy the following advantages over her competitors:

(i) Cheaper and efficient labour

(ii) Greater proximity to the large consuming markets

(iii) Better organisation

(iv) Better service from plant

Japan has to import almost all of the raw materials needed for textile industry. The pioneer attempts to set up industries were made around cotton-growing tracts of Nobi and Kanto regions. Now the major textile centres are located at Chukyo, Hanshin, Toyama, Kyushu and Keihin and also at Osaka and Nagoya.

Spatially, majority of the cotton mills are located within the northern half of Japan. The bulk of the textile goods are produced in following regions: (i) the Kwanto Plain, (ii) Nagowa, (iii) the Kinki Plain, and (iv) along the Northern Coast.

As the industry became more and more export-oriented, textile establishment gradually shifted towards coasts. At the beginning of the decade of 1990s, old obsolete mills closed down their productions. The new mills with updated machineries came into existence. Most of the Japanese textile mills are now using the latest technologies. The priority was given to reduce the cost of production. Soon, Japan became the exporter of not only textile products but also the textile machines. At present, a healthy competition is discernible between small-scale sectors and the big industrial estates of textile industry.

Germany

Germany is one of the leading producers of cotton textile. The history of cotton textile industry in Germany is quite old. Initially, the industry was set up depending upon imported cotton and most of the industries were developed along Rhine river valley. But Ruhr industrial region soon became a leading textile centre.

The cotton manufacturing centres of Germany are grouped into the following three groups:

1. *North-Western:* Consisting of Rhine region towns like Barmen and Elberfield, and Ems-Vechta towns like Pheine and Gronau.
2. *Central:* Consisting of towns along the three mountain ranges which separate Bohemia from Germany, Reichenbach, Chemnitz, Leipzig and Dresden.
3. *South-Western:* Consisting of towns like Augsburgh, Stuttgart and Mulhouse.

The north-western region had the advantage of local market in the industrial populations which also provided it with cheap labour. The other centres had the advantage of water power, pure water and the cheap labour of the mountain populations.

Hong Kong

Hong Kong ranks 7th in production of cotton cloth in the world. The industry in Hong Kong was set up by the refugees from communist China in 1949. Hong Kong is a free trade area and one of the principal entrepot ports of the world. Manufactured goods, particularly textile provide three-fourths of total export earnings. Three major parts of Hong Kong's giant textile industry – the spinning, weaving and finishing business are in a decline from which they may never fully recover. Employment in the industry has plummeted in the past years. Mills are shutting down or leaving machines idle. Local garment makers are importing more and more yarn and fabrics for their needs. The textile industry together with the garment-making industry still is the largest manufacturing industry in terms of sales and employment. The industry's problem is basically one of costs. Higher labour, land and energy costs have made Hong Kong yarns and fabrics more expensive than those from Taiwan, South Korea and China.

The United Kingdom

UK was the leading cotton manufacturing country in the world, but it no longer dominates the world in cotton textile production. The history of cotton textile industry cannot be completed without describing the contribution of United Kingdom. The Industrial Revolution in the 18th century gave the impetus to the development of cotton textile industry in Great Britain. The subsequent invention of spinning machines encouraged the growth. The humid climate and local skilled labour helped a lot during the initial period of development. The cotton textile industry in the United Kingdom attained such a high fame that at end of 19th century the country became the undisputed leader of the cotton textile industry. The early centres were developed around Scottish lowlands, Nottingham, Ireland and Lancashire. Gradually, Lancashire became the most developed textile centre in the world.

The factors that helped in early development of textile industry in UK, especially in Lancashire region were – suitable humid climate, skilled local labours, abundant water resources, availability of local coal, cheap price of land and cotton import facility, etc. Apart from Lancashire, Manchester has also emerged as a leading textile centre. The cotton manufacturing towns of Bottom, Bury, Rochdale, Oldham and Stockport (in Cheshire) are located in a semi-circle around Manchester. The relative position of UK in textile industry has been decreased considerably due to overall decrease of consumption of cotton goods, loss of overseas market and emergence of new textile-producing countries like China, India, Japan, etc.

Other Countries

In *Europe* other cotton textile-producing countries are France, Italy, Switzerland, Romania, Czech Republic, Belgium, Poland and Spain. France's cotton textile industry has had a long history. The textile industry of France was developed on imported cotton, particularly from USA. The industry is concentrated in the north-eastern industrial region. The major centres of textile-producing centres are Belford, Kolman and Nausi.

Italy has also emerged as an important cotton textile producer in Europe. The major centres of textile industry are located in the Po basin and in the Alpine valleys. Milan, Korno, Bergamo, Turin, Genoa, Breccia, Verona and Como are the main centres of cotton textile industry.

Switzerland is having cotton textile industry in the northern part of the country. The most important centre is the Saint Galen.

Romania is also significant in cotton textile production. Its important centres are located at Pitesi, Birlad, Oradea, Guirgui, Bukharest, Brasov, Sibiu, Baia, Mare and Timisoara.

In *Latin America*, Mexico, Brazil, Argentina and Peru are important in cotton textile production. *Mexico* is the major cotton manufacturing country, not only in Latin America but also in the world. The textile industry was first developed in the Orizaba region and later in the Mexico city. The major centres of cotton textile in Mexico are Heroico, Nogales, Ciudad Juarez, Piedras Negras, San Louis Potos, Cudad de Mexico, Toluca de Lerdo and Cuernavaca.

Brazil is another cotton textile-producing country of Latin America and is also important in the world. The important cotton textile centres of Brazil are: Rio Grande do Sul, Minasgerais and Rio de Janeiro.

In *Argentina* textile industry has developed at Buenos Aires, La Plata and Azul, while in *Peru* it has developed at Trujillo, Lima, Calao, Ica and Cuzco.

In *Africa,* Egypt and South Africa are the main cotton textile producers, although Nigeria, Ethiopia and Tanzania also produce some quantity of cotton fabric.

Egypt is famous for its good quality of cotton and has also developed textile industry at Iskandaria, Tanta and Dumyat. Egypt ranks 10th in cotton yarn production and 8th in cotton cloth production in the world.

South Africa also has developed cotton textile industry at Johannesburg, Bloemfontein, Durban, East London and Worcester.

In *Asia,* apart from China, India and Japan, Pakistan, South Korea, Indonesia and Turkey are the leading producers of cotton textile.

Pakistan is a major cotton-producing country in Asia and has also developed cotton textile industry. Cotton mills in Pakistan are located at Lahore, Lyallpur, Multan, Karachi, Sahadra, Montgomery and Peshawar.

South Korea has made good progress in cotton textile industry in recent years. The major cotton textile centres are Inchou, Taegu, Masan, Pusan, Kwangju and Seol.

Indonesia is also a textile exporting country of Asia. Similar is the case with the Philippines.

Turkey is another Asian country having cotton textile industry in prominence. Turkey is a producer of good quality of cotton. Izmir, Izmit, Sivas, Kyseri, Bursa, Erzurum, Usak, etc. are the main centres of cotton textile industry in Turkey.

11

Chemical, Chemical Fertiliser and Paper Pulp Industry

CHEMICAL INDUSTRY

The work through chemicals to affect transformation of matter and molecular structures of planned design has been going on for many years, but its impact on the well-being of mankind was never so far reaching as it was during the last century and as it is today. The chemical industries are considered basic for health, industrial and agricultural development as well as for defence.

The chemical industries are not only concerned with the manufacture of pure chemicals, but also with many kinds of industrial raw materials that are mixtures of substances. The raw materials of chemical industries are derived from various sources such as mines, forests, sea, air, land, oil, gas and brine wells. The chemicals produced serve as essential raw materials for making thousands of articles – medicines, fertilisers, synthetic rubber and fiber, plastics, explosives, etc. Chemicals are also used in many industries to improve or preserve the quality of non-durable and durable goods.

The chemical industry is comparatively a new addition to the manufacturing world. The prosperity of chemical industry in the national economy is the true reflection of the simultaneous development of the industries like engineering, metallurgy and several other manufacturing activities. The industry produces large amount of consumer products. The importance of chemical industry in the day-to-day life of human beings cannot be ignored. The chemical industry is one of the most dynamic, as the processes are ever changing. The industry is also growing very fast.

Chemical Products

There is a large variety of chemical products and their number is still increasing with the new research in this field. According to the standard classification of the US Bureau of the Budget, following chemical products have been identified:

1. *Industrial inorganic and organic chemicals:* Alkalis and chlorine, industrial gases, coal for crudes, dyes, dye intermediates, organic pigments, inorganic pigments, other industrial organic chemicals like acetic, formic, synthetic perfume, flavouring materials and the like. Also, chemicals such as inorganic salts of sodium, potassium, aluminium, calcium, magnesium, etc. are included in this category.

2. Plastic materials and synthetic resins, synthetic rubber, synthetic and other man-made fibres, except glass.
3. *Drugs:* Biological products, medicinal chemicals and botanical products, pharmaceutical preparations.
4. *Soap, detergents and cleaning preparations, perfumes, cosmetics and other toilet preparations:* Soap and other detergents, except cleaners. Specially cleaning, polishing and sanitation preparations, except soap and detergents. Perfumes, cosmetics and other toilet preparations.
5. Paints, varnishes, lacquers, enamels and allied products.
6. Gum and wood chemicals.
7. *Agricultural chemicals:* Fertilisers, agricultural pesticides; other agricultural chemicals, such as soil conditioners and trace elements.
8. *Miscellaneous chemical products:* Glue and gelatin, explosives, printing ink, fatty acids and carbon black.

Because of diversified product structures industries related with chemicals have also been divided as:

(i) *Heavy chemicals:* Such as sulphuric acid, soda ash, caustic soda, chlorine, nitric acid, etc.
(ii) *Petro-chemicals:* Plastics, synthetic fibers, fertilisers, synthetic rubber, explosive, etc.
(iii) *Electro-chemicals:* Fertilisers, nitrate, ammonia, carbides, etc.
(iv) *Pharmaceuticals:* Medicines and drugs.
(v) *Light chemicals:* Insecticides, colours, tars, carbolic acid, synthetic fibers, synthetic rubber, etc.
(vi) *Derived chemicals:* Paints, soap, glass, paper, etc.

Factors of Localisation

Although factors of localisation of chemical industry are similar to that of other industries, e.g. raw material, market, transport, power, water supply, capital, etc. still there are certain specific factors that also determine the site and location of these industries. These are as follows:

Scientific and Technological Know-how

The entire chemical industry is based on scientific and technological knowledge. The technological advancement and attainment of know-how is a prime requisite for chemical industry. Chemical industry also requires updated knowledge, therefore, R&D facilities are necessary.

Capital

The chemical industry is one of the most capital intensive of all industries and the introduction of new products and processes arising from advances in chemical science has accordingly entailed high rates of investment.

Raw Material

Raw materials used for the manufacture of chemicals are bulky and weight-losing. So, some of the plants develop raw material source in their own premises. But, as the products are mostly expensive and basically used in other industries, market plays the decisive role in the localisation of the plant. Several raw materials are generally used in this industry. They are all obtained from different sources. It is most unlikely that all the raw materials will be available at a single place. The market or port locations are preferable, because of the availability of all the raw materials at these places.

Power Supply

Abundant power supply is necessary for the manufacture of chemical products. Formerly, coal, petroleum or hydel-power sources influenced the location but now due to the adoptation of energy efficient technique, the influence of power sources have greatly been reduced.

Availability of Land

Market and raw material sources exert pull on the location of chemical industry. Availability of land is also a significant factor which sometimes influences the location. Only for the availability of extensive lands, chemical industry generally develops not in the urban centres but in the suburbs.

Transportation Facilities

Most of the raw materials used in chemical plants are bulky and weight losing. It is desirable to have a good transportation network. Waterside location is a favoured location.

Production of Selected Chemicals

Although all the chemical products are important, but they are too much in number and it is not possible to discuss all the products. Therefore, production of a few important products have been described; these are:

Sulphuric Acid

Sulphuric acid is the most widely used product in chemical industries. Several industries, e.g. fertilisers, petroleum refining, steel plants, paper, paints, dyes, glass, drugs, etc. use it. The following table indicates the production of sulphuric acid:

Table 11.1

Main producers of sulphuric acid in the world

Country	*Production (in lakh metric tons)*	*Percentage of the world*
China	337.10	33.37
Russia	87.60	8.67
Japan	65.30	6.50
India	60.70	6.00
Brazil	60.50	5.99
Tunisia	48.60	4.80
Canada	38.97	3.80
Spain	38.90	3.80
Chile	28.60	2.83
Poland	16.21	1.60
France	12.8	1.90
Germany	15.3	1.50

Other sulphuric acid-producing countries are Ukraine, Finland, Italy, Lithuania, Indonesia, Greece, UK and USA.

Nitric Acid

Nitric acid is produced from the nitrogen and is used in manufacture of fertilisers (super phosphate), paints, drugs, and explosives. Table 11.2 indicates the main producers of nitric acid in the world:

Table 11.2

Main producers of nitric acid in the world

Country	*Production (in lakh metric tons)*	*Percentage of the world*
USA	67.4	37.5
Poland	20.3	11.3
Germany	15.2	8.4
Belgium	13.2	7.1
China	11.6	6.5
Belarus	11.4	6.5
Canada	10.7	4.9
Spain	9.30	4.3
Bulgaria	7.00	3.9
Japan	6.2	3.5
Italy	5.4	3.0
Brazil	5.4	3.0

Other nitric acid-producing countries are Ukraine, Turkey, Greece, Croatia and Russia.

Soda Ash

Soda ash is an alkali, used in the manufacture of paper, soap, glass and many other chemical products. The main producers of soda ash in the world are as follows:

Table 11.3

Main producers of soda ash in the world

Country	*Production (in lakh metric tons)*
China	242.9
USA	115.0
Russia	28.1
Germany	26.5
Turkey	19.0
India	16.0
Poland	10.5
France	10.0
Ukraine	7.2
Kenya	5.0
Italy	5.0
Japan	4.5

Other soda ash-producing countries are Romania, Pakistan, UK, Australia, Mexico, Botswana, Portugal, Egypt, Taiwan, Ethopia and Ukraine.

Caustic Soda

Caustic soda is used in glass, paper, textile, soap and in oil refining. USA is the leading producer of caustic soda and produces about 29 per cent of the world's total yield. China produces 17 per cent and Japan 11 per cent of the world's total production of caustic soda. Other caustic soda-producing countries are Germany, India, Brazil, Russia, Republic of Korea, Canada, UK, Italy, Spain, etc.

Chlorine

Chlorine is used for washing of textile as well as for purification of potable water. Chlorine is produced by many countries but its major producers are USA, China, Japan, Germany, France, India, Brazil, Republic of Korea, Canada, UK, Russia, Italy, etc.

Ammonia

Ammonia is used as a chemical product in industries. USA is the leading producer of ammonia followed by Russia, Germany, Japan, UK, China, India, etc

Distribution of Chemical Industry

Since chemical industry is based on science and technology, its development is more important in developed countries. But now, so many develcping countries are also important producers of several chemicals. The global chemical industry is mostly controlled by few multinational companies as they have the patent right of the products. The major chemical-producing countries are USA, Germany, China, Russia, Japan, France, India, Brazil, Italy, Poland, Belgium, UK, etc.

USA

The United States of America is the world's leading country in the production of chemical products. It produces nearly 30 to 35 per cent nitric acid, soda ash and caustic soda of the world and also ranks second in the production of sulphuric acid. The factors responsible for the development of chemical industry in USA are:

(i) The development of science and technology.
(ii) High degree of industrial development.
(iii) Availability of raw material.
(iv) Large and expanding market.
(v) Capital through multinational companies.

The centres of chemical industry in USA are widely distributed. The largest concentration of chemical industry is in the northern states of Pennsylvania, Ohio, Kentucky, Indiana, Tennessee, Alabama, Virginia, etc. Some industries often require products of other chemical industries. This interdependence or symbiotic relationship between the chemical plants forced most of the industrial establishments to settle within the same region. The other reasons responsible for this higher concentration in those states are the presence of nearby market, excellent transport facilities and availability of all kinds of raw materials within their periphery.

Apart from these states, almost all other states have at least a few chemical-producing units. The Atlantic coastal tracts ranging from New York, New Jersey, Maryland to the south-eastern state of Florida contribute more than 70 per cent of the chemical output. Of late, states of southern USA are heading for rapid development of chemical industry. The states like New Mexico, Arizona, Utah, Colorado, Kansas, Oklahoma are progressing in such a way that, within a few decades these southern states may equal the production of the north-eastern states.

In US, sulphuric acid is produced in many parts of the country. But the major sulphuric acid-producing states are Kansas, Oklahoma, Colorado, Texas and Louisiana.

The ammonium products are manufactured in the northern states at Kentucky, West Virginia, Tennessee and Indiana.

Soda ash is mostly produced in the states of Ohio, Michigan, New York, Virginia and Texas. Caustic soda and chlorine are produced in the states of Ohio, Virginia, North and South Carolina and Georgia.

All these heavy chemical products have a large and ready market throughout USA. The light chemical plants are the major buyers of these products.

Light chemical industry includes various products ranging from detergents, toilet products to pharmaceuticals. These products are secondary in nature and mostly produced from the basic or heavy chemical products. Several multinational companies control the industry in USA. The internationally famous companies are now operating from USA, i.e. companies like Lever Brothers, Colgate and several other detergent producers, and Max Factor. Helene Curtis in toilet products has dominated international market for several decades. All these factories are also located within Atlantic coastal areas for export advantage.

Germany

Germany is also a leading country in chemical industry. In Germany, the chemical industry began as early as in 1886 with the organisation and early growth of the dyestuffs and potash industry. In Germany, chemical industry has been developed because of the certain favourable factors, such as:

(i) economic stability and research facilities,
(ii) availability of raw materials like salt, potash, limestone, dolamite, sulphur, etc.
(iii) development of thermal power, and
(iv) extensive market facilities.

The areas of chemical industry in Germany are concentrated in Rhine valley and Upper Saxony. The four main areas are the Ruhr region, Frankfurt region, Northern Rhine region and Upper Saxony region.

Russia

Chemical industry is one of the most important industry in Russia. The early chemical-producing centres were largely concentrated around Moscow – Tula and St. Petersburg. The present chemical industry has been developed in the following regions:

(i) Moscow region, having centres at Moscow, Novomoskorsk, Voskresensk, Kazan, Gorky, Dzherzinsk and Yaroslav.
(ii) St. Petersburg region.
(iii) Ural region.
(iv) Siberia and Far-East region.

China

China has now emerged as a leading producer of chemicals, not only in Asia but also in the world. The development of chemical industry in China started in the plan period after 1950, when concerted efforts were made to develop Chinese chemical industry, specially heavy chemical industry. Special care was taken to increase the production of caustic soda, soda ash, sulphuric acid, hydrochloric acid and nitric acid. The effort made was so sincere that in the last three decades production increased threefold.

The major chemical-producing centres in China are located in its northern part. The urban centres of Nanking, Shanghai and Shantung contribute maximum of the chemical output. The other noted chemical factories are located at Manchuria, Fushun, Penki, Dairen and Anshan. The largest of the plants are located at Manchuria.

Japan

The origin of chemical industry in Japan began only after the First World War. But since then, rapid growth of this industry has placed it in a high position. Although, during the Second World War, Japanese industries including the chemical industry were completely devastated. But, with herculean efforts, Japan was able to rebuild its chemical industry within a short period and surpassed its pre-war production level.

Most of the Japanese chemical plants are either newly constructed or completely rebuilt, so output and productivity is very high. All the plants are new, modernised and automated.

Japan is deficient in raw materials. More than 80 per cent of its factories are entirely dependent on imported raw materials. The only raw material abundant in Japan is sulphur, deposited extensively by volcanic eruptions. Most of the chemical plants in Japan are located within the industrial agglomerations of Osaka-Kobe, Tokyo-Yokohoma, Nagoya, Hemagi and Kyushu.

United Kingdom

In UK, chemical industry has been developed in the following areas:
(i) The Tees valley,
(ii) The Mursey valley and southern Lancashire,
(iii) Tyne valley and Avon valley,
(iv) Scotland, and
(v) London region.

The leading chemical-producing centres are Lancashire, Glasgow, Manchester, Birmingham, Yorkshire, Leeds, Norwich, Middlewich, etc.

Italy

Italy is considered as a leading producer of both light and heavy chemical products. The growth rate in the industry is quite high. Several reasons are responsible for the development of chemical industry in Italy. These are:

(i) Presence of vast amount of raw materials within the country, including limestone, dolomite, sulphur and potash.

(ii) Availability of cheap hydel-power.

(iii) Good transport system and market facilities.

The major chemical centres in Italy are Naples, Milan, etc.

France

In France, chemical industry has developed in four areas, i.e. north-eastern region, Lorraine region, Leyons-Marseilles region and Bordeaux-Garonne region. The strong industrial infrastructure, abundant coal reserve, developed petroleum refinery industry and presence of several raw materials like salt, dolomite, limestone and potash facilitated the growth of chemical industry in France.

India

India is now an important manufacturer of the chemical products. India produces 6 per cent sulphuric acid, 6.2 per cent soda ash and 4 per cent caustic soda of the world along with a large variety of other chemical products. The major centres of chemical industry in India are Mumbai, Kolkata, Sindri, Jamshedpur, Chennai, Bangalore, Trombay, Vadodara, Ahmedabad, Kanpur, Amritsar, Delhi, etc.

Brazil

Brazil is a significant producer of chemical products not only in South America but also in the world. It produces 5 per cent sulphuric acid, 3 per cent nitric acid and 4 per cent caustic soda to the world's output. The main centres of chemical industry are Rio de Janeiro, Sao Paulo, Minasgeras, Santos, etc.

Apart from the above, Spain, Belgium, Poland, Australia, Bulgaria, Turkey, Ukraine, Greece, Croatia, etc. are the other important countries, producing chemical products in the world.

CHEMICAL FERTILISER INDUSTRY

The growth, development and productivity of agriculture depends upon soil fertility and the fertility of soil depends upon several factors, especially on its mineral components such as phosphorus, potassium, nitrogen, calcium, magnesium, sulphur, etc. The critical problem of modern agriculture is the maintenance of soil fertility. Each crop removes something from the soil. Our ancestors coped with this problem by following a 'gap season' with no crop on the land, so that it could recover naturally something of what it had lost. But now under the pressure of population, land hardly gets this rest, therefore, loss of soil fertility and lower productivity has now become a common problem.

It was in 1840 when Von Leibig for the first time identified the minerals which are primarily necessary for plant growth. These minerals must be put back into the soil to offset the losses resulting from cropping. With this purpose chemical fertilisers have been developed. The production of chemical fertilisers, although a part of chemical industry, but because of their volume of production and nature, the chemical fertiliser industry now has become an independent and important industry.

The common chemical fertilisers are:

(i) *Nitrogenous fertilisers* in the form of ammonium sulphate, urea, nitro-limestone and ammonium nitrate.

(ii) *Phosphatic fertilisers* in the form of super-phosphate like nitro-phosphate and ammonium phosphate, and

(iii) *Potassium fertilisers* in the form of potassium.

Nitrogen Fertilisers

The primary deficiency of nitrogen in all temperate and tropical countries demands top priority for the manufacture of nitrogen fertilisers. Following are the important nitrogen fertilisers in common use in various countries of the world:

(i) Ammonium sulphate: 20.6 per cent N

(ii) Ammonium sulphate nitrate: 26 per cent N

(iii) Calcium ammonium nitrate: 20.5 per cent N

(iv) Urea: 45 per cent N

(v) Ammonium chloride: 25 per cent N

Nitrogen fertilisers are the most widely produced and most commonly used. Nearly 75 per cent nitrogen is now obtained from air, 20 per cent is derived as a by-product of coke-oven plant in the form of ammonium gas, four-fifths of which is nitrogen and the rest of 5 per cent is obtained from the (mineral) sodium nitrate.

Table 11.4 indicates the production of nitrogenous fertilisers in the world:

Table 11.4

Production of nitrogenous fertilisers in the world

Country	*Production in lakh metric tons*	*Percentage of the world*
China	281.4	24.0
India	106.3	11.0
USA	84.0	8.4
Ukraine	64.4	6.4
Russia	58.2	5.8
Canada	35.9	3.6
Indonesia	28.5	2.8
Pakistan	21.1	2.0
Romania	17.2	1.7
Bangladesh	17.0	1.7
Qatar	16.3	1.6
Poland	15.8	1.5
Egypt	15.4	1.5
Saudi Arabia	12.99	1.3

China is the largest producer of nitrogen fertiliser and contributes 24 per cent of the world's production. India is the second largest producer with 11 per cent of the world's production followed by USA (8.4%), Ukraine (6.4%) and Russia (5.8%). Apart from the countries mentioned in Table 11.5, Netherlands, UK, Germany, France, Spain, Turkey, Iran, Brazil, South Africa and Uzbekistan are the other producers of nitrogen fertilisers.

Phosphate Fertilisers

Phosphate fertilisers, generally known as phosphorus have often been called the master key to agriculture, as low crop production more often is due to a lack of phosphorus. Phosphorus fertilisers are classified into three types, e.g. water-soluble phosphorous, citrate-soluble phosphorus, and insoluble phosphorus.

The fossil remains of animal life in the form of phosphate rock are the largest source of phosphorus today. Most of the rock phosphate reserves of the world are concentrated in North Africa, USA and Russia, as well as in Peru, Egypt, Spain and Nauru island in the Pacific Ocean.

China, Morocco, USA, Russia, Jordon, Brazil, Egypt, Saudi Arabia, Peru, Tunisia, Vietnam are the major producers of phosphate fertilisers in the world. Table 11.5 indicates the annual production of phosphate fertilisers in the world:

Table 11.5

Important producers of phosphate fertilisers in the world (2016)

Country	*Production (in million metric tons)*
China	138
Morocco	30
Western Sahara	30
USA	27.8
Russia	11.6
Jordon	8.3
Brazil	6.5
Egypt	5.5
Saudi Arabia	4.0
Peru	4.0
Israel	3.5
Tunisia	3.5
Vietnam	2.8

Source: U.S. Geological Survey Report.

Other countries producing rock phosphate are India, Belgium, Poland, South Africa, Japan, Belarus, Lithuania, Netherlands, Indonesia and Canada.

Potash Fertilisers

A large quantity of potassium is derived from deposits of potash salts. The largest deposits of potash are found in Germany, Belarus, Russia, France, Spain, USA and Israel-Trans Jordan. Playa deposits in desert areas and the brines of some salt lakes are also rich in potassium. Acid areas usually need potassium fertilisers more than neutral and alkaline soils because acid soils have developed in areas of high rainfall that leaches fertilisers out of available potassium. Japan uses potassium fertilisers on a large scale for rice production.

Table 11.6 indicates the production of potash fertilisers in important countries of the world:

Table 11.6

Major producers of potash fertilisers in the world

Country	*Production (in lakh metric tons)*	*Percentage of the world*
Belarus	113.0	28.8
Canada	80.2	20.4
Russia	54.6	13.9
China	35.9	9.1
Germany	34.8	8.8
Israel	19.1	4.9
Jordan	11.7	2.9
USA	6.9	1.7
Spain	5.8	1.4
UK	5.4	1.4
Chile	4.0	1.0
Belgium	4.0	1.0

It becomes clear from the Table 11.6 that major producers of potash fertilisers are Belarus, Canada, Russia, China and Germany. Apart from the countries mentioned in the table, Brazil, Poland, Republic of Korea also produce potash fertilisers.

Chemical Fertiliser Industry in India

One of the important factors in the success of 'Green Revolution' in India is the use of chemical fertilisers. The crop yield per hectare in India was too low previously. But with the increasing demand and food deficit, the country has given special attention to the production of chemical fertilisers.

As a result, there has been a rapid growth of chemical fertiliser industry in India during last five decades and now India is the third largest producer of nitrogenous fertilisers in the world. India's average annual production of nitrogenous fertiliser is 12 million tons and phosphatic fertiliser is 4.5 million tons.

The Government of India has established a number of industries of national importance. The fertiliser industry is one of them. The Fertiliser Corporation of India is a public sector company, which is the most important fertiliser producer company of India. In India, about 60 factories are actually producing chemical fertilisers in different parts of the country along with about 70 medium and small-scale units.

As a part of agricultural development programme, a large-scale factory of Fertiliser Corporation of India, has been started at Sindri (Bihar). The factory produces mostly ammonium sulphate and to a lesser extent urea and ammonium nitrate. It has a daily capacity of 1000 tons. Other important factories of the Corporation are located at Nangal (Punjab), Gorakhpur (Uttar Pradesh), Trombay (Maharashtra) and Namrup (Assam). In 1966, the Gujarat State Fertilizers & Chemicals Ltd. had set up its factory with seven giant plants near

Baroda. Indian Farmers Fertilizer Cooperative Limited (IFFCO) has set up a big factory at Kandla port. The other major centres of chemical fertiliser industry in India are Neyveli (Ennore), Alwaye, Mangalore, Coimbatore, Paradeep, Korba, Kampti, Guna, Kota, Bhatinda, Barauni, Durgapur, etc. A large number of modern fertiliser plants have been set up using diverse feedstocks and technology to manufacture a wide range of fertilisers like superphosphate, urea, ammonia sulphate, and various grades of complex fertilisers.

PULP AND PAPER INDUSTRY

All types of writing work is done on paper, thus, paper is considered as a base of modern civilisation. There are evidences that paper was first made in China in 105 AD by Ts'ai lun and this art spread in other countries gradually. Until the mid-19th century, rags remained the chief paper making material. The use of wood pulp with rags for making paper began in Germany in 1840 and in USA in 1880. Thereafter, throughout the 20th century, most of the world's paper has been made from wood pulp and this process is still going on. In fact, paper is a forest-based industry. Both pulp and paper industry are complementary to each other. Paper is usually manufactured from wood fibres. The rounded wood and processed wood is converted into wood pulp, which is considered as a principal raw material of paper industry.

The importance of wood pulp is fast growing. The main uses to which wood pulp is at present put to are the manufacture of paper and cellulose which is then used for the manufacture of artificial silk. The chief woods used for the manufacture of pulp are the species of spruce, fir, and pine for 'mechanical' pulps; and aspen, polar and other deciduous trees for 'chemical' pulp. Hemlock is used in considerable quantity in producing pulp for inferior papers. *Mechanical pulps* are made by grinding the wood and are used for inferior kinds of paper. *Chemical pulps* are made by dissolving wood into pulp through chemical solutions. These are generally used for better quality paper. At present, wood pulp is largely used in the production of newsprint only, in the manufacture of which two kinds of pulps are mixed together in proportion of 70 mechanical and 30 chemical. The use of wood pulp for paper of other kinds also is, however, growing fast, owing to the improvements being made in pulp making.

Factors of Localisation

The location of pulp and paper industry is of immense importance because of some specific requirements for this industry. Production of paper, nowadays is done through several integrated processes, where modern technologies are involved. Generally, two types of paper and pulp mills are seen in the world, i.e. (i) raw material-based, and (ii) market-based.

In some countries, mills produce only paper while in other countries they produce wood pulp as well as paper. The pulp is mostly used by paper industries. Therefore, for obvious reasons, pulp and paper industries are always concentrated near raw material source. The mills engaged in the production of only paper generally show affinity towards the market. The composite mills which cover all the manufacturing processes are generally located near the raw material source. The general tendency of the present-day paper mills is to be near the market. The transhipment cost of paper is not very high. Therefore, to be acquainted with the changing mood of customers, paper industries locate within the periphery of consumer centres. In the case of the paper manufacturing units, using waste paper and cardboards, are located near the market, because market is the major supplier of the raw materials.

The locational factors of the pulp and paper industry may be summarised as follows:

Raw Material

Wood is the primary raw material for this industry. Pulp mills must be located near the forests because this minimises the difficulty of transporting the bulk logs as well as cost also. A river-side site is ideal because logs can be floated directly to the mill. The forest in the area must be extensive and capable of supplying large quantities of suitable timber. In paper industry soft woods like Spruce, Cedar, Hemlock, Deodar, Eucalyptus, etc. are used. Several pulp manufacturing units are located near the forest to get abundant supply of wood.

Water

Paper industry requires a large quantity of water. To make 1 ton of newsprint, about 100 tons of water is needed, and since, it is essential to maintain a copious production, vast quantities of clear chemical free, fresh water must be available. These conditions are usually available in thinly populated, forested areas rather than in major industrial complexes.

Power

A ton of newsprint may require about 2,000 kilowatt hours of electricity and thus, vast power sources are essential. Paper plants show an affinity towards cheap hydel-power sources. Canadian rivers have been tapped to provide power to the pulp mills. Similarly, the use of power supplied from rivers in southern USA, has led to the establishment of some of the largest pulp mills in the world in the southern states. In the absence of hydel-power, these mills grow near power plants.

Transport

Transport is one of the most important determinants of paper plant location. The transport cost of newsprint and paper is slightly higher than the transport cost of its raw material. But, on the other hand, raw material reduces its weight considerably during the processing. Whatever may be the cause, for steady supply of raw material, a good network of transport and communication is a prime requisite.

Paper mills are usually situated near the coast, where the rivers on which the log are floated reach the sea, and where paper or pulp can be loaded on ships for export. Most of the mills in Sweden are positioned in this way. In Britain, most of the paper industry is largely dependent on imported pulp, therefore, paper mills are having a coastal position.

Capital

Paper industry is a capital-intensive industry, therefore, large capital is required for sophisticated machinery and other works. The larger the mill the greater are the initial costs. The large paper mills are also associated with the printing and publishing business and often own their own forests.

Labour

Nowadays paper mills are highly mechanised, thus, require lesser manpower. They can be located in remote regions having labour shortage.

Production and Distribution

The production of wood pulp is an important industry in many countries of the world. The major producers of the wood pulp are shown in Table 11.7.

Table 11.7

Major wood pulp producers of the world

Country	*Production in thousand metric tons*	*Percentage*
Canada	11335	32.2
USA	5998	15.3
Finland	3940	11.2
Sweden	2959	8.4
Japan	1674	4.7
Norway	1534	4.3
Germany	1220	3.5
Russia	1025	2.9
France	757	2.1
New Zealand	721	2.0

It becomes clear from Table 11.7 that Canada is the highest wood pulp producer in the world and produces 32.2 per cent of the world production. USA is the second largest producer followed by Finland and Sweden. The other major producers of wood pulp in the world are Japan, Norway, Germany, Russia, France and New Zealand.

Paper is produced in many countries of the world but its major producers are Canada, USA, Russia, Germany, Norway, Sweden, UK, Japan, China, India, etc. There are several varieties of paper produced in the world, among them newsprint paper is very important because of its large quantity of consumption throughout the world. The production of newsprint paper is given in Table 11.8 and paper and paperboard production in Table 11.9.

Table 11.8

Major producers of newsprint paper in the world

Country	*Production in lakh metric tons*
Canada	86.0
USA	65.4
Japan	32.8
Sweden	24.9
Republic of Korea	17.2
Germany	16.0
Finland	14.8
Russia	11.8
UK	10.2
China	8.4

Table 11.9
Major paper and paperboard producing countries of the world

Country	*Production in million metric tons*
China	107.100
USA	72.397
Japan	26.228
Germany	22.608
Republic of Korea	11.569
Brazil	10.357
Finland	10.310
Canada	10.226
Sweden	10.165
Italy	8.840

Canada

Canada is the largest producer of wood pulp, newsprint paper and other types of paper in the world. This has been possible due to its vast resources of coniferous forest, which provide raw material for paper industry. In recent years, apart from newsprint, Canada also expanded production of paper and paper board. In the last 15 years, production of paper in Canada has had about 24 per cent of increase, which is a spectacular achievement.

In Canada, major paper mills are located in three regions, i.e. Quebec, Ontario and British Columbia. The favourable factors responsible for the growth of paper industry are: availability of raw material from coniferous forest, cheap and available hydel-power, transportation facilities specially water transport through rivers and lakes and extensive market. In newsprint production, Canada is supreme and most of the newsprint production is exported to other countries like USA, UK, Germany, India, etc.

USA

The United States of America is a leading country in paper industry. There are several geo-economic factors that favoured the growth and development of the paper industry in this country. These factors are:

(i) Soft wood forest resources are available as raw material;
(ii) Availability of hydel-power resources;
(iii) Good transportation facilities, especially inland waterways of great lakes, which facilitates easy transportation of logs and import of special soft wood from Canada;
(iv) Abundant water resources;
(v) Industrial and economic development of high level enabled her to build up necessary infrastructure for the industry;
(vi) Domestic demand and worldwide market; and
(vii) Capital availability, etc.

The four important regions of paper industry in the US are as under:

The North-Eastern Forest Region

This was the first centre in United States where paper and pulp industry developed. At its early period of growth, the region supplied substantial amount of paper to the country. The major paper and pulp manufacturing units were located around New England states. Several factors were favourable at that time for abundant growth of paper industry in that region.

The Great Lakes Region

This is also a main region of paper industry. The advantage of inland water transportation facility is an additional advantage of this region.

The Western Region

The north-western states like Washington, Oregon, Idaho, Montana and North Dakota contain a large number of mills. The greater concentration of paper and pulp mills occur in the states situated along the Pacific Coast. The narrow coastal belt running through Washington, Oregon and Northern California now contributes substantial amount of paper.

The Southern Districts

Of late, southern paper mills contribute larger share in the production of paper in United States. This region has developed rapidly, because of imported soft wood from Canada and modern productive paper manufacturing process. The states engaged in paper production in this region are North and South Carolina, Georgia, Florida, Alabama, Mississippi, Arkansas and Texas.

Sweden

Sweden is the major paper and wood pulp-producing country in the world. In the last two decades, Sweden's paper industry has developed more than 35 per cent. Sweden is having a forest cover of more than 28 million hectares which is the biggest source of raw material. The cheap availability of hydroelectricity and large European markets are the other causes of its development. Sweden is also an important exporter of paper, not only to Europe but to other parts of the world.

Finland

Finland is also one of the largest paper-producing countries of the world. The major reason behind the phenomenal growth of Finland's paper industry is the vast amount of forest resource within the country. In a country of only 30.46 million hectares, 23.23 million hectares of forest constitutes about 76.26 per cent of the total area. Most of the tree species are of valuable, soft conifers. Apart from raw materials, hydel-power is also available at a much cheaper rate. Due to low consumption of paper in the home market, Finland exports bulk of her paper products.

Japan

Japan is third in paper production and fourth in wood pulp production in the world. The major factors favourable for the rapid growth of Japanese paper industry are:

(i) Vast forest resources of the country. Japan is having 25 million hectares of forest area.

(ii) The cheap hydel-power harnessed from short turbulent mountain rivers.

(iii) Entrepreneurship ability of the industrialists and patriotic zeal of the average Japanese worker.

(iv) Vast market at home and abroad.

(v) Low production cost, due to the adoptation of sophisticated technology and low wage rate of the workers.

The leading centres of paper production are Kwanto plain which includes Tokyo, Kawasaki and Yokohama, Ise Bay including Nagowa and Kitakyushu region.

Russia

Russia produces about 12 lakh metric tons of paper annually and is also important in wood pulp production. Most of the paper industry of Russia is concentrated at Leningrad, Ivanovo, Oblast, Ural and Moscow. Several factors helped in the growth of paper industry. The most important one is the largest forest cover spread over in central and eastern part of the country. The cheap supply of electricity and widespread market are the other causes.

China

China is considered to be the pioneer of handmade paper in the world. The modern paper industry was started only after the coming of communist regime, but soon China became a leading producer of paper and paperboard in the world and also ranks 10th in production of newsprint in the world. The main centres of paper industry in China are located at Canton, Tientsin, Jidong, Hankow, Tianjin, Ningguo and Kyamuje.

Germany

Germany is also a leading producer of wood pulp and paper including newsprint. Although, Germany is not very rich in forest resources. Most of the paper is produced from waste materials. Large internal demand and technological advancements helped Germany to establish large paper plants. In Germany, most of the paper mills are located at Ruhr-Westphalia region and Middle Rhine region. Main centres are Dortmund, Dusseldorf, Frankfurt, Ludwigshanfen, Leipzig and Dresden, etc.

India

In India, paper industry is developing at a fast rate. From a production of about 1 lakh ton in 1950, now its production is more than 40 lakh tons. In the earlier stage, paper industry was predominantly localised in the Hooghly basin of West Bengal. In the later stage there has been growth of paper mills in many other parts of the country, but West Bengal still leads. Other states having paper mills are Bihar, Odisha, Maharashtra, Gujarat, Madhya Pradesh, Uttar Pradesh, Andhra Pradesh, Karnataka, Kerala, Himachal Pradesh and Assam. The Hindustan Paper Corporation Ltd. is a public sector undertaking and has three mills, one located in Nagaland and two in Assam. National Newsprint and Paper Mills was established in 1965 at Nepanagar (NEPA Ltd.) of Madhya Pradesh. Recent trend in Indian paper industry is the production of Indian board. Now India is producing several types of paper and also imports paper for specific purposes to fulfil the growing demand.

In addition to the above, the other paper-producing countries in the world are Norway, France, Italy, Brazil, Republic of Korea, Argentina, Netherlands, Indonesia, Thailand, Poland, Spain, Mexico, Australia, etc.

12

Industrial Regions of the World

Industrial regions are those areas, where concentration of industries has occurred due to favourable geo-economic conditions. These are areas within which manufacturing industry is carried out on a relatively large scale and employs a relatively large proportion of population. The spatial distribution of manufacturing units shows a distinct trend of localisation towards a few selected areas; these regions are referred to as 'industrial regions'. Although, the concept of 'region' and its delimitation is a precise one, the same has not been discussed in this chapter. In this chapter we propose to consider in the broadest outline only the distribution and characteristic features of the industrial regions of the world.

The common characteristic features of the industrial regions are:

1. Large population engaged in industrial pursuits,
2. Large industrial complex in hierarchical order,
3. Integration of some main industries with a group of subsidiary industries,
4. Large banking and credit facilities,
5. A network of communication lines, and
6. A large market for labour supply, etc.

The industrial regions of the world are very unevenly distributed over the face of the earth. Both natural and cultural factors are involved in any explanation of the distribution of manufacturing regions of the world, but the great differentiations in localisation of any industrial region can be explained to a large degree by the availability of resources. Since the development of machinery, many industrial centres have sprung up where there is abundance of coal, or coal and iron, or extensive water-power – the mainsprings of modern industry, and all such towns are more or less business centres.

There are several factors affecting the concentration or localisation of industry. The main localising factors are: the market, the labour supply, the cost of land resources, the situation of raw material, the nature and situation of the natural and human resources, the value of the commodities produced in relation to the cost of the various items entering into their production, and finally, the supply of capital.

It is obvious that the profitableness of large scale operations must depend on the adequacy of the market, which is governed by various condition as:

1. The number of people where the industry is carried on.
2. The purchasing power of the people, a great contrast in this respect being presented by developing countries as compared with developed countries and other semi-developed countries, in which the latter's purchasing power is enhanced by the diffusion of education, and probably still more by the extent of the available undeveloped resources.
3. The nature of the commodity for which a market is sought – cheap goods for peoples of small purchasing power, more valuable commodities for regions in which individual wealth is greater.
4. Facilities for transport in enlarging the range of the market.

The spatial distribution of the industries shows a trend of concentration or agglomeration of industries in few regions where geo-economic conditions of industrial growth are favourable. These industrial regions have variety of industries and other infrastructures and are famous for their production of particular or varied types of industrial goods. The major industrial regions of the world are as follows:

1. North American region, comprising USA and Canada.
2. European region, consisting of the industrial region of UK, Germany, France, etc.
3. Industrial region of former USSR.
4. Asian region, comprising the industrial regions of Japan, China, India, etc.
5. Other isolated industrial regions.

Figure 12.1
Major industrial regions of the world

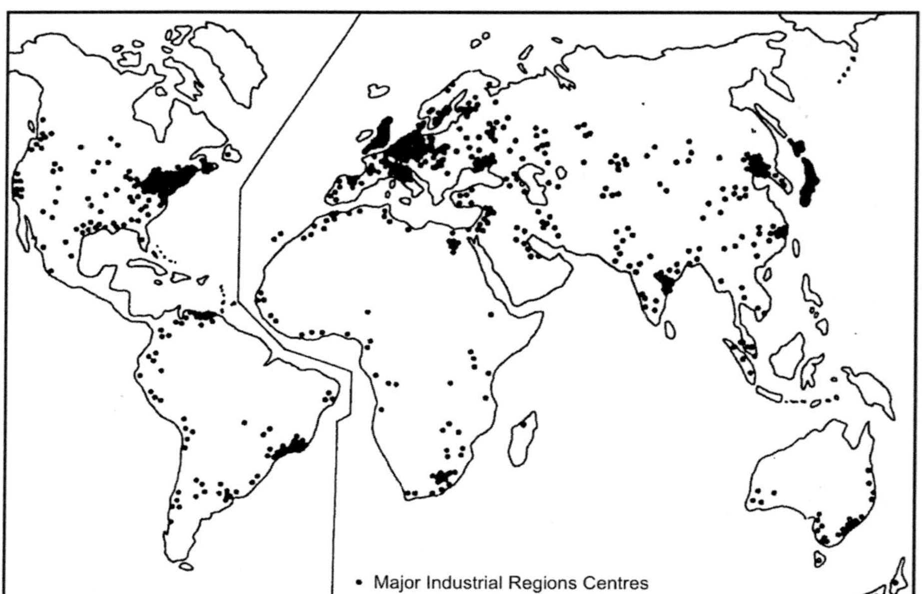

NORTH AMERICAN INDUSTRIAL REGIONS

North American industrial region comprising of USA and Canada is a highly developed industrial region of the world. USA is now the wealthiest and most highly developed nation in the world. Southern Canada is also well developed.

The USA has become the world's greatest industrial country. They had the immense advantages of space and virgin resources. The speed at which the industrial pattern of the USA is shifting and changing today is, in some sense, a measure of their industrial wealth and of the newness of their development. The continent was peopled from the east. The oldest centres of industry lie along the eastern seaboard or in the valleys of the eastward flowing rivers. The industrial centres of the Middle West and of the Pacific coast are more recent. The North American continent has many great industrial centres and a few industrial regions. This is partly the consequence of the widespread nature of the resources of the continent, and partly because of the late date at which industrialisation took place. The development of transport facilities, and in recent years the generation and transmission of hydroelectric power have tended to cut industry adrift from the coalfields. It is now having few areas of large scale concentration. Figure 12.2 shows major industrial regions of North America, particularly of USA and southern Canada.

Figure 12.2

Major industrial areas of USA and southern Canada

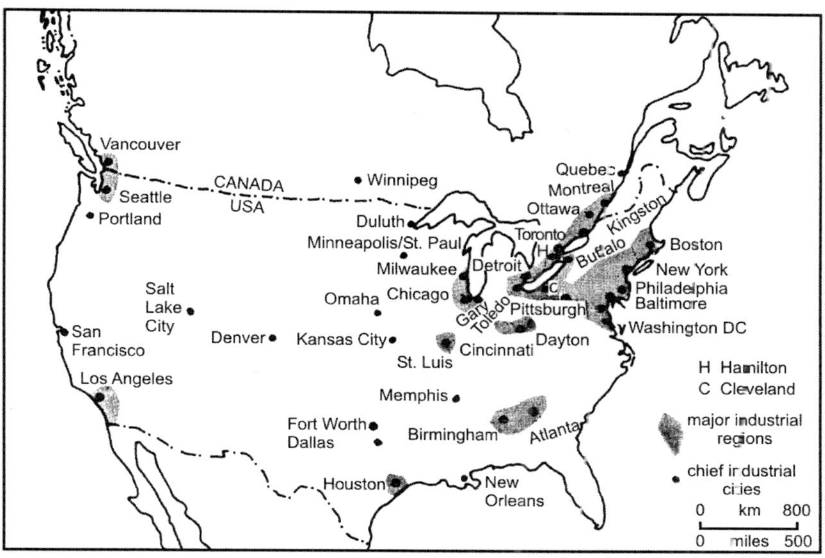

The industrial regions of USA are as follows:

(i) Southern New England
(ii) Mid-Atlantic States
(iii) Pittsburgh-Lake Erie Region
(iv) Detroit Industrial Region
(v) Lake Michigan Region
(vi) Southern Appalachian Region

(vii) Eastern Texas

(viii) Pacific Coastal Region

Southern New England

This part of USA was the earliest to be developed by the settlers from England. Therefore, industrial growth also started earlier in this region. This is one of the oldest industrial regions in USA having a diversified industrial growth. The nucleus of the region is Boston with Connecticut, Massachusetts and Rhode Island are other major centres.

The two dominant industries which developed in this region are shipbuilding and textile, but both have now declined as newer centres with greater advantages have emerged in the Mid-Atlantic States, the Great Lakes and the West. The engineering industry is still important, especially for the production of specialised goods, such as electrical machinery at Springfield, aircraft and armaments in Hartford, instrument-making at Bridgeport and textile-machinery manufacture at Worcester, Lowell and New Bedford. Two towns, Boston and Beverly, are specialised in footwear machinery and the former is a shoemaking centre. The traditional textile towns are Lowell and Providence for woollen textiles; and New Bedford, Worcester and Fall river for cotton textiles; but these now produce mainly high-quality goods. Mass production is now more economic, farther south.

Mid-Atlantic States

This region has a great diversity of manufactures. Inland, the variety of product, from the wrist watch to the giant locomotive; from the coarsest cotton to the finest silk; and from the deadliest and most powerful chemicals to perfumes are the outstanding characteristics of this industrial development. Abundance of cheap and good anthracite coal of Pennsylvania, oil and natural gas from Appalachians have been important factors in encouraging development in the Mid-Atlantic Region. Coal is used in all units of this industrial region as a source of power but oil and gas are also important sources of energy. This is also the most densely populated part of the United States, a main source of skilled labour force, and this is also the main basis for the growth of enormous industrial conurbation from New York to Baltimore.

The main industrial cities of the Mid-Atlantic region are New York, Newark, Trenton, Philadelphia, Wilnington, Baltimore, etc. This vast conurbation from New York to Baltimore is known as *Megalopolis*. New York, situated on Manhattan Island, at the mouth of this important Hudson route from the interior via the Mohawk and Hudson valleys, is the largest city in the United States. It has an excellent harbour, and kilometres of wharves along the shores of the Manhattan Island and Long Island. Leading industries were food and allied products, clothing and other textile products, printing and publishing, chemical and allied products, electrical equipment, transport equipment and instruments. The town of Albany lies near the confluence of the Mohawk and the Hudson, and is noted for iron and steel manufactures.

Pittsburgh-Lake Erie Region

This is the region having greatest concentration of ferrous industries. This region accounts about one-fourth of ferrous and ferro-alloy products of the country. The famous Youngstown-Pittsburgh-Johnstown iron and steel triangle is located in the region. The other steel-producing areas are Wheeling, Cleveland, Louisville, Rookford, Flint, Steubenville and Detroit. The other manufacturing centres engaged in diversified manufacturing activities are Chicago, Anderson, Midland, Iowa, St. Louis, Minneapolis, etc. In cities like Detroit, several industries have developed including motor vehicles, machinery, fabricated metals, machine tools and electronics.

Most of the iron and steel towns are spun in the vicinity of Pittsburgh, such as Mckeesport, Braddock, Carnegie, Homestead and Johnstown. The industry spreads northward up to Shenango valley to Sharon, up the Beaver-Mahoning valley to Youngstown and into Canton, Massillon, and other eastern Ohio towns. It also spreads down the Ohio river to Weirton, Steubenville, wheeling Huntington, Ashland, Ironton and Portsmouth and up the Miami valley to Middletown. Pittsburgh also has the largest glass industry in the United States. Johntown on the Conemangh, to the east of Pittsburgh, has a coal, iron and steel industry. Most of the ore comes from Lake Superior. Cleveland, on Lake Erie, is noted for iron goods, electrical engineering and machineries.

Detroit Industrial Region

This is the greatest automobile manufacturing region of the USA, centred at Detroit. The city was at first a centre for wagon and carriage-making which later led to the assembly of automobiles in the region. It is the headquarters of several giant motor corporations including Ford, Chrysler, and General Motors. Other locational advantages were the large market for cars in the Midwest, where other forms of transport, e.g. railways, were relatively poorly developed in the early 20th century; and the ease of transporting steel from Pittsburgh via Lake Erie. The automobile industry extends to many other towns around Detroit, e.g. Lansing, Flint, Jackson, Pontiac, Dearborn and Toledo; and car assembly is linked with other branches of manufacture such as tyre-making, electrical wires, glass, batteries, paints, polishes, alloyed steel, spare parts and components.

Lake Michigan Region

This area lies on the southern shores of Lake Michigan with Chicago as a main centre. There are some 10,000 factories in and around Chicago, amongst which the iron and steel plants are the most important. The manufacturing industries around Lake Michigan are confined largely to Chicago and Gary where iron ore of the Lake Superior and of north meets coal from the south. Chicago, near the head of Lake Michigan, is now the second largest city in the United States. Its chief advantage lies in the fact that railways from the north-west are obliged to pass through it in rounding Lake Michigan to reach the Atlantic, while it also forms a good centre for railways from the south. Chicago concentrates on motor vehicles and trucks, cement, chemicals, iron and steel goods, furniture, paper, cereal, baby food and pharmaceuticals. Other industries are based on the agricultural products of the surrounding regions, e.g. meat-packing, grain milling and the making of agricultural implements and machinery. Gary near Chicago is important for iron and steel production.

Closely associated with the Chicago metropolitan area are such urban centres as Milwankee, Racine and Kenosha with their extensive iron and steel, motor vehicle, beverage, machinery, meat packing, leather and leather goods establishments. Chicago, Gary and Milwankee depend upon it now for the delivery of Upper Lake ore.

Southern Appalachian Region

This is a very distinctive steel making area centred at Birmingham in the piedmont of the southern Appalachians in the state of Albama. The availability of coal and iron, later supplemented by oil and hydroelectric power from the Fall line are responsible for the growth of this industrial area. Other industrial cities of this region are Atlanta, Gadsden, Bessemer, Anniston and many others. Cotton textiles and chemicals are now manufactured in several industrial towns of this industrial region where water power is available. It makes a very wide range of goods such as metal works, chemicals and machinery manufacture.

Eastern Texas

The industrial development of this region is based on oil, as a source of fuel and as a raw material. The main centres of this region are cities of Dallas and Houston. This region is also rich in sulphur, rock salt and phosphate rock. This makes oil refining and chemical industries the most important in the region. Its situation on the coast have additional advantage of transportation. The capital available by the oil industry helps in industrial development. Dallas has more than twelve oil refineries, chemical plants, synthetic rubber factory as well as steel milling and manufacture of mining equipment and consumer products. Dallas also has clothing and fashion industry and Fort Worth is famous for aircraft and aerospace industries.

Pacific Coastal Region

This region is a narrow coastal strip running through Washington, Oregon and California. This is one of the great industrial agglomeration of the Pacific coast. Its industrial centres are San Francisco and Los Angeles. This region is famous for food and beverages, automobiles, aircraft, metal fabrication, petrochemical and heavy chemical industries. The other industrial centres of this region are Portland, Seattle, Engine, Sacramento, San Diego, etc.

Apart from the above mentioned industrial regions, there are some large isolated industrial centres in USA which are known for their industrial products. St. Louis has meat-packing, flour-milling, footwear, and agricultural machinery industries. Kansas City has similar manufacture of products plus aircraft and oil refining. Others like Omaha, Cincinnati, Indianapolis, Denver, St. Paul and Minneapolis, and Memphis concern themselves mainly with agricultural industries, being located in the midst of America's richest agricultural region. Flour-milling, meat-packing, cotton textiles and food processing are some of the major industrial undertakings.

Bordering the Gulf of Mexico are several towns that serve as the outlets of the Mississippi basin and have industries linked with the oil found in the region. New Orleans has oil refining, chemicals and cotton textile industries.

Industrial Regions of Canada

In North America, Canada is the second largest industrial region. The country is rich in mineral resources like iron ore, petroleum and forest resources and also has abundant hydroelectric power. The three major industrial regions of Canada are: (i) Ontario and St. Lawrence valley, (ii) Prairie Region, and (iii) Pacific Coastal Region.

Ontario and St. Lawrence Valley

This is one of the most important manufacturing regions in Canada. The major products are paper, cheese, flour, agricultural machinery, copper and nickel smelting, iron and steel industry and chemical industry. The major industrial centres are Quebec, Ontario, Ottawa, Toronto, Hamilton, etc.

Prairie Region

As far as manufacturing industry is concerned, this region is not very developed. The major centres of production are Manitoba, Winnipeg, Edmonton, Alberta, etc. Besides agro-based industries, the other noted industries in the region are petroleum refinery and chemical industry.

Pacific Coastal Region

In this region industries like paper and pulp, furniture, agricultural machinery, etc. have been developed. The major industrial centres of this region are Vancouver and Prince Rupert.

EUROPEAN INDUSTRIAL REGIONS

Industrial revolution was first started in Europe, with the result heavy industries on a large scale have developed in many parts of the Europe. In spite of industrial development in many regions of the world, Europe is still a great industrial power. In Europe, industries are distributed in many countries and the manufacturing belt of Europe is not continuous.

Figure 12.3

Industrial belt of North-West Europe

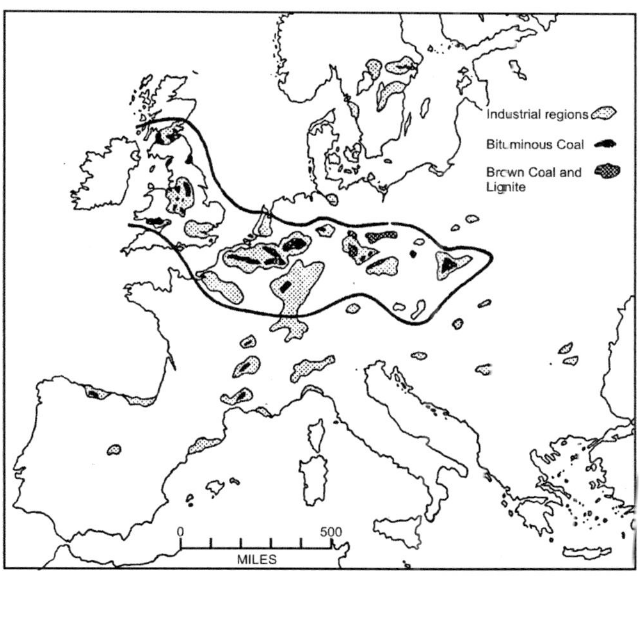

The principal manufacturing zone extends from west to east, from Britain through north-eastern France, Belgium, the Rhineland of West Germany, Saxony-Bohemia to Silesia. Other important industrial areas are found on the Swiss Plateau, northern Italy, in central Sweden and in many large towns and cities throughout Europe such as London, Paris, Berlin and Milan (Figure 12.3).

The leading industrial countries of the Europe are United Kingdom, Germany, France and Italy, while several other regions are scattered in other different European countries. A brief description of important industrial regions of Europe is given below:

United Kingdom

UK was the first country in the world to become highly industrialised. Most of its industrial regions are closely associated with the coalfields. At the present time industry is declining due to cheaper and more efficient production overseas, and with old equipment and labour troubles at home. But still the industrial structure of UK is considered important. In United Kingdom there are certain areas which are more specifically industrial. The major industrial regions of UK are shown in Figure 12.4.

Figure 12.4

Industrial regions of United Kingdom

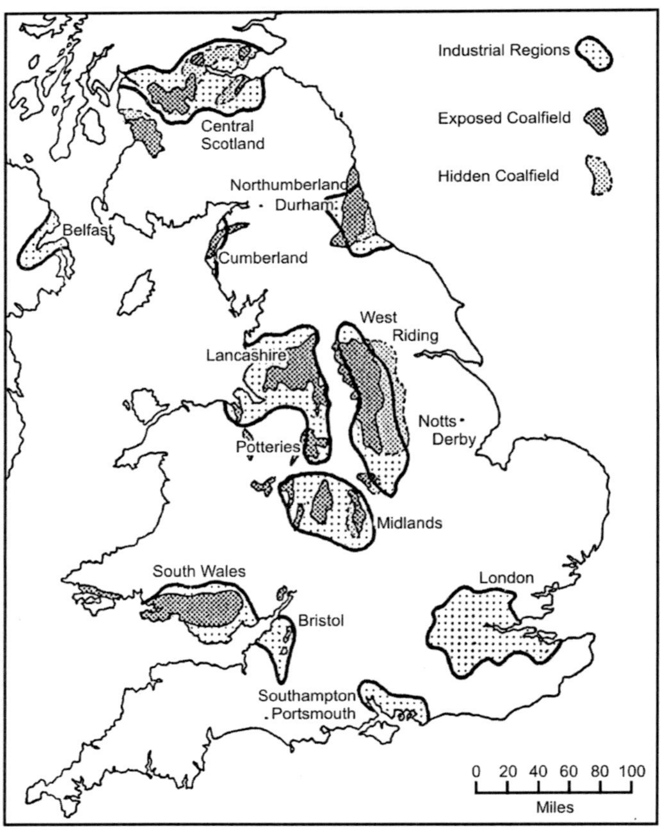

The North-East Coast

The north-east coast industrial region also accords fairly closely with a coalfield, that of Durham and Northumberland. Again the basic industries are coal mining and iron and steel production. Its economic fortunes have not differed greatly from those of West Cumberland in recent years, though a greater variety of steel processing industries and also other industries, such as chemicals, have been established. Foremost amongst these is the shipbuilding industry of the Tyne. Marine, mechanical and constructional engineering are also relatively important. The chemical industries have recently assumed great importance at Billingham.

Cumberland and Westmorland

This region occupies very approximately the coalfield that lies between the Lake District hills and the sea. It is a less specialised region. Apart from coal mining, now of declining importance, iron and steel production is the principal industry.

The West Riding of Yorkshire

This district is dominated by the manufacture of woollen and worsted cloth. Second in importance comes coal mining and iron and steel production. In general, the former occupies the more northerly valleys, centred around Leeds, and the latter, the more southerly, with their focus in Sheffield. The West Riding, unlike the two regions already mentioned, has attracted a large number of subsidiary industries – those which absorb the by-products or work up the main products of the principal industries and those which serve the needs of the large industrial population.

Nottinghamshire and Derbyshire

These counties contain the southern extension of the West Riding coalfield. Here the woollen industry gives way to hosiery, which has, in large measure, replaced the ancient lace industry. Coal mining remains important and many branches of the engineering industry are carried on. Railway and motor engineering, the manufacture of cables, rayon, heavy chemicals and pharmaceutical goods are amongst the products of this area which must count as one of the most varied industrial regions of the country.

Lancashire

Lancashire is dominated by the cotton industry, which is concentrated along the western margin of the Pennines and Rosendale forest. But on the lower land to the west, coal mining and iron, steel and chemical industries are carried on. In Barrow is a shipbuilding industry and along the shores of the Mersey estuary and the banks of the Manchester Ship Canal have developed various elementary and processing industries, based mainly on imported materials. The region may be taken to include the industrialised areas of Cheshire, with their shipbuilding and chemical industries.

The Birmingham Region (Midlands)

The Birmingham region is now much more extensive than the coalfields of South Staffordshire and Warwickshire from which it grew. It is impossible to point to any predominant industry, though the manufacture of motor cars is one of the most important. Few branches of the engineering industry, except shipbuilding, are not represented in the 'black country'. The chemical industries in all their branches are conspicuous; in fact the only significant industry which is poorly represented – it is certainly not absent – is the textile.

Greater London

This region has the greatest variety of industry to be found in any industrial region in Great Britain. None is basic or fundamental to the area in the sense that it could not be carried on equally well elsewhere. Most are concerned with the manufacture of consumer goods; furniture, ready-made clothing, musical instruments, patent and prepared foods. New industries are being attracted to Greater London by its market of over ten million inhabitants, and each brings with it its contribution to the total population and helps to make more probable the appearance of yet further industries. The territorial expansion of London has for many years been presenting difficult problems in transport and supply. The outward spread of London has now been checked by the constitution of the Green Belt, in which non-agricultural development is restricted. At the same time, in order to satisfy the continuing desire of industry to establish itself in the London region, 'satellite' or 'New Towns' have been established beyond the Green Belt.

South Wales

A region of coal and steel, South Wales has been in recent years as depressed as similar areas in the north of England. Attempts have been made here, as in the North, to attract new and more varied industries to the region and the steel industry has itself been greatly expanded by the establishment of large works at Port Talbot and Newport. The tinplate industry has been extended, and oil refining established.

Scotland

Central Scotland contains a number of coalfields and on these local resources a number of varied textile, metallurgical and engineering industries have been built up. The most important concentrations within this region are on the Clyde, where shipbuilding is important below Glasgow, and steel, engineering and textiles above; and in Ayrshire, Midlothian and western Fife, where the textile, linoleum and other manufacturing industries have been established.

Apart from above-mentioned industrial regions there are many large towns that lie outside the regions which are industrial: Bristol, Leicester, Lincoln, Norwich, Ipswich, Portsmouth and Southampton are some. Each has its particular range of industries, some of them, those for example of Bristol and Leicester, are of great national importance. But these towns, and also many smaller towns, Oxford, Bath, Chelmsford, for example, in which highly important industries are carried on, lie isolated from the main industrial areas, so that one does not think of them as part of industrial regions.

Germany

Germany is considered as a highly industrialised country of Europe. The major industrial regions of Germany are as follows:

Rhine Industrial Region

This region is also known as 'Ruhr-Westphalia Industrial Region'. This region is not only a prominent industrial region of Germany but also of Europe. In this region, coal of high quality is available from Ruhr coalfield. Earlier, iron ore was also available but now is exhausted and the ore is obtained from nearby Siegerland and also by import. This region is having an excellent position in relation to transport.

In response to all these locational advantages a wide range of industries, especially heavy industries including iron and steel (at Duisburg, Essen, Bochum and Dortmund); heavy chemicals (around Dusseldorf and Leverkusen); engineering (Gelsenkirchen, Oberhausen, Rheinhausen, Essen and Dortmund) including large interests in armaments; and a number of specialised industries such as cutlery (at Solingen and Remscheid) and textiles (at Krefeld and Wuppertal). The region became a vast industrial conurbation with a population of around 5 million which forms a large supply of labour and also a large local market for smaller manufactured goods, consumer goods and service industries.

The Middle Rhine Industrial Region

The widely spread industrial complex at the confluence of the Rhine and the Main rivers enjoys the advantages of easy water transport, and convergence of rail and road routes. Frankfurt is a railway engineering centre with electrical engineering, automobile and chemicals industries. Mainz has leather, brewing, and engineering industries. Further south, both Mannheim and Ludwigshafen with water-transported raw materials, have developed many industries: chemical, electrical engineering, agricultural implements, iron and steel.

The Hamburg Industrial Region

Hamburg is not a region but a metropolitan city. Here also specialised industries have developed to a great extent. Among the industries, notable are ship-building, light chemicals, tobacco, non-ferrous industries, petro-chemical, petroleum refining and engineering industries.

The Berlin Industrial Region

West Berlin was developed as a major industrial centre under West German occupation. It was the capital of undivided Germany and derived advantage as a seat of administration. Most of the industrial products contributed by this region are of non-conventional type, including electrical, electronics, cosmetics, light chemicals and precision engineering.

Leipzig Industrial Region

Leipzig is an industrial town located in the eastern part of Germany. This region is famous for the production of optical instruments, leather products, engineering goods and machine tools.

In the eastern region of Germany, other industrial centres are Jena, Dresden, Karl Marx Stadt, Magdeburg, Stassfurt and Halle.

France

France is the third industrial country in Europe, next to UK and Germany. The major industrial regions of the France are as follows:

The North-East Industrial Region

This region is the largest industrial area of the France known for iron and steel, textile and engineering. Availability of coal from Nord and Pas-de-Calais and iron from Lorraine make industrial growth possible. A coastal location has allowed the region to retain its position.

The iron and steel towns of Dunkirk, Douai, Denain and Valenciennes also make metal parts and machinery. Lille makes cotton, woollen, linen and synthetic textile. Roubaix, Tourcoing, Armentieres and Cambrai are the other textile towns. Some of these towns also manufacture agricultural machinery and have chemical plants associated with the textile mills.

Lorraine Industrial Region

The Lorraine since before World War I has contributed to the France's economy some two-thirds of total steel and more than three-fourths of total pig iron production. This region is, therefore, recognised as the single most important centre for such manufacturing.

The Lorraine iron and steel plants are grouped in three areas. Outstanding among these is the Metz-Thionvill complex in the Mosselle valley. The mills there contribute about three-fifths of the Lorraine iron steel and iron output, and in view of recent developments, chances for greater industrial expansion within this area have been enhanced considerably.

The second area is the Longway-Villerapt area near the Belgium Luxembourg border, often referred to as the Northern district. This area produces one-third of Lorraine's iron and steel production.

The third area is Nancy. Nancy has large iron and steel works. The best supply of iron in the country are found in the basin of the Mosalle.

The Greater Paris Basin

The capital of France has naturally arisen in the midst of this productive area, and at the best centre of the system of waterways formed by the Seine and its tributaries. Small sea-vessels can reach Paris, and the trade of its port is considerable; but it is not a great manufacture town, and suffers from lack of coal in the vicinity. Its chief manufactures are articles of fashion, as millinery, jewellery and gloves. The city is famous for its art or picture galleries. Important industries are automobiles, locomotives, aircraft and chemicals. From Paris, railways radiate in all directions.

Central Plateau Industrial Region

This region is also known as Dijon industrial region. The Dijon industrial region is flanked by the central Plateau, Coted or, Langres Plateau and Jura. On the southern slopes of the Coted, grape vine is manufactured, and Dijon is a great centre of the burgundy wine industry.

Rhone Sone Valley Region

The Rhone rises on Mont St. Gothard in Switzerland, and flows through the Lake of Geneva before it enters France and joins the Saone at Lyons. Lyons is the centre of the silk industry in France – mulberry trees, on which silkworms are fed, are grown in the lower Rhone valley, and coal can be obtained from the St. Etienne field. The water of the Rhone is, moreover, suited for dyeing the silk. The silk industry is also carried on at Avignon, on the Rhone near the confluence of the Durance and at Nimes, to the west.

Mediterranean Industrial Region

The Mediterranean seaboard of France, west of Marseilles is marshy but east of Marseilles it is extremely picturesque, and warm enough for even oranges and lemons in parts. Marseilles carries on an enormous trade with other Mediterranean ports, and with southern Asia by way of the Suez Canal. Among its industries is the manufacture of soap (which is fostered by the good local supply of olive oil), chemicals, paper and pulp, sugar, leather, silk industry and ship repairing.

Italy

In Italy industrial development began only after the Second World War. The two distinct industrial regions of Italy are northern and southern regions.

The Northern Region

About four-fifths of the industries is concentrated in Northern Italy. The major industrial regions are Lombardy, Piedmont, Liguria, etc. Most of the manufacturing units are concentrated in urban centres, e.g. Venice, Trieste, Genoa, Savona and in Milan and Turin in great Po river valley. Entire region is highly developed with several types of industries. Important among these are textiles, silk, iron and steel, paper, paper pulp, agricultural machinery, aircraft, machine tools, electricals and automobiles.

The Southern Region

This region is far less developed in manufacturing than its northern counterpart. Naples is the only major industrial centre, having textiles, machinery and, iron and steel plants.

Other European Industrial Regions

Most of the European countries have important manufacturing activities. These are outlined in brief below:

Belgium has heavy industries, including iron and steel making and the manufacture of armaments. Liege, Brussels, Antwerp, and Ghent, are the major industrial centres of Belgium.

Luxembourg is known for its iron and steel industry. Luxembourg city has iron and steel as well as engineering industries.

The Netherlands has 40 per cent of its population engaged in the industrial sector and many branches of modern industries are well-represented there. Marine engineering and shipbuilding are important in Rotterdam, Schiedam and Dordrecht. Engineering industries are well-developed in Utrecht (light machinery), and Eindhoven (electrical engineering, home of the Philips electrical company). Chemical plants are found in Pernis and Europoort near Rotterdam, and Maastricht. Groningen is the centre of industries based on the extraction of natural gas from the North Sea. There are a number of towns noted for textiles: Tilburg (woollen textiles), Eindhoven (linen), Enschede (cotton), Arnhem (rayon) and Breda (synthetic fibres). Amsterdam has long been a centre for diamond cutting and Arnhem for tin smelting. Oil refineries are located in Rotterdam, Pernis and Europoort. Dairying, brewing, sugar refining, food processing and oil milling are also important industries in the larger towns in the agricultural polder-lands.

Sweden is the most industrialised country. The main industrial region is in central Sweden, the so-called Lake Depression, with its main centre at Stockholm. Sweden has the richest iron ore resources of Europe, has developed much hydroelectric power and has a long history of technological skills. Some of its internationally-known exports include Volvo cars, Bofors guns, Aga beacons, Electrolux refrigerators, Laval cream separators, Ericsson telephones, Nobel dynamites and Johansson's instruments. Eskilstuna is known as 'the Sheffield of Sweden' and produces excellent cutlery and ornamental goods. Other metal and engineering centres are Vasteras, Falun, Dannemora and Oxelosund. Orebro makes footwear, Norrkoping makes textiles; and Karlstad, Norrkoping, Orebro and Trollhattan make paper.

Norway's leading industries are marine engineering, shipbuilding, fish-canning and the pulp and paper industries. There are aluminium smelting plants at Odda and Ardal, and iron and steel is made at Mo-i-Rana. The capital Oslo, located on Oslo Fiord, and its surrounding region has pulp mills, shipyards, chemical plants and fish-canning factories. The towns of Bergen, Trondheim, and Stavanger are noted for their fishing and shipping activities and Stavanger has become a major port servicing the North Sea oil and gas fields. Electro-chemical industries are well-developed in the Glommen valley and Telemark where cheap hydroelectric power is available. Such plants manufacture fertilisers, plastics, explosives, and smelt ferro-alloys.

Denmark is famous for its dairying and agricultural industries. Other industries developed in Denmark are chemicals, textiles fishing vessels, beer, silverware, machinery, electric equipments, etc. Copenhagen Odense, Flensbug, Esbjerg and Aarthus are the industrial centres.

Switzerland, although a mountainous region, is famous for watch-making, engineering, chemicals and textiles. The Swiss Plateau has the greatest concentration of industrial plants. Zurich, Basel, Baden, St. Gallen, Appenzell, La Chaux-de-Fonds, Biel and Le Locle (Jura towns) are the main industrial centres.

Poland is having an important industrial region in south of the country. Iron and steel, chemicals, textiles and zinc/lead refining are important industries developed in this region. The main industrial centres are Wroclaw, Bytom, Czestochowa, Katowice, Chorzow, Krakow, Warsaw and Gdansk.

Elsewhere in Europe there are a few industrial towns having well-developed industries. These include Barcelona, Madrid, Bilbao, Lisbon, Athens, Budapest, Vienna and the capital cities of the other central and east European countries.

INDUSTRIAL REGIONS OF THE FORMER USSR

Before the revolution in Russian industry which began in 1928, manufacturing was confined to the western parts of the Soviet Union. Its chief centres were Leningrad, Moscow with its ring of smaller towns, and the Ukraine. Also, the Donetz basin, with its reserves of coal and iron, constituted the foremost centre of the metallurgical industries. The development, initiated by Stalin in the First Five-Year Plan was designed to create a series of new industrial regions, with the result USSR became a highly developed industrial nation in the world. Although with the disintegration of the country into several new countries, these industrial regions have also been divided, but still their present pattern shows a general industrial scenario of this region. The well-developed industrial regions are as follows:

The Moscow Region is more extensive, and includes a number of towns; some of them, such as Tula and Kalinin, of very considerable size, located within 160 kilometres of the city. Coal is mined within this region, but in no great quantity. The chief industries are textile, chemical and engineering.

The Ukraine remains the chief centre of the heavy industries in European Russia. Within the Ukraine, the Donetz basin, in which coal occurs, is the centre of the iron smelting and metallurgical industries. To the west, along the Dnieper river, are further centres of the engineering industry, in which high quality steel and aluminium goods are fabricated, and non-ferrous metals refined. Even further to the west is the iron ore field of Krivoi Rog, near which heavy steel industries have been established.

To these industrial regions should be added a number of smaller industrial centres – towns like Kiev, Riga, Kazan and Volgagrad. These are old towns in which the traditional industries have been developed and new industries located.

The Leningrad Region: Coal is lacking, but is, to some extent, replaced by hydroelectric power. Timber is abundant and paper and cellulose are made. These, with engineering, and mechanical, electrical, and textile industries, account for the greater part of the industrial production of the region.

The Ural Region: This range of low hills contains very considerable deposits of iron ore and of various non-ferrous metals. On its borders are not inconsiderable deposits of petroleum. A number of large centres of the metallurgical industry have been set up here, deriving their supply of fuel from the next industrial region to the east.

The Kuzbas Region, in the upper valley of the Ob, has large reserves of coal. These are used, not only to supply the local steel industry, but also that of the Ural region. Subsidiary chemical industries have been established and progress has been made in building up textile and consumer industries.

Soviet Central Asia, or Turkestan, is the only area of Soviet Asia with a significant urban civilisation dating from before the time of the Soviets. Into the ancient towns of Samarkand and Bokhara has intruded a machine civilisation, and this region is important for its textile and light industries.

The Caucasus Region has a very considerable mineral wealth, not only in petroleum but also in coal and metallic minerals. Although these minerals are now being worked, they have not yet given rise to any large-scale manufacturing industries beyond the petrochemical.

The Soviet Far East is an area rich in forests and minerals. It is, however, remote from other parts of the Soviet Union, with which it is joined by the Trans-Siberian Railway. Its exposure has led to the development here of certain 'strategic' industries as part of the defence plans of the USSR.

INDUSTRIAL REGIONS OF ASIA

In Asia, China, Japan and India have done considerable progress in industrial development. Hong Kong, Korea and Taiwan have become major exporters of textile and other goods.

The South-East Asian Region, though traditionally agricultural in outlook, is also developing industries. Singapore is the most industrialised of the South-East Asian countries. Oil is the major resource of Middle East, therefore, oil refining and petrochemical industry have become important in the region. Iran has developed a wide range of industries.

China

Industrial development in China began only after the beginning of Communist rule in 1949, and now China is not only an industrial power of Asia but also of the world. There has been a complete transformation of the industrial system during the last 60 years. Under the new system and policy, China is developing its industrial system in a planned manner. Rapid development has made China a leading producer of iron and steel, textiles, and cheap consumer goods such as toys, household goods and light metal goods. In China, following industrial regions have been identified:

Manchurian Industrial Region

The most important industrial area of China is in Manchuria with centres at Anshan (steel industry), Penki (steel industry), Fushun (coal, lubricating oil, chemicals), Mukden or Shenyang (machinery and tools) and Dairen (mills and shipyards) – all of them near coal and iron ore deposits. Anshan, Fushun and Shenyang form a triangle, within which are numerous large plants. Here, China developed the largest coal mine, by far the largest blast furnaces and almost the only important steel mills, major factories for railway equipment, cement plants, chemical works, military arsenals and factories for the processing of agricultural products. This was principally an area of heavy industry.

Tientsin and Beijing Region

A second industrial area has been developed at the northern end of the North China Plain, near the Kailan coal reserves, with Tientsin, Peking or Beijing and Tangshan as its main centres. This industrial complex centred on Tientsin and extending from Chinwangto southward along the coast past Kaiping, Tangshan and Tangshu, and thence westward beyond Beijing. The presence of coal-fields in Shansi and Hopei has contributed to the rise of the metallurgical and engineering industries here.

Beijing, Tientsin and Tangshan produce coal, steel and machinery making this northern region the industrial centre for the whole of the North China Plain. The industrial economy of the area has much in common with that of Manchuria.

Lower Yangtze Industrial Region

This is China's oldest industrial region because the area has been open to foreign influence since the middle of 19th century. Shanghai is the main industrial town and port of this industrial region. This is an area for the production of consumer goods such as cotton, silk, textile, food, leather, radio, television sets, utensils, leather, etc. Shanghai's population has now increased rapidly. The needs of the city and its productive hinterland led to factories being set up, partly supplied from overseas; these produced foodstuffs and included flour and oil mills. Paper and tobacco factories were also established, and later the first machine repair shops, from which the present-day iron steel and machines industry has developed. The cotton textile mills of Shanghai industrial region are some of the largest in Asia. Shanghai and the lower Yangtze Delta area clearly lead in total industrial output. There are also shipyards, oil refineries, flour mills, steel plants, metal works and a great variety of light industrial products.

The other industrial cities of this region are Hang Chow, Soochow, Nanking and Ningp.

The Middle Yangtze Industrial Region

The industrial centre furthest inland was the one on the middle Yangtze plain around the former tripartile town of Hankow–Hanyang–Wuhan, with the river navigable for large ocean going vessels up to that point. The iron and steel works here are based on Peninsiang coal and Tayeh iron ore. Shipbuilding, metallurgical and heavy industries, railway equipment and chemicals are important items of production. Yangtze forms a magnificent waterway, being navigable for large ocean vessels to Hankow, and for smaller sea vessels to Khang – nearly 1,600 km from its mouth. The next important town is Hanyang. Hanyang lies not far from coal and iron ore deposits and was in fact the cradle of China's heavy industry. Engineering and textile works were later set up, together with foodstuffs factories.

Sichuan (Szechwan) Industrial Region: Sichuan (Szechwan) province above the Chang Jian (Yangtze Kiang) gorge has many important industries around Chongqing (Chungking) and Chengdu (Chengtu). The rich deposits of coal, iron, ferro-alloys and abundant agricultural raw materials have all encouraged industrial development. Iron and steel, textiles, paper and pulp, machinery, cement, and chemicals are made here.

Si Kiang Delta Region

At the mouth of the Xi Jiang (Si Kiang) the port of Canton is the main industrial centre. Canton lacks local raw materials and once was known largely for commerce. Modern industries are centred on silk production; there are silk mills, jute and cotton goods are manufactured, rubber is processed, and there are food-canning and match factories. Iron works and machine factories occupy sites near the docks. The iron ore comes from Hainan Island. There are also mechanised porcelain factories. But, in spite of Cantons many industries, it is firstly a trading centre for the exchange of goods between the interior and countries overseas.

Food processing factories have recently been established at Swatow. Next along the coast come the towns adjacent to Canton-Fatshan which produces textiles and household goods, Shuntak (for silk and sugar), Tungkuan (sugar and food) industries.

In China, many cities are considered to be the industrial cities. Some towns such as Anning, Kiuchuan (iron and steel), Yumen and Hangzhou or Hangchow (oil refining), Lanzhou or Lanchow (chemicals, textiles, mining equipment) and Kunming (chemicals, machinery, textiles) have industrial development.

Japan

Japan is the highly industrialised country of Asia. Despite its shortage in industrial raw materials and solid fuel, it has been able to develop industries at a very fast rate. The reasons of rapid industrial growth in Japan are:

(i) Availability of hydroelectric power.
(ii) Coastal location and large ports which helps in import of raw material and also in export.
(iii) Proximity to mainland of Asia providing a ready market. Now, Japan has a worldwide market for its products.
(iv) Country's large population provides a ready source of labour.
(v) Technological development.
(vi) Government encouragement, etc.

There are four major industrial regions of Japan as shown below in Figure 12.5:

Figure 12.5
Industrial regions of Japan

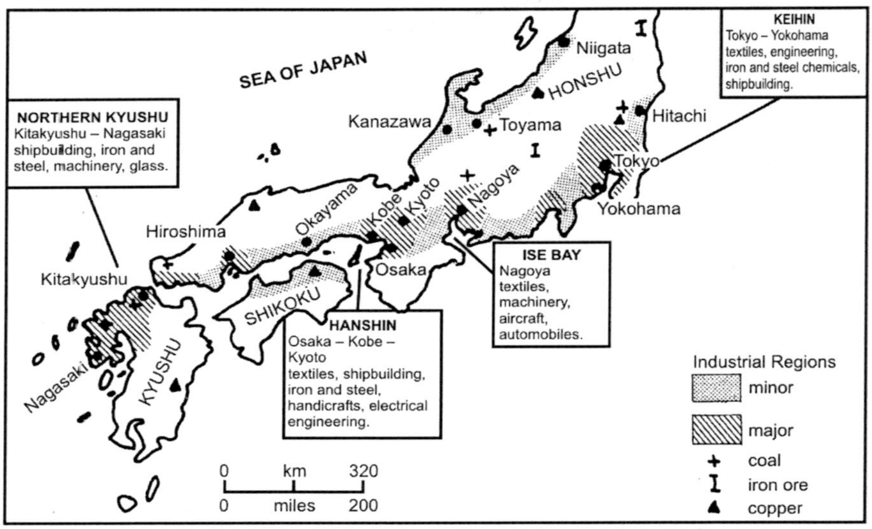

Tokyo-Yokohama Region

The greatest industrial region of Japan is the Kwanto plain and is formed by the conurbation of three chief cities, Tokyo, Kawasaki and Yokohama. Tokyo the capital of the country, is favourably situated in the middle of a small fertile plain known as Kwanto plain, and carries on many artistic industries. Tokyo is noted for electrical engineering such as transistors, radio television sets, washing machines, refrigerators and computers. Today, it ranks high in blast furnaces, steel mills, machines and tools, chemicals, refineries, shipbuilding, airplane, factories of consumer goods, electrical machinery, textile and canning industries, etc.

Yokohama is a port city where manufacturing has been overshadowed by trade. One reason for the slower development of industry has been restricted area of level land suitable for the expansion of factory sites. Yokohama has precision engineering, shipbuilding, oil refining, petrochemicals and port industries.

The third industrial city is Kawasaki. Its Heavy Industries Ltd., Japan's top manufacturer of industrial robots, is planning to bolster production and step up sales, including those in Europe and the USA to meet the growing demand. Though about 90 per cent of robots it makes at present are arc welders for sale to car manufacturers. It will be placing heavier emphasis from now on to the output of robots for other purposes, such as spray painting and assembling.

Osaka, Kobe and Kyoto Region

In the Hanshin or Kinki region are three of the Japan's six great cities – Osaka, Kobe and Kyoto, the first two of which are also among the three great deepwater ports. The manufacturing structure of the Hanshin region is one of great diversity. Until recently at least, textiles lead all other industries. The cotton industry is carried on chiefly at Osaka and other towns in the fertile plain that borders the northern shore of the inland sea.

Osaka is the greatest cotton-textile town and is generally known as the Manchester of Japan. Here the naturally dense population makes labour cheap, and affords a good market. As Osaka has just one poor harbour, it is largely served by the port of Kobe.

The Osaka-Kobe industrial region is as smoky, noisy and unattractive in appearance as are most regions of heavy industry. Kobe concentrates on shipbuilding, oil refining, and petrochemical industries including synthetic textile and rubber manufacture.

The Nagoya Industrial Region

The third industrial region of Japan is Nagoya. Nagoya has textile mills that process local silk, imported cotton and also synthetic fibres; engineering industries, including all kinds of machinery automobiles, locomotives and aircraft. Textile, including silk reeling, cotton spinning, cotton weaving and wool weaving lead all other industries. Much of Nagoya's woollen industry is relatively new and Australian wool is chiefly used. Nagoya is one of the country's foremost aircraft manufacturing centres.

Northern Kyushu Region

This industrial region is located close to the south-western limit of the general manufacturing belt in northern Kyushu. It ranks 4th among the manufacturing concentrations, being credited with nearly 90 per cent of the nation's industrial output. Chikuho coalfield is situated in close proximity of this heavy industrial centre. Textiles are not an important element of the industrial structure of this region; of first importance are the heavy industries, especially iron and steel manufacturing.

Yumata, Kokura, Moji, Fukuoka are the industrial centres of this region. Outside the above four major industrial regions there are several scattered industrial towns. Iron and steel is made at Muroran; oil refining is important at Akita and Niligata; engineering at Hiroshima; shipbuilding at Kure; textiles at Okayama. Hakodate and Sapporo in Hokkaido also have some industrial development.

India

Since gaining independence in 1947, India has gradually emerged as an industrialised nation, in spite of the fact that agriculture is still the base of the Indian economy. The industrial development has occurred through government policies adopted during various plan periods. Both private and public sector industries have been developed, with the result India now is considered as an industrial nation of Asia after China and Japan.

The distribution pattern of Indian industries is varied. Among the states, Maharashtra contributes the largest amount of industrial products, followed by Gujarat, Tamil Nadu, West Bengal, Uttar Pradesh, Jharkhand, Bihar, Karnataka, etc.

The following industrial regions are prominent in India:

The Kolkata Region

The major industries located in this region are jute mills, cotton textile, chemicals, drugs, engineering, machine tool, automobiles, tobacco, paper, etc. The notable industrial centre are Howrah, Liluah, Balley, Konnagar, Chandannagar, Birlapur, Dum Dum, Belghoria, Sodepur, Titagarh, Barrackpur, Shyamnagar, Naithati, etc.

Mumbai-Pune Region

This region stretches from Mumbai metropolis to Pune in the south. Major industrial centres are Andheri, Belapur, Thane, Kalyan, Pimpri and Pune. This is the biggest industrial agglomeration in India. The major manufacturing items produced here are: textile, drugs and pharmaceuticals, chemicals, petrochemicals, paper, leather, engineering, goods, fertiliser and precision instruments.

Ahmedabad-Vadodara Region

This region is having cotton textile, petrochemical, chemical, fertiliser and engineering industry. The main industrial centres of this region are Ahmedabad, Vadodara, Varuch, Surat, Kalol, etc.

Coimbatore-Bengaluru Region

The industries developed in this region are cotton and silk textile, sugar chemical along with several public sector units. Coimbatore, Bengaluru, Madurai, Tiruchirapalli, Mettur, Sivakasi, Mysore, Maducottai, etc. are the major industrial centres.

Chota Nagpur Plateau Region

This area is very rich in mineral resources like iron ore, copper, mica, bauxite, manganese, dolomite, limestone, etc. The region has several industries like steel plants, heavy engineering, machine tools, heavy electricals, locomotive, fertilisers, cement, paper, etc. The major industrial centres of this region are Ranchi, Dhanbad, Jamshedpur, Sindri, Hazaribagh, Chaibasa, Daltonganj, Japla, etc.

Delhi Capital Region

The capital region of Delhi is now emerging as an important industrial region. Adjacent towns of Delhi like, Faridabad, Ghaziabad, Gurgaon, Noida, Mathura, Saharanpur, etc. are now developing as industrial centres. The major industries of this region are textile, engineering, leather, drugs and pharmaceuticals, petroleum refinery, consumer products, etc.

Apart from the above mentioned major industrial regions of India, several other regions/cities have also developed in the country. Among these Kanpur, Lucknow, Meerut, Jallandhar, Ludhiana, Patiala, Jaipur, Bilaspur, Nagpur, Bhopal, Bhubaneswar, Hyderabad, Thiruvananthapuram, Chennai, Alleppey, Quilon, etc. are important.

Other Asian Industrial Regions

The four Asian regions – Hong Kong, Taiwan, South Korea and Singapore are notable for their industrial production. Hong Kong has developed both heavy and light industries. Most of the industries are export-oriented. Hong Kong is famous for toys, plastic goods, domestic appliances, radios, sports goods, handbags and footwear, watches and clocks, photographic goods, jewellery and printed matter. Now, heavier industries like textiles and electrical goods have also been developed. *Taiwan* is located about 200 km away from the south-east coast of China. Taiwan's industrial development includes textiles, electronic goods, plastics, toys, small tools, etc. along with iron and steel industry, aluminium and chemical industries.

South Korea is also considered as an important producer of industrial products not only for its own consumption but for export also. With the help from USA, Japan and some European countries, South Korea now has developed a strong industrial base. South Korea is having a large supply of labour which is cheap and skilled. Today, South Korea is having large steel plants, automobiles, aircraft, and shipbuilding industry and also produces consumer electronics, electrical goods and other types of machines. In recent years emphasis has also been given on machinery manufacture, to produce machines not only for export but to service the increasing local demands.

Singapore with a three million population and expansion of just 600 sq km is specialised in electronic technology, high-tech manufacturing and financial and research services.

Malaysia: Another Asian country having an industrial base of moderate type is the Malaysia. The main industrial regions of Malaysia are in the Kelaung valley between Kuala Lumpur and the sea around.

The Southern Continents

Industrial development in the southern continent has been slowest, not only because of their scanty endowment, but also because of late political independence from colonial rule. The sparse population and underdevelopment of many parts of the southern continents have prevented large areas from being industrialised. However, some countries, especially Australia, South Africa and Brazil, are increasingly dependent upon industrial development.

South America

Industrial development has been most marked in South America, perhaps the best endowed of all the southern continents. It has had the advantage of a large population, and several minerals are available in some countries. The industries of South America are dotted in many centres, none of them very large, around the coasts of the continent.

Brazil is the most industrialised of Latin American countries. The chief industrial region is the south-east and the city of Sao Paulo has diverse industrial activities including steel mills, chemical plants, motor vehicle assembly plants, paper, cement and beer industries. Rio de Janeiro has similar industries with shipbuilding and aircraft engineering in addition. Belo Horizonte is the major metallurgical centre with iron and steel and other metal industries based on hydroelectric power and the rich mineral resources of Minas Gerais.

In *Argentina* and *Uruguay* the main industrial region is along the shores of the Plate estuary extending inland as far as Rosario. The main industries are shipbuilding, at Buenos Aires, Rosario, Cordoba and General Pacheco. The La Plata urban districts have chemicals, textiles, aircraft engineering and steel industries. Meat-packing, dairying and flour-milling are the dominant industries of the Pampas lands.

Chile's main industries are found in Santiago, Valparaiso and Concepcion. Elsewhere in South America, industries are concentrated in the capital cities of the various states, e.g. Lima, Caracas, Bogota and in certain other large towns.

Africa

Africa is the least developed of all the southern continents. The large spell of colonial rule, lack of capital and entrepreneurial skills and political instability as well as underdeveloped economic structure are the main causes of industrial backwardness in many countries of Africa.

The main industries are those connected with either mining or agriculture, e.g. smelting and refining of copper in Zambia and Zaire, and processing of rubber, oil palm fruits, etc. in West Africa. Nigeria also has petrochemicals industries. South Africa is, however, an industrially developed country. The main industrial region is the Witwatersrand where there is not only gold but coal, iron and a range of ferrous and non-ferrous metal deposits, as the basis of iron and steel, engineering, locomotives, and other industries. Chemicals, textiles, cement and light industries are also fairly important. Elsewhere in Africa the main industrial development has been in capital cities such as Salisbury, Dar-es-Salaam, Nairobi, and so on. Such cities have cement, brewing, food processing and light industries mainly geared to import substitution.

Australia

In Australia the main industrial area is the south-east where the concentration of early settlement, the favourable climate, the presence of coalfields around Sydney, and of iron ore resources, led to the establishment of the iron and steel industry, especially at Newcastle and Port Kembla. There are also many engineering industries, including the manufacture of cars, locomotives and aircraft, cement works, chemicals and shipbuilding.

Melbourne has also developed many industries similar to those of Sydney, but based on the Gippsland lignite deposits and the hydroelectric power from the Snowy River Scheme. Melbourne has chemicals, shipbuilding, aircraft engineering, railway equipment and motor vehicles industries. Adelaide, has well-developed agricultural industries such as fruit-canning, flour-milling, dairy industries and woollen textiles. It also has iron and steel (at Whyalla) and engineering industries. Brisbane is the major industrial city of Queensland and is located near the Ipswich coalfield. Locomotives are made at Brisbane, Ipswich, Maryborough and Mackay. In western Australia, Perth is the main industrial city dealing with agricultural products.

13

World Transportation Patterns

"Transportation is a measure of the relations between areas and is, therefore, an essential aspect of geography" (Ullman, 1954: 311). The economic relations between areas is reflected in the character of transportation facilities and in the flow of traffic. Wagner (1960: 129) has stated, "the routes along which men, materials, and messages move bind a society together. They make a reticule on which are strung the sites of work and rest; they are the paths along which flow the myriad streams of raw and half-made goods in process of production; they form the links between each local group of human and the thoughts and presence of its fellows". In the reconstruction of a region or a nation, transport systems invariably play a vital role. The growth and development of transportation provides a medium, contributing to the progress of agriculture, industry, commerce, administration, defence, education, health or any other community activity. In fact, transportation pattern is a reflection of regional and/or national development.

Many factors are involved in the development of a transport system. The present-day transport system of a country or a region cannot be explained by one factor alone, but an outcome of several interrelated factors. White and Senior (1983), in their book entitled, *Transport Geography* considered five basic factors, which influences the growth and development of transport system and the ways in which changes take place. These are:

(i) *The Historical Factor:* This involves the location and patterns of systems, technological development, institutional development and settlement, and land-use patterns.

(ii) *The Technological Factor:* The technological characteristics of each major transport mode are considered together with a discussion of the effects of technological advances.

(iii) *The Physical Factor:* This includes physiographic controls upon route selection, and geological and climatic influences.

(iv) *The Economic Factor:* The structure and nature of transport costs are examined, together with service quality and methods of pricing and charging.

(v) *Political and Social Factors:* These include political motives for transport facilities; government involvement in capital, monopolies competition, safety, working conditions and coordination between modes, transport as an employer and social consequences of transport developments.

Geographical study of transport now has become technical, which deals with network analysis, commodity flow, transport costs, system analysis, planning, etc. In this chapter we are not dealing with technicalities and special aspects of transportation, but discuss only the general pattern of world transport.

Transport systems, which are operated at the global scale, are the expansion of the need for links between both individual nations and trading blocs, and have complex networks. For the purpose of present analysis, i.e. world transportation patterns, the transportation systems can be classified into the following three broad categories:

1. Land transportation
2. Water transportation
3. Air transportation

LAND TRANSPORTATION

The earliest form of land transport was Man himself. They used narrow paths, beaten out and maintained only by use and rarely were specially constructed except at bridges. In some parts of the world human porterage is still prevalent today, e.g. in thickly forested regions or rugged mountains where roads are difficult to build and in sparsely populated regions where the cost of construction is not warranted by the amount of traffic to be expected.

In many countries man himself is the only means of transport. In Central Africa, China and India, men are still employed to carry loads for short distances. The relief and climate of Africa from the Sudan to the Zambesi are such that it very difficult to construct roads and railways. Hired porters carry ivory, rubber, palm nuts and other products of Savannas. The slopes of the mountains may be too steep for animals, as in some parts of the Himalayas and Tibet, or harmful insects may prevent the use of transport animals as in Central Africa, the middle Amazon basin, etc. In such regions, heavy loads are moved by human labour.

After animals had been domesticated a wide range of *beasts of burden* was employed, including dogs, horses and donkeys, cattle, yaks, camels and elephants among others. Man employs many animals in his service and also employs them as his beasts of burden. The horse is the common transporting animal in the temperate lands. In the hot deserts of the Old World, camels carry heavy loads and can travel more than thirty miles a day. Elephants are employed in India and Burma and parts of Africa to carry loads and they rendered valuable service in the teak forests of tropical Asia. Yak is the beast of burden in the mountainous regions of Northern India and Tibet, and the mule is serviceable in the mountain areas near the Mediterranean Sea and Mexico. In the north-west of Canada and in Siberia, sledges are drawn by hardy dogs over the frozen snow. The reindeer has been introduced in Alaska and parts of Canada.

The invention of the *wheel* was another major step forward in the development of transport. The use of carts and wagons, drawn by animals, allowed far larger loads to be carried, or enabled several people to ride in a carriage compared with one on horseback. But these carriages required some medium in the form of cart tracks or roads. Of all land routes, the *road* is most ancient as well as the most universal. Another important means of land transport is the *railway*. Another modern development in transport on land, though as yet of more limited use than the road and railway, is the use of pipeline for carrying liquid commodities of many kinds, e.g. water, milk, mineral oil and gas. But in general the modern land transport means road and railways, which needs detailed analysis.

Roads

Roads and pathways have been stamped out by men since the earliest time. They are the most universal as well as varied form of transport. Roads of one kind or another, ranging from forest paths to the latest highways have several important features. First, wherever a demand exists for a route from place to place a path or road is soon established. Second, roads can be used by a very wide range of transport agents.

The vast importance of contemporary road transport is very much a reflection of this unrivalled convenience to the user, especially in the conveyance of persons. No other form of transport is able to provide such a comprehensive door-to-door or origin-to-destination service, nor does any other mode have such an extensive route network.

Road transport is particularly suitable for short and medium distance travel on account of its convenience. For personal travel, the car is widely used for both work and leisure trips. In case of the former, public transport is usually available as an alternative but for non-work trips the advantage of the private car is even more pronounced, since, flexibility as well as convenience is an additional factor inherent in its use. Over the past 60 years, road transport has become increasingly important for long distance travel due to the construction of motorways (known as 'autoroute' in France, 'autobahn' in Germany, autostrade in Italy and National Highway in India), specially constructed arterial, dual carriageway roads, as well as the straightening, widening, and cambering of the already existing highways. Consequently, roads are now being used for the movement of goods over longer distances: this can be attributed to improvements in vehicle technology and, as in personal travel, to the development of better roads and, more especially, motorways. This trend is in great contrast to the early function of road goods transport which was seen to act as a feeder for rail services. A big advantage of road transport is that it overcomes the transfer problems of rail movement and this certainly appeals to some own account operators. The post-war period has also seen the rationalisation of the public carrier branch of the industry and this has done much to improve the industry's image in terms of responsibility and respectability. Perhaps the major disadvantage of road transport is the limited carrying capacity of the individual vehicles. Just as coaches and buses have gradually increased their carrying capacity, so also road transport goods vehicles have developed greatly increased carrying capacities, e.g. atriculated lorries, special bulk carriers, trailers.

Roads are the most common means of surface transport, but its importance is mostly restricted to national limits. The neighbouring countries may allow or not allow international movement. It depends upon their political and strategic interest. But this much is clear that all the countries of the world are having road transport and more a developed country, more efficient and developed is its road transport connectivity. Even developing countries are having good road network.

All the European countries are having well-developed system of road highways and the road mesh is very close in the more populous and industrialised areas. The countries of North-West Europe like UK, Germany, France, Netherlands, Belgium, etc., and also Spain and Italy have dense road network. Many of the main highways follow age-old routes; in England and France and in many parts of southern Europe, roads are often patterned upon the original Roman network. The French road network is the longest in the Europe, followed by Germany, Belgium, Netherlands, Sweden, Italy and Spain. Eastern Europe is also having good road connectivity, both within the country and with other adjoining countries. The 10,700 km of autobahn in Germany is the largest network in Europe.

The former USSR, with its vast area, has developed road transport system, but in comparison with European countries and USA, its road connectivity is limited. This also is because of the fact that a vast sizeable area is under the cover of ice, and in many other areas of central and eastern part, the topographical conditions are not suitable. In spite of all these conditions, the length of road network has increased more than tenfold since the revolution. During the last twenty-five years, the progress in road transport development is very fast and all the countries of former USSR are developing their internal road transport system.

In North America, the USA has about 34 per cent and Canada around 5 per cent of the roads in the world. The US road network exceeds 6.58 million km in total length, making it the world's longest and biggest road network. Another characteristic feature of the United States is that there are several trans-continental highways. The Trans-Canada Highway links St. John's, Newfoundland, with Victoria on Vancouver Island in British Columbia, a distance of 7,821 km. The interstate highway network in the USA has been depicted in Figure 13.1. The interstate highway network was the largest civil engineering programme in American history.

Most of the roads in Canada lie in the southern parts of the country. Northern Canadian region is still having limited roads due to adverse geographical conditions.

Figure 13.1

Interstate highways of USA

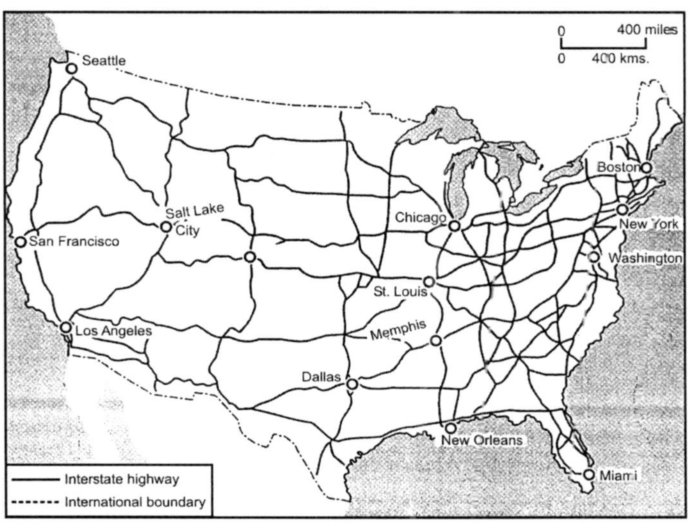

In Latin American countries, road development is limited and varied. Argentina and Uruguay have reasonably adequate highway networks, but extensive areas are ill-served with roads. Brazil had some 1.2 million km of road, but apart from the network in the south-east, which accounts for nearly 75 per cent of the total road length, most of the areas are still not having road connectivity. The Pan-American Highway is a unique feature of the road transport in Latin America. These highways have been designed to link all the countries of North and Latin America. The Pan-American Highway linking Fairbanks, Alaska with Puerto Mont, Chili and Buenos Aires is a longest highway covering a length of approximately 48,000 km. Another international highway is the Garretera Marginal Bolivariana de la selva (commonly known as 'La Marginal') running along eastern foothills of the Andes through Columbia, Peru and Bolivia (Figure 13.2).

In Asia, countries like China, Japan and India have a developed highway system and a dense road network. In other countries of South-East Asia also, road transport is the main source of transportation. While in West Asia, desertic conditions have restricted the road development, but now gradually these countries are also developing their highway system. In China when Communists came into power they began a strenuous programme of highway construction which

Figure 13.2
Important highways of South America

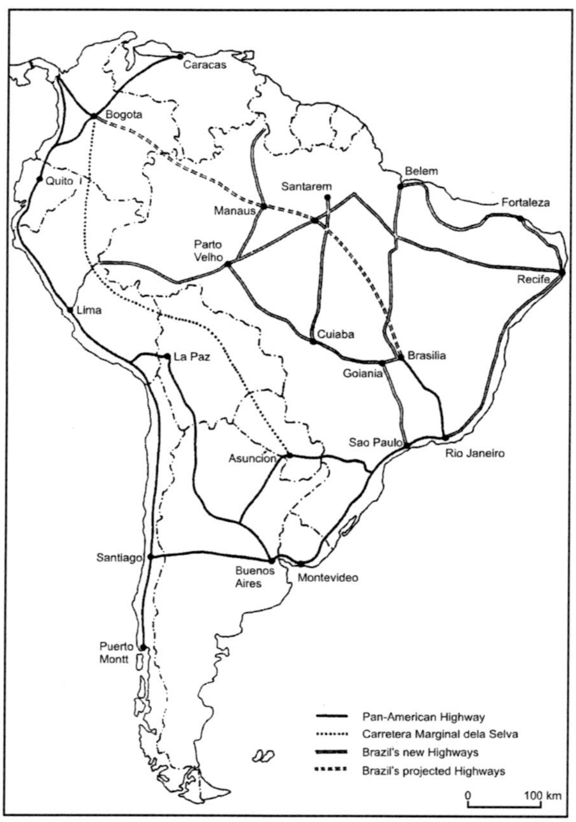

continues to the present and it is estimated that China's total road length is 4,696,300 km in 2017. In Japan, although railways are more important, but the country has also developed a good road network. In Japan, in addition to the A grade expressways that have been constructed, there is a national plan for new arterial highways.

In India, roads are the principal means of transportation. Indian road network is one of the largest in the world. The history of roads in India is as old as its civilisation. In early stages of Indian history, Ashoka and Chandragupta made efforts to construct roads. But, the real progress was made during the Mughal period. A number of roads were laid during the Sultanate and Mughal period. Most modern trunk routes follow the Mughal routes. One such road was constructed by Sher Shah Suri, which connects Peshawar to Kolkata. It was named Grant Trunk (GT) Road and now joins Amritsar with Kolkata. During the British period, a network of roads had not only been planned but were also developed. The first serious attempt to develop roads was made in 1943, when Nagpur Plan was drawn. This plan envisaged increasing of the kilometrage of major roads to 1,96,800 km and of other roads to 3,32,800 km by 1953. In fact, after independence, the Indian government along with the state governments has given this much attention and the process of development still continues. In India, National Highways are the prominent interstate roads constructed and maintained by the central government, while state governments maintained state highways, district and village roads. The length of National Highways increased from 19,811 km in 1951 to 70,550 km in 2010. In 2015, the total road length in India was 5,472,144 km, thus rank second in the world in total road length. A comprehensive plan of National Highway development in the form of Super National Highways, Mega Highways, Express Highways, North-South Corridor and Golden Quadrilateral is also ongoing presently. On the whole, India is developing its road network on priority basis but still has a long way to go.

Africa is a vast continent, but because of its physical conditions and economic backwardness, road development is still limited in many of the African countries. The total road length of Africa is estimated around 2 million km, of which perhaps 20 per cent are paved. Though in the past two decades there have been very substantial improvements, the overall picture is one of complete inadequacy. The need for new and improved roads continues to be a major requirement for African economic development.

The total length of roads in Australia suitable for general traffic is about 8.6 lakh km. Most of the road development in Australia has occurred in south-eastern and south-western part, that too, along the coast. The road development was first focused to connect port towns with its hinterland. All the urban centres are well-connected by roads. Special mention should be made to what are termed as the "beef roads" of northern Australia, which are essential to the cattle industry. New Zealand, although, having a hilly topography but its plain and coastal regions are well-connected by road transport.

Railways

Railways are the most important means of inland transport. Railway was, in a real sense, a product of the industrial revolution and afterwards became a predominant mode of inland transport. Railways solved two important needs: (i) the economic carriage by land of (a) materials in bulk, (b) bulky commodities, and (ii) the relatively rapid movement of large number of people as well as goods. The rails always revolve around its fixed track. This provides guidance for the wheels and also enables very heavy loads to be carried.

The opening of public traffic on September 27,1825 of the Stockton and Darlington Railways is among the great events of history. The date marks the inauguration of the railway era in which we now live. Railways have the following obligations to meet:

(i) the cost of capital expenditure on tracks,
(ii) the cost of maintenance of tracks,
(iii) the cost of rolling stock, and
(iv) the cost of additional restrictions for the safety and convenience of the public.

Railways are providing both long distance as well as short distance mode of carrier. There are national and international railways, while some intercontinental railways are also in function. Rail's main contemporary function, specially in developed countries, lies as a provider of inter-urban travel. Railways are able to achieve higher speeds and also easier access into the heart of cities. New technology has further helped railways to perform their function more effectively. Advance has also been made in improving the design of carriage units which, along with track changes, have promoted a better ride for passengers. Consequently, train speeds of up to 200 kph are now being achieved by high-speed trains. Railways are providing goods service in all countries of the world. The main advantage of rail is for movement of heavy, bulky goods and of coal and mineral ore in particular.

In 2014, *United States* had the world's longest railway network followed by *China* and *India*. The operating length of US rail network is over 2,50,000 km. While China is having railway network of 1,00,000 km, Russia 85,000 km and India 65,000 km. The other major countries are – Canada (48,000 km), Germany (41,000 km), Australia (40,000 km), Argentina (36,000 km), France (29,000 km) and Brazil (28,000 km).

The two categories of railway, i.e. transcontinental and national are important.

Transcontinental Railways

Transcontinental railways are those which are running across the continent. The railways running from the Atlantic to the Pacific Coast in North America are described as "Transcontinental Railways". Such also are the Canadian National Railway, and the Canadian Pacific Railway. But, in common use, all those railways which reach the Pacific Coast from the Mississippi or from Chicago are described as 'transcontinental', whether there is a through coast-to-coast service or not. Other such railways are the Cape-to-Cairo Railway in Africa and the Trans-Siberian Railway in Asia. The Paris-Berlin-Moscow route, Paris-Milan-Brindisi route; and the Berlin-Vienna-Istanbul.

The Trans-Siberian Railway connects Russia with the Far East. It runs from Moscow to Vladivostok on the Pacific, the distance being 9,500 km. Although this line was constructed for strategic purposes, it now carries a large volume of

Figure 13.3

Trans-Siberian Railway

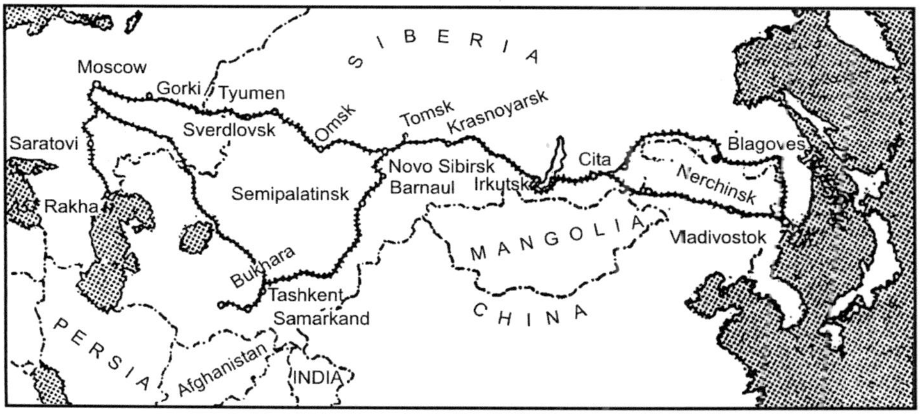

traffic. The settlement of central and eastern Siberia is largely due to this railway system. It has additional value as an alternative route between Europe and Asia on the Pacific for passengers and mails. The line was constructed by the government for the purpose of facilitating the work of administration in Asiatic Russia. It is a single-track system. From Moscow the line goes to Omsk after crossing the Urals and traversing the agricultural lands of northern Steppe provinces where wheat-fields are prominent. From Omsk the line goes directly eastward, crosses the Obi and the Yenisei and soon reaches Irkutsk and Lake Baikal. The line then goes from Lake Baikal to the Amur valley and passes through Manchuria and finally reaches Vladivostok. In Manchuria, a southern branch has been opened at Harbin which connects Port Arthur via Mukden. Mukden is linked up with Peiping by rail.

The Trans-Caspian Railway connects central Asia with European Russia. The line runs from Krasnovodsk, on the Caspian Sea, to the heart of the cotton-growing region of Turkestan, throwing off a branch on the Afghan frontier from Merv to Kushk. Kransnovodsk is connected with Moscow via Tashkent.

The Canadian-Pacific Railway was built during the years 1882–86: The length of the line is 4,340 km. This line connects the Atlantic coast of Canada with its Pacific coast. The line runs from Halifa and St. Johns to Montreal. From Montreal it goes to Winnipeg, the great wheat centre of Canada. The line crosses the plains from Winnipeg via Regina and reaches Medicine Hat in the Rockies. Leaving Medicine Hat, it goes through Kicking-Horse Pass, and ends in Vancouver. This railway system has played a very important part in the political and economic life of the Dominion.

The Chile-Argentina Railway or Trans-Andean Railway of South America connects Buenos Aires with Valparaiso; the distance is nearly 1,440 km. This route was opened for traffic in 1910. As there is a change of gauge both at Mendoza on the Argentian side and at Los Andes on the Chilean, the route is useful only for the carriage of passengers and mails. Of the four transcontinental lines in South America, none is more important commercially than the Chile-Argentian line. The interchange of products between the eastern and western zones of the Continent is small.

Figure 13.4
Transcontinental railways of North America

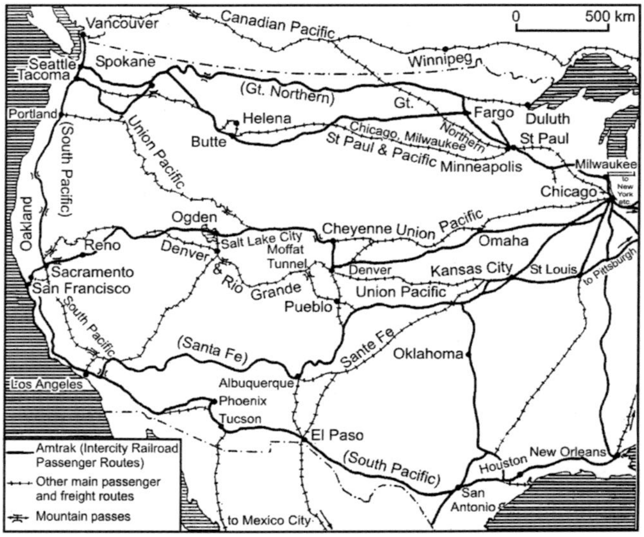

Union Pacific Railway

This railway passes through the central part of the USA. This railway was built in the year 1869 and is one of the longest railways of USA. It starts from Chicago and reaches up to San Francisco located on the Pacific Coast. Its two branches: (a) Chicago to Mississippi and (b) Chicago to New York are also important.

In USA, other transcontinental railways are Great Northern Railway, Northern Pacific Railway and Southern Pacific Railway (Figure 13.4).

Cape to Cairo Railway

In Africa a transcontinental railway was proposed from Cape of Good Hope to Cairo.

There is no transcontinental railroad between North Africa and South Africa. There was a scheme before the World War to construct a railway line from Cape of Good Hope to Cairo. As Egypt was then under the influence of the British, the purpose was to have an all-British transcontinental railway in Africa. The scheme, however, did not work out. A railway line from Cape Town goes up to the border of Congo via Bulawayo and Elizabethville. From Elizabethville, the capital of Katanga, a river-cum caravan route proceeds to Lake Victoria, from where a motor road runs to the Nile gorge. From here steamers maintain regular service to Khartoum. From Khartoum a railway line goes to Wadi Haifa, thence by river-transport Shellal is approached. From Shellal a train runs to Cairo.

Perth-Adelaide Railway

In Australia, a transcontinental railway runs between Perth located at south-western coast to Sydney located at south-eastern coast of Australia. The main in-between stations on this railway line are Kalgoorlie, Koolkordi, Post

Agusta and it also connects Adelaide, Melbourne and Canberra with Sydney (Figure 13.5).

Orient Express Railway is one of the most important railways which connect Paris with Istanbul, the capital of Turkey.

National Railways

Every country of the world is having its own railway system, which is necessary for the development of a country. But development of railways varies from country to country according to their economic development and resources availability. Some physical factors like snow cover, hilly terrain, desertic and marshy conditions etc. have also restricted the expansion of railways within a country.

On the one hand, there are countries like USA, Russia, Canada, China, India, Japan, Germany, France, UK, etc. which have a dense network of railways, while other countries, mostly African, Latin American and Asian, are having limited railway facilities.

The development of railroads in the United States came not only from political considerations, but also from a keen desire to exploit the easily available natural resources and to move them cheaply. Water transportation eased the situation only in areas where it was possible to develop. Thus, it was railroad which ultimately met the demand of the country's economy. The first railway line was built in 1825, and the real construction period began in 1869. USA has now more than 2,50,000 km of rail network.

Figure 13.5
Railways of Australia

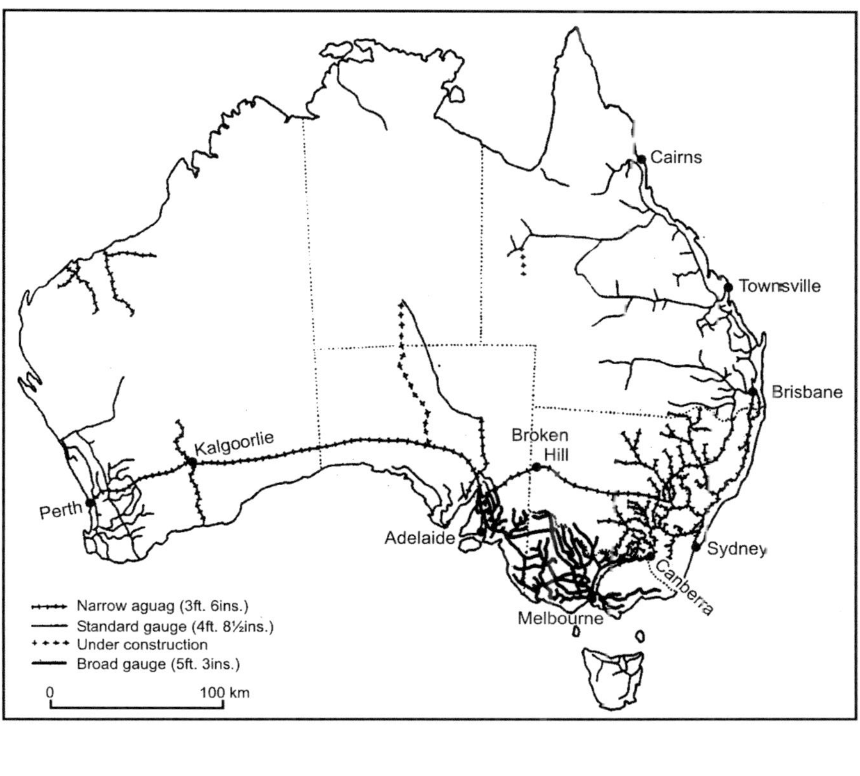

Canada has over 48,000 km of rail network, the beginning of which was made first in 1835. The original purpose of railroad construction was to foster easy communication between the different scattered communities so that they might form into a political unit. The transcontinental lines were built to connect the east coast with west coast. The railroad is the most important factor of Canada's prosperity as it helps in providing outlets in export market for the large surplus of agricultural produce. The latest development of railroad in Canada is its extension to northern sides in the interest of mining industry.

The railroad systems in *Europe* have been influenced by the large number of independent countries in a small continent, each developing the system to meet its requirements as dictated by geographical, economic and political demands. There is no uniformity in respect of gauge. The railroads are being competed by other forms of transport – notably automobiles. The high density of traffic is in the industrial areas of North-West Europe. However, the traffic is heavier in respect of passengers and not of freight, in contrast to USA, where it is heavier in freights.

Germany, because of its location and larger population has the largest traffic transportation. The low passenger traffic in France is due to low density of population. In Italy, however, large arrivals of tourists every year account for a greater volume of railway traffic even though density of population is low. More recent developments has led to the rationalisation of railway networks in many countries and the closure of many lines. There are approximately 41,000 km of railways, most of which are double-tracked or multiple-tracked and on standard gauge. The railways radiate from the main cities, e.g. Paris, Berlin, London, Brussels, Milan, etc. Underground railways are important in many European capitals, e.g. London, Paris, etc. and carry huge numbers of city workers.

Among the developed countries of the world, former *Soviet Union* is unique in its dependence upon railways for its transport needs. Considerable railway development had taken place in Russia during Transit times, and when Communists came into power in 1917, they inherited a fairly extensive network which totalled 58,500 km. Many long distance railway lines had developed, which linked Moscow and St. Petersburg (Leningrad) with peninsular Europe and the Moscow region. The Trans-Caucasus, the Trans-Caspian and the Trans-Aral railway links were completed by 1905. The Trans-Siberian Railway, which links the European and Asiatic parts of the country, and gave thorough communication between Moscow and Vladivostok, a distance of 9,216 km was completed in 1916. During the fifty years between 1917 and 1967 the length of railroutes has been more than doubled. This process continued till the division of Soviet Union into several independent countries. Now, Russia is having dense network of 85,000 km railways. Other countries have also inherited railway tracks and are further developing their own railways according to their needs.

Asia is having moderate network of railways, but its importance varies from country to country. India, China and Japan are having dense network of railways. Before the Communist revolution, *China* had few major railways. Since then the quest for high rate of economic and industrial development has led to the expansion of railways in many parts of the country. Now China is having extensive rail network of 1,00,000 km, but still a large part of western China is lacking in railway facilities. *India* is having about 65,000 km of railway track. The whole country has been divided into eight zones for the administration of railways. Indian railway is a large public sector establishment with a fleet of more than

7,681 locomotives, 39,852 passenger service vehicles, 4,900 other coaching vehicles and 2,14,760 wagons. The railway network in India is quite widespread but still there is a need for its development in many parts of the country.

Japan's railway network is only of about 30,000 km, but because of country's small area, the network is very good and effective. Japanese railways are best developed in the coastal lowlands between the major industrial cities. They are mainly electrified and noted for their speed and efficiency. The Tokyo-Osaka or 'Tokaido' Express is world famous.

Other Asian countries are also having their own railway networks. South and North Korea, Pakistan, countries of South-East Asia etc. also have railway tracks. But in West Asian countries railways are very limited.

Pipelines

Another mode of land transport is the pipelines which are used to transport certain items in liquid and gas form. A pipeline may be defined as a line or conduit of pipe of variable diameter and length, but sometimes hundreds of kilometres long, traditionally used for carrying a liquid or gas from a point of supply to a point of consumption. The use of pipes dates back to the Christian era; water supplies are known to have been piped over long distances since very early times. In China, bamboo pipes were being used in circa 5000 BC, and pipes made of clay or stone were widely used in the ancient civilisations of Egypt, Mesopotamia, Greece and Rome.

The discovery and use of petroleum ushered in a new era in pipeline use. The first crude oil pipeline, constructed of wood, was laid down in the United States in 1861 but this proved to be unsuitable, and the first successful pipeline was made of cast iron in Pennsylvania in 1865. In the early days of the oil industry, pipelines served local purposes, only transporting the crude oil to a nearby refinery or to a rail-head, but gradually the value of piping crude oil or the refined products in bulk came to be recognised and before the end of the 19th century a number of trunk lines had been constructed. Today, nearly half a million kilometres of oil pipeline exist in the world, together with a slightly smaller distance of natural gas pipeline. "The increasing use of pipelines in recent years represents," wrote Manners (1963), "one of the most notable revolutions in the history of transport, especially in the transport of energy."

The United States was the first country to use pipeline transport on a massive scale. In 1955 it possessed 88 per cent of the total world oil and gas pipeline mileage, excluding that in the Soviet Union: of nearly 2,24,000 km of oil pipeline, the United States had 1,84,000 km and of some 2,50,000 km of pipe carrying natural gas it had approximately 2,24,000 km. Since that date there have been phenomenal developments in pipeline usage, especially in other parts of the world. There has been spectacular growth of pipeline system in Western Europe, in former Soviet Union, Middle East, North Africa, Canada and Latin America. Now China, India, Japan and several other countries are using pipelines as means of transportation.

Technological advances have contributed substantially to this recent and rapidly increasing use of pipelines for transportation purposes. The production of relatively inexpensive pipes on a large scale and the development of the technique of electric welding have assisted, more especially, the use of pipelines. By the beginning of the present century, steel had replaced cast and wrought iron as the standard material for pipeline construction.

The main use of pipelines at the present time is for the transport of bulk fluids and gas but increasing attention is being paid to the possibilities of transporting other kinds of commodities by pipeline, especially since roads and railways are becoming increasingly congested, with inevitable delays in delivery, and because of labour problems and difficulties. Considerable research has already been devoted to the practical possibilities of conveying a wide range of commodities by pipeline and, in fact, a number of experimental pipelines carrying solids are in operation.

WATER TRANSPORT

Since, prehistoric times, water transport has been used for carrying both men and goods. Water transport probably developed before the use of animals because waterway formed an easy means of travel in places where dense forests on land hindered movement. The range and importance of water transport was increased when power of wind was harnessed by use of boats or some other medium. At first, boats were small and confined mainly to inland waters and sheltered coastal areas. The gradual increase in size and complexity of sailing craft allowed trade to be established. The Phonecians, Egyptians, Greeks and Romans as well as Arabs and Indians had wide trading contacts. The use of steam has given a new dimension, greater power and speed to water transport to carry larger goods at long distances. The use of diesel and other forms of power has changed the entire scenario of the water transport and today most of the world trade is water-borne. The two greatest advantages of water transport are that it uses oceans, rivers, seas and needs no special tracks, and that it is the cheapest form of transport for large and bulky loads. Water transport can be divided into following two categories: (i) inland waterways, and (ii) ocean transport.

Inland Waterways

There are three types of inland waterways, namely, rivers, rivers which have been modified or canalised, and specially constructed canals. In earlier times much, perhaps most, of the inland carriage of commodities was by water. This was possible when vessels were small, the volume of traffic limited, and the time factor was not particularly pressing. But during the 18th century, ships began to grow in size, trade began greatly to expand, and speed of carriage came to be of greater importance. In order to overcome the limitations of many rivers and, also, to provide many inland towns with water communications, canals began to be built. In England, a pioneer in canal construction, the building of these new man-made waterways became almost a mania. Canal building on the Continent came somewhat later, although there are some examples of early canals, e.g. the Canal du Midi in southern France was constructed in 1681. In 19th century, there was some decline in inland water transport due to development of railways and road transport. But after sometime, water transport has tended to make a comeback, this is closely linked with the cheapness and capacity for bulk carriage of water transport – witness the recent and current developments of the Albert Canal, the canal between Zeebrugge and Ghent, the canalisation of the Moselle, the Rhone Valley Scheme, etc. Inland waterways have both advantages and disadvantages. The chief advantages are:

(i) there is no track to lay or maintain, although dredging may be necessary in the case of natural waterways;

(ii) they may provide the only practicable routes, e.g. in very difficult, mountainous country or in areas of very dense tropical forest; and

(iii) waterways, under favourable conditions, provide cheap transport for heavy, bulky, imperishable commodities such as coal, ore, timber, cement.

The principal disadvantages of inland waterways are:

(i) rivers may involve devious journeys and may flow in the wrong direction from the point of view of trade;

(ii) otherwise navigable rivers may be interrupted by falls or rapids while canals require locks if there are differences in level;

(iii) river levels may change seasonally and freezing may occur in winter causing stoppages in navigation;

(iv) canal construction involves heavy capital outlay and canals require constant maintenance and sometimes dredging, and may also require a water supply;

(v) transport by water is slow in comparison with most other forms of overland transport and carriage by water is generally unsuitable for perishable produce; and

(vi) waterways are less flexible than either roads or railways which can more easily adapt themselves to changing industrial location.

Although water transport is carried on to a greater or lesser degree the world over, there are only six major navigable systems of inland waterways: the rivers of Western and Central Europe, the Volga-Don system, the North American rivers, the Amazon system, the Parana–Paraguay system, and the Chinese waterways.

Inland waterways are best developed in Europe and North America; in other continents their development is moderate. A brief review of inland waterways is as follows:

Europe

In Europe, France, Germany, Belgium, Netherlands as well as Russia, have very extensive inland waterways including rivers and canals. France is having 5,600 km of navigable rivers and another 4,800 km of canals. The major French rivers, e.g. Loire, Garonne, Seine, Rhone, Meuse and Moselle have been modified and are linked by canal systems so as to travel entirely by river and canals from Mediterranean Sea to English Channel or from Rhine to Atlantic Ocean. On the other hand, Germany is having 7,040 km of inland waterways. The important inland waterways of Europe are:

The Rhine Waterway

The Rhine is the busiest navigable river of the world. On both sides of it have developed heavy industries which benefit from cheap water transport. The river is navigable by ocean-going steamers of small size. From the point of economic geography, the rivers prolong the great ocean routes into the interior of lands. Of the "flowing roads" the Rhine is one of the most remarkable. It leads from the ocean into the very heart of the Continent. The Rhine is a "coal river". The lignite of the Aachen basin and the coal of the Ruhr furnish the greater part of the river freight.

The Rhine is one of the rivers most favoured by nature for navigation. The greatest difference between the Rhine from Basle to Strasbourg, and the Rhine from below Strasbourg is the heavy gradient in the upstream stretch, which causes a very swift current. Above Strasbourg the traffic is slight owing to a rapid current, low water and a rock ledge near Istein. But below that point there is a slow current except in the gorge of the Slate Mountain (between Bingen and Bonn). The volume of water is uniform during summer. Rhine navigation is stopped during the months of winter owing to low water.

The Rhine from Basle to Strasbourg is characterised by a torrential regimen betraying its Alpine origin. The seasonal variations – summer floods and winter low water – are the more pronounced and rapid as the gradient increases from Basle to Strasbourg. A barge which carries a full cargo to Strasbourg in summer must discharge half en route in winter. The Rhine navigators invariably allow a margin of 30 cm between boat-keel and river-bed to guard against sudden fall in the waters which may be very rapid in case of drought.

The Rhine empties into a tributary sea of the North Atlantic which lies at the beginning of the largest current of world commerce. This is a privileged position as compared with most other rivers of Europe. To take advantage of this, other rivers near the Rhine have been connected to it by means of canals. The result is that there is no other river in Europe which has so many canal connections as the Rhine.

Waterways of the Germanic-Baltic Lowlands

An extensive network of waterways consisting of east-west canals joining the north-south flowing rivers crosses the northern German plain. The Mittelland Canal, also known as the Midland Canal was built in 1938, joins the three major rivers of Ems, Weser and Elbe. Kiel Canal is 96 km long, links the Elbe estuary to the Baltic Sea. The Dortmund-Ems canal runs north-south and links the Rhine with ports of Bremen and Emden.

Waterways of Southern Germany

Danube is the main river, which flows through seven countries – Germany, Austria, Czech Republic, Hungary, Yugoslavia, Romania and Bulgaria and navigable for about 2,400 km. Canals like Ludwing Canal, Rhone–Rhine Canal provide a good inland waterway.

In Belgium, total length of inland waterway is 1,535 km. Albert Canal (built in 1940) and also other canals on coastal plain serve the towns of Ghent, Bruges, Zeebrugge and Ostend. Netherlands, at the mouth of Rhine, is criss-crossed by its distributaries, and also has extensive man-made waterways.

The former Soviet Union, has developed a system of navigable waterways totalling 1,44,000 km. Most of these waterways are located in European Russia. The Baltic and White Sea Canal, the Moscow-Volga Canal and Volga-Don shipping canals are nodal. There are several rivers like Volga, Dvina, Don, Dnieper and Dneister, which are navigable in many parts. But many Russian rivers remained blocked during winter season. In spite of such defects Russian rivers are very important for domestic and foreign trade.

North America

In North America the rivers of most use for navigation are the Mississippi and Missouri and the most important canals are those of St. Lawrence, which unites the Ontario and St. Lawrence; the Sault Sainte Marie canal, between Superior and Huron; the canal which links the Chesapeake to the Ohio; the New York canal; and the canals between North Allegheny and Erie.

The length of navigable waterways in United States is over 36,072 km. The Mississippi river system, largest of all, provides more than 8,000 kilometres of waterways with depths of 3 metres or more, including the main river trunkline from Minneapolis to the Gulf of Mexico – a distance of more than 12,880 kilometres. The Missouri, a tributary of Mississippi, is navigable for 1,216 km to Sioux city, Iowa.

On the recommendations of The Ralph M. Parsons Company, a private engineering and construction enterprise with headquarters in Los Angeles, a project was set up to carry out technical assessment of water and power potential of North America. The project is referred to by the company as NAWAPA – the North American Water and Power Alliance.

The basic idea behind 'NAWAPA' is to capture the surplus waters of the Fraser, Yukon, Peace and Athabaska river systems in north-western North America and to direct, via an elaborate system of canals, reservoirs and tunnels, the surplus water to deficit areas of Canada and United States.

The St. Lawrence Waterway

The St. Lawrence, with the great lakes, forms a very important commercial route into the heart of North America. The river is, however, ice-bound for about four months every year, and has various rapids and falls which have necessitated the cutting of canals to enable sea-going vessels to reach Lake Superior. Large ocean vessels can pass about a thousand kilometres up the river to Montreal; but here goods have to be transhipped to smaller vessels, because rapids occur, and the canals made to avoid them are not over 3–5 metres deep.

The Canadian government built a 3–5 metres deep canal around the rapids that permitted shallow draft boats to negotiate the St. Lawrence between Lake Ontario and the sea. After the Welland canal and its eight locks were completed in 1931, interest in the Great Lakes – St. Lawrence Seaway was renewed.

The St. Lawrence enters the ocean by a deep estuary due to submergence in the past, but navigation is rendered difficult by the prevalence of fogs and the rapidity of the current. The valley of the St. Lawrence is fertile, and the whole length is lined with villages and towns. Another canal has been made to avoid the falls of Niagara, though a great deal of trade is diverted at Buffalo to the Erie canal and Mohawk-Hudson route to New York. The Sault Sainte Marie or 500 canals were necessitated by rapids between Lake Superior and Lake Hudson, and the traffic on these canals is enormous.

Asia

Asia is not having elaborate system of inland waterways, but rivers in many countries are used as inland waterways.

In China, the rivers have made a significant contribution to the development of commerce. The three great rivers, the Hwang-ho, the Yang-tse-kiang and the Sikiang, cross the country from west to east. China's greatest river is the

Yang-tse-kiang, the most important waterway for navigation in the country. It is doubtful whether there is another equally extensive region of wealth in the world where the people depend as solely upon a single artery of traffic and upon one entrepot as do the inhabitants of the Yangtse basin. About half of the population of China live in this fertile area, utilising the river, its tributaries and its network of canals as their chief means of communication. The Yang-tse-kiang rises in Tibet, and with its tributaries drains the heart of China. It is navigable by steamers up to the port of Hankow. The Sikiang rises in the highlands of Yunan and has a fairly direct course eastward to its mouth. It is navigable for the greater part of its course. The Pei-ho is important for communication and can be navigated up to Tientsin.

Northern India is especially endowed with three large navigable rivers. These rivers are the Ganga, the Brahmaputra and the Jamuna. The Ganga can be navigated by steamers as far as Kanpur from its mouth. This river flows through the most densely populated and fertile plain of India and naturally commands much traffic. Before the development of railways the Ganga was of considerable importance for the movement of goods and persons. The development of railways has greatly reduced the importance of steam navigation, specially in the Upper Ganga. The Lower Ganga is even now very important, and there is traffic all the year round. The Brahmaputra flows through Assam and Bangladesh and is navigable as far as Dibrugarh. Its tributary, the Surma, has made steam navigation possible in Sylhet and Cachar. The Indus in Pakistan is navigable by steamer up to Dera Ismail Khan in the North Western Frontier Province. The river mostly handles wheat, cotton and wool. The frequent shifting of its bed and the formation of sand-bars have caused steam navigation in the Indus to be neglected.

Burma is very fortunate in having a large number of navigable rivers. The Irrawaddy, the most important and the largest, is navigable by steamers for more than 800 km from its mouth and country boats can proceed farther.

Africa

In Africa, some rivers are navigable, that too for a very limited length. The Nile is the most important river in north-east Africa, but its great defect is the succession of cataracts. In its upper course the Nile has rapids and falls; in its middle course there are cataracts. It is navigable in the delta and in its lower course. The rivers of South Africa are of little use for traffic. The Zambesi is navigable for only 350 km, while the Limpopo can be navigated only for a short distance. The Orange is not navigable. In tropical Africa, the Congo provides a magnificent system of waterways. It rises in the highlands between the lakes Tanganyika and Nyasa. But at several places navigation is interrupted by rapids and falls. The Uban, the chief tributary of the Congo, can be navigated almost up to its head. In West Africa the Niger is easily navigable for 500 miles and in the wet season navigation is continued further. The Gambia is navigable for 260 km from its mouth.

South America

South America is having some long rivers but their use as inland waterways is limited. Amazon river is the longest river of the continent. But till now the Amazon system is of relatively little use, because the region through which the river flows is densely forested, scantily populated, undeveloped and largely unexplored. The

Orinoco which flows through Venezuela is a long waterway. But the most useful in South America is the Parana system which penetrates the heart of Argentina, Paraguay, Uruguay and South Brazil. In the southern side of South America, the river Rio Negro drains the sheep-rearing land of Patagonia.

Australia

Australia is deficient in waterways. Her river-system consists of small streams flowing from the highlands to the coast, thus not suitable for navigation purpose. The two most important rivers are Murray and Darling. Darling river remains almost dry during winter and spring seasons. River Murray is partially used as a waterway.

Ocean Transport

Ocean transport is the most important water transport, because it has certain advantages over land carriage. The sea offers a ready-made carriageway for ships which, unlike the roadway or railway, requires no maintenance. Water surfaces are two-dimensional and, although sea-going vessels frequently keep to shipping lanes, ships can travel, within a limited number of constraints, in any direction. Because of floatability and reduced friction, ocean vessels are capable of carrying far greater loads and far greater weights than can be handled even by the longest railway train, the most powerful lorry and trailer, or the largest aircraft; accordingly, ocean transport is usually the cheapest of all forms of transport. Again, except for fog and floating ice, and occasionally stormy weather which may hinder progress, ocean-going vessels have fewer physical obstacles to surmount than those which so often handicap overland transport.

Ships have been used for transport right from early times. During Graeco-Roman times a fundamental distinction was made between longships or galleys, used for military purposes, and round-ships for trade. The Vikings had a similar distinction. During more recent times ships have shown an even greater specialisation and several distinct types of commercial vessels gradually evolved. Today about half a dozen main types of merchant ships are recognised – passenger liners, cargo-liners, bulk-carriers, tramps and coasters and short-sea traders.

The most spectacular development, however, has been the appearance of bulk-carriers, the most important of which are tankers, the product of the oil age. Recent years have witnessed a tremendous growth in the size of tankers, a number of which now exceed 5,00,000 tons dead-weight. Today, more than half of the world's merchant shipping tonnage comprises tankers, a fact indicative of the great importance of oil in the modern world.

Although ships have freedom of movement and are capable of going virtually anywhere on the ocean surface, they tend to keep to certain "lanes". They do so because of: (i) physical conditions, and (ii) economic considerations.

Clearly, ships will go only where there are goods or people to be carried and the most important shipping routes are those linking the most productive and most populous regions. Certain physical conditions also help to determine the routes followed by ships, e.g. the availability of harbours and ports on coasts, weather conditions such as fog and storm occurrence and oceanographical factors such as sea ice and icebergs, submarine banks and shallow waters.

The principal ocean trade routes of the world are as follows (Figure 13.6):

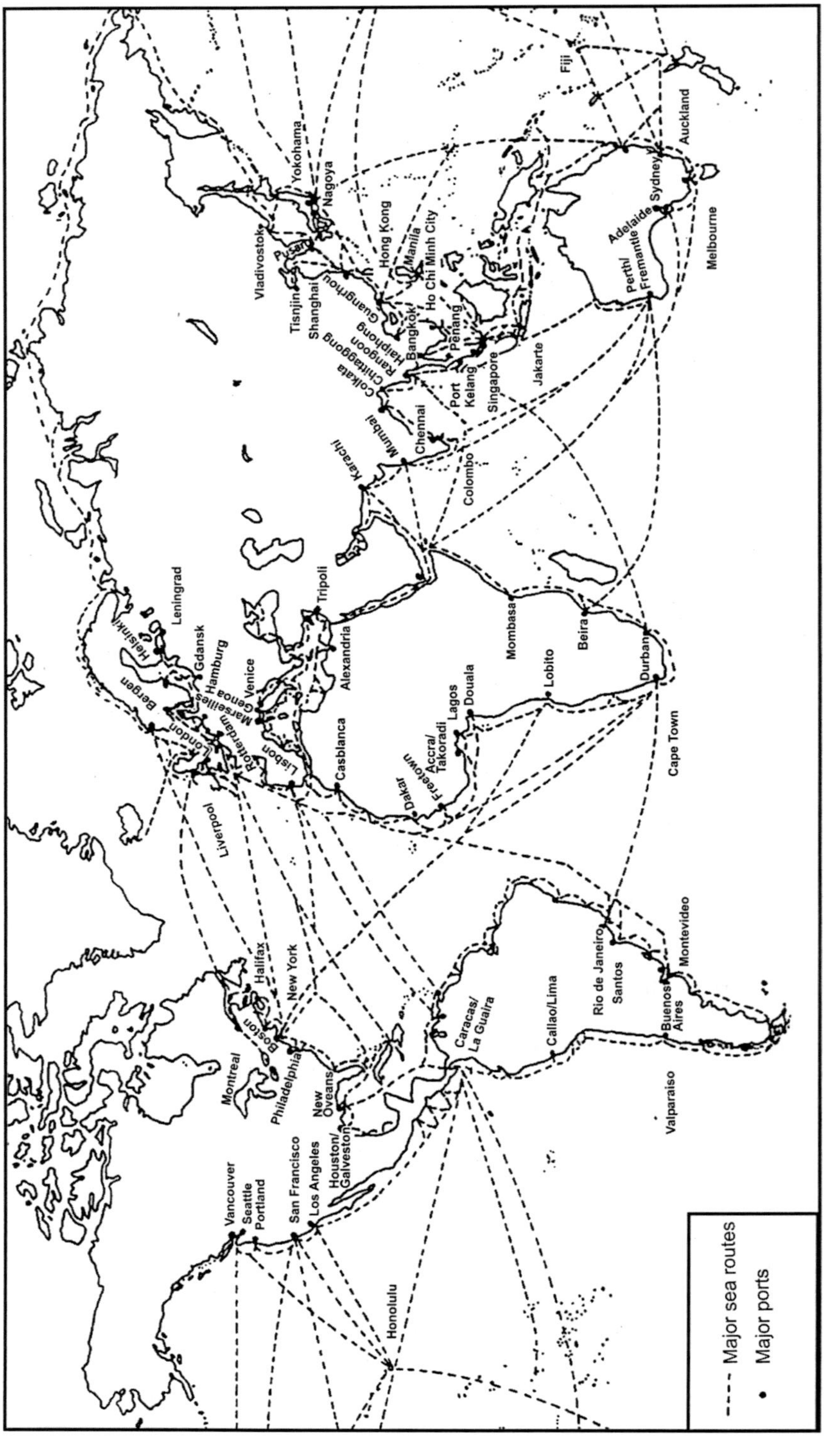

Figure 13.6
Major ocean trade routes of the world

The North Atlantic Ocean Route

The North Atlantic Ocean Route has the greatest traffic of all ocean routes. Nearly one-fourth of the tonnage of the world's merchant vessels serves this route. In volume and variety of cargo, this route far exceeds any other. This route connects the ports of western Europe with those on the east coast of North America. These two regions are the most populous and highly developed regions in the world. North America and western Europe are the world's greatest producers of goods of quantity and diversity. Ports on the western coast of Europe are Glasgow, Liverpool Manchester, Southampton, London, Rotterdam, Bremen, Bordeaux and Lisbon. Ports on the eastern coast of the USA are Quebec, Montreal Halifax, St. John, Boston, New York, Baltimore, Charleston Galveston and New Orleans.

This oceanic route is the busiest trade route of the world. Large quantities of manufactured items: textiles, chemicals, machinery, fertilisers, steel, wine, etc. are exported from these ports across the North Atlantic to the United States and Canada.

The exports of Canada and the USA to Europe are timber, fish, wheat, raw cotton, tobacco, oil, machinery and vehicles, metals, paper and chemicals.

The Suez Canal or Mediterranean Asiatic Route

This route is second to the North Atlantic in respect of volume of traffic. It commands the markets of eastern Africa, Iran, Arabia, India, the Far East, Australia and New Zealand. In fact, the route passes through the heart of the world and touches more lands and serves more people than any other route. Throughout its many ports of call, it reaches about three-quarters of the total population of the globe. After crossing the Red Sea, the route follows two directions – one along the eastern coast of Africa to Durban; another to farther east – to India, Australia, etc. Ports of departure are London, Liverpool, Southampton, Hamburg, Rotterdam, Lisbon, Marseilles, Genoa and Naples. The ports of call are Aden, Mumbai, Kolkata, Rangoon, Penang, Singapore, Manila, Hong Kong, Perth, Adelaide, Melbourne, Sydney, Mombasa, Zanzibar, Mozambique and Durban.

This route is used by Asiatic countries to send raw materials and some food products to the western markets and receive in return manufactured articles – the products of the Far East are rice, tea, sugar and silk; those of India are coffee, tea, pig iron, manganese ore, jute goods, indigo, spices, cotton, teak, silk, skins, leather and oil-seeds and those of Middle East are petroleum, coffee, and dried fruits. From Australia meat, timber, wheat, flour, fruit, wool, butter and wine are sent. China, Australia, New Zealand and countries of South and South-East Asia now use this route for both export and import of commodities.

The Cape of Good Hope Route

This route was once the subsidiary alternative to Suez Canal route, but because of its long and circuitous journey, was avoided by most of the shipping companies. During the closure of Suez Canal in 1967 all the ships had no choice but to take this route. Even after Suez Canal reopened in 1975, much trade continue to follow this route because tankers and other vehicles nowadays are much larger. As the Suez Canal can only accommodate ships of around 20,000 tons capacity and toll charges are high, the Cape route is growing in importance. It has several other advantages. With the greater economic development of the recently independent African nations and the exploitation of their rich natural resources such as gold, copper, diamonds, tin, chromium, manganese, cotton, oil palm, groundnuts, coffee and fruits, the volume of traffic round the Cape of Good Hope and from ports in both East and West Africa is on the increase.

The Panama Canal: West Indian Central American Route

The construction of Panama Canal was completed in 1913. The Panama Canal is 'the gateway to the Pacific' and eliminated the long and hazardous voyage round the Cape Horn. It has benefited on both Atlantic and Pacific seaboard, facilitating trade in minerals, oil, foodstuffs, raw materials and manufactured products. But the greatest benefits have accrued to traffic between the east and west coasts of USA. The Panama route has also greatly facilitated trade in the West Indian islands and the Pacific states of North, Central and South America, especially the Andean states which are rich in mineral resources and have good markets in North America. The Latin American states import manufactured goods and mining equipment from the USA and the western European countries. Much trade destined for the Far East, the Pacific islands and Australasia from North America and Western Europe also goes through the Panama Canal. With the greater economic development of East Asian countries especially China, Japan and the South-East Asian states, the Panama route is assuming a greater role in the exchange of products between the East and West. The distance saved from Auckland to New York via Panama, instead of Cape Horn, is more than 4,000 km.

The South Atlantic Route

This route leads to West Indies, Brazil and Argentina. The chief ports of call on the route are Kingston (Jamaica), Havana, Vera Cruz, Tampico, Pernambuco, Bahia, Rio de Janeiro, Santos, Montevideo, Buenos Aires and Rosario. The exports along the route are sugar, bananas, raw cotton, mahogany, tobacco, coffee, grain, wool and meat, while the imports are manufactured goods.

This route maintains trade connections between Europe on the one hand and West Indies, Caribbean seaboard, Brazil, Uruguay and Argentina on the other.

The Trans-Pacific Route

There are several routes in North Pacific which converge at Honolulu for refuelling and servicing. The direct route further north is a great circle which links Vancouver and Yokohama without calling the Hawaiian Island, reduces the travelling distance by half. The North Pacific trade include Vancouver, Seattle, Portland, San Francisco and Los Angles on the American side, dealing with wheat, timber, paper and pulp, fish, dairy products and manufactured goods. The destinations across the 7,200 km (4,500 mile) wide Pacific are usually Yokohama, Kobe, Shanghai, Guangzhou (Canton), Hong Kong, Manila and Singapore. The east-bound trade from East Asia to North America consists mainly of manufactured goods, e.g. textiles, electrical equipment, from Japan, Hong Kong, S. Korea and Taiwan and tropical raw materials from South-East Asia, e.g. rubber, copra, palm oil, teak, tin and tea. In addition to international links the North Pacific is an important domestic routeway from the US mainland to the isolated states of Alaska, in the north and Hawaii in the mid-Pacific.

In the *South Pacific*, the traffic consists mainly of ships travelling via the Panama Canal between either West Europe or North America and Australia, New Zealand and the scattered Pacific islands. Goods transported are mostly wheat, meat, wool, fruits, dairy products and manufactured articles.

The other important routes are eastern North American-east South American (from New York to Cape Sao Roque), North American-western South American (from New York to Punta Arenas via Panama Canal), North American-Australasian (from New York and Vancouver to Sydney and Wellington via Honolulu), etc.

The analysis of ocean transport cannot be completed without detailed description of Suez and Panama Canals. These two canals have changed the entire pattern of oceanic trade, therefore, it is essential to know the characteristics and importance of these canals.

The Suez Canal

The Suez Canal is one of the great international waterways of the world – cuts across the Isthmus of Suez and provides navigational facilities between the Mediterranean Sea and the Indian Ocean. The history of a canal connecting the Mediterranean with the Red Sea dates back to 13th century B.C. when Nile-Red Sea canal is known to have been in use until the end of 8th century AD. From 16th century onward one or the other of European powers became interested in the idea of either reopening the old waterway or cutting a new one from the Mediterranean. In 1834, Ferdinand de Lesseps, a member of the French Consular service at Alexandria was interested in the Suez Canal scheme. In 1854, he discussed the project with the Viceroy of Egypt (Khedive) and got his approval. A concession to run for 99 years from the date of the canal's opening was granted to de Lesseps, authorising him to form an International Company for the purpose of constructing a waterway. The excavation was started in 1859 under de Lesseps, who took full ten years to construct the canal. It was opened in November, 1869. It is about 160 km long (including distance of lakes) and is 11 to 15 metres deep. The width of the floor is 40 m and varies at the surface. Suez Canal links the Mediterranean Sea with Red Sea. Port Said is located at Mediterranean Sea; while Port Suez is on the Red Sea.

Figure 13.7
The Suez Canal

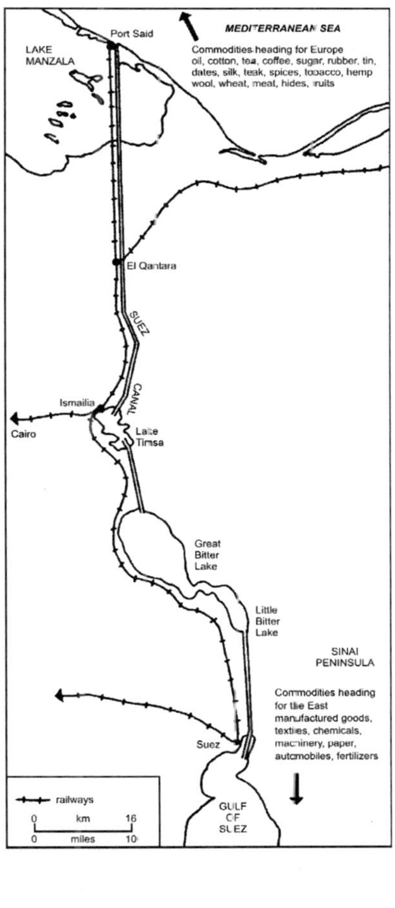

As a ship enters the canal from the Mediterranean Sea, it will pass Port Said, one of the greatest ports in the world and proceeding south will enter Lake Tunisa on the bank of which is the city of Ismailia. From Lake Tunisa to Suez city, a ship will pass through Geat Bitter lake and Little Bitter lake.

No single human enterprise during the past century has done more to affect the destinies of nations through a physical geographical change than the Suez Canal. The opening of Suez Canal route saved approximately 5,820 kilometres on the voyage from London to Mumbai as compared to the Cape route. The opening of Suez Canal had a tremendous effect not only on world trade and commerce but also on international politics, besides opening up to western countries a new route to Africa, Asia and Australia.

The usual trade route between the eastern coast of North America and the Far East was through the Cape of Good Hope. The Suez Canal saved a great deal of distance by diverting the traffic from the Cape of Good Hope route to itself and thus, benefited North America greatly. More than 12,000 vessels pass through the Suez canal every year. The Suez Canal has provided not only the fastest but also the most economical line of transit between Europe and the East. Politically the Suez route is vital because of the oilfields in the Middle East countries on whose products the economy of western Europe is dependent.

There are some problems of the Suez Canal. The canal needs improvements in regard to depth, width, diversion to avoid crossing of ships in the narrow part of canal. The deposition of silt that comes along winds blown from desert also needs regular cleaning. The second problem is the high canal dues levied on ships which pass through the canal. It has been observed that when speed is not essential, many cargo liners follow the Cape of Good Hope route to avoid the high dues. Now many cargo vessels are so big in size that they cannot pass through the Suez

Figure 13.8
The Panama Canal

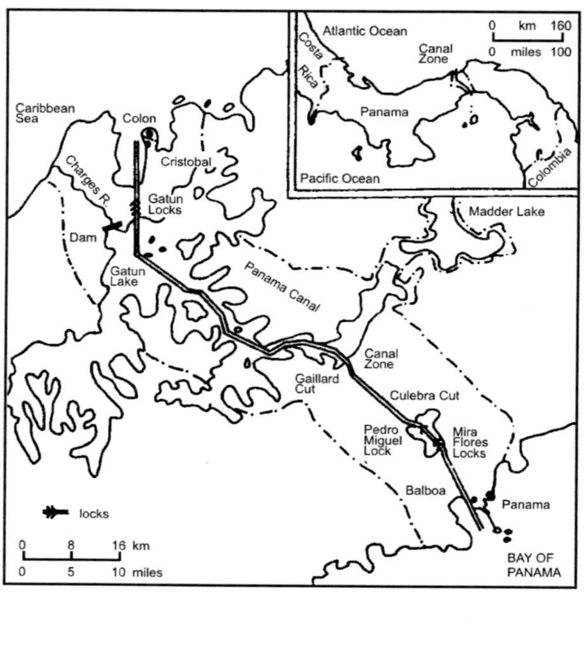

Canal. Political instability in adjoining states of the canal is also a cause of concern. Although, Suez Canal according to international convention is free and open, in time of war as in time of peace, to every vessel of commerce or of war, without distinction of flag.

The Panama Canal

The Panama Canal connects the Atlantic and the Pacific oceans by means of two bays, an artificial lake, a natural lake, and three systems of locks. It has been constructed across the narrow Isthmus of Panama where the long Continental Divide dips to one of the lowest points. The canal is 72 km long from deep water to deep water in the oceans. It was opened on 15 August, 1914 (Figure 13.8).

All the locks are double, so that ships can pass in both directions without any congestion of traffic. The depth of the channel varies from 12 to 26 metres and the width varies from 91 to 305 metres. The time taken to pass through the canal from Panama to Colon is 14 hours.

The Panama Canal passes through a rough country and the engineering difficulties have been much greater than in the case of the Suez Canal, which passes through a level country and needs no locks. The Panama Canal generates its own hydroelectric power with which not only lighting of the region is done, but also electric locomotives are supplied to pull ships through the locks.

The Panama Canal is 'the gateway to the Pacific'. It has benefited countries on both Atlantic and Pacific seaboards, facilitating the trade in minerals, oil, foodstuffs, raw materials and manufactured products. Its greatest benefits have accrued to traffic between the east and west coasts of the United States. The canal shortens the distance between New York and San Francisco by about 12,596 km by sea, and lessens very considerably the distance between western Europe and western America, and between the northern and middle parts of East America and East Asia.

It also slightly shortens the distance between Europe and New Zealand, but it does not lessen that between Europe and Asia or Europe and Australia. Eastern North America and north-western Europe very definitely gained as a result of the canal, for they were placed much nearer by this route to all of western North America, western South America and New Zealand. For eastern North America the canal has meant a great reduction in the distance to Japan and to all of China north of Hong Kong, a factor that has unquestionably contributed to the rapid growth of trade with East Asia.

Comparison between Suez and Panama Canals

Both Suez and Panama Canals are the most important ocean canals of the world and each canal has had its own advantages. From the comparison point of view following points are notable:

(i) The Suez route is well-supplied with coaling stations, etc. as there are plenty of islands and other points of call. The Panama route suffers for want of enough islands and halting stations as the Pacific is a dreary ocean with little commerce.

(ii) Coal is easily and cheaply available on the Suez route, specially as coal occurs in many of the areas served by the Suez route.

The Panama route serves regions which are deficient in coal. It has, however, considerable amount of oil.

(iii) The Suez route serves some of the most thickly populated areas and carries therefore a much larger traffic than the Panama route which generally serves poor mountainous or desert regions like those on the east coast of North America or South America.

(iv) The Suez Canal is longer, has no locks and cost less than the Panama Canal. It is not so deep, however, the practice of tying up, so annoying in the case of the Suez, is not necessary in the case of the Panama Canal.

(v) The Suez Canal dues are higher than those of the Panama Canal.

Other important ship canals of the world are: *The Sault Sainte Marie Canal,* (called Soo), the *Manchester Ship Canal,* the *Kiel Canal,* the *North Sea Canal* between Amsterdam and the North Sea, and the New Waterway between Rotterdam and the North Sea.

AIR TRANSPORT

The use of aircraft and development of air transportation belong to the 20th century. The countries which took the lead in developing commercial air routes in the world were France, Belgium, Netherlands and UK. These countries, after the First World War, put to use their experience of flying and the accumulated planes for commercial aviation, primarily for the purpose of maintaining communication with and defence of there colonies. The USA entered the field of commercial aviation after 1927. Lack of colonial interest was one of the factors for her delay. The real progress of air transportation, however, started after 1946. The World War II gave a great impetus to the development of aerial transport and the period between 1946 and 1956 was characterised by quick development of new equipment and by a big upsurge in the volume of air travel. The greatest innovation of the period was the application of jet propulsion to transport aircraft.

Air transport differs from all other forms of transport in that it is three-dimensional. Since aircrafts are not tied to the surface and have the ability to fly above terrestrial obstacles, air routes, in a purely theoretical sense, can be laid in any direction and, in fact, it is commonly said that aeroplane has the freedom of the air and a freedom of action denied to any other form of transport. Such freedom however, is largely illusory. In the first place, movement for commercial purpose, is normally channeled along carefully prepared routes; secondly, movement may be restricted by political considerations, some countries banning flights across their territory for security or other reasons; thirdly, aircraft need airports just as surely as ships need harbours and port installations and aircraft are tied more closely to ground facilities than is usually imagined; and, fourthly, weather conditions impose a greater control upon air transport than upon any other form of transport.

In the early days of air transport, when aircraft had a relatively restricted range of flight due to their size, speed and limited fuel carrying capacity, air routes were so designed as to avoid extensive ocean crossing, high mountains, uninhabited deserts and vast forest areas. Hence, the very barriers which impeded human travel on the earth's surface also restricted man's movement by air. However, as a result of the greatly improved performance of aircraft and their greater reliability, physical features in themselves now place no limit upon the choice of routes.

In air transport, weather conditions are a limiting factor. But due to technological developments, aircraft have begun to use the stratosphere where they can fly "above the weather". Radar, de-icing techniques, beacons for night flying, and host of other inventions and aids have helped to combat the weather. But, notwithstanding all these things, it must be emphasised that low cloud, ground mist, fog, ice, dust-storms and other weather phenomena, which either interfere with visibility or affect the performance of the aircraft, still hinder flying and create hazards.

Air routes today are primarily determined by: (i) adequate ground facilities for operation, and (ii) availability of traffic for economic working.

Air transport is still, in general, costly. The high cost of air transport is largely the result of the expensiveness of the vehicle and the motive power. The total amount of freight moved by air is still small, less than 2 per cent of the total world figure. Air transport is best suited for the carriage of commodities which are low in bulk but high in value. At the present time most of the air freight is actually carried in the holds of passenger aircraft. But, the expansion of high-technology industries in the Pacific Rim, in North America and in western Europe has generated a growing demand for air cargo services and the highest growth rates have been recorded on US-Far East routes. On an average, 740.2 million tons is hauled as air cargo. The leading international airports in terms of yearly passengers are as follows:

1. Singapore Changi International Airport (55.4 million passengers)
2. Tokyo Haneda International Airport (75.3 million passengers)
3. Incheon International Airport (49.3 million passengers)
4. Munich Airport (42.3 million passengers)
5. Hong-Kong International Airport (68.3 million passengers)
6. Hamad International Airport (30 million passengers)
7. Central Japan International Airport (9.8 million passengers)
8. Zurich Airport (27.7 million passengers)
9. London Heathrow Airport (78.0 million passengers)
10. Frankfurt Airport (61 million passengers)
11. Amsterdam Schiphol Airport (58.3 million passengers)
12. Kansai International Airport (25.2 million passengers)
13. Vancouver International Airport (22.3 million passengers)
14. Tokyo Narita International Airport (39.1 million passengers)
15. Copenhagen Airport (26.6 million passangers)

Air services are of two main kinds:

(i) short-distance services such as those operating between important centres in a country or making short sea crossings, and
(ii) long distance services such as the transcontinental and transoceanic flights.

There is another distinction in services, too: although most aircraft operate to fixed schedules along regular routes, some aircraft, owned by private companies, are operated for charter, that is, they can be hired for special purposes or special journeys. Charter aircrafts are much used nowadays during the summer holiday season, especially in connection with inclusive tours.

Figure 13.9 shows the pattern of air routes in the world:

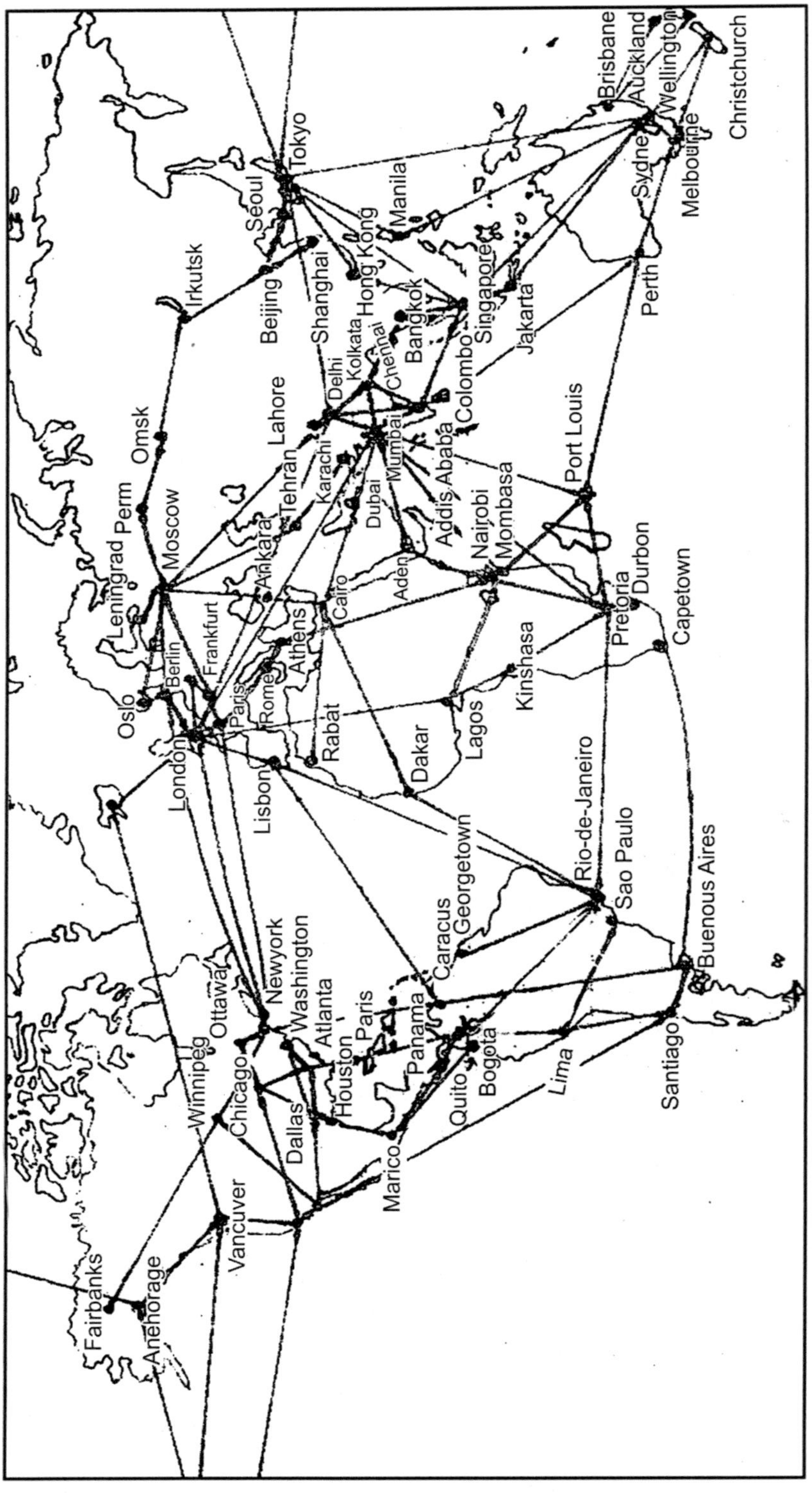

Figure 13.9
Major air routes of the world

The world map (Figure 13.9) showing pattern of routes brings out certain features; these are:

(i) the network shows that there is a worldwide coverage;

(ii) an east-west girdle of routes in the northern hemisphere;

(iii) longitudinal extensions from the latter into the three southern continents;

(iv) a great focusing of routes in three particular regions: western Europe, eastern USA and the Caribbean, and South-East Asia; and

(v) several important foci from which numerous routes radiate, e.g. New York, Chicago, Los Angles, Washington, Seattle, San Francisco, London, Paris, Berlin, Frankfurt, Rome, Moscow, Cario, Delhi, Mumbai, Kolkata, Bangkok, Singapore, Hong Kong, Tokyo, Sydney, etc.

The greatest development in air transport has taken place in United States of America. USA is a country of long distances so that there are no political frontiers with all the customs formalities, to be crossed by aeroplanes. The Atlantic and the Pacific coasts of the United States are among the most developed parts of the country, and the quickest way to connect these areas is by air. Because of this the number of people wishing to use this quick method of contact between the two far-flung borders of USA is very large.

United States alone is served by about 9,000 air terminals, has over 1,50,000 registered civil aircrafts and accounts for almost half of the world's air passenger traffic.

In Canada, the largest airline company is the Trans-Canada Airline, with Montreal, Toronto and Vancouver as the busiest air terminals.

In Europe, most of the countries have their own national airlines. After US, the greatest volume of air traffic is found in Europe. The major air terminals of Europe are London, Paris, Rome, Madrid, Berlin, Warsaw, Vienna, Geneva, Moscow, etc. England-Australia air route is one of the busiest and important air routes. This route starts from London and follows Marseilles, Athens, Alexandria, Cairo, Gaza, Baghdad, Bahrein, Sharjah, Karachi, Delhi, Kolkata, Rangoon, Bangkok, Penang, Singapore, Batavia, Darwin, Brisbane and finally reach to Sydney.

Russian international air routes are mostly controlled by Moscow, Leningrad, Novosibirsk, Irkutsk and Vladivostok. Russia and other countries of former Soviet Union are also well-connected by air service.

Africa is served by international airlines following the East African route through London, Rome, Cairo, Khartoum, Addis Ababa, Nairobi, Johannesburg with Mauritius, Sri Lanka and South-East Asia. The Central African route is through Paris, Algiers, Kano, Lagos, Kinshasa, Johannesburg, Durban or Cape Town. While West African route goes through London, Madrid, Casablanca, Dakar, Freetown, Monrovia, Accra and Luanda. In addition many African countries have their own air domestic service.

Most Asian countries have their own international airlines and many have domestic air service. Important international routes run across the monsoon fringe of Asia and Beirut, Tehran, Karachi, Mumbai, Delhi, Kolkata, Bangkok, Singapore, Hong Kong and Tokyo are all important international airports.

India's location from the point of view of air routes is good, because of its en-route location between Europe, Asia, Australia and Africa. India has air transport agreements with 93 countries and her flights are regularly scheduled to these countries. Air India and Indian Airlines are the main air lines which operate regular international and domestic air service. The major international airports of India are: Indira Gandhi International (Delhi), Sahar (Mumbai), Meenambakkam (Chennai), Dum Dum (Kolkata) and Tiruvananthapuram. Besides these, there are 92 major international and minor aerodromes meant for domestic and other flights. Now, some private airlines are also operating in India.

In China the first air flight between Shanghai and Chungking took place in 1928, but very little progress has been done till 1950. Considerable progress was made in air transport between 1950–1958. Today, there is a well-developed network in China and most of the principal cities have air links. China now has external air links with several other countries. Beijing, Shanghai and Canton are the great hubs of the airways network. But China is still having relatively lesser air transport facilities.

Air transport is well-developed in Japan and operates internal and international services. Tokyo is the focal point of international air transport.

The other countries of South-East Asia are also having international aviation. Similarly, countries like South and North Korea, Pakistan, Bangladesh, Sri Lanka, etc. are well-connected with air transport.

The Central and South American countries have developed air transport and all the capital cities are connected with international flights. The main focal points of air transport are Caracas, Bogota, Lima, Santiago, Buenos Aires, Sao Paulo and Rio de Janeiro.

In a large country like Australia where population is less and widely scattered and half of the people live in or near six major cities, the development of internal air service has been of enormous value. Thus, Australia has a well-developed internal air service and is also well-connected with other parts of world. Sydney is its most important international airport. New Zealand has also well-developed internal and external air transport facilities. Auckland, Wellington, Christchurch and Dunedin are the principal airports of New Zealand.

Part III

Theoretical Economic Geography

14

Theories of Agricultural Location

To the geographer, the study of agriculture is more than how the soil is cultivated, how food crops are raised and how livestock are bred. Geographers are motivated by a quest to describe and document the spatial patterns of agricultural landscape. The geographer then seeks to explain the spatial regularity of agricultural land use and connections between agriculturer's use of land and the happenings in other sectors of the economy and environment. To the economic geographer the explanation for spatial regularity of land use patterns is based on consequences of competitive market behaviour, with how the producer or sector will attain the right to use the land; where, and how changing prices and technology will affect the ability to compete at a particular location.

Unlike manufacturing and services, agriculture is an economic activity that is highly geographically dispersed. There are three reasons for this high dispersion:

(i) agricultural productivity is not the same everywhere for the same type of produce;

(ii) agriculture competes with other land users – including urban and recreational land users – for the use of land; and

(iii) the markets where agricultural products are sold are geographically dispersed.

The economic geographer is interested in the spatial dimension of farming. The earlier geographic characteristic of organised human agricultural activity was the setting aside of land to be used exclusively for agriculture. Such areal specialisation has become highly refined as farming technology has advanced. What is produced where, has a persistent trend and does not change, even though short-term market conditions change. Different crops and livestock systems require differing levels of specialisation of labour and capital. Such specialisation itself can keep a region specialising in a particular product and retards the diffusion of that crop from being farmed elsewhere. The locational analysis of agricultural land use provides an explanation of it. The present chapter deals with some of the locational theories of agriculture and will mainly focus on Johann Heinrich von Thunen's theory of agricultural location.

von Thunen's Location Theory

The analysis of land use patterns has long been one of geography's basic concerns. At first, it might appear as if agricultural land use is little affected by relative location, once the factor of a suitable market has been acknowledged. Indeed, the farmer does adapt his land use to site conditions, climate, land forms, and soils. However, the effects of the market situation cannot be disposed of as easily as all that. Johann Heinrich von Thunen (1983–1850), a German economist and estate owner of the early 19th century, developed a theory of agricultural location that is still worth considering. This model, is based on an econometric analysis of his estates in Mecklenburg, near Rostock in Germany. Most of the data used in explaining his theory were obtained by him through practical experience. He attempted to construct a theoretical model of land use pattern, giving a particular arrangement of towns and villages in a situation experienced in Mecklenburg.

The main aim of von Thunen's analysis was to show how and why agricultural land use varies with the distance from a market. He had two basic models:

1. The intensity of production of a particular crop declines with the distance from the market. Intensity of production is a measure of the amount of inputs per unit area of land; for example, the greater the amount of money, labour and fertilisers, etc. that are used, the greater the intensity of agricultural production.
2. The type of land use will vary with the distance from the market.

The von Thunen's location theory or model states that if environmental variables are held constant, then the farm product that achieves the highest profit will outbid all other products in the competition for location. The competitive position of a crop or livestock activity (namely, how high the bidding needs go to secure a desirable site) will depend on the level of return anticipated from producing at the particular location. A product with a high expected return and therefore, high rent-paying ability will be able to outbid a product with a lower profit level and, therefore, a relatively modest rent-bid ceiling.

By carefully compiling economic data on different farming activities on his own large estate Tellow in north-eastern Germany, von Thunen was able to determine the relative rent-paying abilities of each major agricultural product. Of course, the technology and agricultural products he managed in the early 19th century were different from those of today. But, there are sufficient similarities to allow the analysis to be updated for our purpose. Moreover, his explanation was truly general, allowing his explanation approach to be applied to most contemporary agricultural situations.

Following von Thunen's reasoning, the ranking of agricultural activities on the basis of rent-paying ability in the decreasing order are as follows:

Hierarchy of agricultural crops

1. Truck farming (fruits and vegetables)
2. Dairying
3. Mixed crop and livestock farming (corn belt agriculture)
4. Wheat farming
5. Ranching (yearlings often sold to feedlots of mixed crop and livestock farming)

von Thunen's theory is based on certain assumptions. These are as follows:

1. There is an 'isolated state' (as von Thunen called his model economy), consisting of 1 market city and its agricultural hinterland.
2. This city is the market for surplus products from the hinterland and receives products from no other areas.
3. The hinterland ships its surpluses to no other market except the city.
4. There is a homogeneous physical environment, including a uniform plain around the city.
5. The hinterland is inhabited by farmers who wish to maximise their profits, and who adjust automatically to the market's demands.
6. There is only one mode of transport – the horse and wagon (as this was 1826).
7. Transportation costs are directly proportional to distance, and are borne entirely by the farmers, who ship all produce in a fresh state.

von Thunen's model examines the location of several crops in relation to the market. The location of crops, according to him, is determined by (i) the market prices, (ii) transport costs, and (iii) the yield per hectare. The transport cost varies with the bulk and the perishability of the product. The crop with the highest locational rent for the unit of land will always be grown, since, it gives the greatest returns and all farmers attempt to maximise their profit. Two crops may have the same production costs and yields but difference in transport costs (per ton/kilometre) and market prices influence the decision-making of the farmers. If commodity A is more costly to transport per ton/kilometre and it has a higher market price, A will be grown closer to the market than B (Figure 14.1).

Figure 14.1

Locational rent and distance from market

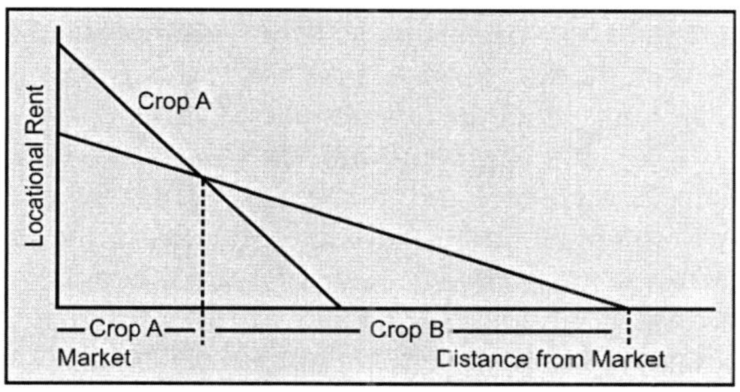

The locational rent of A decreases more rapidly than that of B, because of A's higher transport costs. As the market price of A is greater than B, the total revenue is higher at the market for A than B. Thus, the market of the locational rent of A is greater than B, because production costs are the same and no transport costs are incurred. If the market price of B was greater than that of A, A would not be grown at all.

In his model von Thunen has explained three stages of the growth of agricultural landscape in an isolated state as shown in Figure 14.2.

The single urban centre and undifferentiated landscape of von Thunen's model landscape is portrayed in Figure 14.2. Where are the most desirable farming locations situated? For every farmer, regardless of the crop or type of livestock raised, the answer is indisputable: as close as possible to the central market. The market is the destination for agricultural goods produced throughout the region.

Figure 14.2

Stages of formation of the agricultural landscape in von Thunen's model

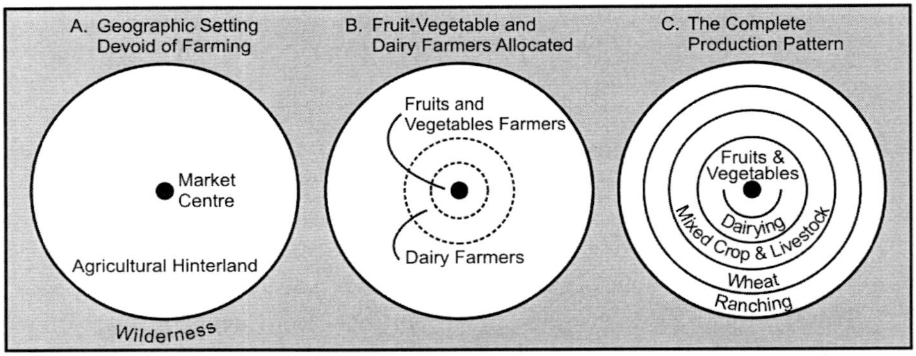

Next, assume that all the land in the heretofore undifferentiated landscape is placed on the auction block at the same time. The myriad of vegetable, dairy, mixed crop and livestock, wheat, and cattle-ranch land users eagerly submit their rent-bids to the landowners. All these actors prefer to purchase the right to use farmland near the market. However, vegetable farmers have a higher relative rent-paying ability near to the market than their competitors; hence, at the auction the vegetable farmers will outbid all the others. The vegetable producers will thereby acquire the right to farm the land adjacent to the market. Since, the undifferentiated landscape presents no advantages of being on a particular side of the market, the land users will distribute themselves circularly around the centre so as to minimise their distance to the town.

The bidding continues after vegetable farmers are accommodated. Since, dairy farmers rank next highest in rent-paying ability, they will successfully outbid the remaining contestants for locations in the next most accessible zone. Dairy farmers, too, arrange themselves in a circular fashion. There arises a definite formation of concentric rings of different land uses circumscribing the market (Figure 14.2-B). The remaining agricultural systems can be arranged concentrically around the market centre in the same fashion, according to their competitive economic positions. The completed pattern of production rings is shown in Figure 14.2-C.

von Thunen's General Theory of Land Use

On the basis of the above-mentioned assumptions, von Thunen constructed a general land use model, having a number of concentric zones around a market town (its three stages of growth have already been mentioned).

The perishable, bulky and/or heavy products, according to this model, would be produced in the belts nearer to the town. The more distant belts would specialise in products which were less in weight and volume but fetched higher price in the market as they could afford to bear relatively higher transportation costs. The final model was conceived as having specialised agricultural enterprises and crop-livestock combination. Each belt, according to von Thunen, specialises in the production of those agricultural commodities to which it was best suited (Figure 14.3).

Figure 14.3
Agricultural zones according to the von Thunen's model

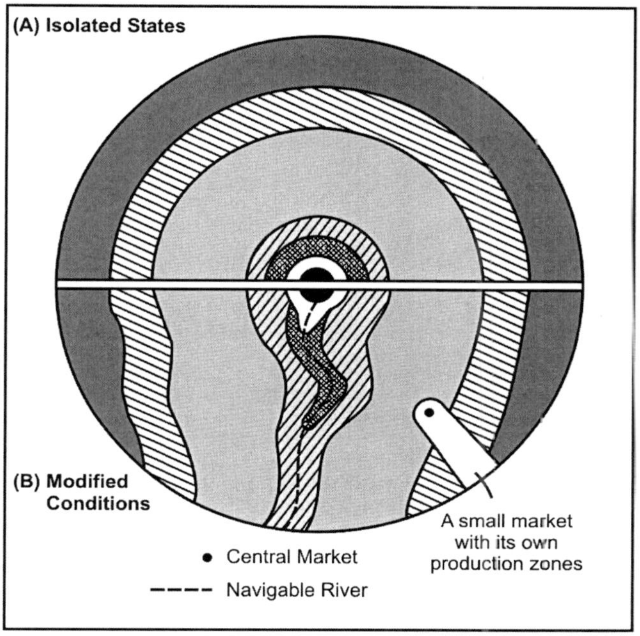

It becomes clear from Figure 14.3 that the production of fresh milk (in the context of Europe) and vegetables was concentrated in the Zone I nearest to the city, because of the perishability of such products. In this zone, the fertility of land was maintained by means of manuring and, if necessary, additional manure was brought from the city and transported to short distances to the farm. The Zone II was used for production of wood, a bulky product in great demand in the city as a fuel in the early part of the 19th century. He showed, on the basis of his empirical data, that forestry yielded a higher locational rent, since its bulkiness meant relatively higher transport cost. The Zone III represents crop farming where rye was an important market product, followed by other farming zones with a difference of the intensity of cultivation. As the distance from the market increased, so the intensity of rye production decreased with a consequent reduction in yields. There was no fallowing and manuring to maintain soil fertility.

In the next Zone IV the farming was less intensive. Farmers used a seven-year crop rotation in which rye occupied only one-seventh of the land. There was one year of rye, one of barley, one of oats, three of pastures and one of fallow. The products sent to the market were rye, butter, cheese, and occasionally, live animals to be slaughtered in the city. These products did not perish so quickly as fresh milk and vegetables and could, therefore, be produced at a considerably greater distance from the market. In the most distant of the zones supplying rye to the city Zone V, farmers followed the three-field system. This was a rotation system whereby one-third of the land was used for field crops, another one-third for pastures and the rest was left fallow. The farthest zone of all, i.e. Zone VI was the one of livestock farming. Because of the distance to the market, rye did not

Figure 14.4
von Thunen: Economic rent considering three crops

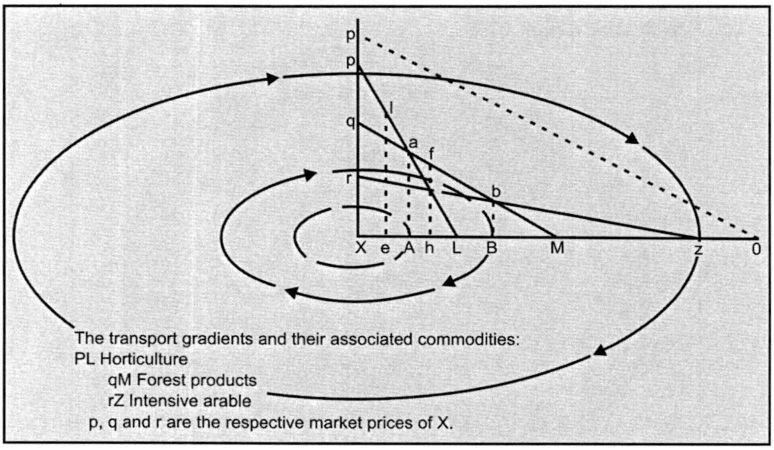

produce so high a rent as the production of butter, cheese or live animals (ranching). The rye produced in this zone was solely for the farm's own consumption. Only animal produce were marketed.

The economic rent considering three crops (horticulture, forest products and intensive arable cereals) has been plotted in Figure 14.4, while Figure 14.5 shows a simplified model of concentric zones. It may be seen from Figure 14.5 that Zone I in which the economic rent is high is devoted to horticulture (fruits and vegetables), while Zone II was devoted to forest products (like fuelwood) as the transportation cost of fuelwood is high. The Zone III is that of intensive arable land devoted to cereal crops.

Figure 14.5
A simplified von Thunen's model

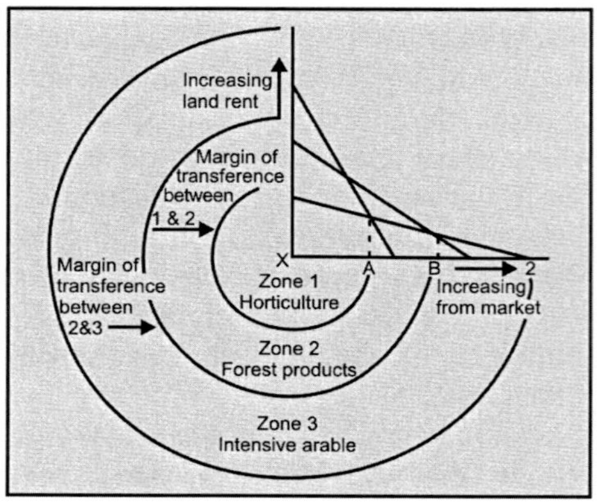

In this model, the distinctive aspects are land values, land use intensity and transportation costs. A brief explanation of these aspects is as follows:

Land Values

For agricultural land users the locations with better access (nearer) to the central market, bids up the value of land. Land values become so high that only those producers who yield the greatest locational rents can afford it. A distance-decay relationship and an inverted cone is revealed, with land values declining as distance from the central peak increases. The locational advantage of proximity to the market is reflected in higher land values; as accessibility declines, so do land values.

Land Use Intensity

In direct response to the land value pattern, land use intensities also decline with increasing distance from the centre. Producers on farmland with better access to the central market must use that land intensively to produce high enough revenues to afford to be located there. This results in high person-hour inputs per unit area of land for central farms, thereby requiring large hired-labour forces.

Farm size is another indicator as to the intensiveness of agricultural production; farm size generally increases with increasing distance from central markets. High land prices encourage farms to be comprised of fewer acres. Thus, in the inner zones, financing may be difficult to obtain on a scale necessary to support large farm operations. Relatively less capital intensive land (such as chicken sheds) will therefore, substitute for relatively more expensive land. The lower value of outer farmland permits the more lavish or extensive use of agricultural space. Because, both the cost of land and farm size change with changing accessibility to the market and aggregate locational rent per farm can be fairly constant across the landscape. For example, the aggregate locational rent for a 50 acre vegetable farm in the inner production ring can be roughly equivalent to a 1,000 acre ranch in the most peripheral zone.

Transportation Costs

The small variation of per farm aggregate locational rent across the Thunian zones is a result of site cost decreasing at approximately the same rate as transportation costs increase (Figure 14.6). High land values near the market are in a sense payments for savings in product-movement costs. Moreover, inner-ring farming is distinguished by the production of goods that do not easily withstand long-distance transportation. Highly perishable commodities such as fruits, vegetables, and dairy products share this low transferability.

Figure 14.6

Increasing transportation costs graphed against decreasing land costs in the isolated state

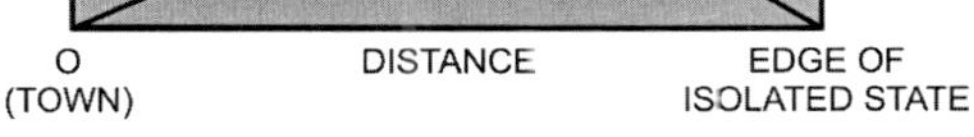

In fact, situations discussed in von Thunen's model was that of early 19th century era. The original Thunian model contained forestry (in its second ring) near to market, because heavy weight wood used for fuel and construction was expensive to transport. By the second half of the 19th century, cheaper rail transportation changed the entire pattern.

Finally, von Thunen incorporated two examples of modifying factors in his classic model. The effect can clearly be seen of a navigable river where transport was more speedy and cost only one-tenth as much as on land, together with the effect of smaller city acting as a competing market centre. Even the inclusion of only two modifications produces a much more complex land use pattern. When all the simplifying assumptions are relaxed, as in reality, a complex land use pattern would be expected. The catalytic factor in von Thunen's model was transport cost and the main assumption was the assumption of an 'isolated state'. In the modified von Thunen model, the influence of fertility, subsidiary town, information, etc. has been incorporated. The concentric zones of the model get modified under the impact of various physical, socio-economic and cultural factors. The influence of availability of information also substantially modifies the concentric zone of agricultural land use.

Critical Analysis

The theory of agricultural location was presented by von Thunen in the early 19th century. Since then, several scholars including geographers have applied it in various parts of the world and have pointed out certain aspects which are not applicable in a way as pointed out by von Thunen. Many aspects of this model have changed due to development in agricultural system, transportation system and also due to other technological developments. There are also certain regional geo-economic factors which not only direct but determine the pattern of agricultural land use. The main points raised by scholars regarding this theory are as follows:

1. The conditions described in this model, i.e. in an isolated state, are hardly available in any region of the world. There are internal variations in climatic and soil conditions. The von Thunen's assumptions that there are no spatial variations in soil types and climate are rare.
2. It is not necessary that all types of farming systems as described by von Thunen in his theory exist in all the regions. In many European countries location of types of farming in relation to market are no longer in existence.
3. The Thunen's measures of economic rent and intensity are difficult to test because of their complexity. The measurement of number of man-days worked in a year, cost of labour per hectare or cost of total inputs per hectare is not uniform in intensive and extensive types of farming. Similar is the case with the measures of intensity.
4. von Thunen himself has admitted that with the change in location of transportation or market centre the pattern of land use will also change.

Figure 14.7(a)
Pattern of land use

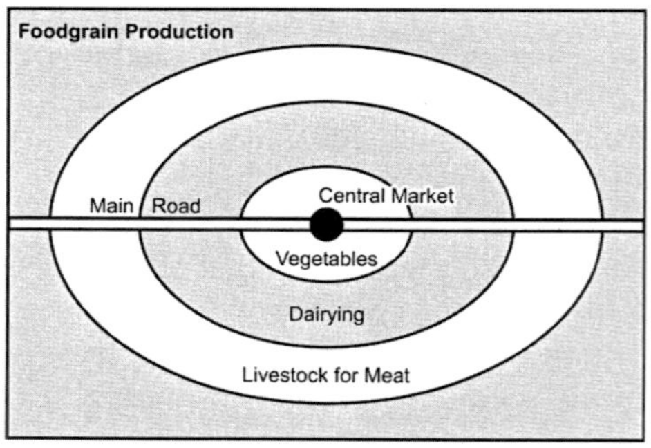

Figure 14.7(b)
Pattern of land use

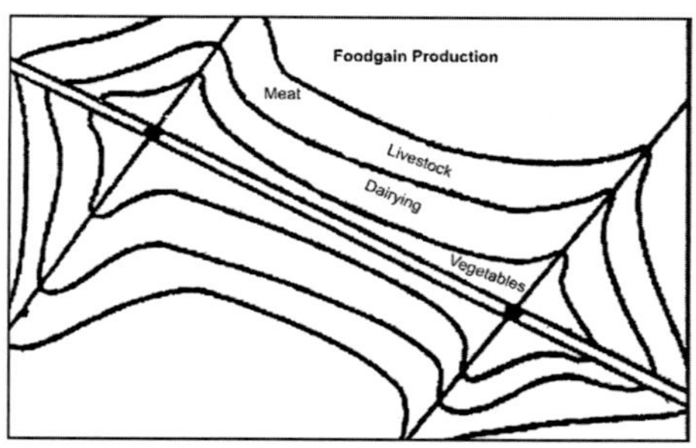

5. The location of transport link and its direction used to change the pattern of agricultural land use is depicted in Figure 14.7 (a) and (b).
6. Similarly, if there are two market centres, the pattern of land use will be according to Figure 14.8.
7. In case of three market centres the land use pattern will emerge like in Figure 14.9.
8. The situation will be entirely different when there are several market centres in a region (Figure 14.10).

Figure 14.8

Location of two market centres and general land use pattern

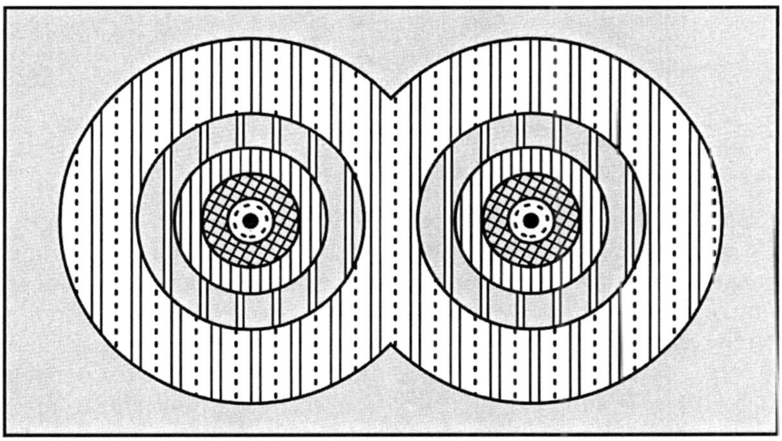

Figure 14.9

Location of three market centres and land use pattern

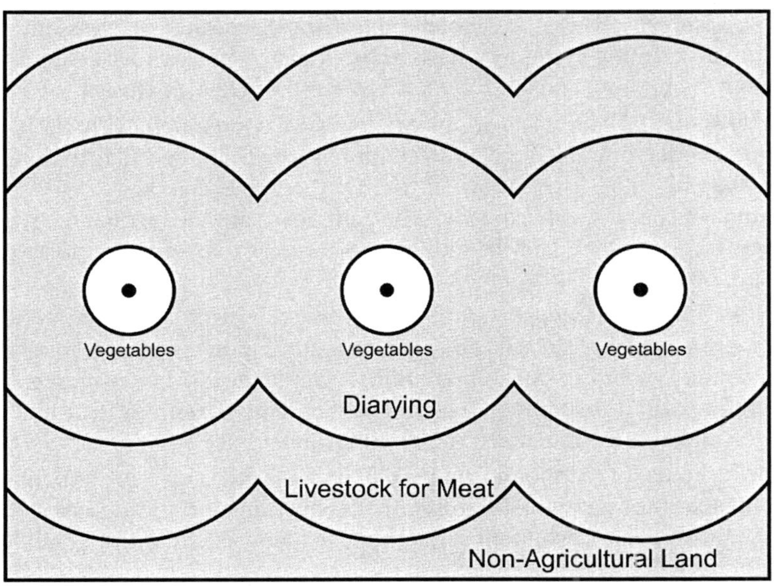

Figure 14.10

Location of several market centres and land use pattern

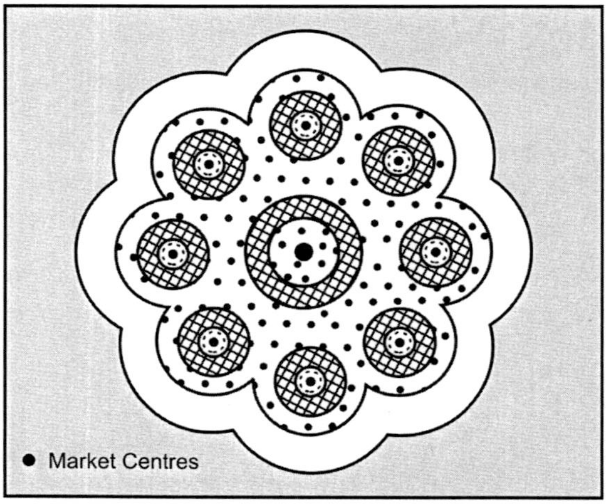

9. During the past 160 years, there have been sizeable changes in agricultural land use and the economy with which it interacts. The most important of the changes have been improvements in transportation technology; these improvements now permit a space-time convergence of distant places, thereby expanding the scale of possible economic organisation. In von Thunen's day, heavily loaded horse-drawn carts moved to market at the rate of about 1 mile an hour. A journey from the wilderness edge to the market centre would require more than two full days, without pauses for rest. Therefore, the truest measure of economic distance in the Thunian model – the absolute mileage beyond which farming was simply too far from the market and could no longer yield locational rent – is in terms of a 50-hour time-distance. If that 50-hour time-distance radius is constant as the Thunian farming system evolves, what would be its territorial extent today? It may be in thousands of kilometres in case of USA or Russia.
10. Environmental variables, as pointed out in connection with the physical limits model, are only a general locational constraint and play a passive role in shaping the distribution of modern commercial agriculture. In the human-technological context, the employment of artificial irrigation, chemical fertilisers, and the like, allows farmers to overcome most environmental barriers.
11. With changes in transportation conditions, the macro-Thunian system has also been modified since its emergence. A continuous process is involved that works to maximise locational utility. Demand for better access begets technological development, which results in transport innovation and culminates into change in pattern of agricultural land use.
12. Three kinds of economic empirical irregularities can be anticipated to influence the national Thunian pattern: transportation biases, distant concentrations of production that appear inconsistent with his model, and secondary markets.

13. The von Thunen model is also static and deterministic. Today, we know that economic growth and changes in demand will alter the spatial patterns of agricultural systems and land use, which in turn influence the rate of change. It might be possible to postulate a dynamic von Thunen model that could be applied to the changing conditions. But, the model, despite these possible manipulations, is really static, since, it represents a land use system at one point in time. von Thunen was not concerned with transitional changes, since, he and most of the direct extenders of his model assumed that any change in technology, demand, or transport cost would automatically be accompanied by an adjustment in the land use system. The Thunian model was developed in the early 19th century, since then, conditions have entirely been changed. Therefore, it is not desirable to accept this model in its original form as observed by many scholars. But this model is still considered to be significant in many ways.

Relevance of von Thunen Model

Almost two hundred years ago, Johann Heinrich von Thunen demonstrated that the geographic pattern of agricultural land use was highly regular and predictable. He first described the pattern of land use within and surrounding his own large estate. Based upon these descriptions he next formulated a hypothesis to explain the geographic pattern. His hypothesis was that the higher the cost of transportation, the lower the amount a tenant farmer would be willing to pay to use the land. He expressed his hypothesis using clear and unambiguous mathematics. He reasoned that by placing reasonable numerical values into his mathematical formulation he could closely predict actual land values and land uses. Among his general conclusions were that land values decline with increasing distance from the market centre; and that land values and land uses change as the various costs of production, transportation, and prices of agricultural commodities change.

Today, the cost and technology of transportation has had a dramatic effect upon the agricultural land use patterns that one would expect by applying von Thunen's logic. Agricultural land use patterns that are evident surrounding market centres are thought to be historic remnants of a bygone era, or the result of administrative institutions whose existence brings about a usage to the historic patterns of land use. At the scale of the continent and the globe we now can observe von Thunen-like market forces and patterns of land use.

The von Thunen logical framework has been important in the evolution of our thinking of how land values and land uses came about in the modern city. Indeed, von Thunen's general theory of land values and land uses has been important in the evolution of thought.

von Thunen was one of the first to adopt the 'new maths' of his era, calculus, and to apply that mathematics to a problem of the social sciences. He was a pioneer in the use of data for the verification of his normative theory. von Thunen's innovative research method was similar in composition to what we would today call computer simulation. Indeed, much of the approach to social science thought today can be traced back to von Thunen's general method of analysis as its precursor. His contribution to modern thinking in the social sciences stands unparalleled. His general approach became diffused through its adoption by the leading scholars of the generations that followed him, and by their adoption of his general method in their own work. von Thunen's application of his general method to his own land use theory became generally accessible only in the early 1950s when Edgar S. Dunn published his interpretation in English. von Thunen is no exception among the greats whose reasoning in time is recognised to have contained an error. The beauty of using mathematics over mere verbalisation to express concepts or hypotheses is that when an error is made it can often be corrected irrefutably. Dunn found an error in von Thunen's treatise and corrected it. It can be recalled from the discussion above that a caveat was to be presented to von Thunen's general theory: once the hierarchical ranking of farming systems was established, the result is, those of lower ranking would always be outbid by those of higher ranking should both happen to be competing for the same land. Instead, Dunn correctly reasoned that since locational rent changed by a different amount for each agricultural product with distance from the central market, then at some locations a lower ranking farming system could indeed outbid a higher ranking farming system, even though positive rents were bid by the higher ranking farming system.

All over the world, scholars have tested and applied the von Thunen's theory of agricultural location. The greatest importance of the theory lies in this fact that it has given a new direction of thinking, resulting into the modified way of its application.

von Thunen himself relaxed certain assumptions of his model. First, he introduced a canal along which transportation costs were lower than by horse and wagon. The effect was to create a series of wedge-shaped land use zones along the canal. Second, he introduced a second and smaller market, around which he postulated that a series of separate zones would be created. Similarly, we could relax the assumptions by introducing yet another means of transport, such as a railroad or allow variation in the physical environment. The extent to which these relaxations affect the simple von Thunen model will depend on how they affect the simple conceptual framework put forward earlier.

Some researchers have used von Thunen's model as a general framework for interpreting the spatial framework of the economy. Others have worked on a more direct basis. Thus, von Thunen's model has been applied to the distribution of European agriculture in 1925.

Muller's interpretation of a normative macro-Thunian model for the United States, anchored by a megalopolis, is shown in Figure 14.11. Its utility for explaining the national pattern of agricultural production is demonstrated as follows:

We begin again by relaxing the normative assumptions of the isolated state model, but this time with the realisation that empirical irregularities will be complex in the sophisticated economic space of the present-day continental United States. However, because we are concerned only with the overall organisational framework of farming regions at a high level of spatial generalisation, the search is not complicated: if macro-Thunian processes have shaped the production pattern, then empirical response to them will be easily discernible. The main task is to set up the investigation by cataloging physical-environmental and economic-empirical irregularities in order to derive an appropriate map of the expected real-world spatial pattern.

Empirical evidence of Thunian spatial systems is also widespread beyond the United States. Figure 14.12-A shows the macro-scale pattern of agricultural

Figure 14.11

The macro-Thunian model for normative United States

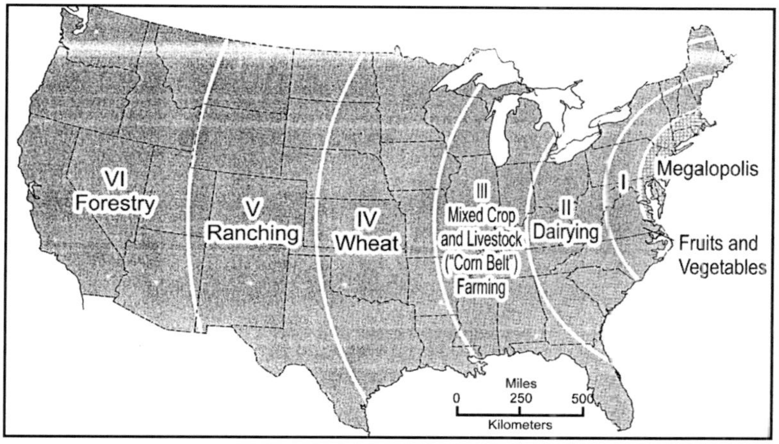

intensity for the European continent, which is sharply focused on the conurbation ringing the southern margin of the North Sea, from London and Paris to Copenhagen. By combining the American and European patterns and proceeding to a yet greater level of spatial aggregation, one can even perceive (in Figure 14.12-B) a global-scale Thunian system focused on the "world metropolis" that borders the North Atlantic Ocean.

Regarding application of the Thunian model in developing countries M.H. Hussain (2010) has observed that in many of the underdeveloped and developing countries of the world, in both the villages and towns, cropping belts are found. In the villages of the Great Plains of India similar patterns can be observed. The highly fertile and adequately manured lands around the village settlements are devoted to the perishable and more fertility requiring crops, e.g. vegetables, potatoes, oats and orchards in the land lying in the middle belt; crops like rice, wheat, barley, pulses, sugarcane, gram, maize, etc. are grown subject to the texture, drainage and other properties of the soils. In the outer fringes fodder crops and inferior cereals (bajra, millets) are sown. After the introduction of tubewell irrigation in the great plains of India, this pattern has, however, been largely modified as the farmers with better inputs are able to produce perishable crops even in the distant fields from the settlements. The consolidation of holdings in India has also modified the crop intensity rings as each of the farmers is interested in growing the commodities for his family consumption as well as some marketable crops for earning cash to clear his arrears of land revenue and irrigation charges and to purchase the articles from the market for his family consumption.

In some of the developing countries like India, Pakistan and Mexico, the introduction of HYV (high yielding variety) has disturbed the application of von Thunen model. The fast development of means of transportation has made it possible to transport the perishable goods at long distances in short period of time. Thus, the model advocated by von Thunen is no longer operative in its original form.

Figure 14.12

Large-scale Thunian system, showing macro-geographical patterns of agricultural intensity for Europe and in the world

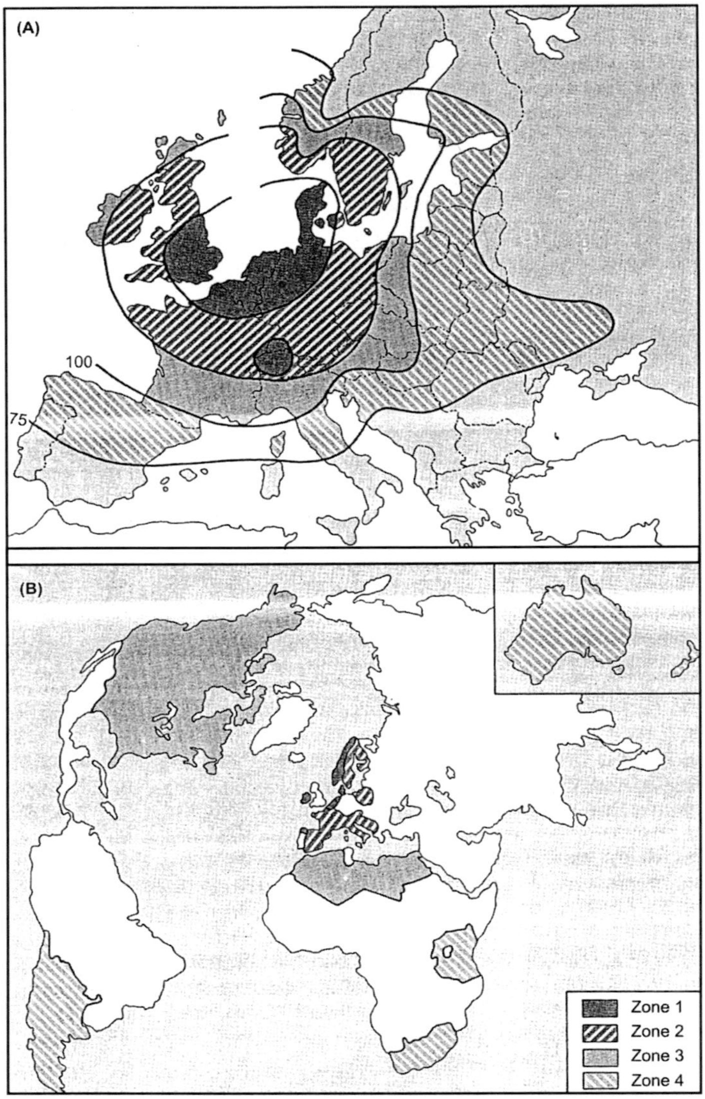

Thunian distance relationships can also be discerned at the national level in smaller developed countries such as Uruguay. Allowing for that nation's empirical irregularities, Ernst Griffin discovered that the expected Thunian pattern accorded nicely with the actual intensity of agricultural land use. Continuing down the level of generalisation continuum from mesoscale to microscale, Thunian influences are often observed to shape farming at the local level. Moreover, local agricultural production in the less developed world, where technological conditions are more comparable to those of von Thunen's days, may even exhibit spatial structures reminiscent of von Thunen's landscape. Ronald Horvath found just such a pattern for the area surrounding Addis Ababa, Ethiopia. Of particular significance was his discovery of an expanding transportation-oriented eucalyptus forestry zone in its classical inner position.

Sinclair's Theory

Robert Sinclair (1967) has suggested an alternative land use pattern. Basically, his thoughts were based on von Thunen theory, but he inverted von Thunen model for the zone of anticipated urban encroachment-distance relationships. Robert Sinclair detected some interesting effects on production in the innermost agricultural land in the path of metropolitan encroachment. Spreading urbanisation appears to influence agriculture several miles in advance of the built-up frontier because farmers realise they cannot compete against the coming much-higher location rents earned by urban land uses. Thus, metropolitan expansion is perceived as a displacement threat in the affected inner rural zone, and this is reflected in the spatial behaviour of farmers. Those closest to the urban frontier feel most threatened and keep their agricultural investments minimised. These investments rise with distance from the frontier to the outer edge of this zone of anticipation, where the specialised agriculture of the region takes over.

Sinclair postulated four types of farming, the fifth zone – specialised feed-grain livestock or Corn Belt agriculture – is the wider regional specialty beyond the belt of expanding urban influence (Figure 14.13). Proceeding outward from the beginning of Sinclair's Zone 1, they are: (i) urban farming, a hodgepodge of small producing units, scattered through the already subdivided outer suburban environment, which favours poultry-keeping, greenhouses, mushroom-raising, and other building-oriented uses; (ii) vacant and temporary grazing, where farmers leave much land empty to sell to urban land speculators at the most opportune moment and allow grazing only under short-term leases;

Figure 14.13

Land use pattern as described by Robert Sinclair

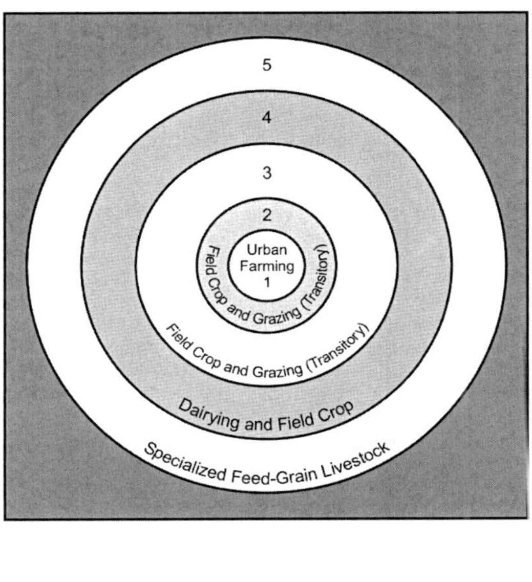

(iii) transitory field crop and grazing, a transitional agricultural type dominated by farm uses, but with definite anticipation of near-future displacement, expressed by little investment beyond the short term; and (iv) dairying and field crop farming, wherein farmers begin to shift to more extensive agriculture with a view towards encroachment in the foreseeable future.

Olof Jonasson's Theory

Olof Jonasson, the Swedish geographer, modified the von Thunen's model, relating to the economic rent of land in relation to market and means of transportations. The modified form of von Thunen's model devised by Jonasson is given in Figure 14.14.

Details of each zone are as follows:

Zone 1: The city itself and immediate environs, green house, floriculture.

Zone 2: Truck products, fruits, potatoes and tobacco (and horses).

Zone 3: Dairy products, cattle for beef, sheep for mutton, veal, forage, oats, flax and fibers.

Zone 4: General farming, grain hay, livestock.

Zone 5: Bread cereals and flax for oil.

Zone 6: Cattle (beef and range); horses (range); and sheep (range); salt, smoked, refrigerated, and canned meats; bones; tallow and hides.

Zone 7: The outermost peripheral area, forests.

Jonasson has applied this model the agricultural landscape patterns of Europe in 1925. He observed that in Europe and North America, zones of agricultural land use were arranged about the industrial centres. In both the continents, i.e. Europe and North America, the most intensive development of agriculture is the hay and pastures region in which the industrial centres are situated. Around these pastures are arranged concentrically the successive grades of land use –

Figure 14.14

Zones of production about a theoretical isolated city in Europe according to Jonasson

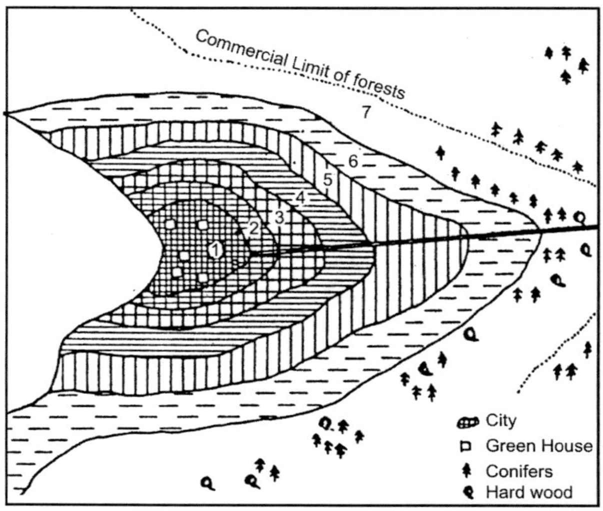

grain-growing, pasturing and forestry. Jonasson advocated a model similar to the model of von Thunen, around a theoretical isolated city in Europe.

Jonasson also found an identical pattern of distribution on Edwards Plateau in Texas. Jonasson's model was also adopted by Valkenburg in 1952, when he prepared a map of intensity of agriculture in Europe.

Apart from above-mentioned modifications in von Thunen's theory, there are several studies that have been done, among them the notable are Gotewald (1959), Chisholm (1968), Hall (1966), Horvath (1969) and Peet (1969).

A few economic and decision-making models/theories have also been presented. Some of the notable models are:

(i) Input-output models.
(ii) Theory of optimum physical conditions and limits.
(iii) Theory of optimum economic conditions and limits.
(iv) Spatial equilibrium models.
(v) Game theory.
(vi) Diffusion models.
(vii) Behavioural models.

All the above-mentioned models/theories have been used to explain the locational aspects of the agricultural land use in some way or other. But the von Thunen's theory still has relevance because it has given a new thinking in geographical studies of the agricultural land use pattern.

15

Theories of Industrial Location

Geographers are interested in location study of industries because it helps in the systematic and rational analysis of spatial distribution of industries to find out the relative merits and demerits of any particular space over the other. We study industrial location in order to understand why plants locate where they do. A different choice of location involves a different mix of costs, as well as different access to the market. Any one location will have a particular set of costs and generates a given level of revenues. Insofar as there is a spatial pattern to these costs and revenues, a clustering of manufacturing plants may occur on the economic landscape. Thus, all manufacturers consider certain basic locational factors or influences in the plant location decision. An industry develops and prospers by virtue of some advantage, natural and/or human, which allows it to outstrip its competitors.

The primary question is, why does a manufacturing plant locate at a particular place? The general answer is, because of certain factors. When a place is selected for a particular industry, it has multiple advantages and few, if any, disadvantages. There may be one or a number of primary factors, which should not only be identified but their impact on the establishment and success of industry should also be examined. The relative advantage of one over other, and the combined cost difference between the places, is the essence of any study. The availability of land, water, raw material, labour, transport and proximity to market, etc. are some of the variables often taken into consideration for the selection of the location of an industry. The different locations have distinct geo-economic character as well as advantages.

The factors controlling the location of industry can be divided into two broad categories as under:

(i) *Geographical factors:* Land, climate, water and power resources, and raw materials.

(ii) *Social-economic factors:* Capital, labour, transport, demand, market, government, policies, tax structure, management, etc.

We are not discussing these factors here because these are general factors having direct and indirect impact on industrial location. This chapter deals with only industrial location theories.

The basic question posed by scholars regarding industrial location has been "where ought industries be located?" The traditional answer has been, "where they derive maximum profits". But this is not so simple because factors are varied and complex in nature and also change with space and time. To explain these complexities several theories of industrial location have been proposed by economists like Weber, Tord Palander, Edgar Hoover, August Losch, Walter Isard, and geographers like George Renner, Rawston, Allen Pred, Smith, etc. Some of the theories had been developed in early 19th century, while others in the 20th century. The prime concern of all the theories of industrial location is to find the 'optimal location', which is economically the best and one that gives maximum profits. There has been a change in factors which distinguish earlier theories with contemporary reality: decrease in importance of transport costs; increased organisational dynamism, interdependence and variety and the rise of corporate enterprise. The real manufacturing landscape, as it exists today, displays a variety of situations some of which have represented ideal locations at one time, but not necessarily now.

Problems in the location search process may arise from the fact that many of the major factors in this process are non-quantifiable or only partially quantifiable. While it is easy to identify some of the prominent factors that may influence a location search, and ultimately site selection, the final determination of the feasibility of a proposed site must be examined in terms of (i) how the proposed site fits into the existing or restructured corporate production network; (ii) its competitive position in the industry as defined by its potential to expand or increase market share or compete with spatial rivals; (iii) its immediate and non-immediate impact on the area in which it locates; and (iv) the anticipated response or actions taken by competitors within the site's sphere of influence.

The first theory of industrial location was given by Alfred Weber in 1909, which has revolutionised the concept of industrial location and given a new line of thought. After Weber's theory several theories came into being and locational analysis became a very important aspect. Some of the theories, formulated after Weber are: the theory of Fetter (1924), the theory of Tord Palander (1935), the theory of Smith (1941), the theory of August Losch (1954), the theory of Melvin Greenhut (1956), the theory of Walter Isard (1956), Renner's Theory (1960), Allen Pred's Theory (1967), and a few other theories. The details of some important theories of industrial location are discussed here.

Alfred Weber's Theory of the Least-Cost Location

Alfred Weber first introduced his famous theory of industrial location in 1909, in his book titled, *Uber den Standort der Industrien* and its English translation was published in 1929 as *The Location and Theory of Industries*. His theory is known as 'Least-Cost Location Theory' or 'Least-Cost Minimisation Approach'. The basic objective of the Weber's theory is to find out the minimum cost location of an industry.

Prior to describing Weber's theory, it is necessary to explain the following terminology used in his theory:

- *Ubiquities* are materials available everywhere throughout the uniform plain at the same cost.
- *Localised materials* are available only at specific locations.
- *Pure materials* are localised materials that enter to the full extent of their weight into the finished product, such as petroleum.

- *Weight-losing materials* are localised commodities that impart only a portion or none of their weight into the finished product.
- *Isodapane* is a line connecting points of equal total transport costs.
- *Isotim* is a line of equal transport cost for any material or product.

The Weber's least-cost approach is based on following assumptions:

1. Firms seek to maximise profits with respect to costs.
2. There is perfect competitive pricing.
3. Transport rates are homogenous, while transportation costs are a function of weight and distance.
4. There is a given buying centre and a given demand.
5. Raw material sources are fixed points.

The Weber's optimal location, depending on the inputs and cost structures, was essentially one where:

1. Total transportation costs per unit of output are at a minimum.
2. Failing this, transportation diseconomies are offset by economies of agglomeration and low labour costs.

Thus, within this Weberian least-cost model, entrepreneurs will site their industries at the points of minimum costs achieved in response to three basic locational factors: relative transportation cost, labour costs, and agglomeration or deglomeration costs. The details of these three factors are as follows:

Transport Costs

In Weber's theory, transport cost was considered the most powerful determinant of plant location. The total transport cost, as stated by Weber, is determined by the total distance of haulage and weight of the transported material. The cost of transportation under two highly simplified conditions is:

- Transport cost with a single market and one source of material supply.
- Transport cost with two supply sources and involves Weber's classic *locational triangle*.

Figure 15.1 a, b, c

Industrial location: one source of material and single market

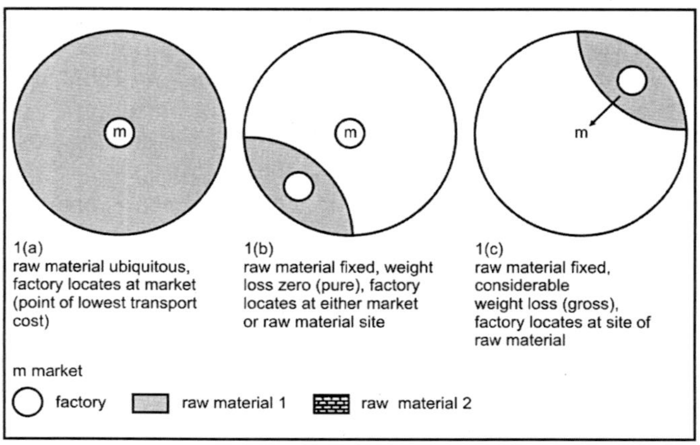

One Market and One Source (Figure 15.1 a,b,c)

- If the material is ubiquitous (actually, many potential sources), then the processing will take place at the market. This location is obvious because it would make no sense to ship an ubiquitous material to a processing point other than the market.
- If the material is pure, processing may occur at the market, the material site, or any place in between. An intermediate location would entail an unnecessary additional handling cost – a cost not recognised by Weber.
- If the material is weight-losing, the processing will be done at the location of material source to avoid transporting waste material.

One Market and Two Sources

The industrial location according to Weber is depicted in Figure 15.2 and 15.3.

- In the first example of the locational triangle, S_1 and S_2 are the two material sources and M is the market location (Figure 15.2). Because the distances (and consequently the costs) between these three points are identical, we may assign each of the three distances a cost of, say Rs 100. Where will processing occur? The answer is, at the market, for the two needed materials can be shipped there at a total unit cost of Rs 200. If processing was to locate at S_1, for instance, there would be the cost of shipping one unit from S_2 to S_1 (Rs 100), the cost of shipping that same unit, now processed, on to the market (Rs 100), and the cost of shipping one unit of the material from S_1, also now processed, to the market (Rs 100). Thus, the total transport cost, if processing was to locate at S_1 or S_2, is Rs 300 versus Rs 200 per unit at the market.
- The situation is different and somewhat more complex when two weight-losing materials are brought together in processing. Let us assume for simplicity that there is a 50 per cent weight loss for each of the two materials. Where, according to Weber, will manufacturing locate? Let the cost of transporting one unit of the weight-losing material be Rs 200 (Figure 15.3). If a market location is selected, one would have to ship one unit of material from both S_1 and S_2 at total cost of Rs 200. If S_1 was selected for processing, the cost of obtaining the material from S_2 would be Rs 200.

Figure 15.2
Weber's locational triangle, with one market and two sources of material supplies.

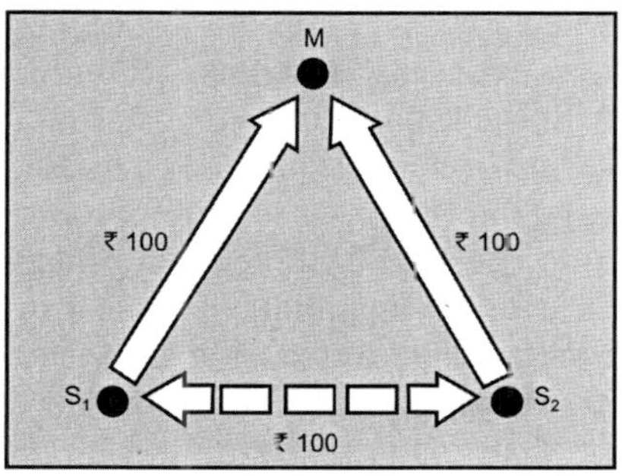

Figure 15.3
Intermediate location

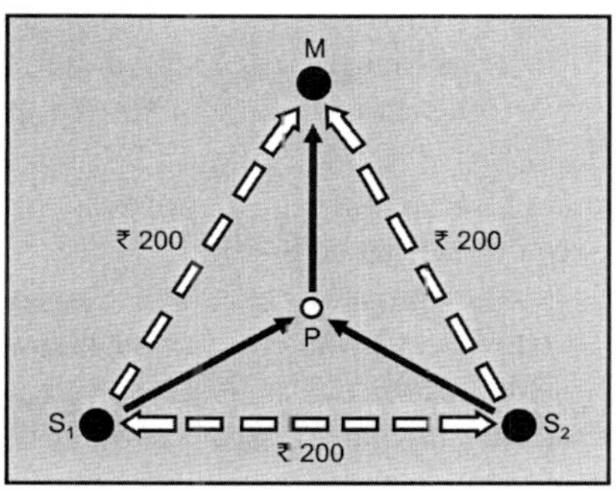

No transport cost would be charged to get the material from S_1 and the cost to transport the product to market with the 50 per cent weight loss would be Rs 200. The market, from S_1 to S_2 would have the same total transport cost.

- Weber, however, was concerned with selecting the least-cost or optimum location. A second look at Figure 15.3 suggests that an intermediate location at P would be optimum, rather than at M, S_1 or S_2, where the transport cost at P would be less than Rs 200. Furthermore, if one material had a greater weight-loss ratio than the other, then the intermediate location for processing would be 'pulled' towards the site of the greatest weight loss.

  On the basis of above analysis three facts emerge which are as follows:

(i) Manufacturing that utilises pure materials will never tie the processing location to the material site, and the location decision is normally made on the basis of other factors.

(ii) Industries utilising high weight-loss material will tend to be pulled towards the material source as opposed to the market.

(iii) Many industries will select an intermediate location between market and material.

Labour Costs

According to Weber, the geographic variation in the cost of labour is a 'distortion' of the basic transport pattern. An area handicapped by high transport cost might nevertheless be attractive to industry because of inexpensive labour. According to Weber's argument, an industry would select the location that has the least cost when transport and labour are considered together. In other words, a trade off may exist between transport and labour costs, and the firm chooses the location with the least combined cost.

To illustrate this, Weber used two devices that he called *isotims* (equal in price) an *isodapanes* (equal in expense). Isotims are isolines of equal transportation cost for each item (raw material or finished product); while isodapanes are isolines joining points of equal transportation cost as shown in Figure 15.4. Here, *m* represents the market and *r* the raw material site. Again, transportation costs are assumed to be the same per ton mile for both raw material and finished product. The isotims around *m* represent transport costs from all points to *m*, and those around *r* represent costs to all points from *r*. Both sets of circles (isotims) represent a spacing of one unit of transport cost per ton. It is assumed that the raw material is gross, and that it loses 50 per cent of its weight in the manufacturing process.

If the factory was located at *r* every ton of the final product shipped from *r* to *m* would cost 10 units of transportation costs (10 intervals from *r* to *m* on the diagram). If the factory, on the other hand, was located at m_1 the cost would be 20 units of transportation charges, since double the quantity of raw material to final product has to be carried.

Alternative locations also exist. At *A*, the total transportation cost would be 18 transport units – 8 units on raw materials (2x4) and 10 units on moving the finished product. An isodapane can now be constructed representing all points that have a total transportation cost of 18 units. Thus, point B carries 13 units on raw materials and 5 cost units on the finished product. All points on this isodapane

Figure 15.4 a, b

Isotims and isodapanes as described by Weber

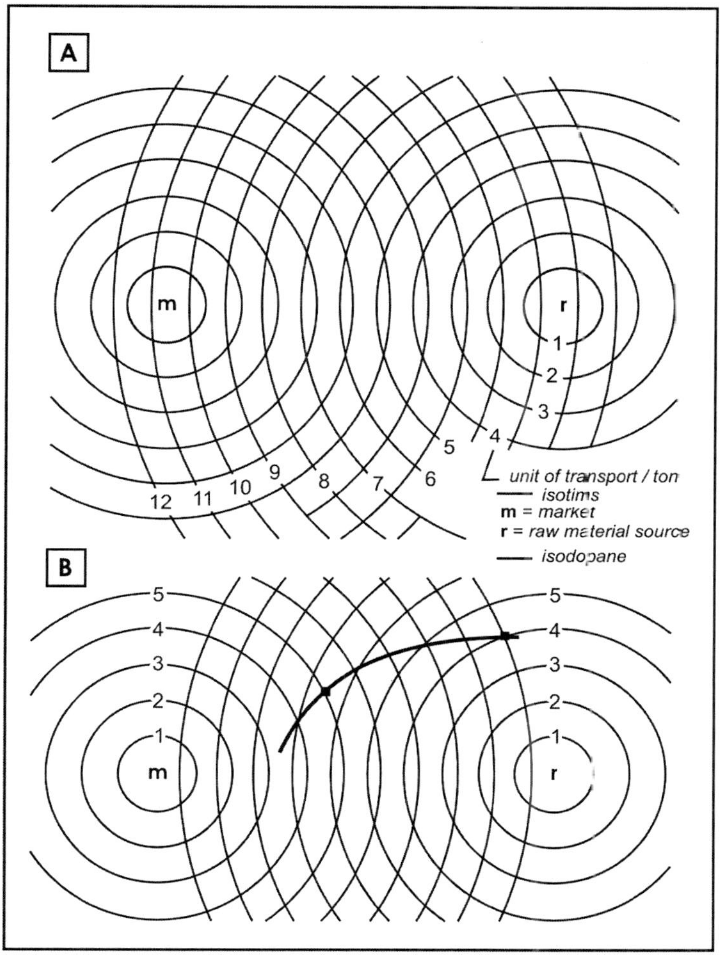

in fact carry 8 units of transportation cost above that obtained at *R*. The isodapanes reveal how great the labour cost advantage would have to be in order to offset higher transportation costs. If any cheap labour site with, say, at least 8 units advantage in cost terms, lies on the isodapane *A–B* in Figure 15.4, then it could represent an industrial site. If its advantage is greater than 8 units, then in economically rational terms it would be an industrial site. If no sites exist with these advantages, then there will be no move to a cheap labour location. If more than one site does, then the firm will move to a cheap labour site – in fact, to the site of the least labour cost.

Agglomeration

Another locational element put forward by Weber for the industries is the 'agglomeration'. He considered agglomeration as the money savings per unit that would accrue to a plant from locating within a cluster of other plants. Specifically,

Weber saw agglomeration not as producing internal-scale economies, but rather external economies (including urbanisation economies). Figure 15.5 illustrates the cost of three manufacturing plants, A, B, and C, which are each independently located at their least-cost point. Around each plant is drawn a *critical isodapane* a line showing where the savings from agglomeration would exactly offset the added transport cost for each firm. In other words, if each of these three firms could locate together, the agglomeration advantages would be just matched along these lines by the higher transport costs. Thus, all firms would benefit from agglomeration savings if they were to locate within the shaded triangle.

On the basis of above mentioned locational elements and their combined interplay of the factors, Weber used *material index,* which is the weight of the localised material inputs divided by the weight of the product. This shows whether the point of 'movement minimisation' (i.e. the optimal site in least costs terms) would be located near the source of raw materials or near the market. In the former case, the index is less than one, in the latter, greater than one. If a firm or industry has a high *labour coefficient* (ration of labour cost to the combined weights of the material input and the product output), then the firm will be attracted to a point other than that with least costs in transport terms alone. Of course, this assumes that the savings in labour costs equal or exceed the transport diseconomies thus incurred. Agglomeration economies could also outweigh transport economies, thus giving rise to a third location type. By combining these factors, Weber was able to distinguish at least fourteen theoretical types of industries that combine transportation costs, labour costs, and agglomeration economies.

Critical Analysis

Weber's theory of industrial location is a landmark in locational analysis because the theory provides a general framework of industrial location. His contribution

Figure 15.5

Intersecting critical isodapanes: agglomeration

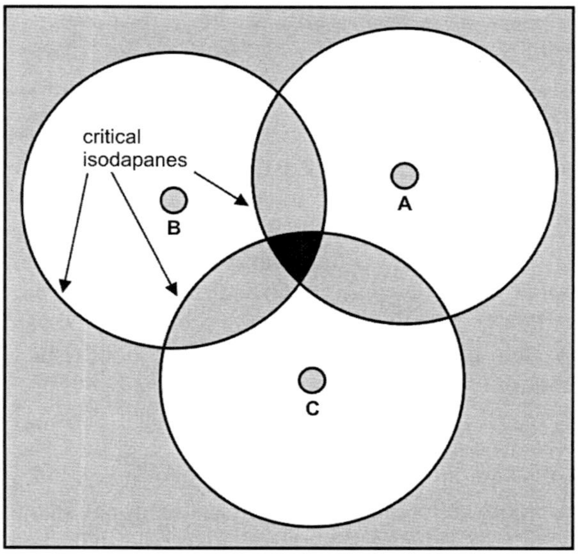

has proved most valuable over the years, however, his work has a number of shortcomings that limit its application in its exact form. The following are the main criticisms of the theory:

(i) Weber did not effectively and realistically take into account geographic variation in market demand, a locational factor of paramount influence.
(ii) There are two major drawbacks to Weber's analysis of transportation costs.
 (a) Freight rates are, in fact, rarely directly proportionate to distance, as assumed in the theory.
 (b) Freight rates are not usually, the same on finished products as on raw materials.
(iii) Weber considered the role of labour costs. He recognised that these could vary spatially and therefore wield an influence on the location of a factory. Thus, savings in labour costs could offset extra transportation costs.
(iv) Labour is normally quite mobile through migration and is not always available in unlimited quantity at any location.
(v) A great many manufacturing plants obtain a large number of material inputs and produce a wide range of products for many diverse markets.
(vi) Weber's treatment of agglomeration was not very satisfactory, and has probably underestimated its effect.
(vii) Weber also underestimates the role of pure materials, overestimates the role of gross materials and ignores the fact that no industry uses just one material.

But in spite of these criticisms Weber's theory is considered as a leading theory of the industrial location. It concludes that the optimum profit maximising location is the location where costs are minimised.

Losch's Theory of Economics of Location

This theory belongs to the 'market area' or 'profit maximisation' approach and has focused on spatial variations in scales potential. August Losch was a German economist and he proposed his theory in 1939 in a book titled *Die taumliches Ordnung Derwirt's Chaff.* Its English translation was published in 1954 as *Economics of Location.* He disregarded spatial variations in production costs by holding them constant, and instead depicted optimal location as occurring where the largest possible market area is monopolised – that is, where sales potential and total revenue potential are maximised. Losch sought to explain the size and shape of market areas within which a location would command the largest revenue. His theory is based on following assumptions:

(i) An isotropic surface.
(ii) For each firm there exists a behavioural pattern such that it seeks to locate at the most profitable of the production points at which it can locate.
(iii) For each location there exists constant costs for the procurement and consumption of raw materials.
(iv) Buyers are evenly dispersed over an area, and have identical demands.
(v) Entrepreneurs act as economic men and their main aim is profit maximisation.

Figure 15.6

Development of market areas from circular to hexagonal

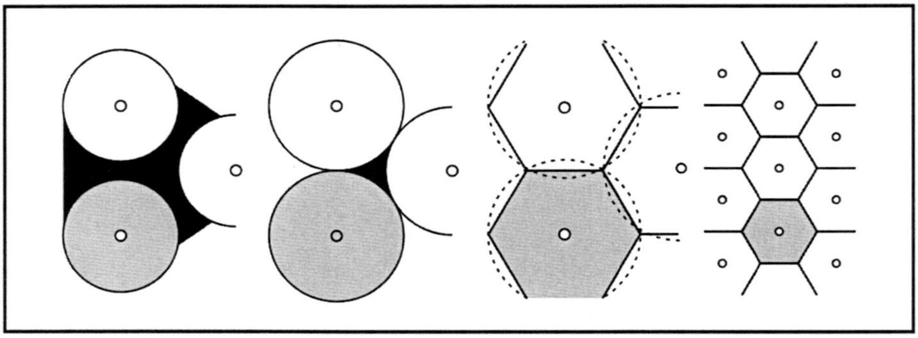

Losch established the hexagon as the ideal market shape, and viewed the trading area of the various products as the nets of such hexagons. Figure 15.6 helps to explain his choice of the hexagonal form. First, a net of hexagonal market forms will completely cover any area under consideration, whereas circular areas will either leave utilised area or will overlap. Second, of all the regular polygons (hexagon, square, triangle, etc.) that will cover an area, the hexagon deviates least from the circular form and in consequence minimises transportation expenditure in supplying a given demand.

Losch then attempts to find the maximum profit location by comparing, for different locations, both the costs of production and the market area that can be controlled. Within the framework of this competitive situation, the location chosen may not be the least-cost location, as the Weberian school predicts. Instead, it will be the maximum profit location built on sales revenues rather than production and distribution costs. Thus, for each commodity or production type, the economic landscape is dissected into a series of hexagonal nets of market areas. These nets are grouped according to the size of their respective market units. After allowance has been made for the minimisation of transport effort, the resulting nets are ordered around a common centre. Thus, according to the model, at the centre of the economic landscape a large metropolis would arise with all the advantages of a large local demand. With population and settlement localised into 'rich' sectors, industries become agglomerated in the same zones to gain economies of scale through linkage. As a result, the greatest number of locations coincide, the maximum number of purchases can be made locally, and the sum of the minimum distances between industrial locations is the least.

A number of criticisms have arisen concerning this Loschian industrial landscape such as, the model is based on the assumption that the price of a commodity is a simple function of the demand for it, and this is frequently unrealistic. In this theory more emphasis has been given on demand. It has failed to take into account the problems arising from locational interdependence of plants. Finally, Losch's calculation of market demand was too crude and ignored many of the difficulties that entrepreneurs encounter in trying to estimate the basis for their locational decision.

Walter Isard's Theory of Substitution

Walter Isard had given the location theory in 1956 vide publication entitled, *Location and the Space Economy*. Isard has modified the Loschian schema, in the attempt to make it more realistic. Isard linked location theory to the general theory of economics through the substitution principle. In economic theory, capital can be substituted for labour, for example. Similarly, the selection of a manufacturing site from among alternative locations can be viewed as substituting expenditures among the various production factors such that the best site is chosen.

Figure 15.7 provides one simple illustration of Isard's substitution principle. In Figure 15.7a we have the Weberian situation of one market, C, and two

Figure 15.7 a, b, c

Isard's principle of substitution

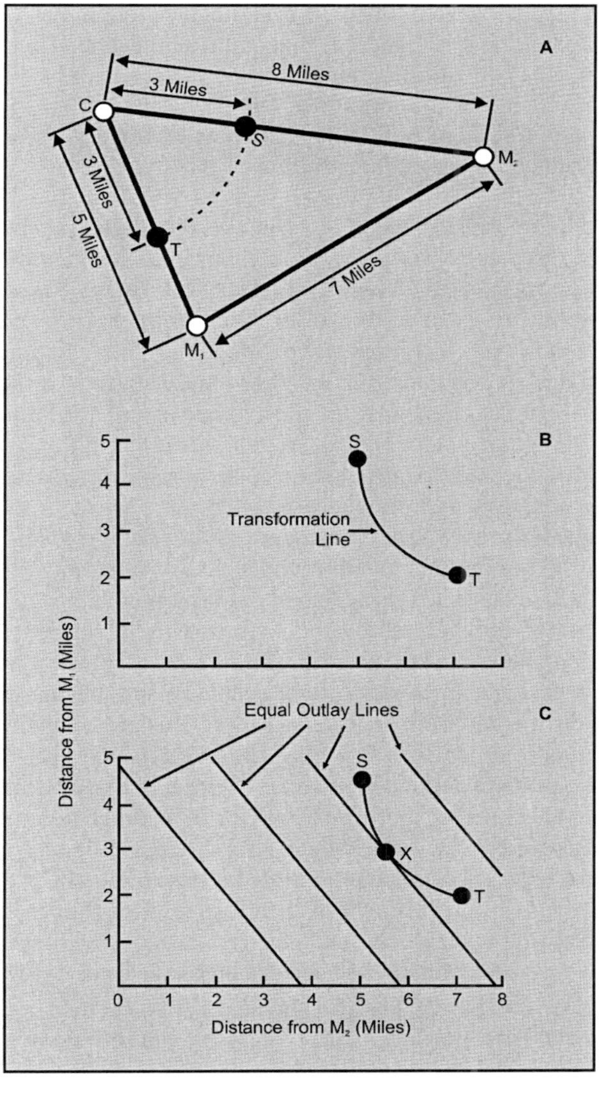

material sources, M_1 and M_2. The line T to S represents a set of possible locations arbitrarily chosen at three miles from the consumption point, C. In Figure 15.7b, the distance from M_1 is plotted against the distance from M_2 with respect to the line T–S, referred to as the transformation line. At location T, distance from M_1 is only two miles, but seven miles from M_2. Conversely, at location S the distances are approximately four miles from M_1 and five miles from M_2. As one moves along this transformation line, distances are increasing with respect to one material site as they are decreasing for the other. If these distances are regarded as transport inputs or costs, then the transport costs for one source are being substituted for the cost of the second material source.

In order to determine the optimum location along the line T to S, equal outlay lines are plotted on Figure 15.7c. These lines depict the costs of transporting material from the two sources. Given the objective of determining the optimum location, the place selected will lie at the point, X, which is the lowest-cost point on the line T to S for that equal-outlay line. Therefore, based on the simple example of substituting among locations at a three-mile distance from the consumption point, the optimum location will be at X with respect to transport costs from M_1 and M_2. The result of this analysis by Isard follows Weber, except for the conceptual emphasis on substitution.

Smith's Theory of Industrial Location

D.M. Smith in his theory has provided a theoretical framework for industrial location. His theory is also known as 'Area-Cost Curve Theory'. Smith has attempted to utilise the perfect competition–least cost approach of Weber with some reference to the monopolistic competition-market area approach of Losch. His conceptual design is quite straightforward and is based on the statements of other location theorists. Recognising the complexity of the industrial location decision, Smith began by simplifying the real-world conditions. He assumed a profit motive. He observed that processing costs vary in space as do revenues. The most profitable location will be where total revenue exceeds total cost by the greatest amount. Figure 15.8 depicts the effect of spatial variations in cost and price and suggests the optimal location and spatial profitability margins.

In Figure 15.8a costs are variable and demand is constant. In this case, with the same revenue everywhere and only costs varying, *o* represents the point of maximum profits, the optimal location. The limits of profitable operation, or *margins of profitability*, *a* and *b*, can also be seen. Beyond this margin costs exceed revenue, and a firm could only operate at a loss. This is essentially the Weberian solution. The reverse situation is shown in 15.8b. Here, costs are the same everywhere, but with spatial variations in price or revenue. In Figure 15.8c the situation becomes more realistic with both cost and price varying from place to place. Maximum profits are obtained at A, where costs are the lowest (profit = $A^1 - A^2$). Here, profits are higher than at the point of highest price ($B^1 - B^2$). The entrepreneur seeking maximum profits will therefore choose the least-cost location, despite the lower total revenue obtainable here.

The following conclusions have been drawn on the basis of Figure 15.8 a,b,c:

1. In a cost-price situation of this type, spatial variations in total costs and revenues impose limits to the area in which any industry can operate at a profit.

Figure 15.8 a, b, c

Smith's model of optimal locations and spatial profitability

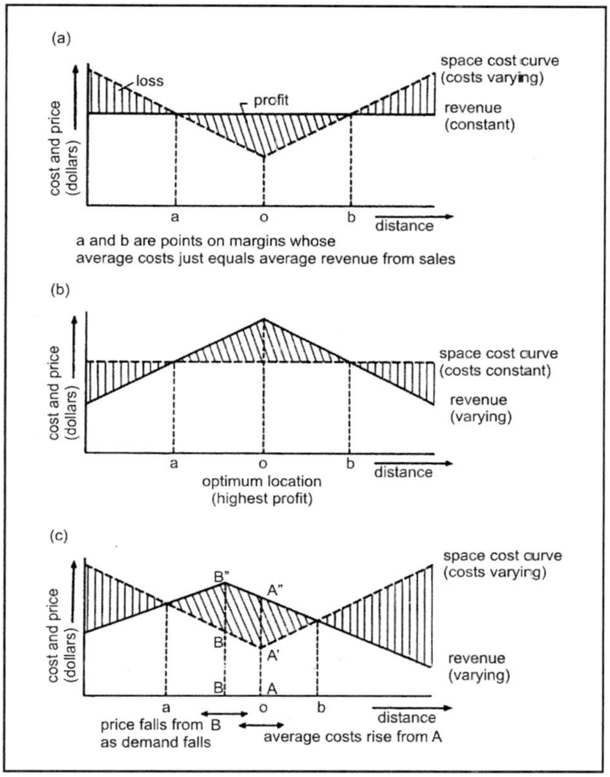

2. Within those limits the entrepreneur can locate anywhere, unless he seeks maximum profits.
3. The steeper the cost or price gradients, the greater is the spatial variation and the more localised the location choice; conversely, the shallower the gradients, the wider is the location choice – unless again maximum profits are sought.

Smith postulates his location model on the following assumptions:

(i) All producers are in business to make profit (but not necessarily the maximum profit).
(ii) All producers are fully aware of spatial variations in costs and profits.
(iii) Sources of production factors like land, labour and capital are fixed, and supplies are unlimited, but no substitution can take place between them.
(iv) Demand (revenue) is constant over space.
(v) No firm tries to take advantage of scale economies.
(vi) No firm influences the location of another firm.
(vii) All entrepreneurs are equally skilful.
(viii) No location is subsidised.

To explain the model Smith has used *isocost lines* and prepared isocost map which indicates the optimum location. Smith has also taken into consideration the factors such as: entrepreneurial skill, behavioural or personal aptitude, existence of subsidies and external economics.

The main drawback of Smith's model is that it is a static one, confined to a particular point in time, with definite locations for optimal points and margins of profitability. In fact, conditions in the real world are dynamic; for instance, the optimal location and the margins of profitability are changing through time as the spatial cost-price situation changes. Manufacturers in fact may never even try to find the most profitable location, because they realise that its spatial location will change. The businessman might therefore choose a location within the broad constraints of the profitability margin, relying on his efficiency and enterprise to build up profits over the long term.

Tord Palander's Theory

In 1935, Tord Palander, a Swedish person had put forward the industrial location theory. First of all Palander determined the boundary between two market areas and explained how two firms making the same product for a linear market distributed horizontally, and how the plant cost or the price charged for the product varied away from the plant. Palander has also described certain variations in the situation by changing the relative values of the plant price and freight charges as illustrated in Figure 15.9.

The following facts become clear from the illustration:

(a) If two firms have equal plant price and the same freight costs per unit of distance the market area boundary is midway between A and B.

(b) There are equal freight rates but lower plant price at location B, which controls more area than A.

(c) B has a higher plant and transport cost than A but is still able to control a small market area by virtue of the higher delivered price from A near B.

(d) When one firm has lower plant price but higher transport costs than the other, it is able to control large section of market area near A where B regains control by virtue of its lower freight cost.

(e) In this case the situation is similar as (d), except that firm B cannot serve the market immediately joining its factory because the price at the point is high. It is only at some distance away from A that the relative low freight rate from B allows the firm to sell at a lower price than A.

The Principle of Substitution

The principle of substitution over space was first put forward by the German economist A. Predohl in 1928. The concept as further developed by Isard and Moses in the late 1950s leads to the conclusion that if one allows for factor substitution and assumes a nonlinear production function, then the optimality of a location will depend on the characteristics of the input, the level of output, and the nature of the demand schedule. Thus, if the process of production is viewed as a combination of inputs to produce a specific output, the principle of substitution will have two components:

Figure 15.9 a, b, c, d, e
Industrial location as described by Tord Palander

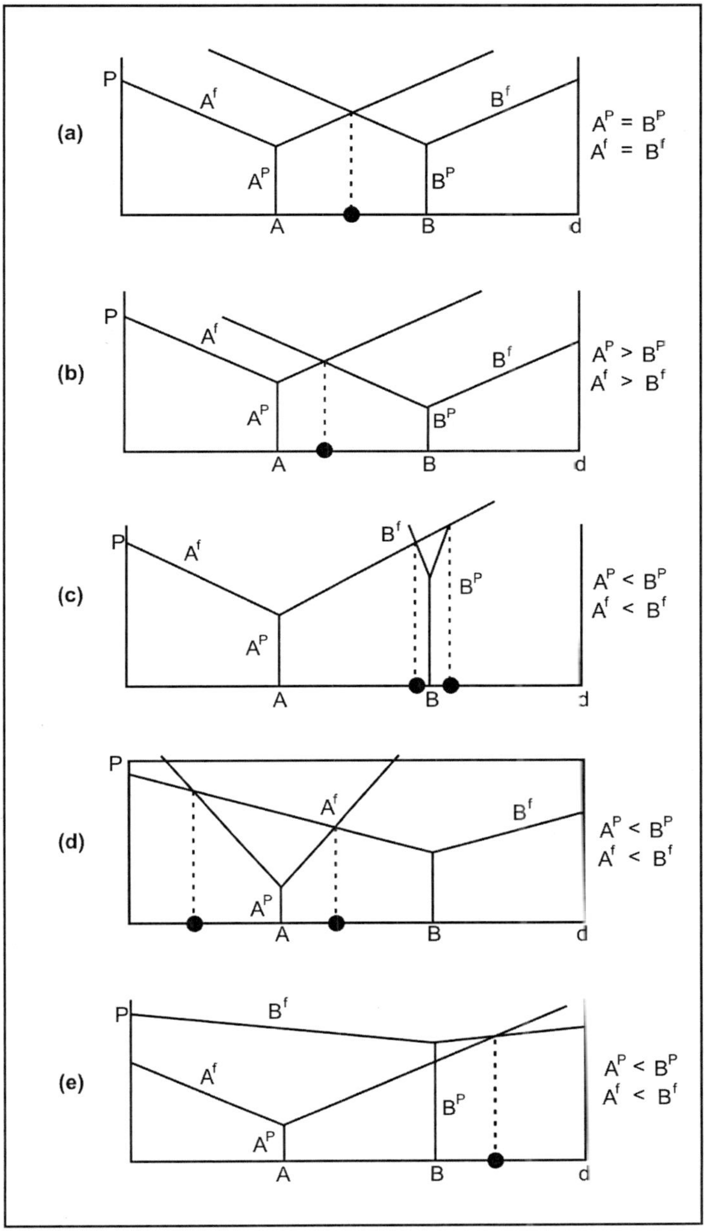

1. A change in the size of operation (level of output) may change the proportion of inputs.
2. For certain production processes, the entrepreneur has, within technical limits, a freedom to choose among alternative proportions of inputs to produce a distinct output or combination of outputs.

Basically, the principle of substitution implies that the entrepreneur has some freedom to change, though within certain limits. Every time a firm is moved over space to effect a saving in some factor, some other factor must also change.

In the mid-1960s R. McDaniel developed a simple locational model based on three types of substitutions:

1. Substitutions between transport inputs (ton miles) and outlays (costs), and revenues associated with the various commodities used in the production process.
2. Substitution among sources of materials.
3. Substitution among markets.

Thus, the whole location process may be conceived as a complex substitution problem in space.

Figure 15.10 shows two sites, c (market) and r_1 (raw material), with a transport link between them. The problem is where should *p*, the production point, be located. Borrowing a concept from production theory in economics, a *transformation line* can be constructed, assuming the same ton-mile cost for the raw material and the finished product. In this case there are two distance variables: distance from *c*; and distance from r_1. When these two variable are plotted, a straight transformation line with a slope of –1 is obtained. Since the transformation line is a straight line, it turns out in this instance that *p* can locate at any point along CR_1.

As another example let us take a more complicated case. Suppose production requires a second raw material available at one source, r_2. Suppose that the distance *pc* is constant, or in other words that *p* can locate any where along *ts*. Again a transformation line can be constructed, though this time it turns out to be a curve (Figure 15.11).

As before we assume that the cost of shipping a unit of r_1 is the same as for r_2, and that one ton of each is required in the production process. A further assumption is that transportation rates are proportional to distance. A series of

Figure 15.10

The substitution principle (i)

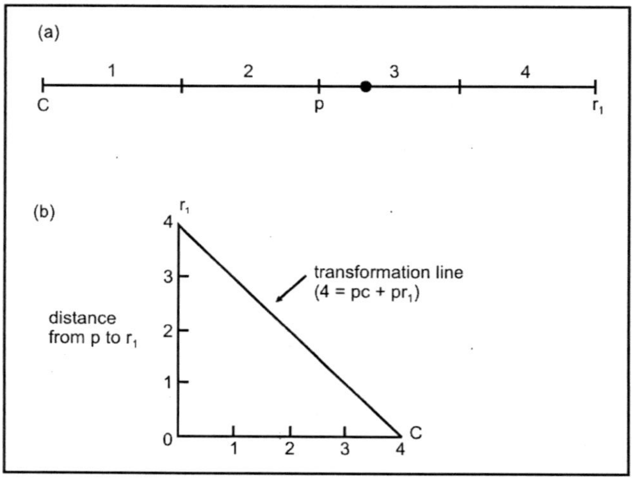

Figure 15.11
The substitution principle (ii)

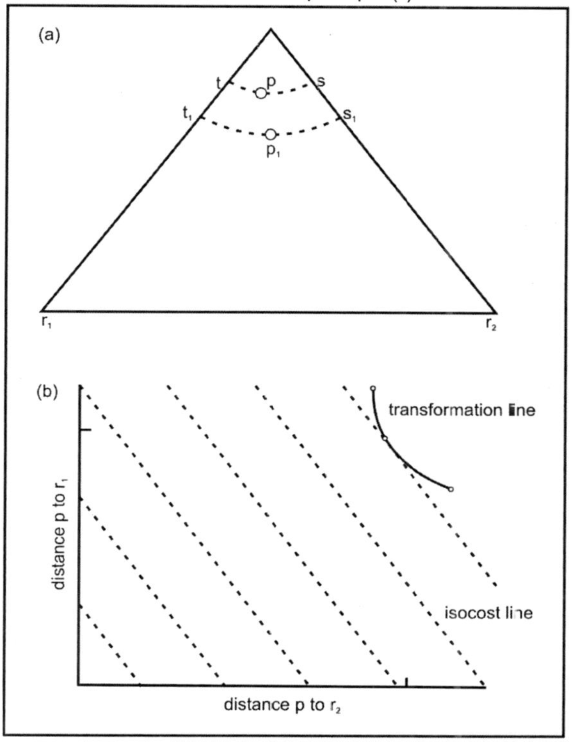

Figure 15.12
Ideal location between market A & B

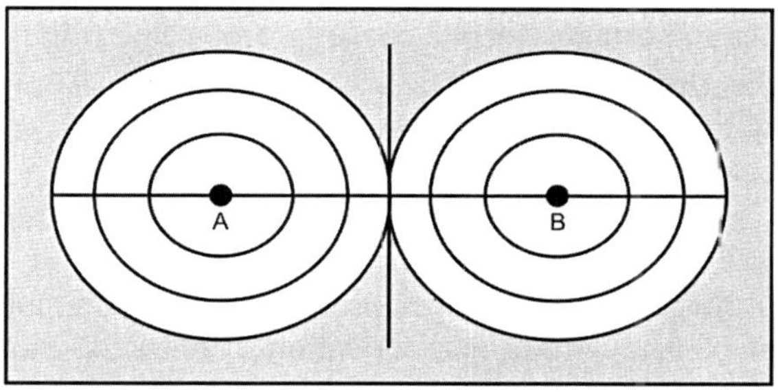

isocost lines can be inserted (Figure 15.11). The least cost transport location is where the isocost line just touches (is tangential to) the transformation line.

Fetter's Law of Industrial Location

In 1924 Frank A. Fetter had proposed the law of industrial location. He proved that all the production can be sold in the markets which are having unlimited demand. In other words, industries have been located according to the demand and consumption. According to Fetter, the place having minimum cost is the place of maximum profit. Fetter's law suggests the following locations:

Figure 15.13

Centre 'A' having higher production, therefore market boundary inclined towards 'A'

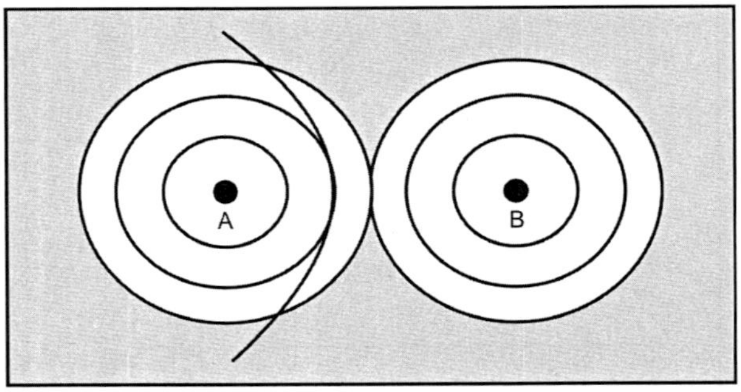

Figure 15.14

Centre 'B' is having higher transport cost, thus market boundary inclined towards 'B'

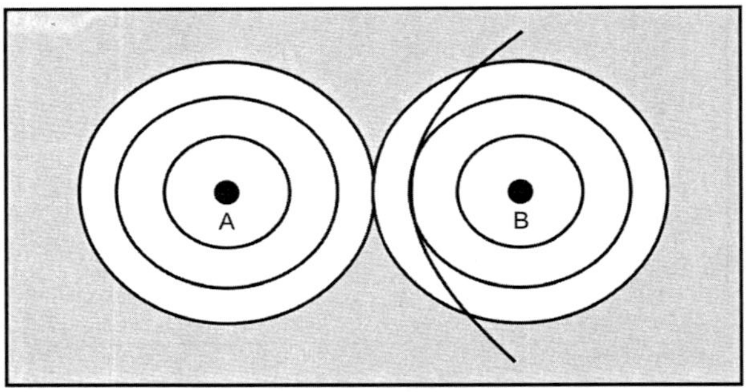

1. If two centres are having same production cost and transportation cost around them, the location of industry will be along centre line (Figure 15.12).
2. If production cost is varied, the boundary of industry will be inclined towards the centre of higher production cost (Figure 15.13).
3. If production cost is similar and transport cost is higher at one centre then the market boundary will be inclined towards the centre having higher transport cost (Figure 15.14).

Palander has further elaborated this principle in 1953 and taken into consideration the factor of competition and allocation of markets. Similarly, in 1956, Greenhunt also based his thoughts of interdependence of minimum cost and localisation of industries.

Renner's Theory of Industrial Location

Renner, in his book titled, *World Economic Geography: An Introduction to Geonomics* (1960), has introduced the industrial location theory which is factor-oriented. Renner identified six factors for the location of industries, these are: capital, transport, raw material, market, power and labour. These factors have direct impact on industrial location but each factor affects differently. In his theory Renner has explained in detail the role of each factor in industrial location as well as localisation of industries and also pointed that there is a tendency that many factors may be available at a particular place. More the factors available at a place more it will be suitable for the industrial location. Renner has given the term *industrial symbiosis* for the combination of these factors. Such symbiosis are of two types:

1. Disjunctive symbiosis, and
2. Conjunctive symbiosis

Disjunctive symbiosis is the condition when two or more different industries in some region are beneficial for each other. Whereas, conjunctive symbiosis occurs when in a region different types of industries function with the help of each other. In such a case product of an industry is utilised by other industry as a raw material.

Renner has pointed out three principles for the industrial location: (i) in the establishment of an industry all the six factors determine the location as well as cost; (ii) industries are generally developed near those factors which are expensive; and (iii) the location of industry also has direct impact on transportation.

The main criticism of the Renner's theory is that due consideration to economic elements has not been given. In regional context there is a difference in price and expenditure which has not been taken into consideration. In spite of some drawbacks Renner's theory is important. Its another characteristic is that it is simple and away from mathematical concepts.

Rawstron's Theory of Industrial Location

E.M. Rawstron has given a simple principle of industrial location, which is entirely based on geographical elements. According to Rawstron, the industries are located at a place where cost is minimum. He pointed out that first of all expenditure on each element is to be examined and then location be determined at a place of maximum profit; in other words, industries are established at a place where the cost is least. He explained certain facts, such as:

(i) Special effective factors for the establishment of industries are raw material, market, land and capital.
(ii) Locational cost of all types of expenditure.
(iii) Cost structure – cost percentage of each item.
(iv) Zone of partial margin to profitability; this is the aspect when profit is converted to loss or loss is converted into profit.
(v) Basic cost – the cost which is different for each element according to amount and quality of the factor.

Rawstron's theory is based on the following assumptions:

1. Mining is also considered as an industry.
2. Transport is only significant with industry. The main importance of transport lies in collection of raw material and distribution of manufactured products; transport cost is always included in product cost.
3. There are physical, economic and technological pressures in the establishment of industries.

On the basis of above assumptions, Rawstron has suggested three principles:

(i) *Principle of Physical Restriction:* The location of industry is always controlled by physical factors. Among physical factors he has given prime importance to availability of minerals. There are several places where occurrence of mineral is possible but it is necessary to find out where its mining is profitable.

(ii) *Principle of Economic Restriction:* Rawstron has given two important economic aspects. These are:
   (a) *Cost Structure of Industry:* including all the expenditure related with establishment and function of an industry, especially expenditure percentage on labour, raw material, transportation, marketing, etc.
   (b) *Spatial Margins of Profitability:* This is a point where cost of industry is more than profit. Therefore, industry is established only after calculation of profit margin and the best location is where cost is minimum. Rawstron's theory is also known as 'Locational Cost Analysis Theory'.

(iii) *Principle of Technical Restriction:* Technical knowledge is a pre-requisite for every industry. It is required more for certain industries. Therefore, due consideration should be given not only to the availability of technology and its knowledge but also its cost.

In brief, Rawstron's theory is basically a theory of least cost and industries are always located at a place where cost is least.

Other Theories

Several other theories and model have been developed to explain the locational pattern of industries.

Edgar Hoover's Theory (1937 and 1948) is based on delivered prices. The delivered prices for any buyer will be the cost of production plus transport cost. This is represented by *isotim* lines joining places of equal delivered prices.

Harold Hotelling Theory (1929) deals with the impact of demand considered together with the idea of locational interdependence, whereby firms in perfect competition arrange themselves spatially for mutual sales.

Allen Pred's Theory (1967) is based on behaviourial approach. The behaviourial approach draws on a human being as a satisfier. Allen Pred published his theory entitled 'Behaviour and Location' in which he devised a behavioural matrix to illustrate an analysis of locational decisions.

The Game Theory, Linear Programming Models, The Multiplier Model, Product Cycle Model, etc. have also dealt with locational pattern of industries in their regional context.

Most of the locational theories treat patterns of contemporary manufacturing in either early 19th or mid-20th century framework – transport costs are strongly emphasised, the actions of individual entrepreneurs rather than corporate bodies are analysed. Now, there is a need to take into consideration the technological changes in transportation, technology, world trade pattern, change in labour requirements, nature of energy source, etc. The factors like globalisation and growth of multinational companies have also become important. Study of the effects of transportation systems and innovations on the location and future development of an area provides insight into the explanation of certain industrial concentrations. All this is necessary, but there is no doubt that industrial location theories developed by economists and geographers are still important and provide a base for further analysis of the locational pattern of industries in the world.

16

Spatial Variations in Production and Transport Costs

SPATIAL VARIATIONS IN PRODUCTION COSTS

Production is the process through which various types of products are produced. This is one of the most important activities performed by man in order to fulfil his needs, and is also a key element of the economy of a nation or a region. The production of any goods or services involves bringing them together within a particular system of various inputs. These are then combined in some productive way in the transformation stage of the system to produce an output for which there is an identified demand. The cost of any product in the process of production primarily depends upon: (i) change in the form of product, i.e. final production of a product from raw material, (ii) price rise, and (iii) place and right of exchange. In the whole process of production, cost factor is considered to be the most important, which not only includes the price of raw material but is also determined by labour, capital, technology, etc.

The particular inputs and the ways in which they are combined to generate output may be expressed as the production function of the system. This is often expressed in the following way:

$$O = f(K, L, Q, T)$$

where

O is the output of the system

K is the land factor of production including physical resources of all kinds

L is the labour used in transforming inputs into outputs

Q is the capital allied in the production process, for instance in buildings, plant, etc.

T is broadly interpreted as the technological of organisational component, the stock of methods and techniques applied in producing output

The essence of the production function as it is expressed above is that the output of a productive system is the sum function of the amounts of land, labour, capital and technology. Although, this represents the system in its most highly generalised form. The main components of production process has been depicted in Figure 16.1.

Figure 16.1
Main components of production process

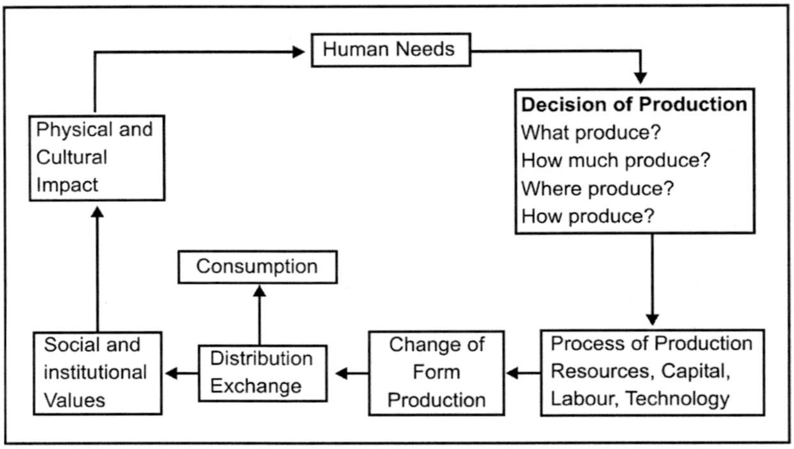

Cost Factors in Production Process

In the production process, cost factor plays an important role and is determined by several factors. Their impact on spatial pattern also varies. The following four factors have a direct impact on spatial pattern of cost in a production process: (i) natural resources, (ii) labour, (iii) capital, and (iv) technical knowledge.

Natural Resources

Natural resources always act as a determining factor of all the human economic activities. This is particularly true about the production process. In the present context, resource means all the resources available on land including soil, minerals, water, forest, air and other living organisms. Some resources such as air and land are found everywhere but most of the resources have very uneven distribution and their impact on spatial pattern of economy is more. The combination of several natural resources and their role in the production process including cost of production varies from places to place. Among the factors affecting the cost of production, the availability of resources is an important one; accordingly resources can be divided into following four categories:

(i) *Ubiquitous Material:* Available everywhere such as air, soil, sunshine, etc.

(ii) *Localised Material:* Available at some particular places such as iron ore, coal, copper, lead, zinc and several other minerals. These resources have direct impact on cost of production.

(iii) *Pure Material:* These are found in pure form in nature itself.

(iv) *Gross Material:* These materials are not pure and found in mixed or impure form such as bauxite, diamond, etc.

Another factor related with resources is the *transportation cost*. Since most of the resources are not available at places of production, they are imported or brought from other places to the place of production. Thus, transport cost also determines the cost of the production. This factor has been discussed in detail in the second part of this chapter.

The other factors affecting cost of natural resources are easy availability of resources, the quantity of resources, the quality of resources, the weight of the resources and cost of technology in obtaining the resources.

The above mentioned aspects of resources not only influences the cost of production but also the spatial economy. The establishment of industries and growth and development of agriculture often depends upon the natural resources. The fertility of the soil have a direct impact on agricultural production and their localisation. Similarly relief, climate, availability of water and forest, etc. influence production of agriculture, dairy and other livestock products, as well as forest products.

Labour

Labour is the basic requirement in a production system. In spite of the increased tendency toward mechanisation and automation, labour cost is still a dominating factor in production cost. The relative importance of the labour factor in the production function varies widely from one activity to another. Where labour is evenly distributed spatially and is flexible in skill and productivity as the simplified model implicitly assumed, then it would have no locational significance. But, in realistic circumstances, labour is unevenly distributed over space and structurally differentiated by skill and productivity. As such, labour does influence the location of economic activity in space.

Weber recognised the importance of labour costs as a "locational factor" and gave it the status of a general regional factor of location along with "the relative price range of deposits of materials and the costs of transportation". He saw all industries as being affected in their location to some degree by labour costs but he also acknowledged that some have a more specific degree of labour orientation due to the greater importance of the labour input in relation to that of other factors.

Within the terms of his analysis, Weber sought to provide some measure of the degree of labour orientation applicable to various industries. His index of labour cost measures the average cost of labour required to produce a given unit weight of product. Thus, those industries with a high index will be more generally sensitive to spatial variations in labour costs than those with a low index. However, the real significance of the labour factor in location depends upon its relative weight as compared with those other elements in the production function of the industry that have an identifiable locational impact. In Weber's analysis the prime component among these was the total weight of materials to be moved for the production of a unit weight of product, that is, the locational weight. Thus, in Weberian terms, the sensitivity of an industry to spatial variations in the cost of labour as an input factor is simply given by the labour coefficient, that is, the ratio of the labour index to the locational weight.

The skill of labour also sometime becomes a factor. There are certain industries which need certain skills. In the past, the existence of such skills exerted a far more powerful locational pull on the craft-based industries. The precision instrument, fashion, gun, jewellery, textile and clothing industries are strongly attracted to particular sites and maintained there by the availability of specialised skills. In spite of modern mechanisation, skill is also considered as a factor of location for certain industries.

Spatial Variations in the Cost of Labour

The cost to a production system of employing labour to perform its transformation or processing operations is expressed in the capitalist system in terms of the wages, salaries, and additional benefits paid to employees per unit of output. There are two variables here: the wages and salaries themselves and the productivity of labour (the amount of output achieved). Wages and salaries may vary from place to place, from time to time, and from industry to industry in accordance generally, although by no means exclusively, with prevailing supply and demand conditions for this factor. Similarly, the productivity of labour varies with space, time, and social conditions. Examining spatial variations in the cost of labour is not, therefore, simply a question of investigating the geographical distribution of wage rates any more than of studying patterns of labour productivity.

For a variety of reasons, social and demographic as well as economic, the supply of labour also varies widely over space. In particular, there is wide variation in the supply of different types of labour: skilled and unskilled, male and female, productive and unproductive. Thus, there are powerful forces at work within the space economy, promoting wage differentials from place to place through inherent imbalances in supply and demand for the factor at various points. The labour is not infinitely mobile and the labour market does not operate freely under conditions of perfect competition. Long-distance labour cost and distance of labour movements have to be examined in the context of migration as a whole. The other factors influencing spatial variations in labour cost are differential capital to labour ratios, differential income elasticities of demand for the products of industrial and agricultural regions; and differential cost of living – all serve to influence the geographical pattern of wage rates with significant disparities within space economy.

The productivity of labour depends upon many things, not least of which is the feature that may be summarised under the heading of labour attitudes. Such problems as high rates of labour turnover, recurring absenteeism, resistance to change in industrial practice, and difficult labour relations in general, profoundly affect levels of productivity. In the search for industrial locations, labour relations and productivity considerations may take precedence over direct wage rates when the significance of the labour factor is considered.

For all the above mentioned reasons, labour supplies and labour costs vary significantly from place to place and exert differential locational attractions.

Capital

Capital is a key ingredient in the production function of any economic activity. Capital, thus, is defined as all those man-made aids to further production such as tools, machinery plant and equipment, including everything man-made which is not consumed for its own sake but which is used up in the process of making other goods.

All economic activities make use of some capital. In general, one can, however, make broad distinction between the relatively labour-intensive service sector, including such industries as wholesale and retail trade, finance, insurance, personal and business services, and construction and the more capital-intensive manufacturing and mining sectors. Within each of the sectors themselves, however, there is also a wide variation in capital intensity from industry to industry.

Spatial Variation in the Cost of Capital

The accumulation of capital within an economic region depends upon the relationship between supply of investment funds and the amount of net capital inflow and the demand for such funds. In some regions, capital may have been accumulating over a long period to give a large basic stock of physical capital in the sense of plant, equipment, and infrastructural facilities as well as an abundant supply of monetary investment capital from savings out of profits and wages. These regions may also be large sources of demand for capital, the high levels of profits within them absorbing internally generated investment funds and drawing in addition from outside.

Other regions, perhaps old-established but less successful, may still exhibit a large accumulation of physical capital and may, from the fruits of a more successful past still accumulate large supplies of investment capital. They may, however, be unable to absorb all of this investment capital within themselves and stand out as regions of capital surplus. At the other end of the scale, developing areas, perhaps new frontiers for settlement, may be sources of a limited supply of capital but may at the same time exert a powerful demand for capital inputs through the potential returns to be had from mining and agricultural ventures.

Thus, over space as well as over time and from one industry to another, there exist variation in levels of supply and demand for capital as a factor of production. In general, therefore, the capital factor is localised in its spatial distribution and is not in any broad sense mobile and the price of capital – the interest rate and hence its cost to the entrepreneurs seeking to use it – varies spatially.

Technical Knowledge

Technical knowledge is a pre-requisite for the production system. This knowledge is accumulated by means of two processes: inventions and innovations. Invention is the introduction of new production processes and techniques to the existing stock of knowledge. Innovation is the adoption of these processes and their translation into actual production processes. We can further distinguish 'autonomous invention' from 'induced invention'. The former represents the long-term, spontaneous, and apparently randomly generated contribution of those occasional geniuses who extend the stock of technical knowledge by the application of intuitive thought to the existing body of technology. Induced invention, by contrast, is the fruit of a deliberate expenditure of time, effort, and resources for the purpose of generating new technical knowledge. The latter is the most volatile element in the modern expansion of technical ability.

All industries require some technology, although some of them are technology-intensive industries, while others need a limited technology. In industries such as aircraft, electronics, communications and scientific instruments, the importance of technical knowledge is very great. For others, such as food, timber, and textiles, there is less drive to expand resources on maintaining new inputs of technical knowledge.

In spatial terms the processes of induced invention – the conscious promotion of new technical knowledge and innovation and the conversion of ideas into practice and process – have much in common. Both depend upon the application of substantial investment inputs and upon the willingness of entrepreneurs to utilise their capital resources in this way. They therefore tend to exhibit a space preference for those locations with ready availability of investment funds. All forms of invention and innovation have a tendency toward spatially localised patterns of evolution.

Technical knowledge, therefore, may be considered a spatially localised factor input for most economic activities. Its localisation tends to be oriented towards the large and more successful existing concentrations of production and the geographical network of communications. In terms of mobility it behaves like the other non-land production factors: It is sensitive to movement over space, it tends to be attenuated by distance, and it is channelled along existing lines of movement and interaction. In view of this, it tends in locational terms to be a strong polarising agent in the evolution of economic activity.

Other Factors

Although, the above-mentioned four factors are the main determining factors of the cost of production, a few other factors also have had their impact on cost of production. These are taxation, large-scale production and substitute of raw material.

Taxation

Taxation is concerned with the government and has a direct impact on production cost. Some taxes are uniform throughout the country but there are several taxes which are imposed by provincial government and other local bodies. These taxes are varied in nature, thus have spatial variations. Apart from tax, there are some subsidies given at some particular place and to some particular items, which reduce the net price in spite of high production cost.

Large-scale Production

If an industry or any production agency is not utilising its full capacity of production the cost will be higher, on the contrary, utilisation of full capacity will definitely reduce the cost of production. Similarly, if the production is at a very large scale, the cost will be relatively less and profit margin will be higher. The production can be increased by the use of improved technology, skilled labour, agglomeration of industries and proper management system, which help in reduction of production cost.

Substitute of Raw Material

The cost of production also depends upon the quality of raw material. If the lower quality of raw material is used, the production cost will be higher. Sometimes change in quality and use of alternative raw material also provide good results. It depends upon the nature of industry and also upon the availability of raw material.

Relationship between Returns of Cost and Production

The returns of cost and production are interrelated. It is possible to substitute among the several elements of production costs. We may, for example, substitute more capital for less labour or vice versa or we may use more energy or fuel and thereby reduce the cost of waste disposal. The higher cost of a better grade of material may allow savings on the energy bills to process this material. Just as various locations have different production cost levels, so too do these locations permit different alternatives for substitution among the production elements. Recent developments of manufacturing in industrial locations have seen massive substitution of capital for labour, leading to increased automation and robotics. The increasing use of computer technology in the workplace has reinforced this trend.

In theoretical terms, if the cost is constant per unit, the production cost depends upon the scale of production. Accordingly, four types of relationships have emerged. These are:

(i) *Constant return to scale*, in which the production increased in proportion to the quantity of cost elements, thus return will be constant.

(ii) *Economies of scale:* In this condition production increased in comparison to the quantity of cost elements.

(iii) *Diseconomies of scale:* When production is lesser than the cost of elements. This in not a profitable stage.

(iv) *Average cost curve:* This is a mixed pattern, in which every firm goes through the three stages during a long period of its production. This is known as 'average cost curve'.

In brief, the production cost is spatially variable. The reasons for this spatial variation are geographical as well as economic and policy related. This spatial variation is the main cause of spatial variation in economy also.

SPATIAL VARIATIONS IN TRANSPORT COSTS

The study of the economic aspects of transport, specially the transport cost, is of prime importance, both to economists as well as to geographers. Until recently, geographers have tended to ignore the fundamental importance of cost and price as influences, but now they intend to study the economic aspects realising that an efficient transportation system in many ways is the lifeblood of the economic system. Therefore, the study of the nature of transport costs and pricing, at least insofar as they affect the spatial patterns of transport phenomena, is a basis to transport geography.

The Structure and Spatial Variations in Transport Costs

In dealing with transport costs, the distinction between private cost and social cost is important. The former, as the name suggests, are costs incurred by the individual or transport operator in providing a particular services. As Lipsey (1971) says, "this is the opportunity cost to the firm (or individual) or the resources used … . These are usually based on the market value of factors purchased". The identification of these costs is not easy. Gwilliam and Mackie (1975) have stated that "the non-storable nature of the product and the differences in the needs for and methods of providing and financing track and terminal facilities between modes, make the transport sector as a complex one even in this respect". On the other hand, social costs are different. Lipsey (1971) defines them as "the opportunity cost to the whole of society of the resources that the firm (or individual) uses". They are costs imposed on society as a whole through an individual making a trip or a transport operator providing a service. These costs are not paid for by the user – social costs are incurred as a result of external effects of the transport activity.

Private transport costs are made up of three main elements:

(i) track costs – of providing and maintaining a surface over which transport services can operate;

(ii) running costs – the cost of purchasing, maintaining and operating a vehicle to run on the track surface;

(iii) interchange costs – the cost of providing facilities at the beginning and completion of a journey.

The two broad categories of transport costs are 'fixed costs' (usually called by economists as inescapable costs) and 'variable costs' (escapable costs).

Fixed Costs

These are costs, which are incurred before any traffic at all passes. They include the costs: (i) of providing the infrastructure (i.e. the roads, the port or the railway line); (ii) of providing, equipping and staffing the terminal facilities (i.e. bus depots, railway stations or airports); (iii) of providing, managerial, administrative and maintenance staff and their offices and workshop. These costs are 'inescapable' because they cannot be avoided except by abandoning the whole operation. They also do not vary with the level of traffic, but remain independent of it. A railway signal-box of the old fashioned kind, controlling a short stretch of line, must be manned (and thus incurs wage costs) whether there is one train or six trains per hour over the line.

Variable Costs

These are costs incurred by the actual movement of traffic and therefore vary with the level of the traffic passing. They include the cost of fuel, crew wages and the maintenance of vehicles due to the operation of those vehicles in traffic service, for example, the replacement of worn bus tyres or routine inspection of an aircraft after so many hours of being airborne. They are called 'escapable' because they can be avoided or escaped by not running a particular train, suspending a particular flight or a private motorist leaving his or her car in the garage and walking to the shops.

But there is one very important consideration, which complicates an otherwise simple concept. In the very short run, to suspend the last bus on Saturday night will probably affect only the fuel and tyre wear, for even the driver will have to be paid the guaranteed minimum weekly wages. Over a slightly longer period, all the drivers' duties could be rearranged and perhaps one of them given notice. In the medium run of several years, bus schedules could be redrawn and four new buses ordered as replacements instead of five. In the long run the whole bus service could be closed down and then all the costs previously regarded as fixed would become escapable. We must therefore, talk in terms of short-medium or long-term escapable costs and must remember that a short-term inescapable cost may become escapable in the medium term.

Because of differences in the basic technology of the various transport modes, the proportion of fixed (inescapable) and variable (escapable) costs in the total costs varies as between those modes. For example, the railway is characterised by having a high proportion of fixed costs in its total costs. It has been calculated (Munby, 1968) that 44 per cent of railway costs are fixed and 56 per cent variable. In contrast, road transport is characterised by a much lower proportion of fixed costs in its total costs (which may of course be higher, equal to or lower than rail costs in a given situation). On an average 22 per cent of road haulage costs are fixed and 78 per cent variable. The identification of fixed and variable costs for the main modes of transport is shown in Table 16.1.

Table 16.1

Fixed and variable costs of the main modes of transport

Mode	*Fixed costs*	*Variable costs*
Private car	Insurance, road fund tax, depreciation, interest	Petrol, oil, vehicle maintenance and tyres
Public service vehicle	Administrative and workshop overheads, depreciation, interest, insurance and licences	Fuel oil, lubricants, maintenance and cleaning, labour costs
Rail	Track, administrative and technical overheads, terminal costs, depreciation and interest	Fuel, vehicle servicing and maintenance, labour costs
Air	Terminal and engineering overheads, insurance, depreciation and interest, central administration	Fuel, landing fees, certain servicing costs and labour costs
Sea	Terminal and engineering overheads, insurance, depreciation and interest	Fuel and oil, in voyage maintenance, crew costs and expenses

The transport costs per unit varies with the increase in traffic, it falls off rapidly in case of rail than road (Figure 16.2). If traffic is light, unit costs of rail are impossibly high, but if flows are very heavy unit costs are greatly reduced and rail becomes very competitive.

All transport operations also give rise to terminal costs (Figure 16.3). These are both fixed and variable. The proportion of terminal costs in the total costs varies between modes. In road haulage the terminal costs can be negligible. On the other hand, to send goods by rail may entail conveying them by lorry from factory to goods depot, loading them into wagons and reversing the process at the other end.

Figure 16.2

Unit cost in road and rail transport

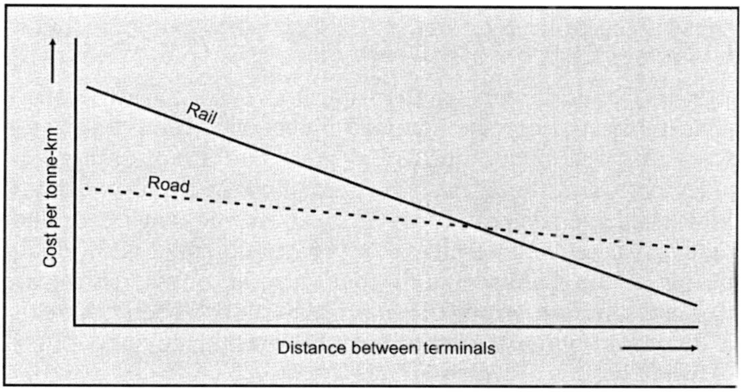

Figure 16.3

Terminal cost in road and rail transport

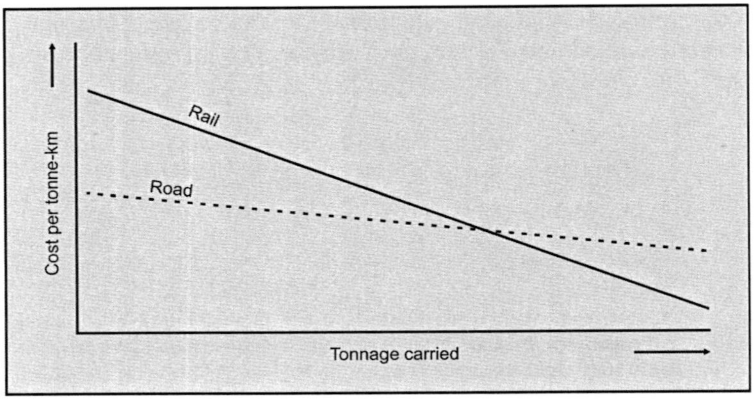

Figure 16.4

Transport cost curves: (A) proportion to distance (B) less than proportion to distance

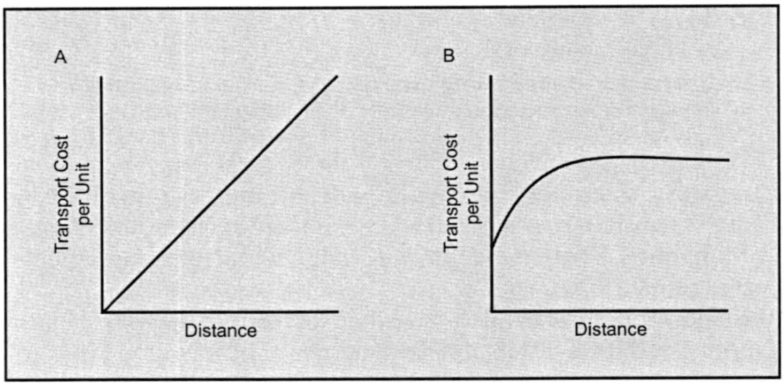

The transport costs are also proportional to distance; in other words, each additional unit of distance added an equal increment of cost to total transportation costs as shown in Figure 16.4.

As result of these varying cost characteristics, each transportation medium offers advantages over different length of haul. Figure 16.4 depicts an idealised transport cost curve for three transportation media.

Marginal and Average Costs

Marginal cost is the additional cost incurred in order to produce one more unit of output. Marginal cost may be incurred by carrying an extra passenger on a bus with seats to spare or another ton of goods on a half-empty lorry or of a wagon on a freight train. It may even mean to allow 25 trains in a day, instead of 20. Marginal costs are, therefore, time-linked and it may be of short-run or long-run nature. Marginal costs do not represent constant additional costs. Up to the capacity of the transport unit (bus, aircraft, train, ship), any further increase in traffic incurs negligible marginal costs. Then, there is a sharp increase at the point, where a second unit becomes necessary. Marginal costs also vary between modes of transport.

Figure 16.5

Idealised transport cost curves for three transport modes

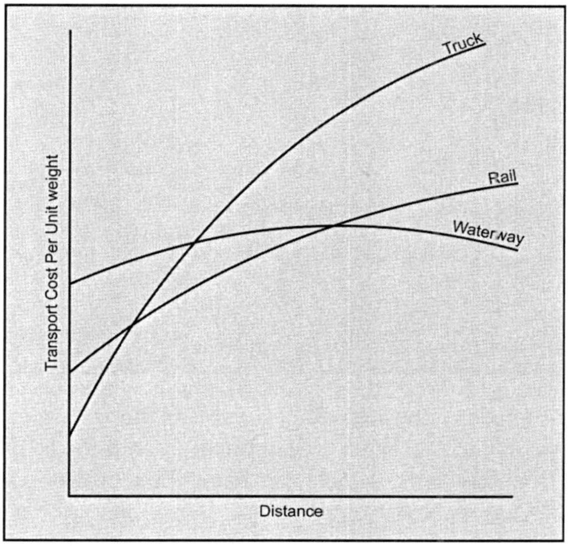

Average costs are obtained by dividing the total costs of the operation by the work done, expressed in terms of passenger-km, ton-km or transport-unit-km. Average cost will of course vary with output, for greater the product the more the fixed costs can be spread.

'Step' freight rates are often applied in case of railways. In such case, calculation of such rates would have been by adopting grouping of rates, i.e. group a number of neighbouring railroad stations together and treat them as a single station from a rate making view. Thus, all the stations in a single group would operate the same rate to any other group.

Geographical Aspect of Freight Rates

Distance is a basic factor underlying cost of service. Transportation costs increase with length of haul, save foreign important exceptions. One exception is the 'tapering principle' of freight rate (Figure 16.6).

Instead of rates increasing as a direct function of distance, they taper off with increased distance or increase in a decreasing manner. For example, if a rate is $1 to ship something 100 km , the rate to ship it 200 km will be less than $2, say $1.80. The longer the shipment, the greater the taper, thus encouraging longer hauls. Tapering rates are justified both because the actual cost of movement is less for longer hauls and because 'terminal costs' can be spread out further to produce a lower ton-mile cost. Also illustrated in figure is the 'stepwise principle'. Rates are calculated by zones, or steps, rather than on a continuous-distance basis, for reasons of simplification. Rates are identical within a given distance zone no matter where the shipment is terminated within that zone. Such an arrangement is similar to parcel post zones and telephone area code districts. If the shipment goes just beyond that zone, the next higher rate will apply. Stepwise rates are devised to avoid the burden of an overwhelming number of rate calculations for every possible point along the way.

Figure 16.6

Graph showing the tapering and stepwise rate principles of transportation

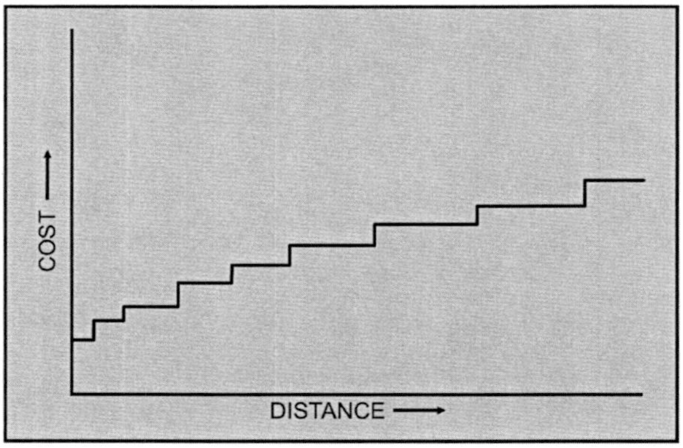

Related in rationale to the stepwise principle is the 'grouping principle'. The operation of this principle also reflects a significant exception to the idea that rates increase proportionately with length of haul. For classes or categories of commodities, rates are quoted from one area to another, rather than among all possible points. Normally, a major city or shipping point is taken as the centre or control point for the determination of rates. Several proximate shipping points will also be included in that group; all points in that group or area have the same rates to any other group of shipping points. A state, for example, may be divided into several areas or groups of shipping points. The value of this system is, of course, to simplify the publication and quotation of rates. A short-distance shipment that crosses a group boundary suffers a high payment in terms of the actual costs involved, whereas a shipment that crosses a single group boundary but that is sent from the extremity of one region to the farthest point in the other will benefit by a rate lower than distance alone would suggest.

There are numerous reasons for rates to vary with direction, such as different shipping volumes, differences in operating conditions, empty-car movement involving back-hauls and differences in competition. For these same reasons, there are even many cases in which the rate is not the same in both directions. For rail shipments the 'short line principle' provides that the rate must be based on the mileage of the shortest route over which the traffic can be transported without transfer of the cargo. In the absence of several routes radiating outward from the shipping point, it is to be expected that rates determined on this principle will vary by route direction.

Most of the principles of rate structure were first applied to the railroad and later substantially adopted by truck transportation. Yet the costs of rail and truck transportation differ considerably. Joel Dean (1973) has suggested five factors important in determining the optimum trucking costs per ton-mile for any given traffic:

1. Mileage utilisation of equipment and empty return ratio.
2. State highway weight limits.
3. Length of haul (road mileage).

4. Degree of metropolitan concentration and other terminal characteristics.
5. Type of equipment required.

Isotim

The word 'isotim' refer to lines on a map connecting points of equal transport cost. Figure 16.7 shows a hypothetical pattern of isotims.

It becomes clear from Figure 16.7 that if a firm is located at the market, *M*, there will be no cost of distributing the processed good. The only transport costs will be the assembly costs from *S*. By examining the isotims for assembling the material, we see they increase irregularly away from the source location, reaching the level of 30 cents per hundred weight at the market. The distribution costs also increase away from the market location, and in this example they rise more rapidly than those for assembly. Thus, an individual locating at *S* would have no assembly costs, but the distribution costs would be 40 cents per hundred weight. A location at point *I*, an intermediate location, would incur a 20 cent charge to assemble a unit of materials and another 20 cent cost to distribute the product to market, for a total of 40 cents. It is obvious in this example that the lowest-cost transport location is at *M*, the market.

Figure 16.7
The isotims lines (lowest-cost location is the market-M)

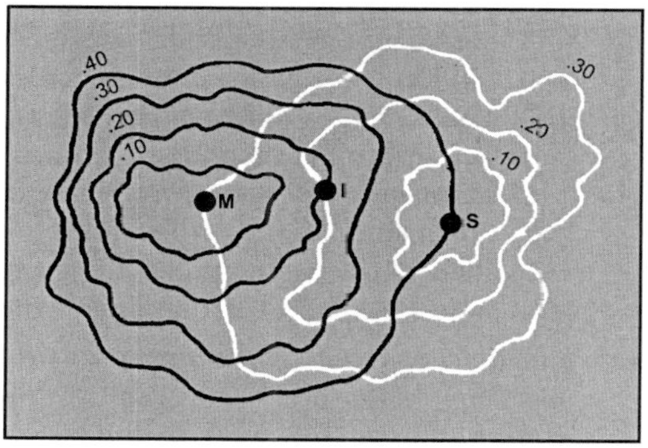

The illustrations of the effect of freight rate on the location of economic activity, though elementary, point up some of the basic considerations entrepreneurs and locational analysts comfort. The pricing of transportation can have a strong influence on the location a firm selects and on the success the firm enjoys at that location. Because freight rates are part of the cost of making a good available, these rates are passed on, in one way or another, to the buyer. A uniform increase in rates will normally raise the price of the goods, whereas selective increases on different commodities or on different routes may or may not, depending on the competitive situation. When rates are upped on some routes but not on others, the advantages and disadvantages are unevenly spread, and some productive readjustments may result at these location.

Variations in Freight Rates

According to Commodities

The transportation costs varies markedly according to the general characteristics of commodities involved. Just as the tapering of freight rates has its origin in the existence of fixed costs, so these same costs encourage transport operators to vary their rates to cover these costs. The result is a considerable degree of discrimination between commodities in the level of freight rates and the existence of rates that are above or below those justified by the actual costs of transportation.

This rate discrimination by commodities is mainly because of two basic causes: differences in the cost of providing a transportation service for various commodities and differences in the ability of various types of traffic to stand high transportation charges.

(a) *Differences in the cost of service:* A number of factors contribute to differences in the cost of service:
   (i) *Loading characteristics:* Of particular importance is the weight-density of the commodity (weight per cubic foot). Consequently, light though bulky articles are likely to incur higher freight charges than heavy, compact articles. This explains the common practice of charging more favourable rates on "knocked-down" than on "set-up" articles.
   (ii) *Size of shipment:* Up to a point there is a direct relationship between the size of shipment and the level of transportation costs. Large, single consignments of goods permit economies in administrative, terminal, and in some cases, line-haul costs, per unit weight.
   (iii) *Susceptibility to loss or damage and risk liability:* There is considerable variation between commodities in their susceptibility to loss or damage. As a result, freight rates must often be calculated to cover such contingencies. The more fragile and perishable a good – such as delicate instruments and components, on the one hand, and vegetables and fresh fruits on the other – the higher the rate is likely to be.

(b) *Elasticity of demand for transportation:* It is generally accepted that goods of high unit value are better able to "bear" relatively higher transportation charges than goods of lower unit value. This, as Hoover has pointed out, is related to the good's elasticity of demand for transportation, which is less for goods of high unit value. Such variations allow the transportation agency considerable flexibility in rate making. High-value goods are generally charged at least the full cost of the service, including overhead charges, while goods of low unit value may be charged rates that do not meet the actual costs involved.

According to Traffic Characteristics

Traffic characteristic such as competition between various transporting media, traffic density and direction of haul over a given route have an impact over variations in freight rates. A brief explanation of these factors is as follows:

(i) *Competition between transportation media:* Where only one effective form of transportation exists, the operator can set rate levels to cover costs and, in the absence of government intervention, there is considerable scope for establishing high rate levels. But, as we have seen, in the major transportation media, each one has an advantage over certain distances. If, for example, railroads wish to compete with trucks for traffic on short hauls they must keep their rates down to a comparable level. A similar effect occurs because of competition between different routes of the same transportation medium, particularly railroads. The general effect of competition, then, is to lessen the rate difference between direct competitors.

(ii) *Traffic density:* Where demand for transportation is really concentrated with the consequent heavy volume of traffic over certain routes there is a justification for setting lower rates, because the greater the traffic density, the lower is the unit cost of transportation as the fixed costs can be spread more extensively. Conversely, areas or routes with light traffic may charge higher rates.

(iii) *Direction of haul over a given route:* A common practice is for freight rates to be lower along a route in the direction of light traffic flow. Such a difference is based on the fact that the railroad cars, trucks, or other vehicles must in any case be returned to the point from which the major traffic originates. Where a return journey has to be made, it costs little more to carry a freight load than to return empty. Thus, more favourable "back-haul" rates can be offered and these have been significant in a number of cases.

Transport Costs and Quality of Service

Quality of service is of equal importance to cost of service, and in many cases users are prepared to pay for quality. As Table 16.2 shows, the attributes of quality vary as between passengers and freight.

Table 16.2

Quality of service: Not necessarily in order of importance

Passenger	*Freight*
Reliability	Reliability
Frequency	Speed
Speed	Freedom from damage and pilferage
Comfort	
Safety	

Passenger looks for reliability above all, the likelihood that the service will fulfil the promise of the timetable. For urban bus passengers the most frustrating experience is to wait 15 minutes for the next bus on a 5 minute service at the end of which time three buses come along together. For short journeys frequency is important, as this reduces waiting time. Speed is important for a businessman as he is prepared to pay higher fares for a faster service. Conversely, for the student, money is important than time and he will be prepared (if he cannot hitch) to go by motor coach, slower but cheaper than rail, at least before the introduction of railcars. Comfort is another quality that passengers are prepared to pay for. To provide first-class accommodation in trains and aircraft is more costly to the operator because fewer passenger can be accommodated in a given space. First-class fares are therefore higher, but some people are prepared to pay these. Very often, passengers demand safety and for this they are willing to pay additional coast.

The freight shipper may be prepared to pay more for better quality service, as this may allow him to reduce his total transport costs. Although rates for air cargo are higher than by surface routes, it may pay the shipper to use the air, as the extra cost may be outweighed by the reduction in cost of packing and insurance (due to greater freedom from pilferage and breakage) and the reduction of the quantity of goods in transit due to greater speed. If the service is reliable and frequent, warehouse charges can be reduced or altogether eliminated.

17

Decision-making Process

"Economic activity consists of several closely related stages: the generation of wants and needs known collectively as demand; the transmission of information about the nature of demand to firms; the transfer of information from firms to resource owners about the demand for resources; the response of resource owners by mobilising their resources; the movement of resources to firms in return for income; the manufacture of goods; the transmission of information from firms to consumers about the availability of goods; the movement of goods to consumers in exchange for payment; the consumption of goods by final consumers. All these aspects of economic activity refer to those tangible, often visible, processes which are apparent in everyday life and whose energy creates the economic landscape. But it will already be clear that there is another and perhaps more fundamental aspect of economic activity – decision-making – which provides the impetus and direction for these processes" (Hodder, 2008: 27).

Decision-making is the choice of one particular strategy to achieve some end. Human and economic geographers have studied decision-making in the context of industrial location, residential choice, migration, response to environmental hazards, and shopping behaviour and have used two major concepts: movement minimisation and place utility. In the earliest models of decision-making, economic man was seen as the decision maker, but this concept has generally been replaced by that of the satisfier who is not blessed with perfect knowledge, who works with bounded rationality, who seeks only a satisfactory solution and is therefore sub-optimal. Decision-making is of great interest to behavioural geographers, who express the variety of incoming information and the range of the individual's abilities to use that information in a behavioural matrix.

Sets of Decisions

Generally, all economics have three fundamental and interdependent sets of economic decisions. These are: (i) allocation decisions, (ii) production decisions, and (iii) distribution decisions.

Allocation Decisions

In a society where economic activity consists of the concerted action of large numbers of individuals, decisions about which goods and services and in what quantities these goods and services are to be produced are exceedingly complex. Individual views on the most effective use of scarce productive resources will vary widely, so that the economy must make value judgments about the kinds of goods to be produced and quantity judgments about how much of each good should be produced. In all economies the criteria of efficiency and utility should govern the decisions because locative efficiency is measured by the ratio between useful output and total input. The effect of such decisions is to allocate resources to those productive agencies capable of producing the chosen goods.

Production Decisions

Having decided on the type and amount of goods to be produced, the next set of decisions involves the organisation of production. Production is a process involving firms in the acquisition of premises at a suitable location in order to combine resources in an efficient productive ratio and to set in motion the distribution of the finished products. Both resources and demands are distributed unevenly over the surface of the earth. Some communities, therefore, must attempt to compensate for their lack or relative scarcity of certain resources by utilising their limited resource endowment in ratios which make extensive use of plentiful resources and intensive use of scarce resources. Alternatively they may, by military or economic conquest, extend their access to a wider range of resources or, by developing trading connection, import those goods which are demanded by their consumers but which are difficult, if not impossible, to produce with their own resource endowment. As a result of these considerations, decisions about methods of production need to be made at the same time as decisions about which goods and services are to be produced, because the output of goods depends not only upon utility priorities and resource endowment, but also upon the ways (production techniques) in which the resources can be combined in productive service.

Distribution Decisions

In a subsistence economy the producer of goods and services not only provides his own factors of production but is also the consumer of the finished product. There is no need for complex arrangements to facilitate resource allocation, production, or distribution of the finished product, as all processes are under the control of one individual or a small group of individuals. However, in a society in which substantial specialisation of occupation has developed, each individual produces only a small fraction of his own personal requirements, and in certain occupations (for instance, the manufacture of component parts of machines) the individual may not produce anything of direct use to him or to his family. Clearly, some means of distributing the bundles of goods to satisfy the demands of the members of such a society is necessary. Furthermore, the amount of goods distributed throughout the economy must be equal to the amount of goods that it is possible to produce with the available resources, and the type of goods must bear some relation to the demand priorities of the consumer households. Decisions must, therefore, be made both about the quantity and type of goods each member of the society should receive. These distribution decisions are thus closely related to both allocation and production decisions and must be taken at the same time.

Other Types of Decisions

Apart from three sets of decisions as described above, there are decisions based on time and space as well according to the needs. The following are the other types:

Routine and Important Decisions

Some decisions are routine decisions, which everyone is used to taking about his or her needs or about their routine work. Such decisions do not need much thinking and they often become part of the work in one's life. On the other hand, some decisions are important, which may be about some policy, future plan or big investment, etc. Such decisions are taken after proper consideration and analysis of the facts.

Organisational and Personal Decisions

There are decisions related with some particular organisations – economic or social. Such decisions are usually taken by an organisational team, while personal decisions are related with individual affairs.

Programmed and Non-programmed Decisions

Programmed decisions are those which are taken in a systematic manner for a specific work. Such decision are followed for similar work, for example, decision regarding sick leave to employees. On the contrary, non-programmed decisions are taken according to the problem or on some specific occasions, such as to provide aid for some work, to give additional incentive to a particular person, etc.

Policy and Operating Decision

The decision taken for some particular basic policy is the policy decision. Policy decisions are always taken by the supreme authority with the assistance of a particular group. Such decisions have a long impact. While operating decisions are often routine decisions, usually taken for the regular work.

Enterprise, Inter-departmental and Departmental Decisions

There are decisions which have had their impact on the management of whole enterprise. While departmental decisions are related with a particular department, there are certain decisions which are inter-departmental also.

Elements Working in Decision-making Process

A wide range of physical, economic, political and socio-cultural elements enters into the decision-making process. These are: (i) scale, (ii) labour, (iii) land, (iv) capital, (v) transfer, and (vi) demand and supply.

All these elements are interrelated with each other. Figure 17.1 depicts direct and looped relationship between decision-makers.

Scale

Considerations of scale are fundamentally important because they may condition not only the profitability of any enterprise but also its vocational requirements. The scale at which any activity takes place affects not only its cost of production but also its level of profitability. Since considerations of cost and profitability underline both optimising and satisfying behaviour, the factor of scale becomes a significant element in the decision-making process.

Land

Land is needed for one activity may be equally needed for other activities. Every economic activity have had its own demand of a particular activity. For example, housing development, normally requires well-drained and flat land in close proximity to existing or future places of employment and service provision. Similarly, land is needed for agricultural, industrial, commercial, transport and recreational purposes. The amount and type of land that is needed at any time and at any location is basically determined by the prevailing level and pace of economic growth and development, as well as motivation of decision-making entrepreneurs in all forms of economic activity.

Labour

All forms of human activity require a supply of labour, but requirements vary considerably between different firms, industries and locations. The requirements of larger firms are different from those of a small firm in the same business, not only in terms of the total number of workers required, but also in certain circumstances, in terms of their types and skills. Spatially too, labour requirements vary considerably because of the tendency for human activity to agglomerate at certain

Figure 17.1

Elements of the decision and their interrelationship

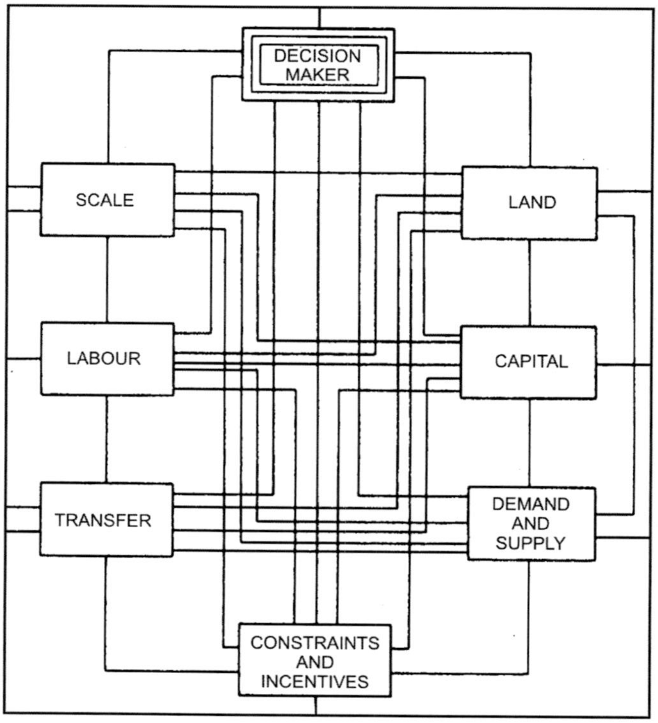

locations that have at some time possessed an initial advantage with respect to other locations. The availability and cost of labour have a direct impact in the decision-making process.

Capital

Growth in any economic system is only made possible through the substitution of capital for the other factors of production, land and labour. The mechanism by which capital is generated and allocated within the system constitutes a crucial aspect of spatial organisation and have had direct impact on decision-making process. Capital affects the possibilities of the organisation, location and profitability of human activity.

Transfer

In a landscape system where locations are geographically separated by distance, the transfer of goods, materials and individuals is an inevitable necessity of spatial organisation, since both producers and consumers are located at different points in geographical space. Considerations of transfer, consequently constitute a further element that has to be considered by entrepreneurs in the vocational decision-making process.

Demand and Supply

In the vocational decision-making process, considerations of demand and supply occupy a position of central importance since together they determine the economic viability of the firm. The volume of demand for a product determines the scale of its production and its selling price. Price, however, conditions the volume of demand so that demand and supply mechanism operate through the complementary mechanism of price adjustment. Supply and demand are thus related through the determination of price and location which in turn are related to supply and demand conditions in an apparently self-regulating control subsystem.

All of these elements of the decision-making process are mutually interrelated and affected each other to varying extent. Some of their relationships tend to be self-regulating so that some of the mechanism of control system are essentially of a negative-feedback nature, but others tend to be rather more self-perpetuating, and thereby give rise to mechanism of a positive-feedback nature. Decision-makers may therefore find it necessary to introduce a series of constrains and incentives to their own decision-making. It is not a simple system but a complex of direct, indirect, series, parallel and feedback relationships among the personal characteristic (age, sex, education, income, occupation and mental ability), information, preferences and motivation of different individuals and groups as shown is Figure 17.2.

The Mechanics of Decision-making

Decision-making processes operate under various conditions which may be regarded as lying along a continuum. At one end, decisions are made by a central authority with power to govern the elements of an economy; that type of economic system resulting from such an organisation is known as a command economy. At

Figure 17.2
The decision-making system

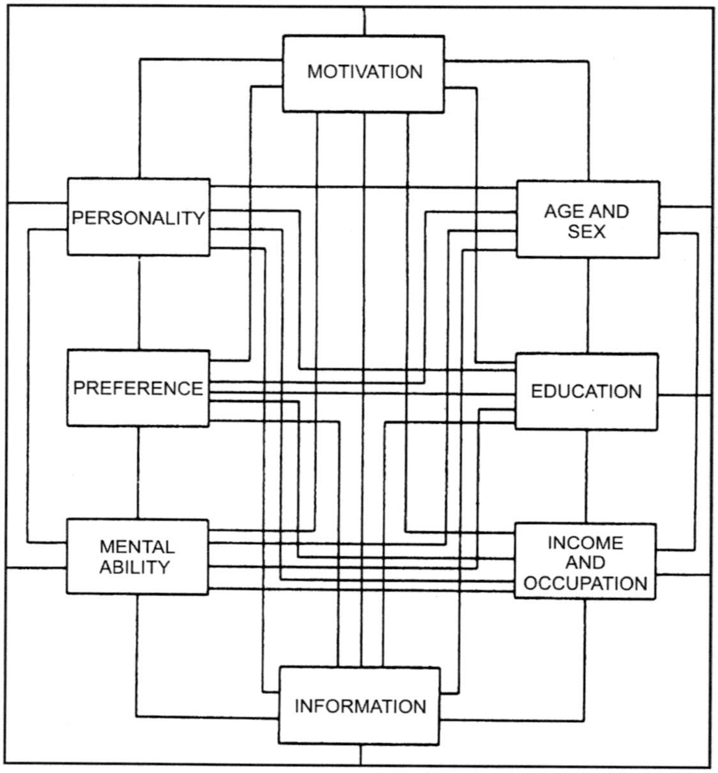

the other end of the continuum, decisions are made entirely by the individual consumers, firms and resource owners without any interference from a central authority; this is known as a capitalist or market economy. In reality, however, few economies nowadays operate in either of these two ways, most economies more realistically being described as 'mixed', in which both private and public decision-making contribute to the end result. Nevertheless it is pedagogically convenient, as well as a common practice, to make this distinction between three broad types of economic organisation – command, capitalist and mixed.

In a command economy the means of production are collectively owned and the decisions made by a central administration which needs to gather all relevant information together and keep it constantly updated. Three sets of information are required: the size and nature of the demand for goods; the different ways in which resources may be combined in alternative production methods; and the size and nature of available resources. With these data to hand, the decision-making process involves the drawing up a list of priorities for the use of productive resources, choosing efficient methods of production, matching these methods of production with the list of priorities and deciding upon the criteria for distributing goods and services amongst the community. Clearly, in such an economy both the data-collection processes and the decision-making processes are complex, large and exhausting tasks and whilst there are many advantages in a command economy, associated with its ability to extend the range of criteria for decision-making, it is hardly surprising that mistakes may be made by the central authority to the detriment of the economy as whole.

Some of the advantages and disadvantages of this system for economic-geographical decision are being explored in a small body of literature dealing with the behaviour of decision makers within planned economies. For example, decisions about industrial location in eastern Europe are, according to official sources, based upon ten principles or objective laws of socialist location (Hamilton, 1970). The ten laws, or principles, have been outlined and examined by Hamilton and state that activities should be located:

1. Close to the resources or inputs they use.
2. Close to the market they supply.
3. Inter-regionally to develop maximum regional specialisation of production.
4. Between regions to achieve maximum regional self-sufficiency.
5. As evenly as possible to exploit regionally or locally under-utilised resources.
6. In a dispersed fashion throughout the countryside to create 'proletarian bastions of socialism'.
7. Preferentially in backward, national minority, or underdeveloped regions.
8. To eliminate cultural, economic and social differences between town and country.
9. As strategically as possible to meet war eventualities.
10. To achieve international and intra-bloc division of labour and optimum trade flows within COMECON (Council for Mutual Economic Assistance).

The complexity of the decision-making process in planned economies relates to the conflicting and overlapping nature of the ten principles and the hierarchical manner in which they are applied. This has caused their application to vary over space and time and between the different economic sectors. Figure 17.3 shows generalised patterns of interaction among decision-makers in a planned economy.

In fact, decision-makers cannot work objectively in applying the principles because their behaviour is itself conditioned by several environmental influences. These include the temporally variable strength of their ideological beliefs; a conflict-ridden decision-making system created by pressure groups, the emergence of which is itself associated with changes in the acceptance of Marxist-Leninist philosophy; an economic environment stripped of market pricing which cannot provide any clear rules or data on economic efficiency but which is nevertheless shifting towards economic criteria and away from those of ideology; an environment in which spatial concepts are inadequately researched and distorted by the decision-makers' identity with a home area, by various spatially defined pressure groups and by an imperfect supply of data. The tendencies towards industrial dispersion or concentration embodied within the principle of location and observable at different times in eastern Europe appear to be associated with fluctuations in the decision-making environments, rather than with the objective application of the principles, and so result in a reduced supply of information feedback about locational alternatives and data for locational selection.

Figure 17.3

Generalised patterns of interaction among decision-makers in a planned economy

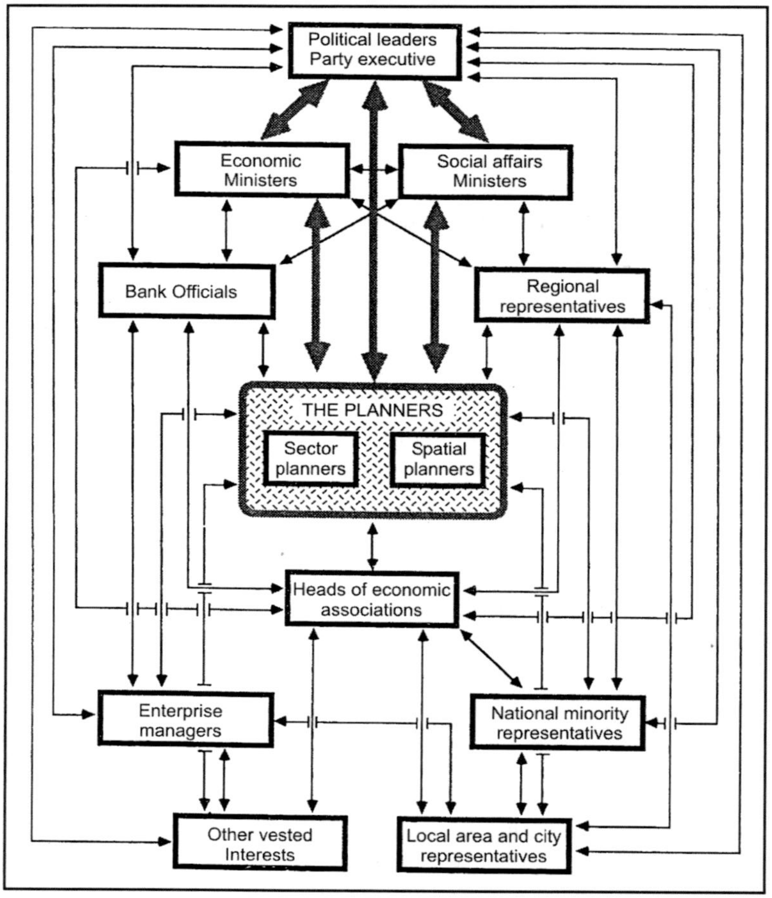

In capitalist, and to some extent, in mixed economies, the decision-making process is decentralised from the government to other elements in the system. Decision-making in a decentralised economy is based upon private ownership and gain and is undertaken by households – as consumers and as owners of resources – and by firms. Consumers choose the type and quantity of goods that will yield them the greatest utility. But, the extent of their freedom of choice will depend in part upon their knowledge of alternative commodities and upon their spending power which, in turn, is determined by the income they receive as resource owners. Firms, as agencies of production, must decide which lines of production, what techniques of production and what locations of the producing units will yield them the greatest benefit. If we accept the assumption that firms are motivated largely by economic considerations, this 'benefit' is measured by profit, or the excess of incoming revenue over outgoing costs. Production, decisions will affect the amount and type of resources used in the production process and householders, as owners of these resources, will attempt to maximise their incomes by selling their resources to the highest bidder. Again, if we assume that owners of resources are rational in an economic sense, then income will refer to financial gain. However, job satisfaction, a sense of vocation, simple ignorance of alternative uses to which resources may be put, or a weak bargaining position can easily distort this simple objective of income maximisation.

In any economy certain fundamental decisions must be made. The more complex the economy and the more specialised its individual elements, the more difficult it becomes to organise decision-making. The price mechanism provides one way of overcoming this problem, but it has many shortcomings, the most important being that it tends to respond to the actions of the most economically powerful rather than the most needy. The cumbersome and labour-intensive administrative decision-making process associated with command economies is perhaps equally open to abuse, but it does have the advantage of being able to incorporate a wide variety of economic, social and political criteria in decision-making. The intermediate solution of a mixed economy is regarded with suspicion by those who doubt the arbitral ability of capitalist governments concerned with the maintenance of maldistributed economic power. In any case, the ability of governments in economic management is by no means proven and the priorities of resource allocation change with the evolution or revolution of political ideology. In brief, all economies, developed or less developed, urban or rural, industrial or agricultural, command or capitalist, are comprised of the same essential decision-making elements of consumers, firms and resource owners. It is to their decision-making roles, whether undertaken for themselves or by a government, that we now turn.

Firms always act as prime factor in decision-making, specially in capitalist economy. In a spatial context, firms are the main productive and decision-making agents (Chisholm, 1970: 7) and effectively decide the geographical structure of capitalist economics.

One of the sources of the economic power of firms is the essential organisational link that they provide between consumers and resources. This function involves firms in several sets of interrelated activities. First, they must attempt to assess the needs and desires of consumers as expressed by the demand in the market for goods and services, assess their own abilities to provide for this demand and create alternative demands or extend their technical ability for production. Second, by using appropriate criteria of judgment they must make four sets of interrelated production decisions (Figure 17.4): (i) the range and type of goods to be produced; (ii) the quantity to be produced; (iii) the techniques to be used; and (iv) the location of production. Third, firms must organise and execute the production thus decide upon. Finally, they must undertake or at least initiate the distribution of their products to the consumers. All these functions cause firms to take executive action in the form of decision-making, and technical action in the implementation of the decisions.

Location and Land Use Decision-making

The term *location decision* refers to changes in the number, location, and size of establishments, and to the nature of activities occurring within them. Accordingly, land use decision refers to changes in the number and size of units (e.g. farms, forests) and types of land use occurring on them. In this field, different

Figure 17.4

Decision and process of production

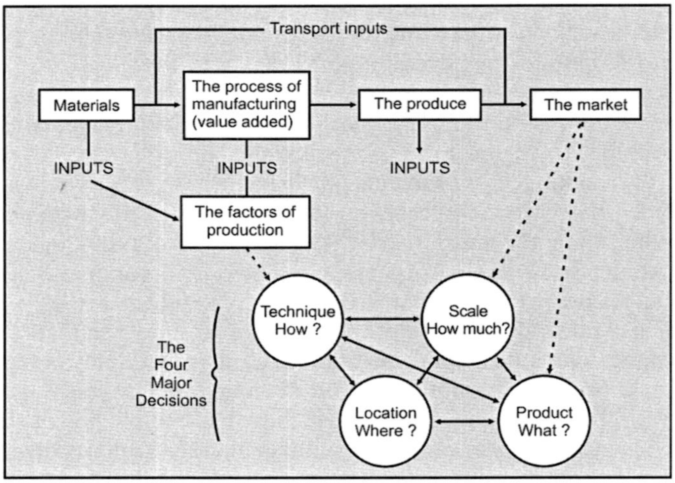

theoretical perspectives have been developed in economic geography. The approaches developed to explain the nature of location and land use decision-making can be grouped in three categories, i.e. neo-classical, structuralist and behavioural approach.

Neo-classical Approach

In traditional approaches to economic location, the decision-maker is assumed to be economically rational (economic man), with the ultimate goal of maximising profitability (optimiser). This necessitates complete knowledge and remarkable range of information regarding such factors as the costs of transporting products from the factory/farm to the market, costs, and the desirability of producing one product/crop vis-à-vis others. Profit maximisation can be phrased in terms of finding the least-cost site (e.g. Weber) or the point of maximum demand (e.g. Losch). Weber, for example, assumed perfect competition in his analysis of a single firm reacting optimally to locational factors, with the ultimate aim of cost minimisation.

Although the limitations of neo-classical models are now widely recognised, they do retain a capacity to solve practical problems where the objective is to locate a single unit of production at the point of least operating cost.

To counter the problems surrounding economic rationality and profit maximisation, extensions to neo-classical theory have been proposed. The concept of 'spatial margins to profitability', for example, was developed by Rawstron (1958) and Smith (1966). This demonstrates how both costs and revenues vary over space, causing total cost and total revenue curves to intersect and enclose an area in which it is possible for a firm to make some profit, although not necessarily the maximum profit. The point of minimum costs is still the optimum location (unless revenue is higher at somewhere other than the least-cost point), but at every point within the spatial margins some profit is earned. The concept helps in the interpretation of patterns but it has received little attention outside geography; two factors have limited its practical application: first, the difficulty of empirical identification; and secondly, its limited value as an explanatory device (Smith, 1979).

The concept of spatial margins to profitability also has limited explanatory power because it cannot explain the choice of final location within the margins; however, it remains useful for demonstrating how certain areas may be more profitable than others for certain industries and plants (Watts, 1987). Behavioural and structuralist approaches have attempted to overcome this deficiency by respectively concentrating upon the decision-making behaviours of individuals and the broader economic structures within which the entrepreneurs operate.

Further extensions to neoclassical theory have been outlined by Smith (1977 and 1979), in terms of the spatial aspects of welfare economics and territorial-production complexes.

In summary, location and land use decisions are according to neoclassical theory, a response to a search for profits.

Structuralist Approach

The structuralist approach is concerned with describing and explaining real world behaviour, rather than with predicting behaviour on the basis of various assumptions. Structuralists interpret decision-making behaviour as a product of the system (e.g. capitalist/socialist) in which individual business is set, and of its place within that structure.

Central to the approach is the view that investment in a capitalist economy is an attempt to increase profits and accumulate capital. Farmers and industrialists, for example, are becoming increasingly dependent on wider 'circuits of capital'. The nation of the circuit of capital has been depicted in Figure 17.5.

In the circuit, money (*M*) is used to purchase commodities (*C*) like materials and labour. These in turn are transformed by the process of production (*P*) and thus acquire increased value (*C'*). When exchanged for money (*M'*) this increased value can be used to purchase more inputs for the production process and so the circuit continues. If one firm, farm, or company is able to improve its efficiency, find cheaper sources of inputs (i.e. materials and labour), or make a better commodity than its competitors, then the difference between *C* and *C'* will increase and profits will be enlarged. In a capitalist economy, this will threaten the profits of competitors, who are forced to respond and produce more *C'*, but in so far as they are successful this will in turn force competitors to do the same. The structuralist approach argues that this continuous process is necessary for businesses to maintain their profit, leave alone increase them.

An extension to, or modification of the approach, *realism* recognises that individuals make decisions within the constraints set by economic processes. In order to understand how real casual processes affect location and land use decision-making, a distinction has to be made between *necessary* (internal) and *contingent* (external) relations. A necessary relationship is a dependent relationship, it may also be asymmetric, where one is dependent on the other but not vice versa.

Figure 17.5
The basic circuit of capital

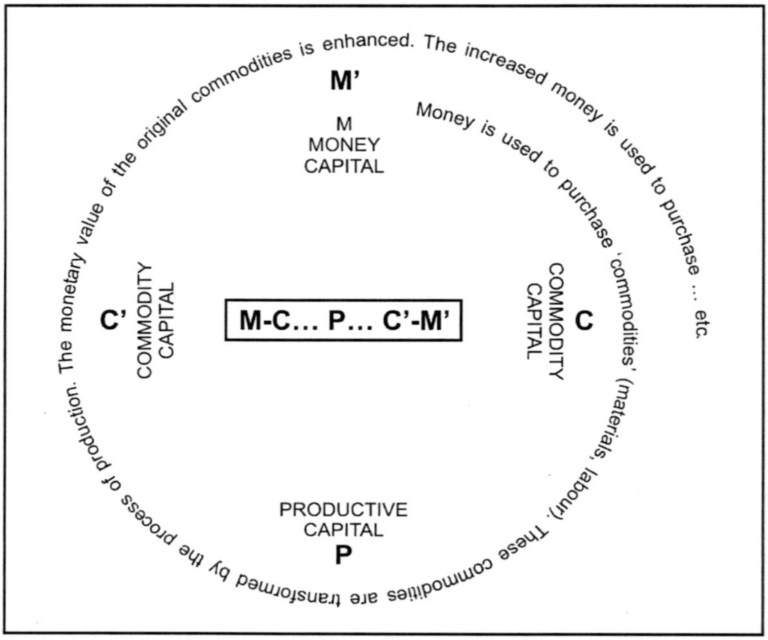

Behavioural Approach

Whereas neoclassical and structuralist approaches assume that location and land use decisions are determined by the need for profitability, the behavioural approach suggests the entrepreneurs have other goals than just profit maximisation. For example, in a large firm where management is separated from ownership a production manager put in charge of searching for a new location would tend to emphasise a low-cost site, while a sales manager charged with the same task would probably emphasise a location which would facilitate high sales. Stability, security, pride of ownership, and independence are often advocated by decision-makers above the making of maximum profits.

Most work adopting a behavioural approach in economic geography has examined various aspects of the locational behaviour of individuals or groups and attempted to see whether there is any systematic variation in their behaviour. An important aspect of this work has been to investigate how individuals/firms make location and land use decisions and the factors which influence them. Individual and group decision-making takes place within an environment of uncertainty; all decision-makers are faced with this, but the actual decisions made will vary because individuals have different goals, different levels of knowledge, and they vary in their aversion to risk and uncertainty (Worlpert, 1964). In the light of this uncertainty, entrepreneurs attempt to make satisfactory decisions and the 'satisfier concept' has been put forward as a more realistic alternative to optimising behaviour.

Figure 17.6

A model of decision process for office firms

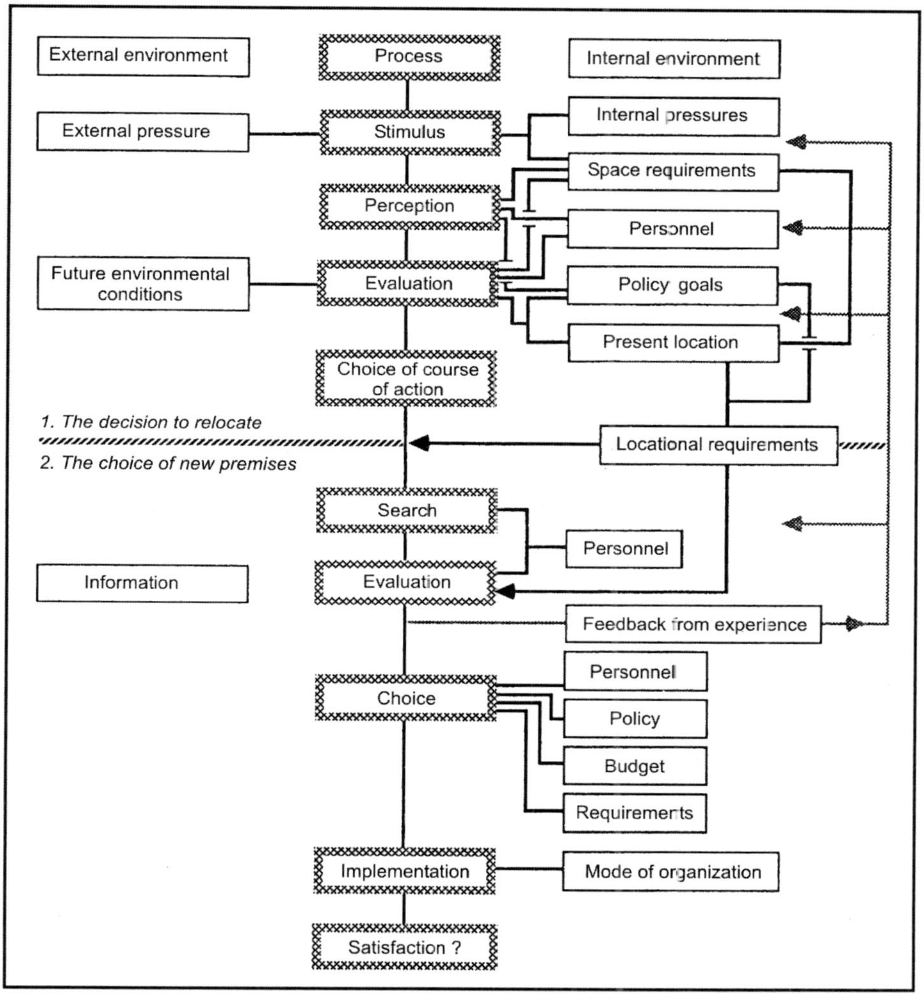

Many scholars have given general models of the location and land use decision-making process in the different economic sectors. Most tend to include a number of distinct stages, including the stimulus, search, evaluation, and choice, and to recognise that firms, farms, and offices are influenced by internal and external pressures and constraints. Internal pressures and constraints include changes in organisational structure, marketing, and policy, whilst external ones include the cost of inputs such as labour and materials and competition. Edwards (1983) developed such a model for office firms (Figure 17.6) where the location decision process is divided into two stages; first, the decision to relocate; and second, the choice of new premises. For new offices starting up for the first time, stage one is ignored and the second component is immediately utilised. Stage one in the decision-making process is initiated by "a mismatch of the requirements of an establishment and its relationship with the environment in order to fulfil these requirements" (Edwards, 1983: 1333).

In brief, "decision-making is of great interest to behavioural geographers, who express the variety of incoming information and the range of the individual's abilities to use that information in a behavioural matrix"(Pred, 1969). Decision-making is an internal party of economic management and essential for the sustainable development.

18

Economic Regions and Regionalisation

The study of regions has for long been regarded as the principal aim of geography, because region is an area of the earth's surface differentiated and given unity by specific characteristic or a set of criteria. The potential bases for such differentiation are innumerable, e.g. relief, climate, soil, agriculture land use, industries, transportation, population density, quality of life, etc. In *Dictionary of Geography* Mayhew (2006: 419) has defined region as, "any tract of the earth's surface with either natural or man-made characteristic which mark it off being different from the areas around it". A region is thus a territorial, internally heterogeneous whole, a spatial expression of processes of concentration of various masses and of the emergence and growth of centres of various type that subordinate to themselves the development and location of masses in the areas around them.

Regions are often based on 'homogeneity' and 'wholeness', but apart from it there are a number of characteristics which determine a region.

A region is characterised by its own measures, which are:

(a) Measures of centrality in the light of the uneven location of 'masses' of the productive forces.

(b) Measures of concentration which the internal heterogeneity of the region. In practice, use is usually made of measures of concentration based on the comparison of the actual location of 'masses' with the average.

(c) Measures of compactness, which are especially important for purposes of control.

(d) Measures of coherence which express the very essence of the formation of regions. The available measures are usually based on an analysis of the total number of ways in a system's connecting points (units) within it, that is, an analysis of the internal structure (anatomy) of the spatial system of the region. But these measures fail to take into account the functioning of the region system, of its 'life'. It appears to be advisable additionally to take account of the "total intensity of the contacts" between the units in the region;.

(e) Measures of the typicalness of the parts of the established region, or of the units located within it. In establishing the measure of typicalness one should start from the fact that 'typicalness' is not analogous to 'uniformity', and that the region must have a definite 'set' of typical parts or units characterised by different but not random features. Productive use of the 'image identification' method, which consists in having a known set of 'type nuclei' and their 'identification' among the entire set of units within the boundaries of the region, 'sifting' those of them which least of all correspond to the 'type nuclei' (standards).

These five types of measures characterising regions are inapplicable to homogeneous areas. Indeed, if one assumes (as some scientists do) that the internal homogeneity is the region's chief feature, these measures likewise become inapplicable with the exception of the measures of compactness, and then only in its elementary geometrical form.

Consequently, the region is an internally heterogeneous territorial entity, a spatial expression of the concentration of various 'masses' and the emergence and growth of various types of centres which subordinate the development and location of the masses on the territory adjacent to them. The region as an entity tends towards the greatest compactness that facilitates its control and that stimulates a faster rate of its development. Any region (but not an internally homogeneous area) is a complex spatial system, because it consists of two or more also fairly integral parts which are connected with each other by stronger links than they are with neighbouring regions.

Regions may also be defined at a whole range of different spatial scales, from global, e.g. climatic regions like tropical rainforest, tundra, etc. to local, e.g. urban regions such as Central Business District and high-class residential district, etc. While this may be a much less widely held view today, there are aspects of regional study which are currently deemed to be important; e.g. the investigation of *function regions* as spatial systems and integral elements in the organisation of society, and the considerable interest in the theories and problems of regional development.

Generally, three approaches have been taken to defining regions. The first approach emphasises the 'homogeneous' or 'uniform' region, that is, the homogeneity or similarity of one or a combination of physical, economic, social or other characteristic. The second approach emphasises the 'nodal' region, that is, polarisation or centralisation around some focus or node, which is usually a central place. The third approach emphasises the 'policy-oriented area', a more or less arbitrarily defined unit erected mainly for administrative coherence or convenience.

These three approaches are not mutually exclusive; in fact, they are really variants on the homogeneity criterion. The difference lies in what kind of homogeneity is sought. Thus, an administrative region is homogenous in being entirely under one jurisdiction, a nodal region is homogenous in its dependence upon certain trading links, and uniform regions are homogenous with respect to certain physical, economic or social characteristic. But much of this seems doubtful in the light of systems analysis. Perhaps the pragmatic, problem solving approach of J.L. Fisher (1955) is the most acceptable one: "The most helpful region in many instances is what might be called the *economic development region* … . The emphasis is on development of policies, programs, and actions to move the region from where it is economically toward predetermined economic objectives."

Economic Regions

A region is a spatial entity characterised by certain properties. Thus, economic region includes all aspect of economy, i.e. agriculture, industries, resource potentialities, transportation, marketing, etc.

The theory of regions, their formation, development and prospects has become the core of all the geographical sciences, and has largely determined the boundaries of the system of geographical sciences as a whole. The extent to which the theory of regions has been elaborated is an indication of the maturity of this or that geographical science. The formation of economic regions is closely connected with the territorial (geographical) division of labour. N. Baransky (1960), a leading Soviet economic geographer, stressed: "The geographical division of labour is a fundamental concept of economic geography". It helps to make economic geography an exact science, to introduce the systemic approach in its spatio-temporal expression, broadly to apply economic calculations, and to go on to modelling the whole, its parts and their interaction. The territorial (geographical) division of labour is the scientific basis for considering economic combinations on the scale of one country or on an international scale as complex integral systems, consisting of a number of parts.

Development of Economic Regions

The formation and development of economic regions is a contentious process and their characteristic also change during the growth process. The question of the stabilisation of the region as a whole and of the system of regions is closely bound up with the stages in the formation of economic regions. Kolosovsky (1969) has suggested five stages in the development of economic regions, primarily along socialist lines, but applicable in other economies also. These five stages are as follows:

(i) *Reserve territories* with poorly-developed productive forces and little involvement in the territorial division of labour. But these have a large natural potential like mineral deposits, water resources, forests, etc. Since the economic specialisation of these territories has yet to crystalise, they are 'joined' to some neighbouring developed economic regions merely on the principle of transport gravitation.

(ii) *Regions of pioneering economic development* with proved natural resources, which have a population for the initial stages of development, for which the establishment of a regional territorial production complex has been planned, and the specialisation of the economy on the scale of the whole country determined, but the use of whose natural resources is selective. Such regions are characterised by small-scale settlement and small-scale development of production.

(iii) *Regions of large-scale economic development* with established major industrial centres and transport arteries with adjacent economically developed zones. Alongside these centres and zones, where the main branches of specialisation are located, there are reserve territories which are being gradually involved in economic complexes.

(iv) *Regions of powerful seats of economic development*, which are well-formed economic complexes, but only in the main, because many of their elements are still in the process of construction and some have only been projected. In short, this is the 'scaffolding' stage.

(v) *Fully formed complex-economy regions* with an established structure of production, considerable involvement of natural and other local resources, a well-defined place in the territorial division of labour, many-tier development of the regional complex, including the 'upper' tiers, that is, manufacturing, many branches of science, etc.

In the light of above-mentioned stages, scholars have observed that stabilisation of economic regions is mostly seen at the fourth and fifth stages of development. The greatest changes in the network, lines of economic development, specialisation, and place within the system of the territorial division of labour tend to occur in regions at the second and third stages of development, with the latter being the most 'latent' with new regions, for they already have within them powerful forces which could generate and then give shape to new regions on the reserve territories within their boundaries.

Large-scale natural resources are a powerful factor behind the emergence of new economic regions and stabilisation of existing regions. Their appearance and initial exploitation tend to 'explode' some regions and even to create 'upheavals' within the system of regions as a whole.

Economic regions are also stabilised by major transport arteries, which serve as region-forming 'axes' and by large cities serve as region-forming centres.

Types of Economic Regions

Economic regions are varied according to their size, purpose and part of total spatial or total economic landscape. Five types have been identified, viz., small economic region, city region, natural resource region, institutional region and the economic development region.

Small Economic Region

Areas drawn together by close economic bonds, such as those of commodity flows, labour supplies, or flows of capital, are often known as small economic regions. The concept is comparable to that of R. Vining's 'economic community'. Vining (1949) bases his analysis on flows, structure, and stages of production. "In broad outline, ... an area can be divided into an irregular patchwork of subareas, each characterised by some form and substance ... lines of union along with matter and energy flow connect these subareas into some kind of functioning system of entities."

Similar to Vining's ideas are Losch's systems of economic areas, developed on a homogenous plain on which population is distributed, and over which labour specialisation and transportation costs occur in response to population needs. The interrelationships of these marked areas or economic regions are very complex, and in reality may be quite difficult to identify. A clear economic region would seem to be a fortunate accident rather than a natural subdivision of the landscape. Still, beneath a regional substructure of varying importance existed: "The economic landscape is a system of different markets; an organism, not merely and organ." Despite this complexity, Losch identified three types of economic areas: simple market areas, nets or subsystems of such areas, and systems of nets. The simplest is dependent upon trade within a closed system; the most complex is also based on trade, but with areas external to the basic subsystem.

The City Region

A second type of economic region is the city region complex. Here, trading links are still very important, but there are also many spatial links consisting of flows of passengers, telephone calls, newspapers, and so on. A metropolitan community has been defined by Bogue (1949) as "... an organization of many communities, distributed in a definite pattern about a dominant city, and bound together in a territorial division of labour through a dependence upon the activities of the dominant city ... the metropolitan community is not independent of the physical environment, but is, rather, an adaptation to the environment. It utilises the techniques of production and exchange which are common to populations with industrial commercial cultures in order to exploit environmental resources ... ." The complete structure of the metropolitan community may include the functions of finance, government, education, religion, and innumerable other aspects of the institutional composition of the individual hinterland community.

Within urban city regions, there are a number of *regional cities*, small in size and performing fewer functions than a primate city. Below these are the towns in lower order hierarchy. Between some of the cities are regions of interdependency, the elongated corridors along principle transport routes.

Natural Resource Region

A third type of economic region is the natural resource region. Here the area is identified by the homogeneity of certain features that distinguish it from surrounding areas. For example, it is a common administrative device in water resource management to use a river basin as a regional unit, as is done by the Tennessee Valley Authority. The validity of such all-purpose regions based on a single resource has been questioned, particularly in urban industrial areas where the particular resource may be of little relevance to development.

Institutional Region

A fourth type of economic region in the total spatial system is the arbitrary region, chosen as an aid to decentralised administration by many institutions such as government agencies, businesses, and banks. These institutional regions also arise on an international basis, through nation states that are willing to participate in such institutional arrangements as preferential trade areas or economic communities.

A number of such supranational regional organisations exist today. One of the oldest of the European economic regions was Benelux. It began in 1921 with an economic union between Belgium and Luxembourg, and was joined by the Netherlands in 1944. Common tariffs were established for many goods, and plans were set in motion to eliminate such factors as import licenses and quotas. Another celebrated regional union was the Organization for European Economic

Cooperation (OEEC), set up in 1948 to administer the Marshall Plan in Europe. In 1961 this was replaced by the Organization for Economic Cooperation and Development (OECD), which is now concerned with economic stability, aid to developing regions, and expansion of world trade.

The present European Union (EU) was formed in 1950 by six European countries, but has now become a leading economic organisation of with more than 35 European countries.

At present, there are a number of economic organisations and trade blocks in the world based on mutual understanding. The notable economic organisations are World Trade Organization (WTO), European Free Trade Association (EFTA), Latin American Free Trade Association (LAFTA), Association of South-East Asian Nations (ASEAN), The South Asian Preferential Trading Agreement (SAPTA), Organization of Petroleum Exporting Countries (OPEC), Asia-Pacific Economic Cooperation (APEC), etc.

Economic Development Region

These regions have been identified either for certain economic problems and or for opportunities that can be best treated on a regional basis. Therefore, economic development regions are considered popular. One of its subtypes is the *depressed region*, or economic problem area – an area with a declining or stagnant economy, which offers only modest development prospects, and provides many of the migrants areas of new growth. *Frontier region* is also included in this category. Frontier region is an area of economic opportunity, which would be greatly aided by investment in resource development and transportation networks. Fisher (1955) observed, "each economic development region has a particular problem or set of related problems; each has a susceptibility to a particular kind of policy and program which will reduce its problems and help in realising its opportunities".

The economic region on the whole, as a complex system has a definite spatial structure. The scientific and technological revolution intensifies the concentration of the population, production, science, education, recreation and other functions. The territorial concentration and spatial contrast of many economic phenomena tend to grow. These processes have an effect on the formation of regions because in many instances, concentrations of people and production become the 'nuclei' and axes in the formation of economic regions, thereby predetermining their internal heterogeneity and territorial structure.

The boundaries of economic and physico-geographical regions (and ecosystems) do not, as a rule, coincide, and there is good reason for this because the largest and most promising economic centres and their groups, which become region-forming seats, tend to grow fastest at the points of contact between integral natural formations and regions. As a rule, the more diversified the natural territorial structure of an economic region the greater its potentialities for complex development and the more grounds for its parts having economic diversity. Thus, the diversified natural structure of the territory of a region tends to influence the character of its spatial economic structure and the intra-regional division of labour.

The intra-regional division of labour helps to 'grind down' the spatial distinctions, which spring from the configuration of economic seats and centres, natural distinctions, dissimilar population patterns and other historically rooted spatial distinctions. It shapes the intra-regional system of subregions (districts), which are the basis for the regional territorial structure. The ties established between the districts in the process of the intra-regional territorial division of labour is the basis for the complex development of the economic region. However, this process does not necessarily have to continue: it is impossible to continue endlessly to urge the need for the complex development not only of an economic region but also of its subregions, of their parts, etc. for this calls for circumspection and sobriety. In some instances, some elements of the complexness will suffice. Everything depends on the real economic efficiency of the complex development of an urban settlement, a section of a district or a whole district.

Economic regions are also stabilised by major transport arteries, which serve as region-forming 'axes' (the Volga, the Siberian Railway), and by large cities which serve as region-forming centres (Moscow, Leningrad, New York, London, Mumbai, etc.).

Generally speaking, regions are stabilised by large-scale investments and the accumulation of various resources, which ensure their future development.

Economic Regionalisation

According to *Oxford Dictionary of Geography* (2006: 420), regionalisation is the demarcation of regions such that there is little variation within each region while each region is sharply distinct from the others. The bases for regionalisation vary so much that different regions may be delimited according to the criteria used. Small and Witherick (1995 : 205) have explained regionalisation as "a form of classification in which areas are divided into regions on the basis of some specific characteristic".

Regionalisation is a means of arranging this 'point information' in space, discovering regularities in it and establishing definite theories, systems, aggregations and structures. It is simultaneously the result of the generalisation of such information and a means of processing it. Regionalisation permits the extensive application of mathematical formalism for processing primary information. Conversely, mathematical methods help in the scientific establishment of the region grid, that is, the division of the territory into integral parts. Regionalisation is becoming an ever more efficient means of management, including control over many processes, a touchstone of practical recommendations and verification of their fulfilment, and a key method in the spatial organisation of numerous natural and social phenomena.

With the ever broader application of systems analysis and mathematical methods of processing and generalisation of primary material in the geographical sciences, regionalisation comes to play an ever greater part. This is undoubtedly promoted by the objective course of various processes intensifying the spatial contrast both in nature which is being modified by social production, and in the productive forces. The stronger the spatial contrast of phenomena, the clearer the contours of regions and their frontiers, and the greater the practical importance of regionalisation.

Regionalisation is of special importance for the control of various processes. Indeed, it is one of the key constituents of control, blending with it. The connection between regionalisation and control is such that control becomes effective and achieves it purpose when it has to deal with ordered, organised systems which are hierarchically or otherwise subordinated or connected. It is regionalisation that has the function of bringing out ordered, organised spatial systems, thereby creating the basis for various types of territorial control. This includes not only spatial planning according to the country's economic regions, or state administration of the basis of a system administrative and political districting, or again the holding of elections on the basis of legislative regionalisation, but also the regulation (control) of the country's water resources by means of hydrological regionalisation, forest management on the basis of forest-management regionalisation, etc.

The most important thing in regionalisation is to achieve the internal integrity of the region, which takes shape as a result of the development of the country (zone, etc.) of which the region is a part.

'Homogeneity' and 'integrity' are in a sense antithetical concepts: homogeneity leads to internal uniformity, similarity; integrity leads to a synthesis of different phenomena, to an accentuation of their mutual connections, to the formation of a new quality as compared with the aggregate of different individual phenomena, to the emergence of a system.

Regionalisation from 'below' rules out the possibility of subjectivism, since the marking out to regions as spatial systems developing in time through an analysis of the 'fields of force' in the interaction between primary 'cells' and centres makes it possible to produce a more precise analysis of reality.

Soviet geographers take the view that regions exist objectively. Physico-geographical, natural (that is , environmental), economic, industrial and other regions exist independently of our thinking. It is up to science to discover these regions and to make it possible to control their development, and the impact of society on them, which is now and again so profound that their substance and boundaries tend to be modified. But recognition of the objective existence of regions has nothing in common with objectivism, that is, a passive attitude to systems of regions.

Regionalisation is inseparable from territorial planning, which is why economic regionalisation is of state importance in the socialist countries. Under socialism, the integrity of the economic region is combined with the integrity of the planning of the economic region, design, development and construction of the whole aggregation of its enterprises. That does not happen under capitalism, where the objective integrity of the economic region contrasts with the fragmented private-property attitude to the design and development of enterprises and their economic ties. The integrity of the region is a vast potential which can be tapped fully only under socialism.

Kolosovsky (1969) formulated the tasks of economic regionalisation in socialist society as follows: "The socialist economic region is a combined economic system of production and commodity turnover, an element of the national economic system ..., developing on the basis of the principle of achieving the highest labour productivity with the lowest possible inputs, and attaining full economic and political equality for all the nationalities and former fringe areas, and realising other basic principles of the socialist location of the productive forces." That is an expression of the main tasks in present-day economic regionalisation in socialist countries, which is regionalisating for the purpose of optimising the development and location of the productive forces in the interests of society as a whole.

Bibliography

Alexander, J.W. and Gibson, L.J. (1979), *Economic Geography*, Prentice-Hall of India, New Delhi.

Alexonderson, G. (1967), *Geography of Manufacturing,* Prentice-Hall of India, New Delhi.

Allen, S.W. (1966), *Conserving Natural Resources,* McGraw Hill, New York.

Bamford Roy, P. (2005), *Economic Geography,* New Central Book Agency, Kolkata.

Baransky, N. (1960), 'Economic Geography', *Economic Castography*, Moscow, p. 80.

Berry, B.J.L. (1960), 'An Inductive Approach to the Regionalisation of Economic Development', in N. Ginsburg (ed.), *Essays on Geography and Regional Development*, University of Chicago, Chicago, pp. 78–107.

Berry, B.J.L. (1967), *Geography of Market Centres and Retail Distribution,* Prentice-Hall of India, New Delhi.

Boech, H. (1964), *A Geography of World Economy,* D. Van Nostrand Co., New York.

Bounge, D.J. (1949), *The Structure of the Metropolitan Community*, University of Michigan Press, Michigan.

Chisholm, G.G. (1999), *Handbook of Commercial Geography,* Longmans, London.

Chisholm, M. (1968), *Rural Settlements and Land Use* (2nd ed.), Hutchinson, London.

Dean, Joel (1973), 'Competitive Pricing in Railroad Freight Rates', in Martin T. Farris and Paul T. McElhiney (eds.), *Modern Transportation*, Houghton Mifflin, Boston, pp. 333–45.

Dunn, E.S. (1954), *The Location of Agricultural Production,* University of Florida Press, Gainesville.

Edwards, L.E. (1983), 'Towards a Process Model of Office Location Decision-Making', *Environment and Planning*, A., pp. 1327–42.

Fisher, J.L. (1955), 'Concepts in Regional Economic Development Programs', *Papers and Proceeding of the Regional Science Association,* Vol. I, II W I–W.

Gotewald, A. (1959), 'von Thunen in Retrospect', *Economic Geography,* Vol. 35, pp. 346–55.

Griffin, Ernst (1973), 'Testing the von Thunen Theory in Uruguay', *Geographical Review,* 63(October), pp. 500–16.

Guha, J.L. and Chattoray, P.R. (2009), *A New Approach to Economic Geography,* The World Press Private Ltd., Kolkata.

Gwilliam, K.M. and Mackie, P.J. (1975), *Economics of Transport Policy*, Allen & Unwin, London.

Haggett, P. (1965), *Locational Analysis in Human Geography,* Edward Arnold, London.

Hall, P. (ed.) (1966), *Von Thunen's Isolated State (Der Isolierte Staet),* translated by C.M. Wartenbarg, Pergamon Press, Oxford.

Hall, P. (ed.) (1966), *von Thunen's Isolated State,* Oxford University Press, Oxford.

Hamilton, F.E.I. (1970), 'Aspects of Spatial Behaviour in Planned Economics', *Papers and Proceedings of Regional Science Association,* 25, pp. 83–105.

Hartshorne, T.A. (2009), *Economic Geography* (3rd ed.), PHI Learning Pvt. Ltd., New Delhi.

Hartshorne, T.A. and Alexander, J.W. (1988), *Economic Geography,* Prentice-Hall of India, New Delhi.

Hodder, B.W. and Lee, Roger (2008), *Economic Geography,* Rawat Publications, Jaipur.

Hoover, E.M. (1948), *The Location of Economic Activity,* McGraw-Hill, New York.

Hurst, M.E. (1972), *A Geography of Economic Behavior,* Duxbury Press, California.

Isard, W. (1956), *Location and Space Economy,* MIT Press, Cambridge.

Jonasson, O. (1925), 'The Agricultural Regions of Europe', *Economic Geography,* Vol. 1.

Jones, C.F. and Darkenwald, G.G. (1950), *Economic Geography,* Macmillan & Co., New York.

Knox, Paul, Agnew, J. and McCarty, L. (2008), *The Geography of the World Economy,* Hodder Education, London.

Kolosovsky, N. (1969) *The Theory of Economic Regionalisation* (in Russian), Moscow: Mysl Publication, pp. 57–72.

Leong, Goh Cheng and Gillianc, Morgon (1995), *Human and Economic Geography,* Oxford University Press, Oxford.

Lipsey, R.G. (1971), *Introduction to Positive Economics,* Weidenfield and Nicholson, London, p. 207.

Lloyd, P.E. and Dicken, Peter (1972), *Location in Space: A Theoretical Approach to Economic Geography,* Harper and Row, London.

Losch, A. (1967), *The Economics of Location*, translated by W.H. Woglomand, W.F. Stopler, New York.

Manners, G. (1963), 'The Pipeline Revolution', *Geography*, Vol. 47, pp. 153–63.

Manners, G. (1971), *The Geography of Energy,* Hutchinson, London.

Martin, Ron (2003), 'Institutional Approaches in Economic Geography', in E. Sheppard and T.J. Barnes (eds.), *A Companion to Economic Geography,* Blackwell, Oxford.

Mayhew, Susan (2006), *A Dictionary of Geography*, Oxford University Press, Oxford.

McCarty, H.H. and Lindberg, J.B. (1966), *A Preface to Economic Geography,* Englewood Cliffs, N.J.

McFarlane, J. (1937), *Economic Geography,* Pitman & Sons, London.

Michael, E.H. (1972), *A Geography of Economic Behavior,* Duxbury Press, California.

Michael, J.H. and Brian, W.I. (1990), *Location and Change: Perspectives on Economic Geography,* Oxford University Press, Oxford.

Morgan, W.B. and Munton, R.J.C. (1971), *Agricultural Geography,* Methuen, London.

Munby, D.L. (ed.) (1968), *Transport: Selected Readings,* Penguin, Harmondsworth.

Paul, K., John, A. and Linda, M. (2008), *The Geography of World Economy,* Hodder Education, London.

Peet, J.R. (1969), 'The Spatial Expansion of Commercial Agriculture in the Nineteenth Century: A von Thunen Interpretation', *Economic Geography,* Vol. 45, pp. 283–301.

Pounds, N.J.G. (1970), *An Introduction to Economic Geography,* John Murray London.

Pred, A. (1969), *Behavior and Location: Foundations for a Geographic and Dynamic Location Theory,* Part II, University of Lund, Lund Studies in Geography, B., No. 28.

Prest, A.R. and Turkey, G. (1966) *Survey of Economic Theory,* Vol. III.

Renner, G.T. and others (1957), *World Economic Geography,* Prentice-Hall, New York, p. 4.

Richardson, H.W. (1971), *Urban Economics,* Penguin, Harmondsworth.

Robinson, H. and Bamford, G.B. (1978), *Geography of Transportation,* Macdonald and Evans, London.

Royan, Von W. and Bengston, N.A. (1971), *Fundamentals of Economic Geography,* Prentice Hall, New York.

Saxena, H.M. (2004), *Marketing Geography,* Rawat Publications, Jaipur.

Saxena, H.M. (2005), *Transport Geography,* Rawat Publications, Jaipur.

Shaw, E.B. (1955), *World Economic Geography,* John Wiley, New York.

Sheppard, E. and Barnes, T.J. (eds.) (2003), *A Companion to Economic Geography,* Blackwell, Oxford.

Sinclair, A.R. (1967), 'von Thunen and Urban Sprawl', *Annals of the Association of American Geographers,* Vol. 57, pp. 72–87.

Small, J. and Witherick, M.E. (1995), *A Modern Dictionary of Geography,* Hodder Arnold, London.

Smith, D.M. (1966), 'A Theoretical Framework for Geographical Studies of Industrial Location', *Economic Geography,* Vol. 42, pp. 95–113.

Smith, D.M. (1971), *Industrial Location: An Economic Geographical Analysis,* Wiley, New York.

Smith, D.M. (1977), *Human Geography: A Welfare Approach,* Edward Arnold, London.

Smith, D.M. (1979), 'Modelling Industrial Location: Towards a Broader View of the Space Economy', in F.E.I. Hamilton and G.J.R. Linge (eds.), *Spatial Analysis and the Industrial Environment in Industrial Systems,* Wiley, Chichester, pp. 37–56.

Smith, G.H. (1965), *Conservation of Natural Resources,* Wiley, New York.

Smith, J.R. and Phillips, M.O. (1950), *Industrial and Commercial Geography,* Constable and Co., London.

Stamp, L.D. and Gilmour, S.C. (1954), *Chisholm's Handbook of Commercial Geography,* Longmans, London.

Taaffe, E.J. and Gauthier, H.L. (1973), *Geography of Transportation,* Englewood Cliffs, N.J.

Thoman, R.S, Yeates, M.H., Conkling, E.C. and Timber, J. (1968), *Geography of Economic Activity,* McGraw Hill, New York.

Thoman, R.S. and Conklin, E.C. (1967), *Geography of International Trade,* Englewood Cliffs, N.J.

Toyne, P. (1974), *Organisation, Location and Behaviour: Decision-Making in Economic Geography*, Macmillan, New York.

Ullman, E.L. (1954), 'Transportation Geography', in P.E. Jones (eds.), *American Geography: Inventory and Prospects*, Syracuse Press, Syracuse.

Vance, J.E. Jr. (1970), *The Merchant's World: The Geography of Wholesaling,* Englewood Cliffs, N.J.

Wagner, P.L. (1960), *The Human Use of the Earth*, Free Press, Illinois, pp. 129–30.

Watts, H.D. (1987), *Industrial Geography*, Longmans, New York.

Welner, A. (1909), *Uber den standort der industrien,* translated by C.J. Friedrich (1929) as *Alferd Weber's Theory of the Location of Industries*, Chicago.

Wheeler, J.O., Muller, P.O., Thrall, G.I. and Fik, T.J. (1998), *Economic Geography,* John Wiley & Sons, New York.

White, H.P. and Senior, M.L. (1983), *Transport Geography*, Longmans, New York.

Wood, A. and Roberts, S. (2011), *Economic Geography: Places, Networks and Flows,* Routledge, London.

Worlpert, J. (1964), 'The Decision-Making Process in a Spatial Context', *Annals of the Association of American Geographers*, Vol. 54, pp. 537–58.

Yeates, M.H. (1968), *An Introduction to Quantitative Analysis in Economic Geography*, McGraw Hill, New York.

Zimmermann, E.W. (1972), *World Resources and Industries,* Harper and Row, New York.

Index